Fascinating Challenges

Studying Material Culture with Dorothy Burnham

Judy Thompson, Judy Hall and Leslie Tepper,
in collaboration with Dorothy K. Burnham

**Mercury Series
Canadian Ethnology Service
Paper 136**

**Published by
Canadian Museum of Civilization**

© Canadian Museum of Civilization 2001

NATIONAL LIBRARY CANADIAN CATALOGUING IN PUBLICATION DATA

Thompson, Judy, 1946- .
Fascinating challenges: studying material culture with Dorothy Burnham

(Mercury series, ISSN 0316-1854)
(Paper/Canadian Ethnology Service, ISSN 0316-1862; no. 136)
Includes an abstract in French.
Includes bibliographical references.
ISBN 0-660-17841-9

1. Athabaskan Indians — Costume — Canada.
2. Ntlakyapamuk Indians — Costume — Canada.
3. Woodland Indians — Costume — Canada.
4. Inuit — Costume — Canada.
5. Native peoples — Costume — Canada.
6. Native peoples — Material culture — Canada.
I. Hall, Judy, 1950- .
II. Tepper, Leslie Heyman, 1947- .
III. Burnham, Dorothy K., 1911- .
IV. Canadian Museum of Civilization.
V. Canadian Ethnology Service.
VI. Title.
VII. Series.
VIII. Series: Paper (Canadian Ethnology Service); no. 136.

E99.A86F37 2001 391.'0089'972 C2001-980000-2

PRINTED IN CANADA

Published by
Canadian Museum of Civilization
100 Laurier Street
P.O. Box 3100, Station B
Hull, Quebec
J8X 4H2

Senior production officer: Deborah Brownrigg
Design: Roger Langlois Design

Front cover: Dorothy K. Burnham at the Canadian Museum of Civilization, October 1999. Photograph by Harry Foster.

OBJECT OF THE MERCURY SERIES

The Mercury Series is designed to permit the rapid dissemination of information pertaining to the disciplines in which the Canadian Museum of Civilization is active. Considered an important reference by the scientific community, the Mercury Series comprises over three hundred specialized publications on Canada's history and prehistory.

Because of its specialized audience, the series consists largely of monographs published in the language of the author.

In the interest of making information available quickly, normal production procedures have been abbreviated. As a result, grammatical and typographical errors may occur. Your indulgence is requested.

Titles in the Mercury Series can be obtained by calling 1-800-555-5621;
by e-mail to <publications@civilization.ca>;
by Internet to
<http://www.cyberboutique.civilization.ca>;
or by writing to:

Mail Order Services
Canadian Museum of Civilization
100 Laurier Street
P.O. Box 3100, Station B
Hull, Quebec J8X 4H2

BUT DE LA COLLECTION MERCURE

La collection Mercure vise à diffuser rapidement le résultat de travaux dans les disciplines qui relèvent des sphères d'activités du Musée canadien des civilisations. Considérée comme un apport important dans la communauté scientifique, la collection Mercure présente plus de trois cents publications spécialisées portant sur l'héritage canadien préhistorique et historique.

Comme la collection s'adresse à un public spécialisé, celle-ci est constituée essentiellement de monographies publiées dans la langue des auteurs.

Pour assurer la prompte distribution des exemplaires imprimés, les étapes de l'édition ont été abrégées. En conséquence, certaines coquilles ou fautes de grammaire peuvent subsister : c'est pourquoi nous réclamons votre indulgence.

Vous pouvez vous procurer les titres parus dans la collection Mercure par téléphone, en appelant au 1 800 555-5621,
par courriel, en adressant votre demande à <publications@civilisations.ca>, par Internet, à <http://www.cyberboutique.civilisations.ca> ou par la poste, en écrivant au :

Service des commandes postales
Musée canadien des civilisations
100, rue Laurier
C.P. 3100, succursale B
Hull (Québec) J8X 4H2

Canada

Abstract

In 1990, Dorothy Burnham, a renowned authority on textiles and former curator at the Royal Ontario Museum in Toronto, began work with three curators at the Canadian Ethnology Service of the Canadian Museum of Civilization. This book marks the 10th anniversary of this rewarding collaboration. It celebrates Dorothy Burnham's many contributions to ongoing research on the Museum's ethnographic collections from the Northern Athabaskan, Arctic, Plateau and Eastern Woodlands regions of North America. Eight papers highlight the important role that comprehensive study of museum collections – in particular, the understanding of garment cuts and techniques of weaving, sewing and decorative work – can play in material culture studies. Three papers by individuals working in contemporary Aboriginal communities illustrate the value of this detailed information to those seeking to revive traditional skills.

Résumé

En 1990, Dorothy Burnham, spécialiste reconnue en matière de textiles et ancienne conservatrice au Musée royal de l'Ontario, à Toronto, a commencé à travailler avec trois conservatrices du Service canadien d'ethnologie du Musée canadien des civilisations. Le présent ouvrage marque le 10e anniversaire de leur fructueuse collaboration. Il met en lumière les multiples contributions qu'a apportées Mme Burnham à la recherche permanente sur les collections ethnographiques que possède le Musée relativement aux Athabaskans du Nord, à l'Arctique, au Plateau et aux régions boisées de l'est de l'Amérique du Nord. Huit des articles du livre illustrent le rôle important que l'étude approfondie des collections des musées – en particulier la compréhension de la coupe des vêtements, des techniques de tissage, de la couture et de la décoration – peut jouer dans l'étude des cultures matérielles. Trois articles rédigés par des personnes travaillant dans des communautés autochtones contemporaines illustrent combien cette information détaillée peut être utile à ceux et celles qui cherchent à faire revivre les techniques traditionnelles.

Table of Contents

Abstract
Résumé iii

List of Illustrations vii

Acknowledgements xiv

Preface
Andrea Laforet xv

Introduction
Judy Thompson, Judy Hall and Leslie Tepper 1

Fascinating Challenges
Dorothy K. Burnham 9

SECTION 1: ATHABASKAN STUDIES

Traditional Summer Clothing of the Dena'ina and the Gwich'in: Variations on a Theme
Judy Thompson 17

The Oldest Athabaskan Garment?
Judy Thompson 67

The Gwich'in Solution
Dorothy K. Burnham 91

Revitalization
Judy Thompson 97

Table of Contents

My People Did This: The Re-making of a Gwich'in Garment
Karen Wright Fraser 99

The Gwich'in Traditional Clothing Project
Ingrid Kritsch. 107

SECTION 2: ARCTIC STUDIES

"Following the Traditions of Our Ancestors": Inuit Clothing Designs
Judy Hall 115

Masters of Design
Dorothy K. Burnham. 143

SECTION 3: PLATEAU STUDIES

The Old Made New Again: James Teit and The Revitalization of Cultural Knowledge
Leslie Tepper 149

The Making of a Traditional Nlaka'pamux Silver-Willow Cape
Pearl Hewitt. 177

The Observant Eye: Analyzing Nlaka'pamux Woven Mats
Leslie Tepper 187

SECTION 4: EASTERN WOODLANDS STUDIES

"To Make Them Beautiful": Porcupine Quill Decorated Moccasins from the St. Lawrence-Great Lakes
Judy Hall 237

Epilogue. 263

List of Contributors. 268

List of Illustrations

Unless otherwise noted, all drawings are by Dorothy K. Burnham; descriptions by Dorothy Burnham in the figure captions are indicated by (DB). Names for quillwork techniques were developed by Dorothy Burnham to reflect the actual process of applying the quills and the number of quills used. In the drawings of quillwork techniques, a running stitch secures the quills; a backstitch was also commonly used. The term "cut" refers to the component parts of the garments.

Unless otherwise noted, maps were produced by Joanne Purich.

Section 1: Athabaskan Studies

Map Athabaskan territories and cultural groups referred to in text.

1.1 Gwich'in man's outfit. National Museums of Scotland, Edinburgh 564.

1.2 Gwich'in man's tunic. National Museums of Scotland, Edinburgh 564.

1.3 Dena'ina man's tunic. Peter the Great Museum of Anthropology and Ethnography, St. Petersburg 620.40a.

1.4 Cut of Gwich'in man's tunic, c. 1860. National Museums of Scotland, Edinburgh 564.

1.5 Cut of Dena'ina man's tunic, c. 1840. Peter the Great Museum of Anthropology and Ethnography, St. Petersburg 620.40a.

1.6 Cut of Dena'ina style woman's dress, c.1840. National Museums of Scotland, Edinburgh L357.9.

1.7 Dena'ina woman's dress, c. 1842. National Museum of Finland, Helsinki VK174.

1.8 Gwich'in woman's dress, 1860. Smithsonian Institution, Washington 884.

1.9 Gwich'in style woman's dress, c.1900. Royal Ontario Museum, Toronto 953.160.5.

1.10 Cut of Gwich'in style woman's dress illustrated in Figure 1.9. Royal Ontario Museum, Toronto 953.160.5.

List of Illustrations

1.11 Cut of Gwich'in girl's hooded tunic. Royal Ontario Museum, Toronto HD 5397.

1.12 Component parts to tunic Canadian Museum of Civilization VI-Z-10 (see Figure 1.40) superimposed on two barren ground caribou hides.

1.13 Dena'ina moccasin-trousers, c. 1842. National Museum of Finland, Helsinki VK 168.

1.14 Gwich'in moccasin-trousers, (from outfit illustrated in Figure 1.1). National Museums of Scotland, Edinburgh 564.

1.15 Cut of Gwich'in moccasin-trousers. National Museums of Scotland, Edinburgh 564.

1.16 Cut of Athabaskan moccasin-trousers: Variation A. Canadian Museum of Civilization VI-I-77.

1.17 Cut of Athabaskan moccasin-trousers, Variation B. Canadian Museum of Civilization VI-Z-244.

1.18 Woven-in-place quillwork.

1.19 Folded, sewn quillwork technique.

1.20 Loom-woven quillwork technique.

1.21 Fringe technique.

1.22 Technique used in wrapping fringe strands with porcupine quills.

1.23 Method of making tags, commonly seen on Dena'ina tunics.

1.24 Method of making tags, commonly seen on Gwich'in tunics.

1.25 Line technique using porcupine quills and sinew.

1.26 Line technique using bird and porcupine quills.

1.27 Technique used in making garters for moccasin-trousers.

1.28 Method of attaching garter on the Gwich'in moccasin-trousers illlustrated in Figure 1.14.

1.29 Gwich'in style outfit. Bata Shoe Museum, Toronto 87.74.

1.30 Dena'ina style outfit. Bata Shoe Museum, Toronto 83.161.2.

1.31 Tunic (front view), "Kenai, circa 1800". Canadian Museum of Civilization VI-Y-5.

1.32 Tunic (back view),"Kenai, circa 1800". Canadian Museum of Civilization VI-Y-5.

1.33 Pacific Coast of Alaska, with Native peoples referred to in text.

1.34 Cut of tunic illustrated in Figure 1.31.

1.35 Folded quillwork technique: reinforced, straight, single quill.

1.36 Detail, reinforced folded quillwork on breastband of tunic illustrated in Figure 1.31.

1.37 Tunic, c. 1800. Peter the Great Museum of Anthropology and Ethnography, St. Petersburg 633-31.

1.38 Ahtena woman's dress, 1841. Peter the Great Museum of Anthropology and Ethnography, St. Petersburg 593.10.

1.39 Quillworked breastband, 1794. British Museum, London Van.206.

1.40 Gwich'in style tunic (front view), late 19th century. Canadian Museum of Civilization VI-Z-10.

1.41 Gwich'in style tunic (back view), late 19th century. Canadian Museum of Civilization VI-Z-10.

1.42 Gwich'in sleeve design.

1.43 Cut of the Gwich'in style tunic illustrated in Figures 1.40 and 1.41.

1.44 Karen Wright Fraser, at the Canadian Museum of Civilization, Hull, June 1999.

1.45 Members of the Gwich'in Traditional Clothing Project Team, at the Canadian Museum of Civilization, Hull, February 2000. Left to right: Renie Martin, elder, Inuvik; Rosie Stewart, elder, Ft. McPherson; Rosie Firth, elder, Ft. McPherson; Alestine André, Director, Gwich'in Cultural Institute.

Section 2: Arctic Studies

Map Northern Canada showing places and names referred to in text.

2.1 Man's outer parka (front view). Copper Inuit (Kilusiktormiut). Canadian Museum of Civilization IV-D-960.

2.2 Cut of man's outer parka. Canadian Museum of Civilization IV-D-960.

2.3 Woman's outer and inner parka (front view). Copper Inuit (Kilusiktormiut). Canadian Museum of Civilization IV-D-944 a,b.

2.4 Kila and Kanneyuk, Copper Inuit women. Photograph by George H. Wilkins, Bernard Harbour, 1916. Canadian Museum of Civilization 51249.

2.5 Woman's outer parka (back view). Copper Inuit (Kilusiktormiut). Canadian Museum of Civilization IV-D-944 b.

2.6 Cut of woman's outer parka. Canadian Museum of Civilization IV-D-944 b.

2.7 Cut of woman's inner parka. Canadian Museum of Civilization IV-D-944 a.

2.8 Man's outer parka (back view). Caribou Inuit (Qairnirmiut). Canadian Museum of Civilization IV-C-924.

2.9 Cut of man's outer parka. Canadian Museum of Civilization IV-C-924.

2.10 Woman's outer parka (front view). Caribou Inuit (Qairnirmiut). Canadian Museum of Civilization IV-C-628.

2.11 Cut of woman's outer parka. Canadian Museum of Civilization IV-C-628.

2.12 Woman's inner stockings. Iglulingmiut. Canadian Museum of Civilization IV-C-665

2.13 Cut of woman's stockings. Canadian Museum of Civilization IV-C-665

2.14 Women on board ship. Photograph by Albert P. Low, Fullerton Harbour, 1903-04. National Archives of Canada, Ottawa C51.

2.15 Elsie Nilgak from Ulukhaqtuuq (Holman), Northwest Territories, wearing fabric parka at the Canadian Museum of Civilization, November 1992. Photograph by Judy Hall.

Section 3: Plateau Studies

Map Nlaka'pamux Traditional Territory.

3.1 James Teit and his wife, Susannah Lucy Antko outside their home. American Museum of Natural History Library, New York 1686.

3.2 Sinsimtko, Kwolalp, Roi.pellst, TekwitlixkEn and XaxalExkEn worked with James Teit to record Nlaka'pamux traditions. Photograph by James A. Teit, 1914 Canadian Museum of Civilization 27000.

3.3 James Teit holding a shield now in the collection of the Peabody Harvard Museum, Cambridge. Photograph courtesy of Sigurd Teit.

3.4 People wearing woven garments, Nicola Valley, British Columbia, early 20th century. Princeton and District Pioneer Museum Collection, Princeton.

3.5. Mandy Brown, Mabel Joe and Theresa Albert working with the collections. Photograph by Steve Darby, Canadian Museum of Civilization.

3.6 Cut of woman's deerskin dress. Canadian Museum of Civilization II-C-626.

3.7 Cut of man's deerskin shirt. Canadian Museum of Civilization II-C-354.

3.8 Silver-willow bark cape and headdress. Canadian Museum of Civilization 94-60.

3.9 Construction of silver-willow bark cape. Canadian Museum of Civilization II-C-604.

3.10 Mary Anderson presenting model silver-willow bark cape to community, Lytton. Photograph by Leslie Tepper.

3.11 Summer hats made from tule reeds. Hat with tall crown made by Maggie Shuter. Hat with low crown made by Sarah McLeod. Canadian Museum of Civilization II-C-921 and II-C-922.

3.12 Pearl Hewitt presenting the finished cape to the community, Spences Bridge. Photograph by Chief David Walkem.

3.13 Gathering the materials. Rose Marie Charlie stripping silver-willow bark near Spences Bridge. Photograph by Chief David Walkem.

3.14 Hemp preparation. Pearl Hewitt removing the outer bark of the hemp stem. Photograph by Chief David Walkem.

3.15 Pearl Hewitt spinning hemp thread. Photograph by Chief David Walkem.

3.16 Pearl Hewitt and Carolyn Lytton preparing the silver-willow warp threads. Photograph by Chief David Walkem.

3.17 Twined weave.

3.18 Twined weave with one added warp.

3.19 Twined weave with two added warps.

3.20 Twined weave, weft turning.

3.21 Children's capes made by Pearl Hewitt. Left to right: Chief David Walkem, Mandy Jimmie, Pearl Hewitt and Vincent Wilson. Photograph by Leslie Tepper.

3.22 Floor mat made of rushes and silver-willow bark. Woven using tabby and twine techniques. Canadian Museum of Civilization II-C-333.

3.23 Mat tipi. Photograph by James A. Teit, 1914. Canadian Museum of Civilization 26628.

3.24 Taking down mat tipi. Photograph by James A. Teit, 1914. Canadian Museum of Civilization 27038.

3.25 Technique of rush mat weaving.

3.26 Technique of grass mat weaving.

3.27 Technique of small rush mat weaving.

3.28 Technique of rush mat weaving.

3.29 Technique of twining used for skin blankets.

3.30 Tent mat. Canadian Museum of Civilization II-C-288.

3.31 Construction A: plain weave.

3.32 Construction B: plain weave, starting edge.

3.33 Construction M: twined weave.

3.34 Construction N: twined weave, starting edge.

3.35 Construction C: plain weave, selvage treatment I.

3.36 Construction D: plain weave, selvage treatment II.

3.37 Construction O: twined weave, selvage treatment.

3.38 Variations of selvage treatment within one mat. Canadian Museum of Civilization II-C-323.

3.39 Construction E: plain weave, finishing treatment I, front and back views.

3.40 Construction F: plain weave, finishing treatment II.

3.41 Construction G: plain weave, finishing treatment III.

List of Illustrations

3.42 Construction H: plain weave, finishing treatment IV, front and back views.
3.43 Construction R: twined weave, finishing treatment I.
3.44 Construction S: twined weave, finishing treatment II.
3.45 Construction P: twined weave, addition of warp thread.
3.46 Tent door mat showing variegated texture. Canadian Museum of Civilization II-C-285.
3.47 Food mat showing undulating weave pattern. Canadian Museum of Civilization II-C-325.
3.48 Undulating weave technique.
3.49 General purpose mat showing diamond pattern. Canadian Museum of Civilization II-C-326.
3.50 Construction T: decorative technique, diamond pattern.
3.51 Construction U: decorative technique, U-shape additions.
3.52 Wrap-around skirt showing dyed warps and inset decorations. Canadian Museum of Civilization II-C-358.
3.53 Shaman's cape with painted design. Canadian Museum of Civilization II-C-321.
3.54 S-Twist spin.
3.55 Z-Twist spin.
3.56 Tabby weave.

Section 4: Eastern Woodlands Studies

Map   St. Lawrence-Great Lakes area referred to in text.
4.1   Moccasins. Northeastern North America. Musée de l'Homme, Paris 78.32.265.
4.2   Line, whipped running stitch technique.
4.3   Folded, zig-zag, single quill technique.
4.4   Edging technique, single quill.
4.5   Moccasins. Northeastern North America, 18th century. Museo de América, Madrid 13953-1,2.
4.6   Moccasins. Northeastern North America, probably early 18th century. British Museum, London 1921.10-14.84.
4.7   Sa Ga Yeath Qua Pieth Tow (Sagayenkwaraton), a Mohawk Chief, by John Verelst, 1710. Oil on canvas. National Archives of Canada, Ottawa C-92419.
4.8   Quill wrapping.
4.9   Moccasins, decorative style attributed to the Iroquois (Seneca), early 19th century. Canadian Museum of Civilization III-I-1309 a,b.

4.10 Line, overcast core, decorative technique.

4.11 Folded, straight, two-quills, alternating and interlaced technique.

4.12 Folded, straight, six-quills, interlaced technique. Moccasin (detail). Indianermuseum der Stadt Zurich, Zurich Nr 5.

4.13 Folded, zig-zag, two-quills, alternating technique.

4.14 Folded, zig-zag, two-quills, alternating and interlaced technique.

4.15 Folded, zig-zag, three-quills, interlaced technique. Moccasin (detail). University of Pennsylvania Museum, Philadelphia NA 4945.

4.16 Folded, zig-zag, four-quills, interlaced technique. Moccasin (detail). Peabody & Essex Museum, Salem E26,326.

4.17 Moccasins, decorative style attributed to the Huron-Wendat, late 18th century. Canadian Museum of Civilization III-H-432 a,b.

4.18 Nicholas Vincent Isawanhoni, a Huron Chief, La Jeune Lorette near Quebec, 1825. Edward Chatfield. Hand-coloured lithograph. National Archives of Canada, Ottawa C38948.

4.19 Cut of moccasins illustrated in Figure 4.17. Canadian Museum of Civilization III-H-432 a,b.

4.20 Loom-woven technique.

4.21 Join between weaving.

4.22 Folded, zig-zag, two-quills, double layer technique.

4.23 Moccasins. Huron-Wendat type, early 19th century. Berne Historical Museum, Berne, Switzerland Po 74.403.18 a,b.

4.24 Moccasins made by Richard Froman (Wa-La-Has-Keh), Mohawk, 1987. Bata Shoe Museum, Toronto P87.0152 a,b.

Acknowledgements

The research described in this book centres on collections of the Canadian Museum of Civilization (CMC), but has involved as well ethnographic and archival collections in many other institutions. The authors would like to thank their many colleagues and friends in museums in Canada, the United States, Europe and New Zealand who over the course of a long research process have contributed information, photographs, research facilities, time, and expertise.

We also gratefully acknowledge the support and assistance of CMC staff and colleagues. Kelly Cameron and Ann Rae of Collection Management Services assisted with access to collections on numerous occasions. Harry Foster, Head of Photographic Services photographed Dorothy Burnham for the cover of this book and he and Steven Darby photographed many of the CMC artifacts illustrated in this volume. Staff of the Conservation Services Division cheerfully provided working space for Dorothy in their busy laboratory. Deborah Brownrigg, Head of Production, Publishing, helped us turn a manuscript into a book.

Finally, we would like to express our special thanks to Dr. Andrea Laforet, Director, Canadian Ethnology Service, for her support of our research and of this publication.

Preface

Andrea Laforet

Few aspects of my work at the Canadian Museum of Civilization over the past ten years have been more rewarding than watching the evolving collaboration among Dorothy Burnham, Judy Thompson, Judy Hall and Leslie Tepper. It was our good fortune that Dorothy Burnham moved to Ottawa to enjoy her retirement. It was almost serendipitous that the Museum had three curators working in the ethnology division with strong interests in clothing from very different regions. Although they arrived at their expertise by different paths, and conducted their research quite independently from one another, the work the curators did with Dorothy Burnham illuminated their common interest even as it gave precision and clarity to the stylistic features of the clothing they studied.

Dorothy Burnham's expert eye and precision of line brought a welcome dimension to the study of the clothing made by the Dene, Inuit, Nlaka'pamux and people of the Eastern Woodlands. As she recalls in her paper, *Fascinating Challenges*, line drawings were once an essential feature of the documentation of a collection, at a time when it was far more common to publish descriptions of collections than it is now. Drawings have long been superseded in most instances by photographs, and now are often made only when components of an object are to be discussed in a publication. While the camera lens can make an admirable record, anyone who has squinted patiently (or not) at the grainy print of a "record shot" of an intricately detailed object has learned to appreciate the benefits of a careful drawing made with an inquiring mind, discerning eye and trained hand. What distinguishes this body of drawings, however, is that it was compiled in the context of ongoing, evolving research, with almost constant consultation between Dorothy Burnham and the curator concerned while each drawing was being made. In each area the research benefited from consultation with Aboriginal people undertaken over a period of several years.

Preface

This work has resulted in an astonishing number of drawings useful to people with a wide range of interests. However it is also remarkable for its scope. The first conversation between Judy Thompson and Dorothy Burnham began with the Canadian Museum of Civilization collection and the broader work has kept that collection as its focus, but it has also included and made accessible clothing housed in several different countries.

Museum research is often fragmented. Curators, including the three who have produced this book, have many different responsibilities. Work begun in one year must often be finished in another, and can be expected to be interrupted many times. The four people who undertook this work sustained a common interest and focus through ten years of interruptions and challenges, and Dorothy Burnham's unflagging intellectual curiosity and engagement with the collection did much to make that possible.

Introduction

For many readers of this volume, Dorothy Burnham will require no introduction. In the course of a long career in museum work she has been a friend, colleague and mentor to many, and through her research, exhibitions and publications has reached countless others who have not had the pleasure of knowing her personally. Dorothy joined the staff of the Royal Ontario Museum in Toronto in 1929 and became the first curator of its newly formed Textile Department in 1939. Working closely with her husband Harold, she conducted seminal research on the history of Canadian handweaving. Together they accumulated an outstanding collection of Canadian textiles at the Royal Ontario Museum, and wrote a groundbreaking publication on early handweaving in eastern Canada. Dorothy continued research in these areas following her husband's untimely death in 1972.

Officially "retired" in 1977, Dorothy went on to curate a major exhibition of traditional Canadian spinning and weaving at the National Gallery of Canada, and then to research and mount an exhibition on the textile traditions of the Canadian Doukhobor community. In 1992 she brought a long-standing research project on the painted hide coats of the Innu of the Quebec-Labrador peninsula to a magnificent conclusion with the publication of *To Please the Caribou*.

Dorothy Burnham's contributions and achievements have been recognized nationally and internationally. In 1984 she was made a Member of the Order of Canada, and in 1998 Trent University in Peterborough, Ontario awarded her an Honourary Doctorate.

Dorothy Burnham's work with curators in the Canadian Ethnology Service of the Canadian Museum of Civilization began early in 1990. This volume is, therefore, intended both to mark the tenth anniversary of a very rewarding collaboration, and to celebrate her many contributions to our on-going research. Although common threads run through all her work with us, each project has involved distinctly different ethnological collections and research topics, not to mention three different curators, each with her own *modus operandi*. The organization of this book reflects those divisions, starting with

Introduction

the following section of this introduction, which contains our personal accounts of working with Dorothy.

Athabaskan Studies (Judy Thompson):

The Athabaskan component of this book reflects a recent, decade-long, collaboration with Dorothy Burnham, but she has been part of my museum life for much longer. My first introduction to her work came in 1969, when I joined the Canadian Ethnology Service as a young and inexperienced Cataloguer. Dorothy and her husband Harold had recently studied all the textiles in the ethnographic collection and compiled a series of binders with descriptive analyses of each artifact. These binders became my "bible", an invaluable resource to which I referred many times over the years. They served not only as a source of information about the collection, but also as a model of how to approach the study of an artifact.

I saw Dorothy sporadically over the next twenty years, as she visited the storerooms of the Canadian Ethnology Service while researching Aboriginal textiles and Innu caribou hide coats. During the same period, I was developing a research passion of my own – the study of Northern Athabaskan clothing. Athabaskans do not have spinning and weaving traditions and Dorothy's work in those years reached only occasionally into the western Subarctic. Nevertheless, her publications became standard reference works on my office shelf. I loved the way she wrote about material culture, managing to convey both a sense of wonder at the miracle of human creativity and solid, thoroughly researched information about how an artifact was made. I had great admiration and respect for her professional achievements, but never dreamt that one day I would have the opportunity to work with her, or to know her as a close personal friend.

Then, in the fall of 1989, returning to work at the Canadian Museum of Civilization after a year's leave, I learned that Dorothy Burnham had moved to Ottawa from Toronto. This was very welcome news. Knowing she would be interested and intrigued by the beautiful Athabaskan garments I was working on, I invited her to spend a day with me in the ethnology storeroom. The rest, as they say, is history.

Our work together began with the analysis of a quillworked, ochre-painted caribou hide garment which had an intriguing, but unverifiable, collection history (Figure 1.31). Eventually, we examined and described, and Dorothy produced measured drawings of, 29 examples of traditional Athabaskan clothing in the Museum's collection. Clothing artifacts from other collections were added to this corpus as opportunities presented themselves. When the *Crossroads of Continents* exhibition was installed at the Canadian Museum of Civilization in November 1991, we were able to add an early, documented summer garment from southwest Alaska to our study (Figure 1.3). Dorothy examined and drew the cut (the shape of component parts) of a girl's outfit and of a woman's dress in the Royal Ontario Museum collection (Figures 1.11 and 1.9). Together we studied several examples in the McCord Museum of Canadian History, Montreal. In 1993, we travelled to Scotland, working first with the marvelous and extensive Athabaskan clothing collection of the National Museums of Scotland, Edinburgh, then with a rare example of Gwich'in women's winter clothing in the Glasgow Art Gallery and Museum. Dorothy carried on to London, where she examined and drafted drawings for three garments in the British Museum's collection.

In 1993, armed with a worksheet, a camera, and instructions from Dorothy as to what and how to measure, I spent a week studying examples of Dena'ina clothing from the National Museum of Finland, when the collection was exhibited at the Alaska State Museum in Juneau, Alaska. On my return, Dorothy worked with photos, written descriptions and measurements to provide sketches of garment cuts. These sketches were important to the understanding of this early collection, and useful for comparison with other clothing artifacts with which she had had "hands-on" experience.

Dorothy Burnham's contribution to this research project constitutes a remarkable achievement. Over a ten-year period she has produced 51 beautifully crafted, scaled (1/10) drawings of the cuts of Athabaskan garments, and 60 diagrams illustrating Athabaskan sewing and decorative techniques. Many of the drawings and diagrams are accompanied by detailed written analyses. Her work has greatly furthered my understanding of how individual garments were cut, sewn and decorated. It has also facilitated comparison of garments, both within a given cultural area and from different parts of the Athabaskan territory, and enabled us to draw conclusions about regional approaches to cut, construction and decoration. This work stands as an important resource to researchers and students engaged in the study of this important aspect of Athabaskan culture. In a very practical sense, it is also a body of information that contemporary Athabaskans are already drawing upon, as they seek to revive traditional sewing and decorative art skills and reconstruct traditionally styled garments true to their particular cultural heritage.

Arctic and Eastern Woodlands Studies (Judy Hall):

Like many researchers of material culture, my knowledge of Dorothy Burnham and her work began long before I met her. As a graduate student of Anthropology and Museum Studies at the University of Toronto in the early 1970s, I was privileged to spend many fascinating hours in the exhibitions and anthropology department at the Royal Ontario Museum. One of the exhibitions I particularly remember was *Keep Me Warm One Night: Early Handweaving in Eastern Canada*, a wonderful collection of textiles curated by Dorothy Burnham and Harold Burnham. *Keep Me Warm One Night* was an inspiration - it helped to focus my career on material culture research and museum work.

Introduction

In the late 1970s, **Dorothy Burnham** was doing research for the exhibition *The Comfortable Arts: Traditional Spinning and Weaving in Canada*, which was to open at the National Gallery of Canada in 1981. By that time, I was working with the ethnographic collection at the National Museum of Man (now the Canadian Museum of Civilization) in Ottawa. Dorothy came to the Museum to study early examples of First Nations weaving. Over a number of days with Dorothy in the collection, I was impressed by her meticulous approach to the analysis of each object.

My next professional encounter with Dorothy came in 1987, when she was completing her long-term study of Innu painted caribou-skin hunting coats for her book *To Please the Caribou*. The ethnographic collection had just been moved to Quebec. Dorothy arrived as the collection was being unpacked, so she was provided with the only space available - a table outside the storeroom amidst constant activity, boxes and packing materials. She didn't seem to mind - I think she had had a lot of experience working in less than optimum conditions in museum storerooms around the world. She was very pleased when people inquired about her work and she could explain her drawings of the cut and decoration of the coats. Her passion and admiration for the material was obvious and we all learned a great deal from her visit.

By the early 1990s, I was working on the Inuit component of the exhibition *Threads of the Land: Clothing Traditions from Three Indigenous Cultures* that opened at the Canadian Museum of Civilization in 1995. During the research for the exhibition, it became evident that some clothing styles had not been made since the 1920s and seamstresses in the northern communities of Ulukhaqtuuq (Holman) and Qurluqtuuq (Coppermine) were interested in recreating the traditional garments. Detailed patterns of clothing in the Museum's collection could contribute to this process. Dorothy had since moved to Ottawa and was working with Judy Thompson on Athabaskan clothing. Being aware of her remarkable ability to analyze the cut of garments, I approached her to see if she would like to look at a few items of Inuit clothing. She seemed quite pleased with the idea of expanding her knowledge of northern clothing traditions, although I'm sure she didn't realize the amount of work that would be involved in the project (see *Masters of Design*, this volume). Working in the Conservation Division, Dorothy painstakingly drew the intricate and complex patterns of five items of Inuit clothing illustrated in this volume. Her drawings highlighted details that are often difficult to see on the original garment and contributed enormously to my understanding of this material.

At the same time that I was working on *Threads of the Land*, I became the Curator of Eastern Woodlands Ethnology at the Museum. I started a research project which involved examining porcupine quill-decorated objects from northeastern North America. In 1997, I asked Dorothy if she would like to look at a few of these objects. Dorothy came to the project with considerable experience and knowledge, having researched quillwork techniques for the exhibition *The Comfortable Arts*, as well as for her more recent work on

Athabaskan clothing. Thus began many fascinating hours of stimulating conversation in the Museum's storeroom, spent marvelling at the skill of generations of women quillworkers. As Dorothy remarked in the storeroom one day: "It's a humbling experience working with this material. When I see what these women do, I admire their skills." We made a good team. I was able to identify details and variations of technique and design; Dorothy excelled at "unravelling" the complex interweaving of the quills to produce the drawings. During our work, we developed an innovative system for identifying different techniques, which are often very difficult to see even with a high-powered magnifying glass. We took detailed photographs of the quillwork, then had the photographs enlarged. It was remarkable how much clearer the elusive techniques became. Working together about once a month over a period of two years, we looked at all the objects decorated with porcupine quills from northeastern North America in the collection. Our discussions broadened my knowledge and appreciation of the skill of these remarkable women artists.

I have known, or known of, Dorothy Burnham for over 25 years. She has an amazing knowledge of textile arts from a broad range of cultural traditions that she has shared with scholars from all disciplines. Dorothy has transferred her enthusiasm for the objects and the people who made them to many others who have pursued careers in museums and material culture research. I am one of these fortunate people.

Plateau Studies (Leslie Tepper):

I first encountered Dorothy Burnham's work in the early 1970s, through her book *Keep Me Warm One Night*. My mother, sister and I had recently learned to weave and Dorothy and Harold's book on nineteenth century Ontario coverlets was a wonderful source of new ideas and designs. The traditional patterns of Wheels and Roses, Overshot and Summer/Winter, could be woven in a wide range of colours and yarns. By doubling or slightly changing the threading sequence, we could create fabrics with a bolder, more contemporary appearance. The book's introduction told a fascinating story of early Ontario crafts people. It included not only the expected accounts of housewives and farm women who wove their family's blankets, but also the history of professional weavers who traveled from farm to farm, using their client's loom and homespun yarns to make the coverlets which would become family treasures. *Keep Me Warm One Night* linked us to a long tradition while serving as a sure guide and interesting companion during the hours my family and I designed and wove our own treasures.

Dorothy's book *Cut My Cote* was my second introduction to her work. It would sometimes take months to create sufficient fabric to make a garment, and it was difficult to find dressmaking patterns that would not waste woven material. Dorothy's pattern book revealed the construction of both historical garments and the clothing of many cultures. She showed how cloth could be

Introduction

transformed into a 'cote' while preserving the work of the weaver. This small book became my favourite resource and guide for new projects.

Several years later, I met Dorothy when she was working on her exhibit *The Comfortable Arts*. We discussed my thesis research and she offered suggestions for comparative materials and alternative resources. It was my first encounter with her lively curiosity, her extensive knowledge of material culture, and her generous support and stimulating interest in projects proposed by students and colleagues.

During the past ten years, Dorothy and I have worked together on two projects. *Earthline and Morning Star* was an exhibit and publication on traditional and contemporary clothing of the Nlaka'pamux, an Interior Salish speaking community living on the British Columbia Plateau. The second collaboration was a study of Nlaka'pamux twined reed and bark mats in the collection of the Canadian Museum of Civilization. The papers written for the present volume are derived from these research projects on Plateau material culture.

The Canadian Museum of Civilization exhibit on Nlaka'pamux clothing opened in 1995 as part of the larger exhibition *Threads of the Land*. It was the first time the Museum focussed on the important assemblage of Plateau material culture it had acquired almost 75 years earlier. The collection includes a variety of Nlaka'pamux clothing, some of which were made of tanned skin and others woven from cedar or willow bark. Many of the garments have painted designs or are decorated with animal fur, bones, teeth or claws. These decorations are said to refer to dreams or visions, or to indicate the wearer's relationship to a supernatural guardian.

Dorothy drafted diagrams of the cuts of Nlaka'pamux skin garments, including a dress, two types of shirts, and two styles of moccasins. Her eye for detail directed our attention to unusual sewing techniques and methods of attaching ornaments and fringes. She made separate drawings of these technical elements. Dorothy's analyses and drawings illuminated the underlying art and craftsmanship of Nlaka'pamux skin clothing and, when joined with the artifacts and written text, helped to communicate the unique character of this material culture.

Working with Dorothy on the willow and cedar bark clothing was a special pleasure. Part of my enjoyment came from the uniqueness of the study. Museum collections of woven clothing from North American Native cultures are rare, and the Canadian Museum of Civilization is fortunate to have examples of Nlaka'pamux hats, capes, leggings, and slippers. Comparative clothing from that area and time period (probably made by the same weavers) is available in museums in New York, Boston, Victoria and Washington. These collections include samples of woven vests and a willow bark shirt. By combining the study of the objects in these various collections we had examples of men's and women's garments from head to toe. The objects themselves also made the research an enjoyable work experience. Nlaka'pamux women were master weavers who were able to shape the garments by the addition or removal of warp threads or by increasing and decreasing the tension of the weft threads. Their decorative techniques included complex manipulation of dyed and neutral warp strands, and fringing using extra warps. Dorothy analyzed and illustrated these various twining, shaping and decorative techniques.

Our next project together, the study of Nlaka'pamux mats, was a continuation of our work on woven garments. Several capes in the collection were identified as rain capes as well as household mats. Such multi-purpose textiles were an integral part of everyday material culture. They provided a clean work surface, a place to sit, to serve food, to dry meat or berries or to wrap-up and store extra food, tools or other small objects. In a rainstorm the capes kept people and household objects dry. Yet the simplicity of their construction and design made them almost invisible in museum collections. Our study looked at the range of weaving techniques and decorative elements present in the mats. The research revealed that such utilitarian objects provided women with a venue to explore colour and design, as well as personal aesthetics. Such studies of material culture provide a fascinating challenge in understanding the history and context of the different communities, and discovering the crafts people who expressed themselves through the objects they made.

The history of Plateau material culture has come into greater prominence in the past few years. New publications have highlighted basketry and beadwork, and recent exhibits have focussed on Salish communities in eastern Washington, Idaho and Montana and British Columbia. Dorothy Burnham's analyses of traditional garments and mats are important elements in this growing field of study. Not only have other scholars and the general public appreciated her work, but the First Nations communities, in particular, have welcomed her many contributions. Recently the cut and decoration of dresses and shirts for powwows and feasts on the Canadian Plateau have been based on Plains and Northwest Coast styles. Although knowledge of many of the techniques of weaving garments had been lost, Dorothy's drawings have inspired weavers and seamstresses to create clothing in the Plateau style. Her work has helped to make old things new again.

Conclusion

At the start of the new millenium, Dorothy celebrates a career in museum work that spans more than seven decades. In the Canadian Ethnology Service, we feel enormously privileged to have benefited from her knowledge, expertise, and friendship during the past 10 years. The papers in this volume highlight some of her important contributions to our work, particularly her drawings of the cuts of garments from the ethnological collections, and of the techniques of sewing and decoration employed in the manufacture of these artifacts. The drawings number over 140, each one an informative and elegant work of art

Introduction

in its own right. They constitute a tangible legacy upon which future generations of researchers, students and Aboriginal people will continue to draw. But there are other, intangible, components of Dorothy's gift to us, for which we are equally grateful. These include the many hours of collegial discussion which furthered our understanding of the artifacts and stimulated our thinking, her generous sharing of a lifetime of knowledge and experience related to material culture studies, her wonderful, infectious, sense of curiosity about each new artifact, and her delight in and appreciation of the skills of bygone generations of Aboriginal artisans.

For all of this, we thank you, Dorothy.

Fascinating Challenges

Dorothy K. Burnham

At the age of 78 an offer of work is both startling and intriguing. The offer came in January 1990 and this is how it happened. I had had a long and varied career with the Royal Ontario Museum in Toronto and in 1977 I had retired from my last position there, Curator of Textiles and Costume. I was 65 with sufficient income to pursue my own research, travel, writing and enjoyment of a life connected with my museum interests. At the time of the work offer, I was in the throes of coping with the complicated publication details of a book I had written on some very beautiful caribou-skin garments made by the Innu of Quebec-Labrador. It was work that had trickled along through some thirty years of other activities. I felt strongly that, when it was published, the time would be right for me to sever my active connection with my old museum and retire again, this time firmly and finally. In anticipation of that I moved to Ottawa. I like the city. It is a beautiful place to live. I had family there and, apart from the friendships one makes with colleagues in other institutions, no museum connections. I really thought my museum life was ending. How wrong I was and how glad I am that I was wrong! A wonderful ten-year extension to my enjoyment of museum research was about to open up before me.

In the course of my work I had come to know and like a number of those on the staff of the Canadian Museum of Civilization. One day Judy Thompson, Curator of Athabaskan material, telephoned to ask if I would be interested in going to the Museum to see some caribou-skin garments from the western Subarctic that she was working on. They were spread out in the storage area for easy examination and she thought I might like to take this opportunity to see this interesting material. It was a chance I could not resist and we made a date. I had a marvelous day. I saw beautiful garments from a part of Canada I did not know and was able to examine them closely, comparing them with those I did know. I could check details of cut (the shape of component parts) and decoration, marveling and exclaiming over the skill and artistry of the women who made them, with a kindred spirit - Judy Thompson.

I was still in a glow some days later when she again telephoned, this time to ask, rather diffidently, whether I would consider doing a few drawings for her projected publication of the material we had been enjoying so much together. She would just like to have a few diagrams of the construction of the tunics similar to those I had done for my Innu book, and she suggested a short term contract from the Museum to do this work.

It was quite wonderful to get this strong assurance, at my advanced age, that I was still considered useful enough to be paid for my services. I savoured the thought for awhile. Then I turned the contract down, but said I would like to try doing the work as a volunteer. Ten years later I am still doing it.

I have been working with Judy Thompson on artifacts from the western Subarctic, with Judy Hall on Inuit clothing and beautiful material from the Eastern Woodlands, and with Leslie Tepper on garments and weaving from interior British Columbia. What a fascinating mixture of challenges! Fortunately, my three favourite ethnologists do the scientific research and the writing while I am allowed to do what I enjoy most. I look long and carefully and then simply record what I see with a scale drawing and sometimes a few added words. To me this is a perfect division of labour and some of the results of this three-fold collaboration can be found in this book.

I find it fascinating that the skill that made my help desirable was simply a refinement of the drafting skills I was taught when I started my long museum career in 1929. When I left school my art teacher, who knew Dr. C.T. Currelly, Director of the Royal Ontario Museum of Archaeology, recommended me for a drafting position that she had heard was open at the museum. I knew the museum well. I was born just a few blocks away from it and, as a child, had haunted its galleries. I loved the place but never dreamed of being able to work there. I got the job and, at 18 years of age, I found myself the most junior of juniors, on a small but interesting and very kind staff who took over the task of bringing me up. I had the impressive title of second assistant draftsman and the princely salary of eight dollars per week.

In those almost prehistoric times, many museums used pen and ink scale drawings for identification, as well as illustration. It was cheaper than photography. I was taught the basics needed for museum drafting, how to take and reduce accurate measurements, how to indicate bulk and texture and most importantly, how to handle fragile objects. I drew everything from English porcelains and Chinese bronzes to prehistoric stone axes. Much of the work was routine and inclined to be a bit boring, but the atmosphere of the office was stimulating and I enjoyed both the people and the close connection I had with the material. My main work was drawing, but the staff was small and flexible, and slowly I found myself involved in a wide variety of museum tasks, cataloguing, caring for material, arranging cases, writing labels, in fact anything that needed to be done. In those early days it was possible to work one's way up in an institution. I was only too aware of my lack of university training, but I was working under some very outstanding scholars and that was a liberal education in itself. I filled in many gaps with night courses, reading and as much travel as I could squeeze in. The particular virus that infects those of us who love museums had entered my blood stream and I worked hard but with great enjoyment.

Ten years later I was put in charge of the newly formed department of textiles and costumes. A door opened in front of me and I walked through it into a challenging and fascinating life. I was no longer making drawings for other people but I continued using that method of research and communication in all my own work. A few years later Harold Burnham and I were married. This certainly enriched my life immensely, but it also complicated it. We had a family and with Harold's work we had to move away from Toronto. Reluctantly, I gave up even the small connection I had maintained with my museum work.

As a hobby, Harold had become a very skilled weaver, fascinated with the making of textiles and their history. He became involved in international work concerning textile terminology. To make a long and complicated story short, in 1958 he was offered a position on the staff of my old textile department working with my successor, Betty Brett. Her interests lay mainly with costume studies and with textiles that were embroidered, painted or printed. With Harold's weaving knowledge they made a strong team and the department flourished.

I found myself in a rather strange position on the outside. Harold had done a lot of volunteer museum work with me during the first years of our marriage. We liked working together and now we reversed the roles. He was paid. I was the volunteer. This proved to be very productive, and whatever research was done, the drafting skills were an integral part of it. I did dozens and dozens of drawings, many of which are in our publications or have been borrowed by other authors.

Harold's untimely death in 1972 put an end to that most enjoyable partnership. I was bereft. Work is a godsend at such times. Fortunately, I was asked to return full time to my old department and that saw me through a bad stretch of time. After retirement I was able to complete a couple of our joint projects and was in a receptive frame of mind when I received Judy Thompson's request for a few drawings.

With increasing age people too often find themselves sitting on the shelf, comparatively inactive, the knowledge and skills acquired over a long working life dropping away from them unused and forgotten. Judy Thompson's request and my fortunate decision to take on the work as a volunteer spared me from that fate. True, I have worked long and hard, I have been exhausted and frustrated at times, but I have actively enjoyed the work.

I find that my three colleagues have taken a lead from the Native people they work with: I am treated gently and lovingly as a respected elder. I like that. It makes growing old worthwhile and even fun. My most grateful thanks go to the Canadian Museum of Civilization for opening its doors to me, to the Canadian Ethnology Service and its director, Dr. Andrea Laforet, and to my three bosses and very dear friends, Judy Thompson, Judy Hall and Leslie Tepper.

Life and Career

Born and educated in Toronto. Joined the staff of the Royal Ontario Museum (ROM) in Toronto as a draftsman after leaving school in 1929.

Did archaeological drafting and general museum work. Took training in spinning, weaving, textile chemistry, and costume pattern drafting. Travelled to other museums to study their collections. Worked for two summers at the Victoria and Albert Museum in London, England.

1939 A Textile Department was created at the ROM and I became its first Curator.

1944 Married Harold B. Burnham

1947 Launched the Textile Department's major research project on the history of Canadian handweaving.

1949 Left the ROM to bring up our family. Moved away from Toronto due to Harold's work, but maintained connection with museum research.

1954 Moved to the Niagara Peninsula and set up as professional handweavers, Burnham & Burnham.

1959 Harold joined the staff of the ROM's Textile Department, later becoming a most outstanding Curator of that department.

On returning to Toronto, I again worked at the ROM, first as a volunteer in the Ethnology Department and then as a part-time research assistant in my former department of Textiles. Intense work followed by both Harold and myself on Canadian handweaving. This resulted in a major exhibition in 1971 and was followed by the publication of *Keep Me Warm One Night: Early Handweaving in Eastern Canada* in 1972.

1972 Harold died and I returned to full-time work at the ROM, first as Associate Curator and then as Curator of the Textile Department.

1977 I retired from the ROM, but continued as Research Associate.

1978 Retained by the National Gallery of Canada to gather and present a major travelling exhibition of Canadian traditional spinning and weaving.

1981 Exhibition *The Comfortable Arts: Traditional Spinning and Weaving in Canada* opened at the National Gallery of Canada in Ottawa and then travelled to Guelph, Ontario; Regina, Saskatchewan; and Vancouver, B.C. Catalogue published in English and French.

1983 Received a grant from the Explorations Program of the Canada Council to research the textile traditions of the Doukhobors, a Russian group of religious dissenters who settled in the Canadian west in 1899.

This resulted in the publication, in 1986, of *Unlike the Lilies: Doukhobor Textile Traditions in Canada*. I was then asked to be a guest curator for an exhibition of the same name organized by the Provincial Museum of Alberta in Edmonton. This exhibit opened at that museum in the autumn of 1988 and travelled to various museums in western Canada over a two year period: Winnipeg, Saskatoon, Victoria, Langley, Castlegar and Red Deer.

For approximately twenty five years as time and opportunity permitted, I studied a group of rare painted caribou-skin coats of the Innu of the Quebec-Labrador area. The coats were made and worn between 1700 and 1930 and my research focussed on their connection with European fashion costume. This has been an interesting project bringing together two of my textile-costume interests, fashion and Native skin clothing. Travelling in North America, Great Britain and Europe I have been able to catalogue practically all of the early specimens and many of the later examples.

A volume with detailed analysis of sixty of the most important examples with introductory historical and technical chapters was published by the Royal Ontario Museum in association with the University of Washington Press, Seattle. It is entitled *To Please the Caribou: Painted Caribou-Skin Coats Worn by the Naskapi, Montagnais and Cree hunters of the Quebec-Labrador Peninsula*.

1990 to present
>   Research Associate, Canadian Ethnology Service, Canadian Museum of Civilization

Currently working with curators of the Canadian Ethnology Service on their magnificent collections of Athabaskan, Inuit, Eastern Woodlands and Plateau clothing and textiles.

2000 Curator Emeritus, Royal Ontario Museum

Awards

1980 Alberta 75 Civic Committee Certificate for Outstanding Voluntary Services to the Cultural History Department, Glenbow Museum, Calgary, Alberta.

1982 Award of Merit, Canadian Museums Association

1984 Member of the Order of Canada

1985 John Mather Award, Canadian Guild of Crafts

1987 Diplome d'Honneur, Canadian Conference of the Arts
1988 Fellow of the Ontario College of Art
1994 Honourary Member, Canadian Crafts Council
1995 Barbeau Medal, Folklore Studies Association of Canada
1998 Honourary Doctor of Laws, Trent University, Peterborough, Ontario

Main Publications

1967 *Costumes for Canada's Birthday: the Styles of 1867*. Eight folders. Toronto: Royal Ontario Museum.

1972 *Keep Me Warm One Night – Early Handweaving in Eastern Canada* (with Harold Burnham). Toronto: University of Toronto Press.

1973 *Cut My Cote*. Textile Department, Royal Ontario Museum, Toronto.

1974 Handweaving and textiles (with Harold Burnham). In *The Book of Canadian Antiques*, ed. D.B. Webster, 282-295. Toronto: McGraw-Hill Ryerson.

1975 *Pieced Quilts of Ontario*. Toronto: Royal Ontario Museum.

1976 Canadian Textile Traditions. In *Textile Collections of the World*, Vol.1, United States and Canada, ed. Cecil Lubell. New York: Van Nostrand.

1977 Constructions used by Jacquard Coverlet Weavers in Ontario. In *Studies in Textile History: In Memory of Harold B. Burnham*, ed. Veronika Gervers. Toronto: Royal Ontario Museum.

1980 *Warp and Weft: A Textile Terminology*. Toronto: Royal Ontario Museum.

1981 *The Comfortable Arts: Traditional Spinning and Weaving in Canada*. Ottawa: National Gallery of Canada.

1985 Textiles, Woven. In *The Canadian Encyclopedia*. Edmonton: Hurtig Publishers, Limited.

1986 *Unlike the Lilies: Doukhobor Textile Traditions in Canada*. Toronto: Royal Ontario Museum.

1992 *To Please the Caribou: Painted Caribou-Skin Coats Worn by the Naskapi, Montagnais and Cree Hunters of the Quebec-Labrador Peninsula*. Toronto: Royal Ontario Museum.

Section 1
Athabaskan Studies

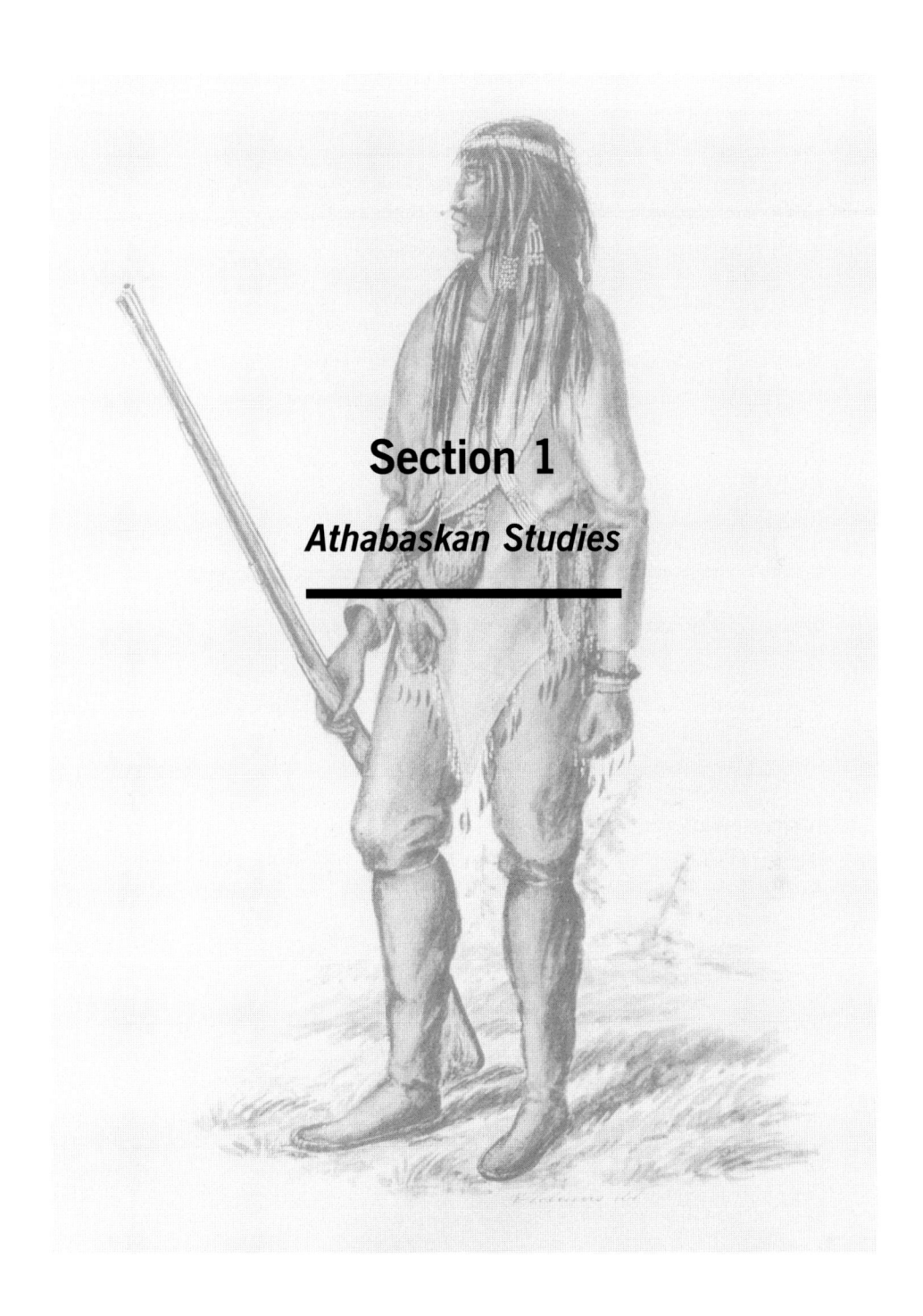

Gwich'in Man. Watercolour by Edward Adams, 1850-1854.
Courtesy of the Glenbow Museum, Calgary AE58.31.1.

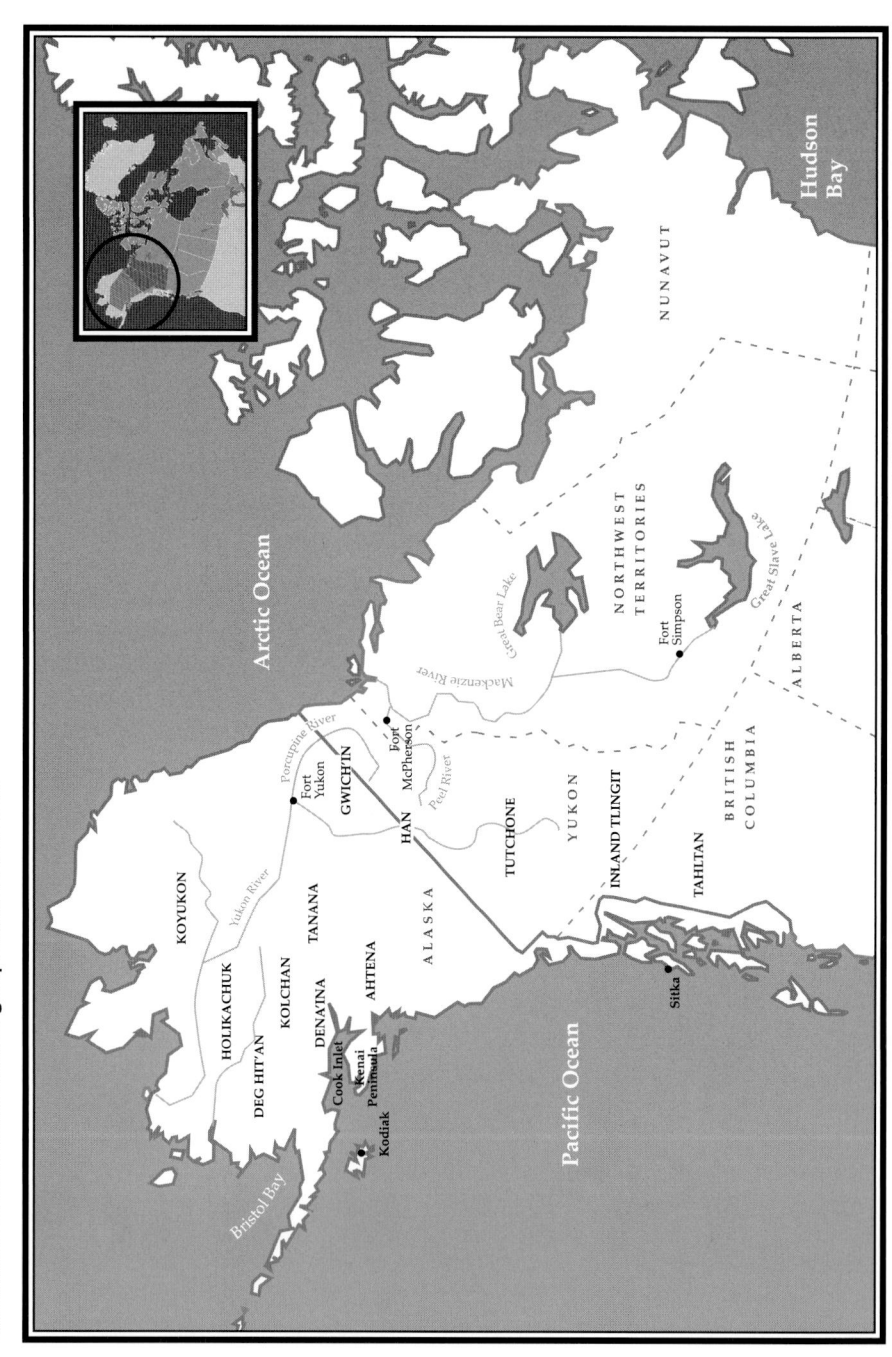

Athabaskan territories and cultural groups referred to in text.

Traditional Summer Clothing of the Dena'ina and the Gwich'in[1]: Variations on a Theme

Judy Thompson

Introduction

Distinctive, beautifully made summer garments are a signal feature of the traditional culture of many Northern Athabaskan peoples. A major clothing style, illustrated in Figure 1.1, consisted of multi-piece outfits made from tanned caribou hides and decorated with porcupine quills and fringing. The two principle components were a sleeved, pullover tunic (often cut to a point at front and back), and a lower garment (moccasin-trousers) which combined trouser with footwear. Mittens and detached hoods and accessories such as bags and knife sheaths often completed an outfit. Decoration of this clothing was aesthetically pleasing, accentuating the lines of each garment and providing colour and contrast in texture.

The sophisticated design and skilled craftsmanship of the earliest examples testify to a tradition which was already ancient and highly developed when white people first penetrated North America's western subarctic regions. Of the many centuries of development and evolution this tradition underwent before the late eighteenth century, and of its distribution in ancient times, virtually nothing is known. The earliest written and pictorial records and twentieth century ethnographic studies suggest that during the late eighteenth and early nineteenth centuries, clothing of the type seen in Figure 1.1 was worn throughout a region extending from Cook Inlet on the Alaska coast to the lower Mackenzie River in Canada's Northwest Territories.[2]

As with other aspects of the material culture, following the arrival of fur traders and European goods in the western subarctic Aboriginal clothing of

1.1 Gwich'in man's summer outfit, collected by Reverend W.W. Kirkby, 1860. Courtesy National Museums of Scotland, Edinburgh 564.

this type was gradually displaced by new fashions. At various times during the nineteenth century, traditionally styled hide garments were first modified by the incorporation of glass trade beads into their decoration, then replaced completely by new modes of dress.[3] The last "old-style" summer tunics and moccasin-trousers were made about 1900.

Fortunately, these beautiful and distinctive garments were often sought after by visitors to the far north. Throughout the nineteenth century, explorers, fur traders, missionaries, scientists, government officials, sportsmen and tourists collected traditional Athabaskan clothing items, usually transporting their acquisitions back to home cities in other parts of the world. A legacy remains: over 150 examples of the two principle garments, tunics and moccasin-trousers, are preserved in North American and European museums.

These museum collections confirm a broad distribution for the clothing style illustrated in Figure 1.1. Garments of outwardly similar appearance are attributed to at least eleven Athabaskan groups - Dena'ina, Ahtena, Deg Hit'an[4], Koyukon, Inland Tlingit, Tutchone, Tanana, Holikachuk, Kolchan, Han and Gwich'in. That so many different Athabaskan peoples dressed alike is not surprising. These groups inhabited contiguous territories and were closely related culturally and linguistically. They exploited the same natural resources and lived similar lifestyles, traded with each other and intermarried. Clothing such as that seen in Figure 1.1 would have served all of them well.

At the same time, common sense tells us that regional variations on the common clothing theme must also have existed. These would have developed in response to local life style, aesthetics, and resources, and undoubtedly would have been recognized by Athabaskans of the day. With the passage of time, much information about such sub-styles in Athabaskan clothing has been lost. Contemporary written accounts and illustrations are vague about the details of clothing and twentieth century ethnological field studies, while often recording valuable data related to traditional clothing, did not produce the kind of detailed information that would help in the definition of regional styles. Today, extant collections have greater potential than any other source to shed light on this subject. Clothing artifacts are primary sources of information, for they come to us virtually unchanged from the hands of their makers and users.

As this paper will document, study of a large number of examples and, in particular, the drawing out and comparing of garment cuts (that is, the shape of component parts) as well as of sewing and decorative techniques, has revealed subtle variations in the way garments were made. The recurrence of certain traits, or combinations of traits, on more than one garment has indicated approaches to design and decoration that once may have been common to a given cultural group or region. Where these could be linked to artifacts of known provenance, a picture of regional styles within the broader Athabaskan clothing tradition has emerged.

This picture is by no means complete. Although, as previously noted, a diversity of Athabaskan peoples is represented in extant collections, coverage and documentation is uneven. The majority of reliably documented examples are attributed to one of two groups – Dena'ina or Gwich'in. These collections in particular, therefore, lent themselves to analysis and comparison aimed at identifying and describing regional approaches to design and decoration of clothing. The fact that Dena'ina and Gwich'in territories are geographically distant, at opposite sides of the region within which clothing of the type being discussed here was worn, was fortuitous but helpful. It could be anticipated that differences in clothing would be more pronounced, and therefore more easily recognizable, as a result of this physical distance.

The purposes of this paper are two-fold. The first is to describe, in greater detail than has heretofore been possible, aspects of design and decoration integral to a major nineteenth century Athabaskan clothing style. The second is to compare, using mainly Dena'ina and Gwich'in examples, regional approaches to the cut and decoration of the two principal garments, the tunic and the moccasin-trouser. The paper comprises three main sections. The first, "The Collections", presents an overview of collection histories and current repositories for documented examples of nineteenth century Dena'ina and Gwich'in clothing; the second, "The Design of Garments" describes and compares the cuts of men's and women's tunics and moccasin-trousers from these collections; and the third, "The Decoration of Clothing", discusses techniques and other aspects of the decoration of garments from the two groups.

The Collections

Dena'ina

The Dena'ina, or Tanaina as they have been known until recently, are the only Northern Athabaskan people with territory bordering a seacoast. In the nineteenth century, the Dena'ina lived in the mountainous region around Cook Inlet, in southwestern Alaska, hunting and fishing in a land rich in both sea and land resources. Their proximity to the coast resulted in early contacts with explorers and fur traders who approached northwestern North America by sea. British, Russian and American voyagers reached the area in the late eighteenth century, and during the late eighteenth and early nineteenth centuries Russians established trading posts and redoubts in Athabaskan territory, on Cook Inlet and the lower Kuskokwim and Yukon rivers.

Given the strong Russian presence in the region, it is not surprising that the most important early collections of Dena'ina clothing are found today in two northern European museums, one in Finland and the other in Russia. The National Museum of Finland (NMF) in Helsinki has eleven Dena'ina tunics and six pairs of moccasin-trousers. These were collected by Arvid Adolf Etholén, a Finn who managed the Russian American Company from its headquarters at Sitka, Alaska between 1841 and 1845. Pirjo Varjola, the author of a definitive catalogue of the Helsinki collection, has noted that a Russian scientist, Ilya Voznesenskii, probably contributed items to Etholén's collection and assisted in cataloguing the material (Etholén's catalogue is in Voznesenskii's handwriting).[5] Voznesenskii was in the Cook Inlet region in the summer of 1842, assembling "zoological, botanical, mineral, and ethnographic collections" for the Russian Academy of Sciences;[6] in the following spring of 1843, he spent two months in Sitka.

The second major repository for pre-1850 Dena'ina clothing is the Peter the Great Museum of Anthropology and Ethnography (MAE) in St. Petersburg.[7] This institution also holds a number of closely comparable garments attributed to other, neighbouring, Alaskan Athabaskan groups – specifically, to Ahtena, Deg Hit'an, and Kolchan. Erna Siebert has published the collection as a whole.[8] It includes six Dena'ina tunics and moccasin-trousers, three Ahtena tunics, four Kolchan tunics and one Deg Hit'an tunic. The principal collector of this material was the same Ilya Voznesenskii referred to above. A few items were acquired by Lavrentii Zagoskin, a Russian military officer and pioneering ethnographer who travelled in the Lower Yukon and Norton Sound region from 1842-45,[9] and by A.E. Kashevarov, a commander of Russian American Company ships in the north Pacific between 1833 and 1844.[10]

A later collection of traditionally styled summer garments is housed in Germany, in the Stäatliches Museum für Völkerkunde (SMV) in Berlin. This collection includes two Dena'ina summer tunics and three pairs of moccasin-trousers collected specifically for the Museum für Völkerkunde by Captain J.Adrian Jacobsen in 1881-83.[11] Less well-documented, but probably Dena'ina in origin, are garments (three tunics and four moccasin-trousers) in the Field Museum of Natural History (FMNH) in Chicago, acquired in 1887 on the Alaska coast by Edward Ayer, an American industrialist and collector of ethnographic material. James VanStone has published this collection.[12] Finally, the Alaska State Museum (ASM) in Juneau has a comparable collection from western Alaskan Athabaskans, collected in 1888 by an American seaman, Ewald Schmieder.

Gwich'in

In the nineteenth century, the nine regional bands which make up the Athabaskan group known as the Gwich'in occupied a large area extending from north-central Alaska east across the Yukon to the lower Mackenzie valley in Canada's Northwest Territories. Although like other Athabaskans, the Gwich'in fished and hunted a wide variety of animal resources, their economy centered on the caribou, an animal which provided them with food and materials for clothing, shelter, and tools.

Direct contacts between the Gwich'in and white men began in 1789, as fur trader/explorer Alexander Mackenzie encountered people at summer fishing camps along the lower reaches of the river that was later to bear his name. Mackenzie's expedition opened up a region rich in furs to Euro-Canadian traders. Within a few decades, several more-or-less permanent trading posts were set up in the Great Slave Lake-Mackenzie River region. The Forks (later Fort Simpson), created in 1803, and Fort Good Hope, established in 1804, drew Gwich'in from the Mackenzie Flats region to trade. With the setting up of Fort Yukon and Peel River Post (later Fort McPherson) in 1840 and the establishment of Lapierre House in 1848, the Gwich'in had trading posts located within their own territories.

The oldest examples of Gwich'in clothing stem from the collecting activities of personnel attached to these posts, or of others (missionaries, travelers, sportsmen) who used the resources of the posts as they traveled through the northwest. Bernard Ross, a Scottish fur trader stationed at Fort Simpson on the Mackenzie River in the early 1860s, was the most important single collector. With the assistance of colleagues and contemporaries such as fur trader Charles Gaudet and Reverend William Kirkby, an Anglican minister, he assembled collections for both the Royal Scottish Museum (NMS) in Edinburgh and the Smithsonian Institution (SI) in Washington, D.C.[13] As a result, two multi-piece Gwich'in summer clothing outfits and one tunic are in the Edinburgh collection, and the Smithsonian Institution has six outfits and three tunics. Another item, a child's outfit in the Field Museum of Natural History, probably was collected by Robert Kennicott, a naturalist sponsored by the Smithsonian Institution who travelled through the Mackenzie region and west to Fort Yukon in 1860.

Later examples of Gwich'in clothing are scattered through several different institutions in Canada, the United States, and England.[14] Documentation of many of these late nineteenth century garments is fragmentary. Examples with at least some collection history include a magnificent five-piece outfit in the Fenimore House Museum in Cooperstown, New York, collected by Captain Henry Phillips Dawson between 1882 and 1883 at Fort Rae, Northwest Territories, and an outfit in the American Museum of Natural History in New York that probably was collected by Caspar Whitney, a sportsman and writer who made a trip to Great Slave Lake and to the Barren Grounds beyond in 1894. James McDougall, an important figure in the Hudson's Bay Company during the latter nineteenth century, collected another example, which is now in the Manitoba Museum of Man and Nature, Winnipeg.

The Design of Garments

Men's Tunics:

Figures 1.2 and 1.3 illustrate typical nineteenth century Gwich'in and Dena'ina men's summer tunics.[15] It can be seen that, in outward appearance, these garments have much in common. Both are made from softly tanned,

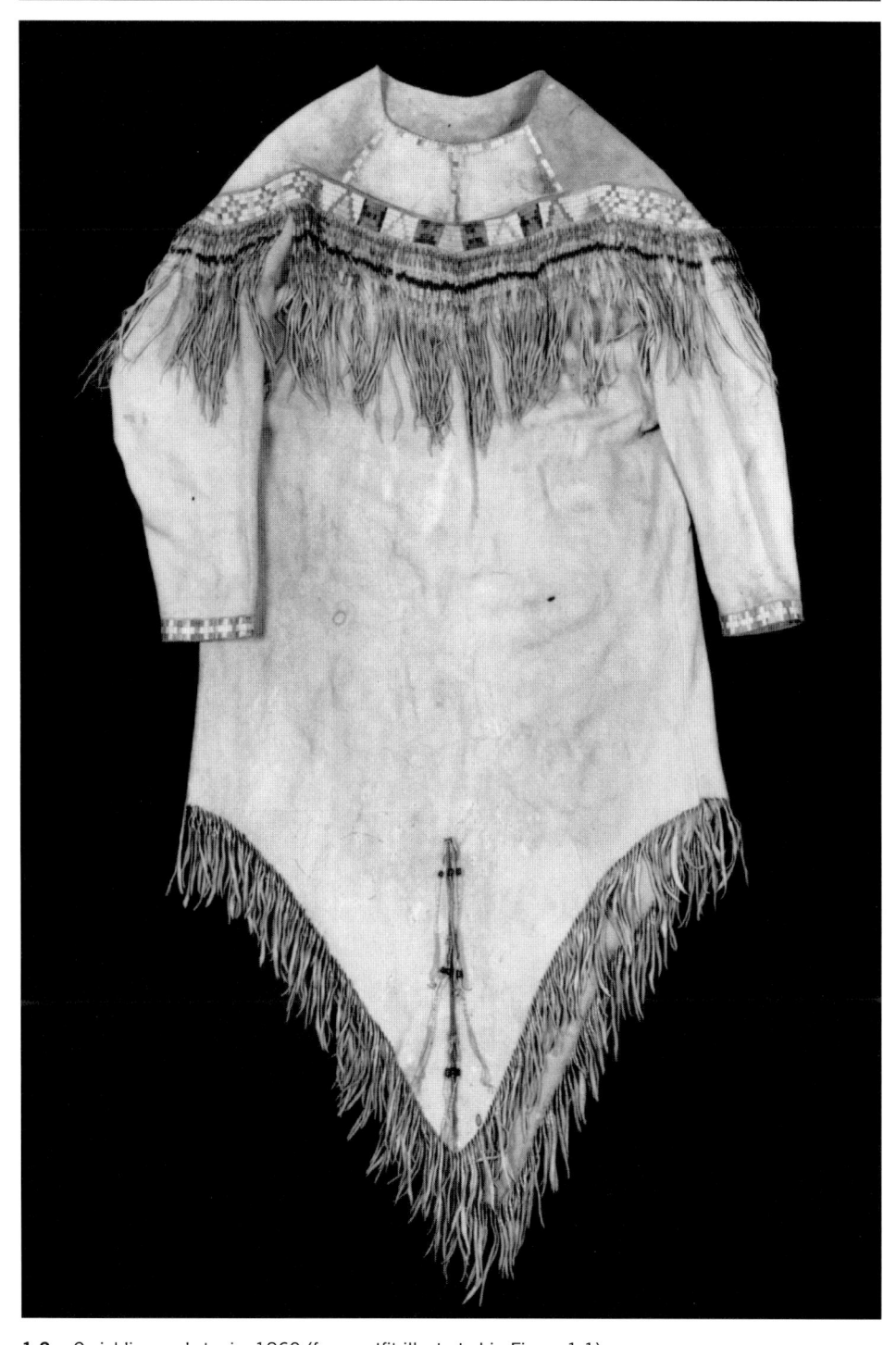

1.2 Gwich'in man's tunic, 1860 (from outfit illustrated in Figure 1.1).
Courtesy National Museums of Scotland, Edinburgh 564.

1.3 Dena'ina man's tunic. Collected by Ilya Voznesenskii, 1842.
Courtesy Peter the Great Museum of Anthropology and Ethnography, St. Petersburg 620.40a.

light-coloured (almost white) caribou hide and similarly decorated with porcupine quills and fringes. The shapes of these two garments are alike as well. In each case, the body hangs straight and is cut to a deep point at front and back. At its greatest length, each garment would fall to about knee level on an individual approximately 1m 65cm (5'5") in height. On the upper front of each tunic, diagonal seams (one on each side) run from the neck edge to the armhole. Neck openings are round, and sleeves taper to the wrist.

These general similarities notwithstanding, detailed examination of the two garments brings to light some significant differences in the way they are constructed. The first difference, revealed by drawings of the cuts of the tunics (Figures 1.4 and 1.5), concerns the shape and relative size of component pieces, and the manner in which they are sewn together. On the Gwich'in tunic (Figure 1.4), the hide piece which forms the back is slightly larger than that used for the front. It crosses over the shoulders, and is joined to the front in diagonal seams running from neck edge to armhole and in vertical seams at the sides. The Dena'ina tunic design (Figure 1.5) also involves a larger hide piece for the back of the garment, and it too crosses over the shoulders and is seamed on the upper front with diagonal seams running from neck edge to armhole. In this case, however, rather than being sewn to the front at the sides, the back wraps around the sides to form the lateral portions of the front as well. A relatively narrow panel forms the centre front of the garment. Furthermore, darts, a tailoring feature not normally associated with North American Aboriginal skin clothing, are taken in the upper front of the Dena'ina garment – one on each side, extending from above the diagonal seam to under the breastband.

The second important difference in the cut of these two garments concerns the sleeves. The sleeves on the Gwich'in garment are (to a modern seamstress's eye) most unusual in their design. As clarified by Dorothy Burnham (page 91, this volume), the sleeve head has an angular configuration, corresponding to the opening created by the joining of the garment front and back. The sleeve seam runs up the inner arm, meeting (approximately) with the diagonal seam on the upper front of the garment. When the sleeve is inserted, the upper back of the garment is pulled around toward the front. The result is a sleeve positioned forward of the tunic's median line and curving to the front of the garment.[16] The Dena'ina tunic has a far less complicated sleeve design. The sleeve shape is trapezoidal; sewn up, it forms a tapered sleeve with no extra depth or fullness at the underarm. This relatively simple sleeve is sewn into a straight armhole.

The differences in the cut and construction of the Gwich'in and Dena'ina examples illustrated here are not unique to these two tunics. The distinctive sleeve shown in Figure 1.4 was a characteristic of virtually all Gwich'in tunics examined in the course of this research; and these garments also were seamed from the underarm and made without darts on the upper front. Dena'ina tunics, on the other hand, often had darts in the upper front, were made with

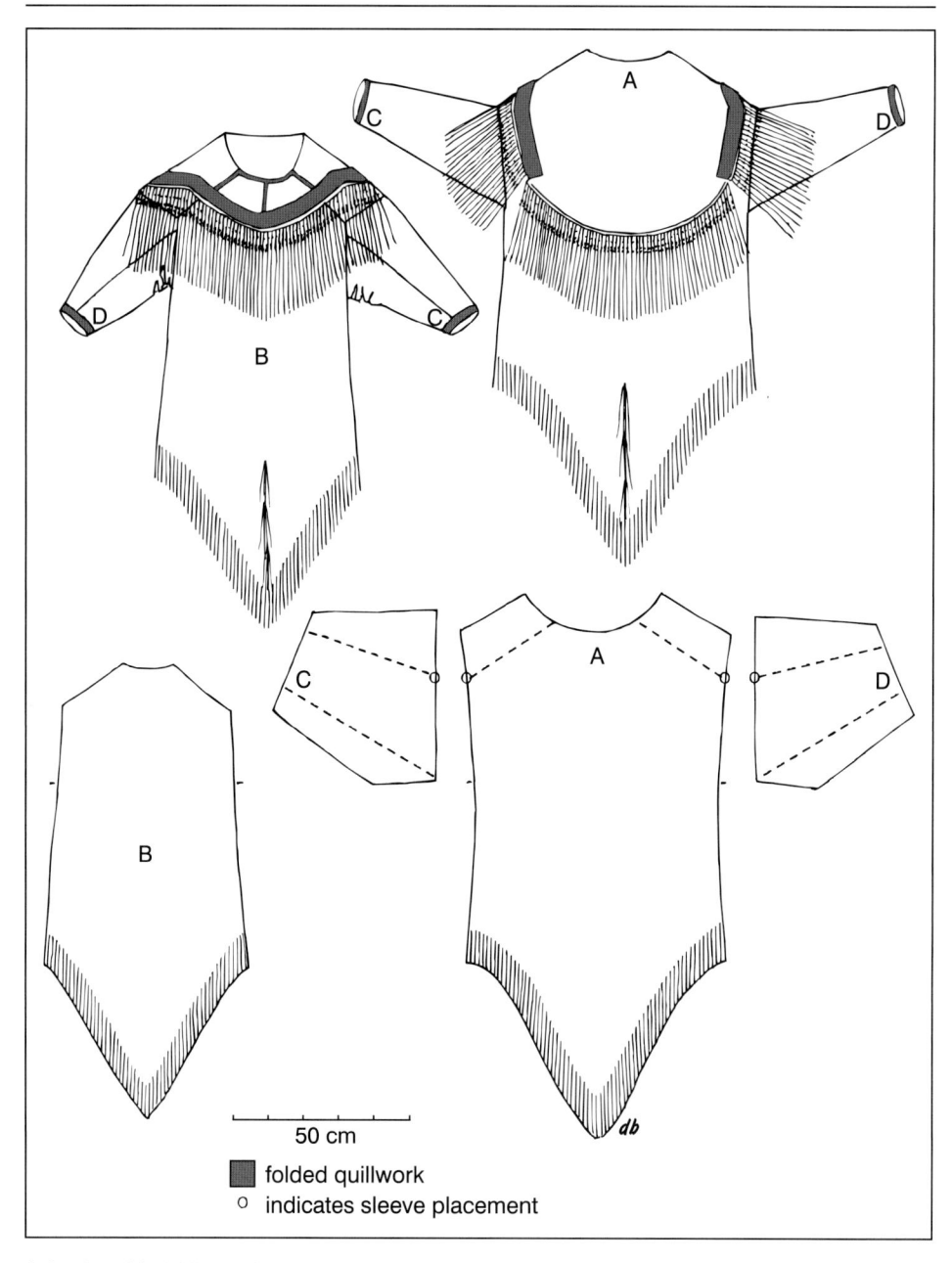

Traditional Summer Clothing of the Dena'ina and the Gwich'in

1.4 Cut of Gwich'in man's tunic (illustrated in Figure 1.2), c. 1860. National Museums of Scotland, Edinburgh 564.

a single hide forming not only the back of the garment, but parts of the front as well, and had a simple sleeve design.

Because of the paucity of documented examples from other regions, it is difficult to determine how widespread these particular approaches to cut and construction might have been, beyond the territories of these two groups. However, on the evidence of a very few garments from neighbouring groups to the south and west of Gwich'in territory, it seems probable that Athabaskans in these areas wore upper garments similar to those of the Gwich'in in cut and construction. For example, the tunic of a summer outfit that probably was made in southwest Yukon about 1870 has the same cut, as does a child's hooded shirt collected at Fort Reliance, Alaska, in Han territory.[17]

In contrast, although the "Gwich'in style" cut must have been known to seamstresses in southern and western Alaska, it was not common in this area. Rather, the majority of tunics attributed to Dena'ina, Ahtena, Deg Hit'an, Holikachuk, Koyukon and Kolchan were made like the Dena'ina example shown in Figure 1.5. For example, the use of a single hide to form not only the back of the tunic, but parts of the front as well was seen on at least 14 tunics attributed to the Dena'ina and on one Kolchan garment.[18] In some cases, the wraparound portions were relatively small, as on the garment shown in Figure 1.5. In other instances, they formed the greater part of the front of the garment, so that only a narrow front panel was required to complete the body. Sometimes, a single hide seamed up the centre front of the garment was used, and a triangular gusset inserted at the lower centre front to increase the width of the garment. Darts on the upper front of tunics were another characteristic feature of garments from these groups, appearing on at least seven Dena'ina tunics and on one attributed to the Kolchan.[19] A simple, tapered tube sleeve sewn into a straight armhole was also common to tunics from this region.

Women's Tunics:

> *At the head of [Cook] Inlet and on the rivers emptying into it from the north we find these people...dressing in buckskin shirts and trousers, the men and women almost alike.*[20]

Ivan Petroff's observation, quoted above, about the similarity between Dena'ina men's and women's clothing was echoed by other nineteenth century observers of Athabaskan fashion. In general, women's upper garments, like other clothing items, closely resembled those worn by men: the materials used were the same, as were sewing and decorative techniques and the general look of the garment. The specifics of these shared attributes, as well as some differences between men's and women's upper garments, are evident when individual garments are closely examined and their cuts drawn out. At the same time, as was the case with the men's garments, a comparison of Gwich'in and Dena'ina

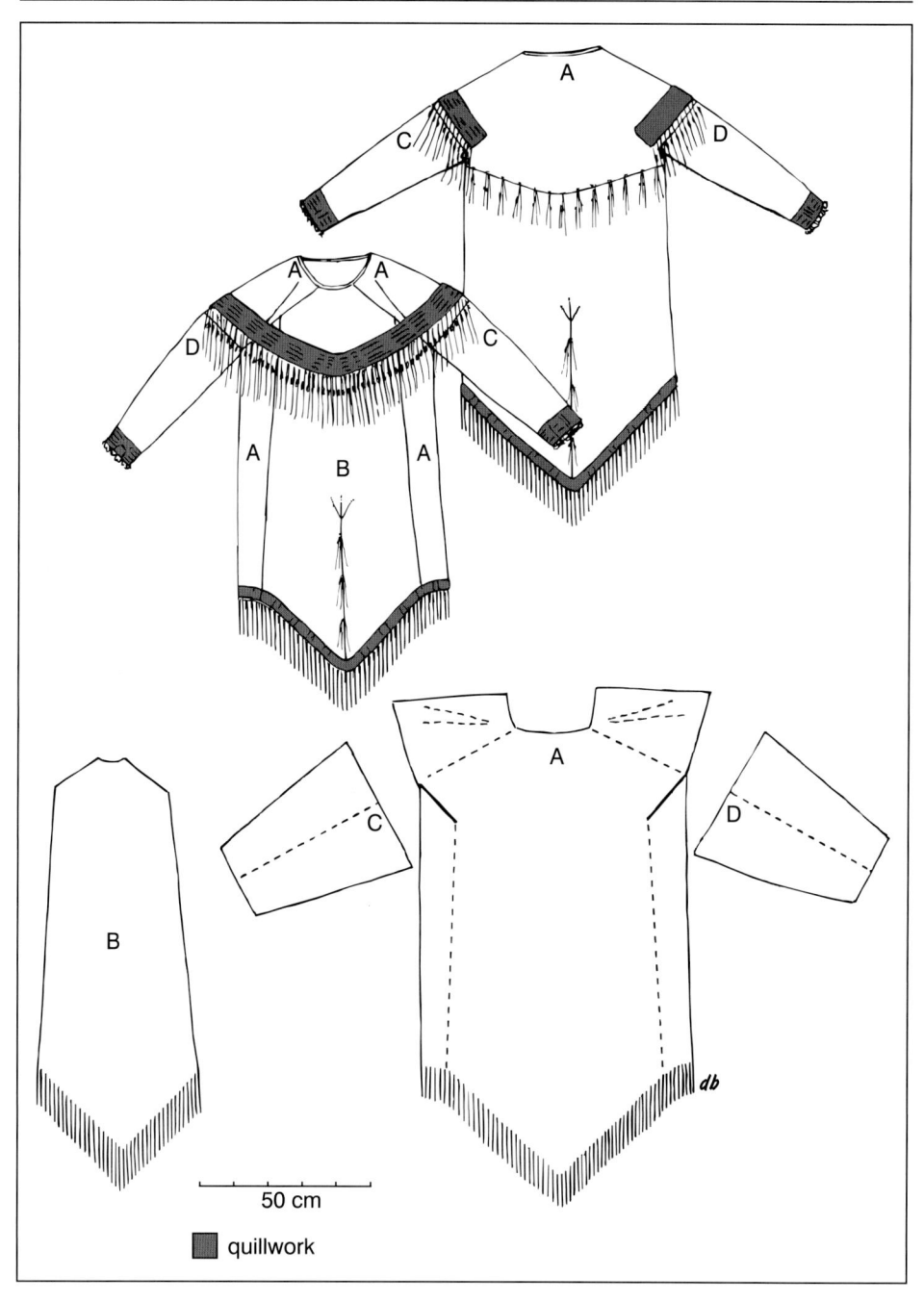

Traditional Summer Clothing of the Dena'ina and the Gwich'in

1.5 Cut of Dena'ina man's tunic (illustrated in Figure 1.3), c. 1840.
Peter the Great Museum of Anthropology and Ethnography, St. Petersburg 620.40a.

examples highlights distinct regional approaches to the cut and decoration of women's tunics.

One of the conundrums faced by researchers studying traditional Athabaskan clothing is whether or not women ever wore tunics with the deeply pointed lower edge so characteristic of men's upper garments. Although we will probably never have a complete and final answer to this question, artifact collections and ethnohistorical sources support the view that, at least in the western Alaskan region, they did. The collection in St. Petersburg includes four garments, identified as women's, which are closely comparable to men's tunics in every respect, including having a pointed lower edge in front and back. These women's pointed tunics include a garment collected by Kashevarov, attributed to Dena'ina[21], two others, collected by Voznesenskii, attributed to Ahtena and Dena'ina,[22] and another, collected by Zagoskin, identified as Deg Hit'an.[23] The Museum für Völkerkunde in Berlin has another Dena'ina example, collected by Jacobsen in 1883.[24]

In his writing, Zagoskin corroborates this artifactual evidence. According to him, the "Yunnaka-khotana" (that is, Koyukon) and "some others":

> ... *make their summer clothing of deer or moose rawhide...This garment is similar in cut to a long shirt, fitting around the neck and ending front and back in the shape of a wedge. With the women the top of these wedges comes halfway down the calf; with the men it stops at the knee.*[25]

In addition to the women's pointed tunics found in western Alaskan Athabaskan collections, there are also several examples of a different style of woman's upper garment - a long (ankle length) dress with straight-cut bottom edge. The body of this longer garment is formed from two large caribou hides of approximately equal size, joined by seams at the sides.[26] Two, slightly different, approaches to the construction of the upper part of this dress were noted. Several examples resembled pointed tunics from this region in having diagonal upper front seaming, darts, and set-in sleeves.[27] Figure 1.6 illustrates the cut of a garment with these features. Other garments of similar appearance have shoulders formed from separate, rectangular, hide pieces. As seen on the example illustrated in Figure 1.7, these inserts join the body of the dress in horizontal seams high on the garment front.[28] Similar seams appear on the upper back of the dress.

No documented examples of a Gwich'in woman's tunic with pointed bottom edges have been located, and ethnohistorical sources are inconclusive on this aspect of clothing. Alexander Mackenzie implied that eastern Gwich'in women, at least, wore this style of upper garment: his detailed description of Gwich'in men's tunics which "taper[ed] to a point" is followed by the assertion that, "The Womens dress is the same with the Mens, only their Skirts are longer, and have not a Fringe on the Breast."[29] A more specific reference to the

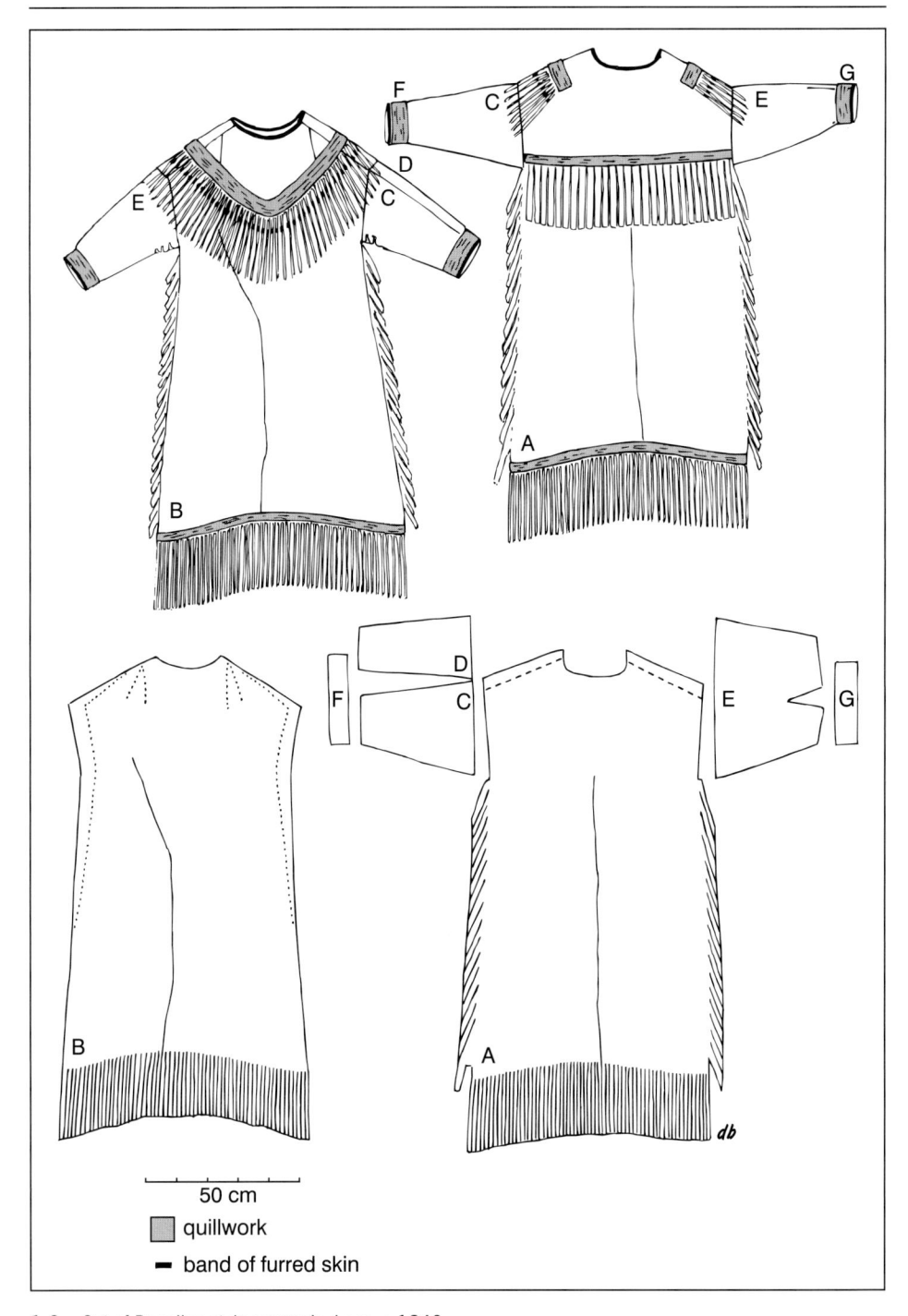

Traditional Summer Clothing of the Dena'ina and the Gwich'in

1.6 Cut of Dena'ina style woman's dress, c.1840
National Museums of Scotland, Edinburgh L357.9.

Fascinating Challenges

1.7 Dena'ina woman's dress.
Collected by Arvid Etholén,
c. 1842.
Courtesy National Museum of
Finland, Helsinki VK174.

wearing of pointed tunics by Gwich'in women is found in the writings of Emile Petitot, an Oblate missionary in the Mackenzie region in the 1860s. Petitot observed that, "[Gwich'in] Women's skin dresses, furnished with points in front and back, are only a little longer than those of their husbands."[30]

Other nineteenth century sources describe Gwich'in women's upper garments which do not have a pointed cut. For example, fur trader Alexander Hunter Murray, at Fort Yukon in 1848, described and sketched a woman's dress that was cut straight at the front: "The women dress nearly the same as the men, only the capot is a leetle [sic] longer, and with no point in front".[31] The dress style noted by Murray is probably the same as two examples collected in 1860 by Bernard Ross for the Smithsonian Institution.[32] These dresses are cut straight in front at approximately knee level; the back is longer and dipping at the centre, but not pointed (Figure 1.8).

1.8 Gwich'in woman's dress. Collected by Robert Kennicott on the Peel River, circa 1860. Courtesy Smithsonian Institution, Washington 884.

Fascinating Challenges

1.9 Gwich'in style woman's dress. Collected by D.A. Cameron in the region of Dawson City, Yukon, 1901-08. Courtesy Royal Ontario Museum, Toronto 953.160.5.

Another version of the Gwich'in woman's dress was longer, approximately ankle length, and cut straight across the bottom, with front and back of approximately equal length. Figures 1.9 and 1.10 illustrate a garment of this type from the Royal Ontario Museum collection.[33] A similarly cut little girl's hooded tunic is illustrated in Figure 1.11. If we compare the cuts of these Gwich'in dresses, with that of the Dena'ina version illustrated in Figure 1.6, we can see that the differences in sleeve design and the presence or absence of darts observed on comparison of men's tunics, also apply here.

Another difference between Dena'ina and Gwich'in versions of the longer, straight-cut woman's dress is in the sizes of the caribou hides used to form the body of the dresses. Dena'ina versions are made with larger hides, resulting in a looser, fuller appearance to the finished garment. For example, the piece forming the back of the garment illustrated in Figure 1.6 measures over 1m

Traditional Summer Clothing of the Dena'ina and the Gwich'in

1.10 Cut of Gwich'in style woman's dress illustrated in Figure 1.9. Royal Ontario Museum, Toronto 953.160.5.

50cm (60") in length. It was large enough that side and bottom fringes (each about 20cm (8") in length) could be cut out of the same piece. That used in the Gwich'in dress (Figure 1.10) measures only 1m (39 ½ ") in length, and required the addition of a second piece, approximately 25cm (10") wide, to make an ankle-length garment. In this case, fringing along the bottom is added separately, and there are no side fringes.

Discussion

Whether they were Dena'ina or Gwich'in, or members of one of the other groups believed to have worn the kind of clothing discussed here, the makers of summer tunics worked with like clothing materials and sewing technologies, and started with an outwardly similar end product in mind. How, and why, did variant approaches such as those noted above develop?

An explanation for some differences in the cuts of tunics may lie in the size of hides available to these seamstresses. Gwich'in seamstresses sewed mainly with the hides of barren-ground caribou (*Rangifer tarandus groenlandicus*). An adult male of this species averages 1m 80cm (71") in length; a female, 1m 66cm (65 ½") in length.[34] Two tanned hides in the Canadian Museum of Civilization collection measure 1m 35cm (53") X 95cm (37 ½") and 1m 70cm (67") X 1m (39 ½").[35] The Gwich'in tunic design used such hides efficiently: normally, one each for back and front, and a third for sleeves and fringing.[36] In exceptional cases, if the hides were of a good size and quality and the seamstress was skilled, two hides could suffice for the body of the garment. Figure 1.12, in which component parts of a tunic are superimposed on two hides of the dimensions given above, illustrates how this might have been done.

If extant clothing collections can be taken as representative, the Gwich'in rarely used hides other than caribou for summer clothing. A few garments are made from a slightly heavier weight skin which lacks the warble fly scarring typical of caribou hides. This heavier skin is probably moose (*Alces alces*).[37] Some Gwich'in also hunted mountain sheep (*Ovis dalli*) and used their hides for winter clothing. It is possible, but has not been confirmed, that summer garments were made from these hides as well. Moose in particular produces a much larger hide than that of a barren-ground caribou. Average lengths for male and female moose, for example, are 2m 57cm (101 ½ ") and 2m 32cm (91 ½"), respectively.[38] A tanned moose hide in the CMC collection measures approximately 2 m (79") in length and the same in width.[39]

Perhaps because they rarely used these larger, heavier, hides for summer clothing, Gwich'in women did not change their normal cutting and sewing procedures when they did sew with them. Gwich'in upper garments made from hides other than caribou – for example, a man's moose hide tunic in the National Museums of Scotland collection[40] – closely resemble caribou hide

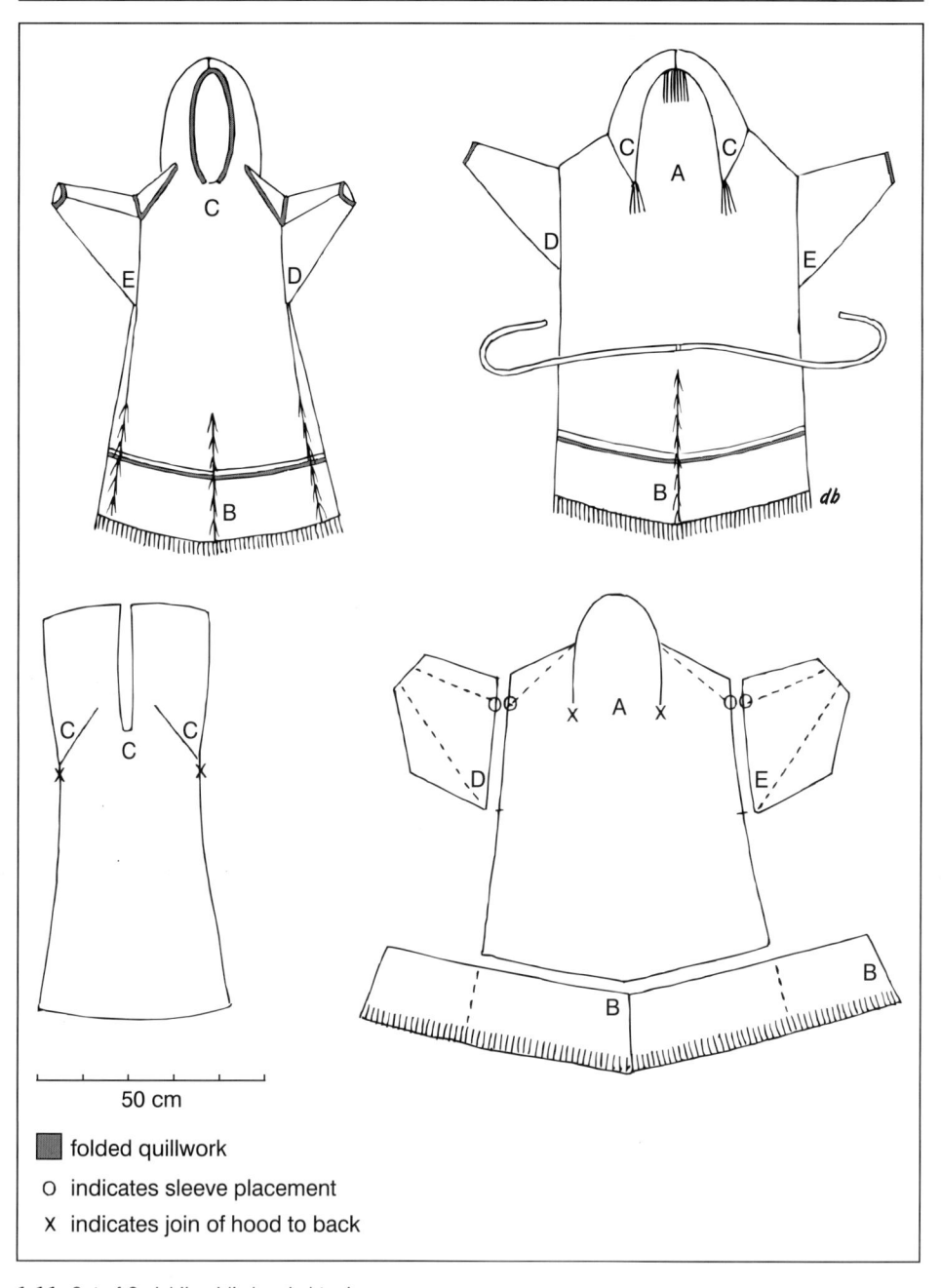

Traditional Summer Clothing of the Dena'ina and the Gwich'in

1.11 Cut of Gwich'in girl's hooded tunic.
Royal Ontario Museum, Toronto HD 5397.

examples in size of component pieces, sleeve design and the way backs and fronts are joined.

Dena'ina clothing collections reflect a different situation with respect to types and sizes of hides used for summer clothing. The earliest, that is, pre-1850, tunics are virtually all made from caribou hides. As already noted, the size of the component parts of many of these garments suggests that the hides from which they were cut were larger than those used in making Gwich'in garments. Figure 1.6, the drawing of the cut of a Dena'ina-style woman's dress, brings to light another feature indicative of the availability of large caribou hides. The hides used for both front and back sections of this garment have each been cut for part of their length, roughly down the middle, the edges stitched together and the hide then treated as a single piece. The cut section corresponds to the part of a hide most subject to scarring and holes from warble fly infestation. Clearly, the original hides were large enough that damaged sections could be removed and the hide still be of sufficient size to be used in making an upper garment – even one of generous proportions, such as the woman's dress illustrated here. This feature is seen on a number of upper garments from this region.

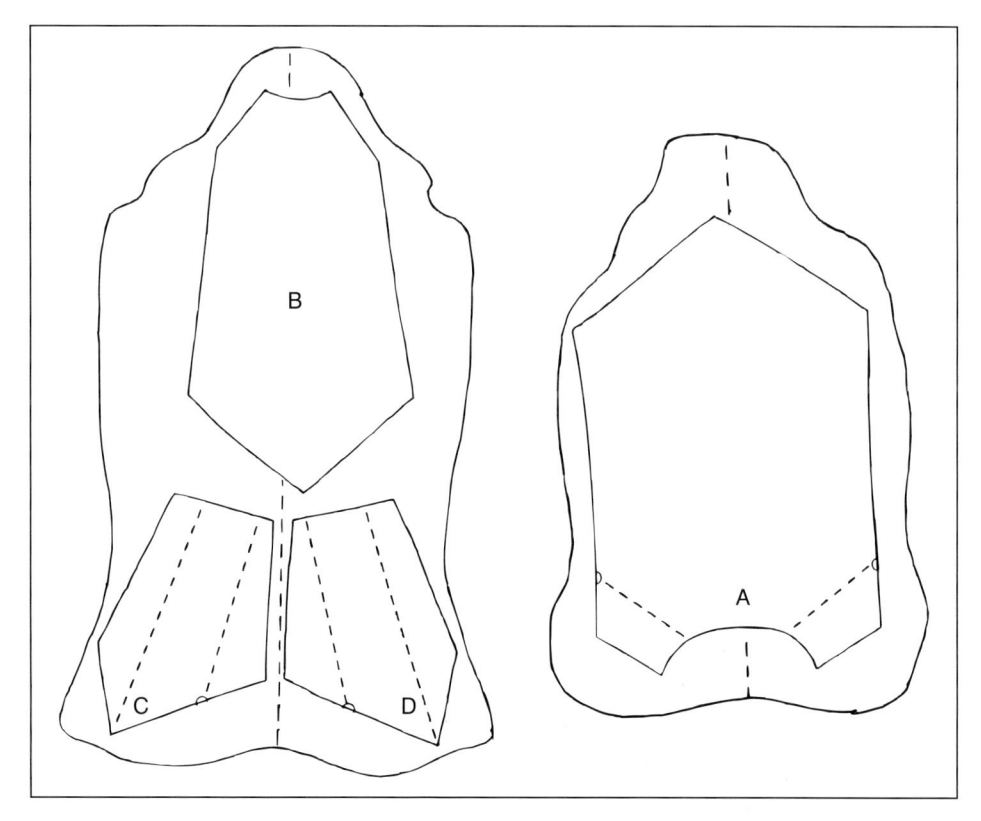

1.12 Component parts to tunic illustrated in Figure 1.40 (Canadian Museum of Civilization VI-Z-10), superimposed on two barren ground caribou hides.

The later Dena'ina tunics, those collected in the 1880s, are almost all made from moose hide. This ascendancy of moose over caribou as a summer clothing material reflects the increasing importance of this animal in Dena'ina economy in the nineteenth century. Moose were "generally more common" than caribou throughout Dena'ina territory[41] and, although the Dena'ina continued to hunt caribou, this animal was not abundant, or available everywhere. For example, by the end of the nineteenth century, caribou populations on the Kenai Peninsula had declined to the point where they were no longer of economic significance.[42]

In light of this, the almost exclusive use of caribou hide for the pre-1850 garments is surprising. The large size of the hides used is also striking. According to ethnohistorical studies,[43] Dena'ina hunted *Rangifer tarandus granti*, a sub-species of barren-ground caribou so like the *Rangifer tarandus groenlandicus* found in Gwich'in territory that a major authority on mammal populations recommended the two sub-species be considered as one.[44] However, a more southerly habitat and better nutrition resulted in greater growth of the animals in Dena'ina territory, and this may be the reason for the larger hide components to Dena'ina tunics.[45] Furthermore, Dena'ina may also have hunted woodland caribou (*Rangifer tarandus fennicus*) and this, too, is a larger animal than the barren-ground caribou utilized by the Gwich'in. Woodland caribou are found in the southern part of Alaska, from the Kenai Peninsula to the valley of the Copper River.[46] A contemporary writer, Ivan Petroff, who conducted surveys and interviews in Alaska in the 1870s, wrote that, "The deer here [that is, in Dena'ina territory] is apparently a larger cousin of the reindeer, the woodland caribou."[47] Dena'ina also may have compensated for a scarcity of indigenous caribou hides required for clothing by importing skins from other regions. There is the intriguing, but equally unverifiable, possibility that some of the hides used in these garments are from a closely related, but geographically distant source – Siberian reindeer (*Rangifer tarandus tarandus*). In the mid-nineteenth century, reindeer hides were an important trade item in the North Pacific, changing hands in a complex Aboriginal trade network that involved the Chukchi of Siberia, Eskimos of the Alaskan coastal regions, and Athabaskans of the Yukon drainage.[48] Unfortunately, it has not been possible to establish whether Siberian reindeer and barren-ground caribou indigenous to Dena'ina territory differ with respect to size.

Whether made from caribou or moose hides, Dena'ina tunics reflect familiarity, and considerable expertise, in sewing with large hides. Most, if not all, differences in the cut and construction of Dena'ina tunics, as compared to those of the Gwich'in, can be interpreted in this light. For example, rather than divide a large hide, Dena'ina seamstresses developed complex folding and trimming strategies so that a single, uncut hide could form not only the back of a tunic but part or all of the front as well. Their skill was such that, where a hide was large enough, they would cut parts of sleeves from the same piece.[49] In one extraordinary example, an entire garment, sleeves included, was made from a single moose hide.[50]

The tapering tucks, or darts, seen on the upper front of many Dena'ina upper garments are, as far as is known, the only instance of this tailoring feature on North American Aboriginal skin clothing. They can be understood as yet another accommodation to the use of large hides in the making of a fitted garment. The positioning of these darts varies: usually, they extend from some point along the diagonal seam to under the breastband; sometimes they appear on the shoulder side of the diagonal upper front seam. Whatever their position, the function of these darts appears to have been the same – to draw up excess hide on the upper front of the garment and ensure a smooth fit in this area.

So prevalent were these "large hide" adaptations, that they appear to have influenced the way the Dena'ina made garments from smaller hides as well. For example, sizes of the back components to the two tunics seen in Figures 1.4 and 1.5 are not, in fact, greatly different. Yet, on the Dena'ina garment, a relatively wide (compared to the Gwich'in example) extension is left to cross over the shoulder, requiring darts on the upper front to achieve the desired fit, and the back wraps around the sides to form part of the front as well.

Moccasin-Trousers:

Athabaskan upper garments of the type discussed above were worn with lower garments equally remarkable in their design. The combination moccasin-trouser made of tanned caribou or moose hide was a close-fitting but flexible garment. It was designed for both mobility and comfort, while at the same time providing protection against brush, rough terrain and biting insects. As the soft sole wore out, it could be patched from inside or outside, or removed and replaced without sacrificing the body of the garment.

Moccasin-trousers are essentially one-piece footed leggings joined with an inset in the crotch. Figures 1.13 and 1.14 illustrate Dena'ina and Gwich'in versions of this garment. Each is made from well-tanned, lightly smoked caribou hide. The Dena'ina garment has been pieced in the crotch, seat and right foot, but, basically, both garments are cut in the same way. As can be seen from the drawing of the Gwich'in example (Figure 1.15), the legs of the garment are each formed from one skin piece, seamed down the inner leg and extending on the outer side to form the side waist as well. The seat of the pants, crotch area, and mid-front of the pants are made from another piece. The sole is a separate, oval-shaped element, drawn up for a short distance around the edges of the foot and gathered slightly at heel and toe. The upper foot is covered by a triangular insert which extends over the ankle front to the bottom of the leg of the garment.

This particular cut apparently had a widespread distribution. Virtually all of the Gwich'in and Dena'ina examples included in this study were made in this

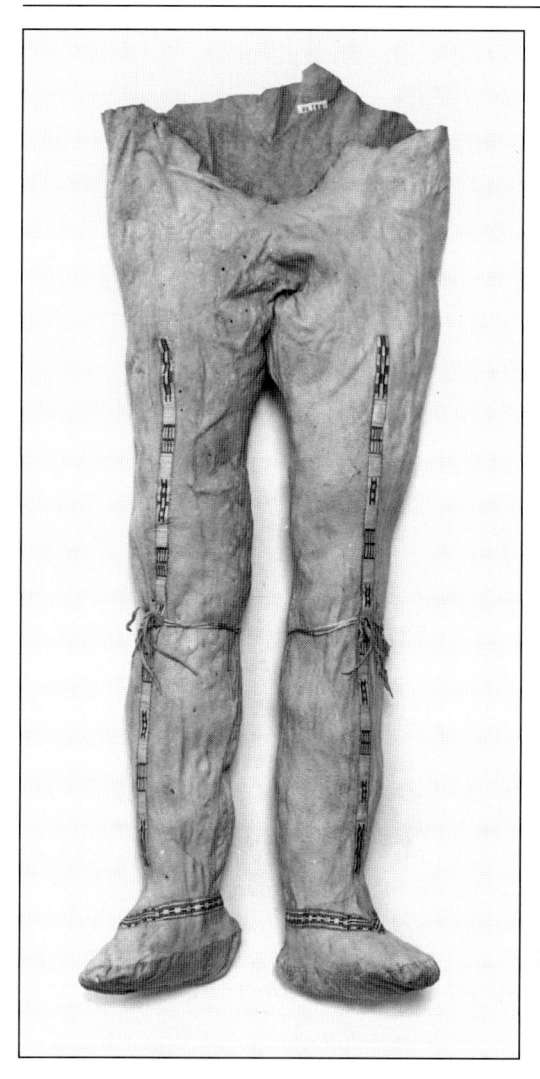

1.13 Dena'ina moccasin-trousers. Collected by Arvid Etholen, c. 1842. Courtesy National Museum of Finland. Helsinki VK 168.

way. Men's, women's and children's versions were alike. Two minor variations in the cut and seaming of the foot of the garment were noted. In the first (Variation A), the leg and upper foot of the moccasin-trouser are one continuous piece and the sole is another piece, turned up around the edges of the foot. A garment in the Field Museum of Natural History, collected among the Tlingit in 1902 and attributed to Southern Tutchone, is made in this way.[51] Figure 1.16, a drawing of an undocumented garment in the Canadian Museum of Civilization collection, illustrates this cut. In the second variation (Variation B), the upper foot is covered by an instep piece which is sewn to the base of the legging at the ankle front, with a basically horizontal seam; that is, there is no inverted v-shaped extension up the front of the leg. The CMC collection includes two examples made in this way. One was collected at Ross River in the Yukon in 1913 and is attributed to Tutchone. The other, from which the cut drawn in Figure 1.17 was taken, is undocumented but, on the basis of its

Fascinating Challenges

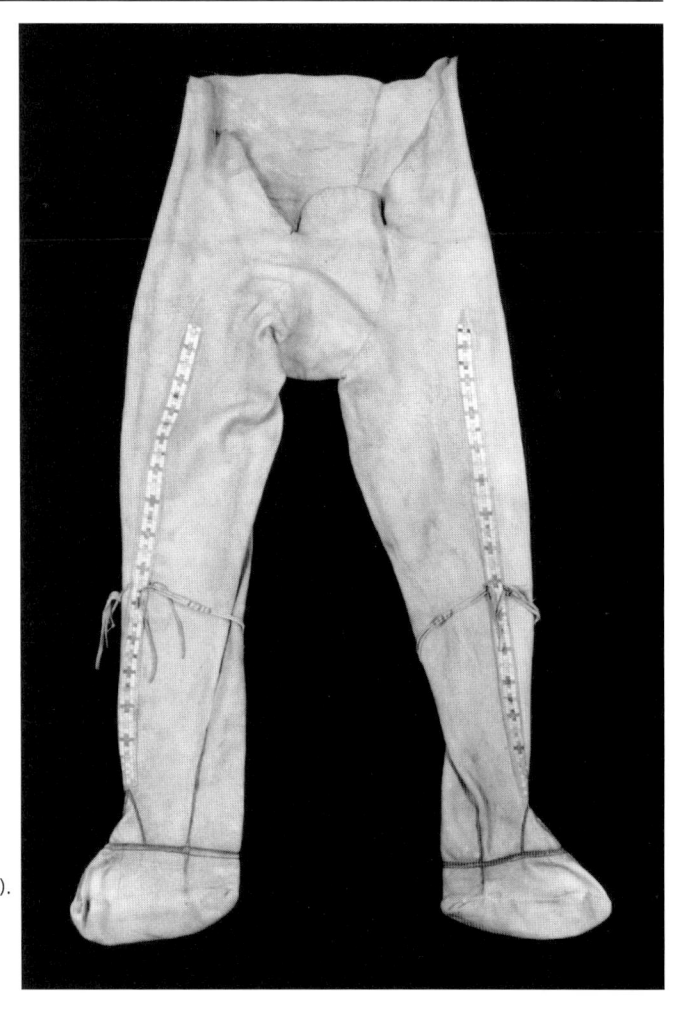

1.14 Gwich'in moccasin-trousers (from outfit illustrated in Figure 1.1). Courtesy National Museums of Scotland, Edinburgh 564.

decoration, is thought to have originated in the southern Yukon.[52] Unfortunately, examples of these variant approaches to the cut of moccasin-trousers are too few and too poorly documented, to offer conclusive evidence of a regional approach or sub-style. Such information as there is links moccasin-trousers with these cuts to the southern Yukon. In the context of this paper, the important point is that neither variation was characteristic for Dena'ina or Gwich'in moccasin-trousers.

How was the moccasin-trouser held up? Most extant examples, including those illustrated here, have wide unfinished-looking waists, with no apparent mechanism for drawing the trouser in at this point, or for preventing it from sliding down on the hips. Possibly, a simple, unattached, thong belt tied around the outside of the trouser at the waist would have served this purpose. A few Dena'ina examples have the waist edge turned to the inside and sewn to form a casing through which a thong belt is drawn.[53] A more common (and probably more satisfactory) method may have been suspenders. Many extant examples

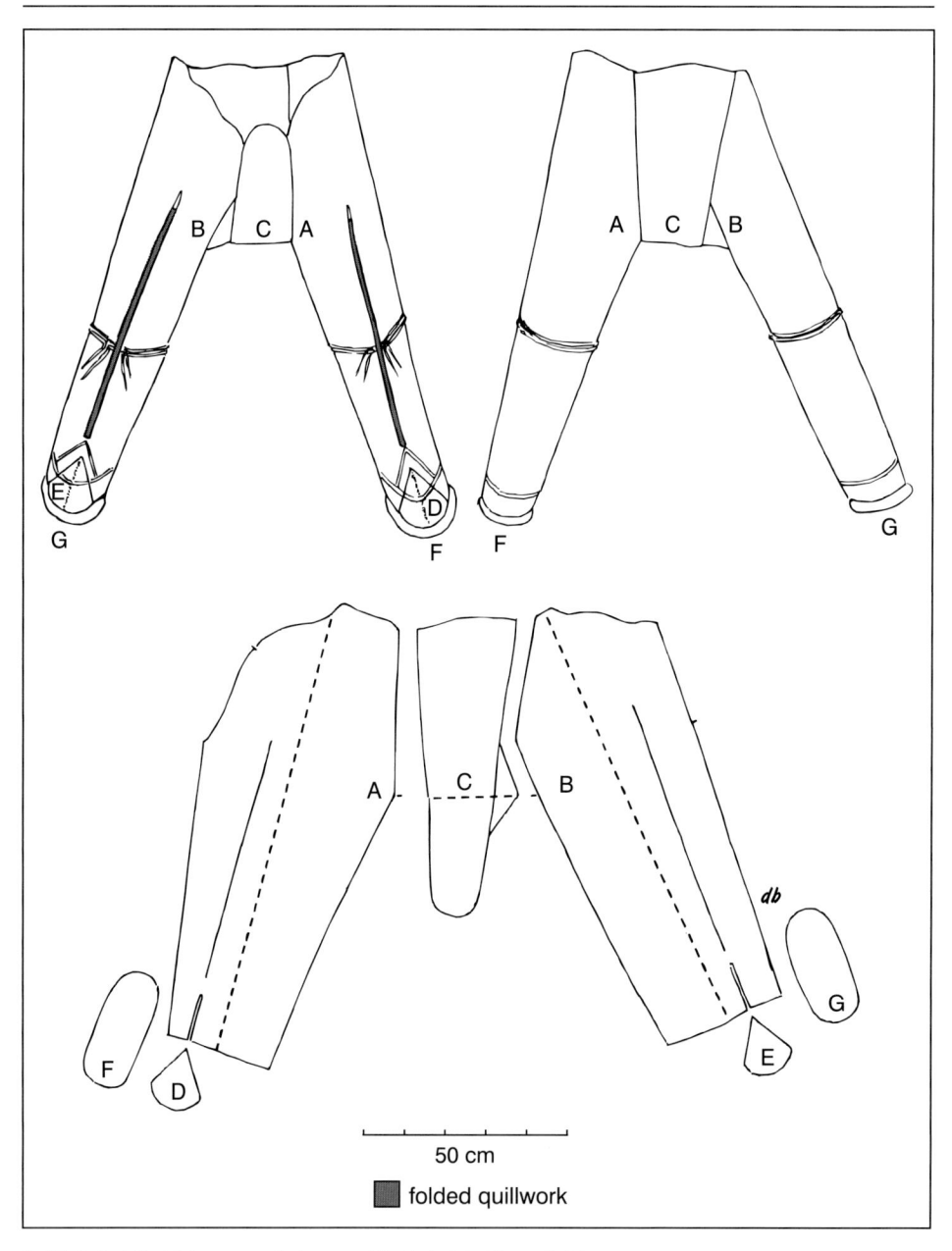

Traditional Summer Clothing of the Dena'ina and the Gwich'in

1.15 Cut of Gwich'in moccasin-trousers illustrated in Figure 1.14.
National Museums of Scotland, Edinburgh 564.

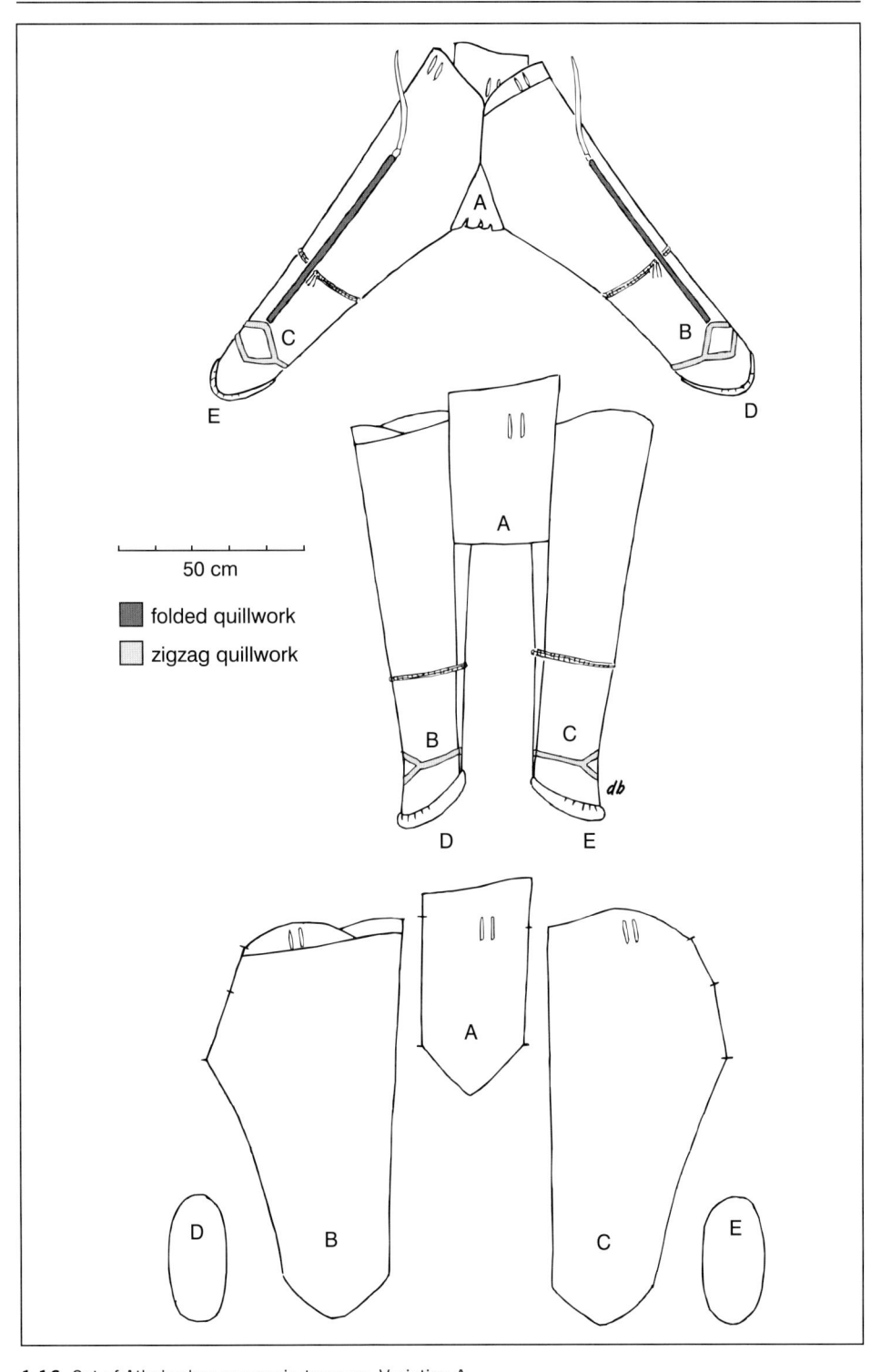

1.16 Cut of Athabaskan moccasin-trousers: Variation A.
Canadian Museum of Civilization VI-I-77.

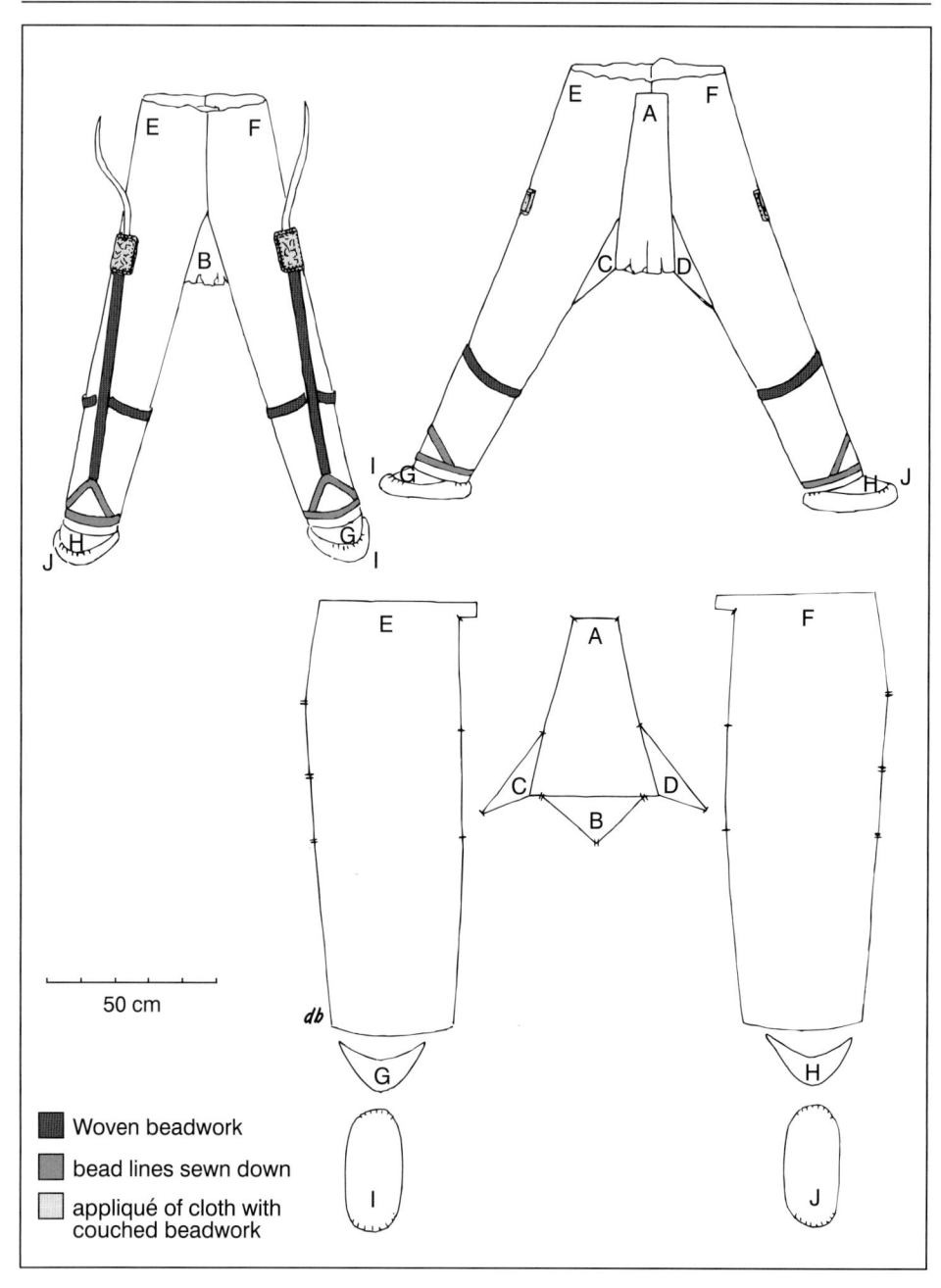

Traditional Summer Clothing of the Dena'ina and the Gwich'in

Woven beadwork
bead lines sewn down
appliqué of cloth with couched beadwork

1.17 Cut of Athabaskan moccasin-trousers, Variation B. Canadian Museum of Civilization VI-Z-244.

have long, tapered, undecorated bands of tanned hide attached by sewing at the upper thigh, at the top of the decorative band that runs down the centre leg. These can be seen, for example, on the garments illustrated in Figures 1.16 and 1.17. Although on most museum specimens, there is no clear indication of how these skin strips functioned, a garment in the Field Museum of Natural History has them sewn to the center back waist, thus forming suspenders.[54] Probably, adding length to the skin strips to make them long enough to go over the shoulders and attaching the free ends to the back of the garment were final adjustments to the moccasin-trouser, made the first time it was worn.

To conclude, it has not been possible to distinguish different Dena'ina and Gwich'in approaches to the cut and construction of moccasin-trousers. For this garment, it has been the decoration, rather than the cut, which indicates cultural affiliation.

The Decoration of Clothing

Men's Tunics:

Extensive, beautifully executed decorative work in porcupine quills and fringes is a striking feature of Athabaskan upper garments. As the Dena'ina and Gwich'in garments shown in Figures 1.2 and 1.3 illustrate, there was a common approach to this decoration. The materials used - porcupine quills, thongs, and ochre - were the same throughout the region, as were the main elements - quillworked bands, fringes, and "tags". The most striking component of the decoration was the broad, fringed, band of quillwork which crossed the upper chest. Fringing finished the bottom edge of the tunic, and thong tags marked the mid-line on lower fronts and backs.

Differences between Dena'ina and Gwich'in tunics can be seen, however, in the techniques used to produce decorative work. Some variation can also be seen in the placement and colours of this work. With few exceptions, Dena'ina tunics were decorated with a form of woven quillwork which in this paper will be called "woven-in-place". The garment illustrated in Figure 1.3 is typical in this respect, with bands of this woven work sewn to the upper front, at the wrists, and bordering the lower edge. Figure 1.18 illustrates the technique. Sinew threads formed the weft in this work, and the warp consisted of porcupine quills alternated with sinew. The sinew weft elements were stitched to the hide backing at either side of the work, as the weaving progressed. Very fine quills, carefully sorted for consistency of size, were used. Design motifs in woven-in-place quillwork are usually intricate arrangements of rectangles and elongated triangles, built up through alternation of small segments worked in natural white and dyed ochre-yellow and brown quills. Wide bands were produced by working two, three, or four closely juxtaposed strips simultaneously.

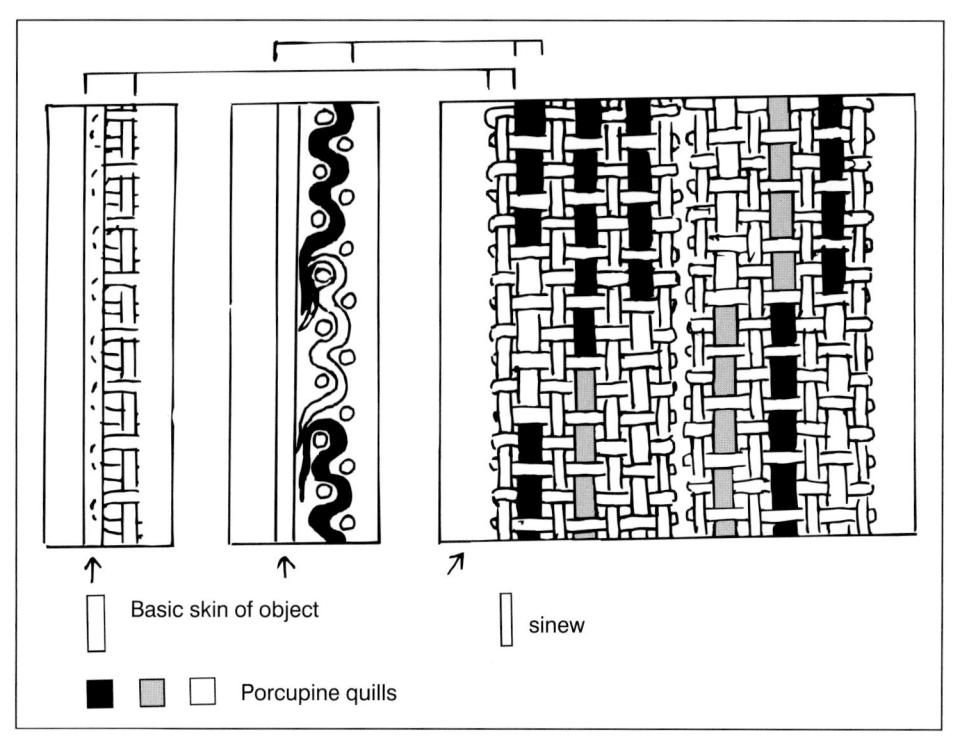

Traditional Summer Clothing of the Dena'ina and the Gwich'in

1.18 Woven-in-place quillwork.
Alternated porcupine quills and sinew thread form the warp, the weft is sinew thread. Warp elements are free from the hide backing, except where they are anchored at the start and finish of the piece. The sinew weft takes a small stitch into the hide backing at each side of the width, as it turns. In the actual piece, the sinew of both warp and weft is almost entirely hidden by the closely packed quills. (DB)

The quillwork seen on most Gwich'in men's tunics, on the other hand, is a form of sewn work, in which flattened quills were attached to the surface of a hide backing by folding them over two parallel lines of stitches. The usual technique, which in this paper will be called "folded, straight, single quill", is illustrated in Figure 1.19. On the Gwich'in garment shown in Figure 1.2, five lanes of this type of quillwork on a hide backing form the breastband. Single lanes in the same technique, worked directly on the hide of the garment, appear on the upper front of the garment above the breastband (crossing the neck front, and in three lines from neck front to breastband). Three lanes worked on a hide backing decorate the wrists. Motifs are simple, repeated, combinations of rectangles, triangles and crosses worked in quills dyed red and blue against a background of natural white quills. Quills are broader than those used in the Dena'ina work.

Although, as already noted, the great majority of Dena'ina men's tunics were decorated with woven quillwork, and those of the Gwich'in with folded, sewn quills, this division was not absolute. No documented examples of Dena'ina folded sewn quillwork have been located, but its presence on an Ahtena

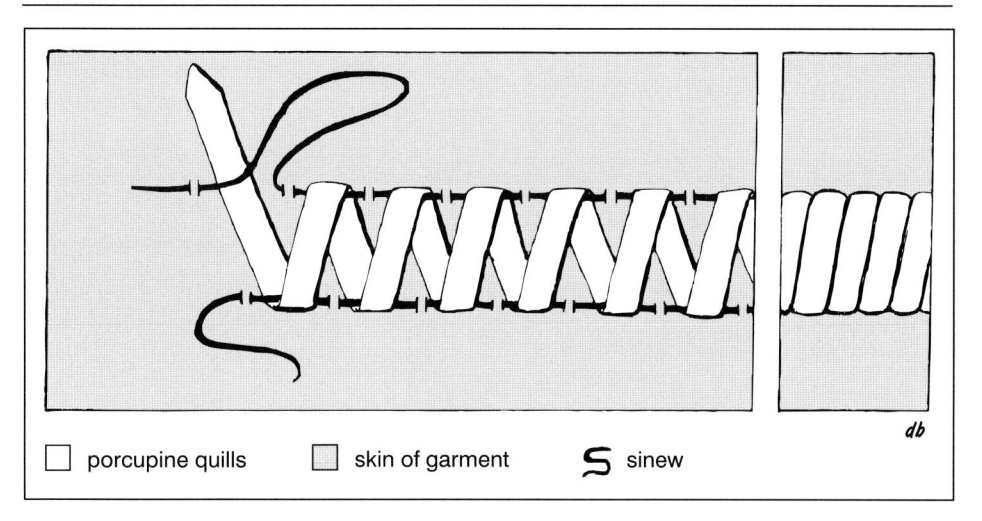

1.19 Folded, sewn quillwork technique: straight, single quill.
In this type of sewn quillwork, moistened porcupine quills are folded back and forth over two parallel lines of sinew stitches. Note that while the technique is illustrated here using a running stitch, modern Dene quillworkers use a tiny backstitch, taken through the surface of the hide immediately after each fold of the quill.

woman's tunic (Figure 1.38, following paper) suggests that seamstresses in this region at least occasionally produced it. There is also evidence that Gwich'in women sometimes used woven quillwork in the decoration of clothing. A Gwich'in outfit (tunic and moccasin-trousers)[55] collected "near the mouth of the Mackenzie River" in 1860 is decorated with woven-in-place quillwork, as are the mittens and knife sheath of the outfit illustrated in Figure 1.1 of this paper. Another type of woven work, produced with the aid of a bow loom, also is occasionally seen on Gwich'in garments. For example, a tunic in the CMC collection (Figure 1.40, following paper) has loom-woven bands around the wrists; another, in the Smithsonian Institution, has bands of loom-woven quillwork forming the breastband and sewn to the front above the breastband.[56] This technique is illustrated in Figure 1.20.

Fine, dense, thong fringing is another important aspect of the decoration of Dena'ina and Gwich'in tunics. As can be seen on the two examples illustrated here, fringing crosses the upper front and back and finishes the bottom edge of the garment. However, although they are very similar in appearance, the fringes on the two examples shown here were made using different techniques. On the Gwich'in garment, the breastband fringe is formed from a succession of two-strand units, each consisting of a thong drawn through two holes 1 cm (3/8") above the lower edge of the breastband (Figure 1.21). The fringe on the Dena'ina tunic, on the other hand, is formed from a length of tanned hide cut into narrow segments, then sewn along its top (uncut) edge to the breastband. In the research to date, these differing methods do not appear to represent distinct regional approaches. Rather, it appears that a variety of closely related ways of making fringes were used across the region.

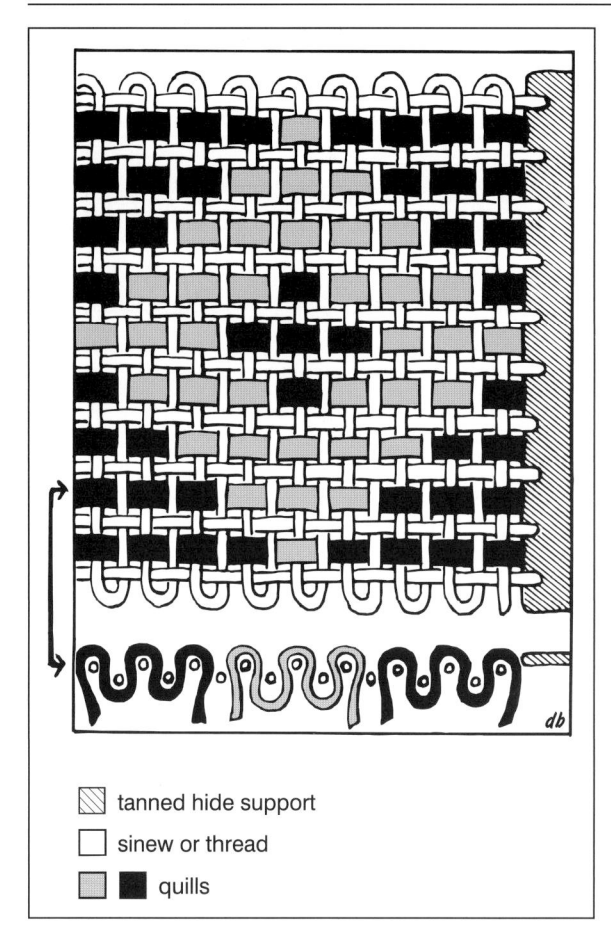

Traditional Summer Clothing of the Dena'ina and the Gwich'in

1.20 Loom-woven quillwork technique.
In an actual band, only the quills show. Every second warp thread is held firmly on a bow; the intervening warps are supplied by porcupine quills inserted by the weaver. As the short length of a quill runs out, or if another colour is desired, the end of the quill is pushed down to the back and a new quill worked in. (DB)

Techniques employed in making fringes varied, but a single technique for decorating fringes was employed. Individual fringe strands were wrapped with porcupine quills using the technique illustrated in Figure 1.22. Normally, as well, a single silver willow (eleagnus) seed was threaded on each segment, partway along the quill-wrapped portion. Fringes on the Dena'ina garment (Figure 1.3) are decorated in this way; on the Gwich'in example (Figure 1.2), red and blue glass trade beads are used in the place of the indigenous seed.

Another decorative element common to Dena'ina and Gwich'in garments is the line of thong tags marking the mid-line on the lower front and back of the tunic. As was the case with fringing, a number of different techniques were employed in making these tags.[57] In the case of tags, however, regional preferences can be discerned. For example, the method of making tags illustrated in Figure 1.23 was common to most Dena'ina tunics, including the garment illustrated in Figure 1.3. In this technique, each tag is a thong which has been split for half its length and the unsplit end drawn to the inside, then back to the outside of the garment. The split ends are decorated with quill-wrapping and silver willow seeds, as with the breastband fringe. On Gwich'in

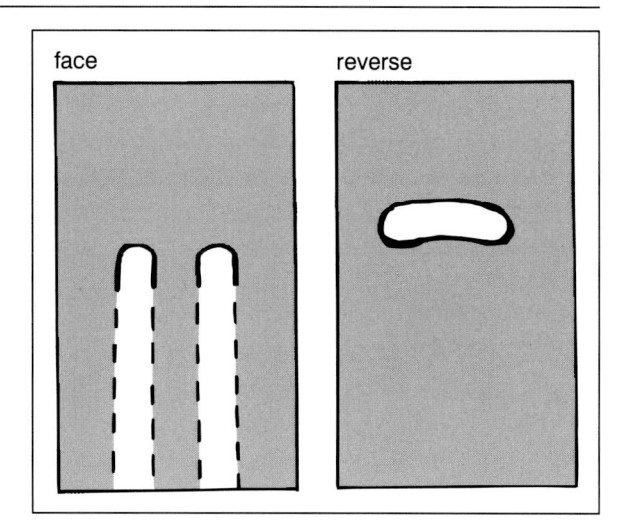

1.21 Fringe technique: A thong is threaded in and out of a hide backing, producing a two-strand unit.

tunics, on the other hand, the most common method for making tags is that shown in Figure 1.24: each tag is a small skin rectangle sewn along its upper edge to the garment and cut into three fine strands. Tags on the Gwich'in tunic pictured in Figure 1.2 are made in this way.

Painting with red ochre is another element of the decoration of most Dena'ina and Gwich'in tunics. Common to garments from both groups is the use of ochre to draw guidelines for the placement of breast and upper back bands, for the quillwork on the upper front of the garment above the breastband, and for the line of tags on lower front and back. More specific motifs drawn in ochre were not found on any Gwich'in garments, but were observed on some examples from western Alaskan groups. For example, on some Ahtena and Dena'ina garments (including the example illustrated in Figure 1.3), the vertical tag line on the lower front and back flares to a two or three-pronged fork pattern at its upper end. A western Alaskan (as opposed to Gwich'in) association for this motif is reinforced by the fact that the same mark is found incised on a wide variety of Bering Sea Eskimo artifacts. In the latter instances, it is thought, in some contexts, to represent a raven's foot and to signify membership in the raven "clan".[58] Dena'ina and Ahtena also had clans associated with raven, and a similar meaning for this motif on their garments is entirely possible. Another Alaskan Athabaskan garment, a man's tunic that may be Dena'ina, has a small bird motif drawn in ochre on the back.[59]

A final point of comparison between Dena'ina and Gwich'in men's tunics relates to the finishing of the neck edge. Dena'ina upper garments, as well as those attributed to Deg Hit'an, Ahtena, and Kolchan, often have a narrow band of furred skin sewn around the neck opening. The pelt, where the hair is still preserved, is brown in colour and soft-textured. On garments in the Etholén collection in Helsinki, it has been identified as otter;[60] on the tunic pictured in Figure 1.3, as beaver. Usually, the underside of this fur trim is stained red, probably from ochre or plant or berry juice. Similar furred bands

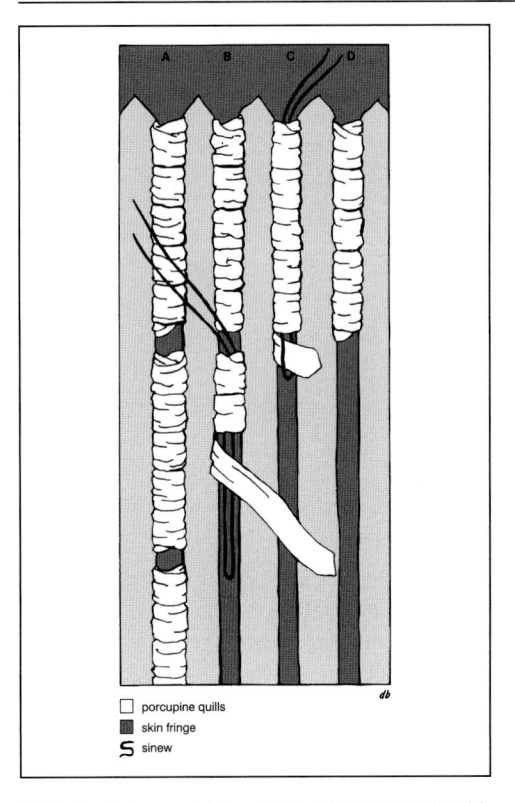

1.22 Technique used in wrapping fringe strands with porcupine quills:
 A. Finished strand
 B. Finished section and incomplete wrapping showing insertion of sinew loop
 C. Quill end enclosed in sinew loop
 D. Finished section with quill end drawn up and sinew removed

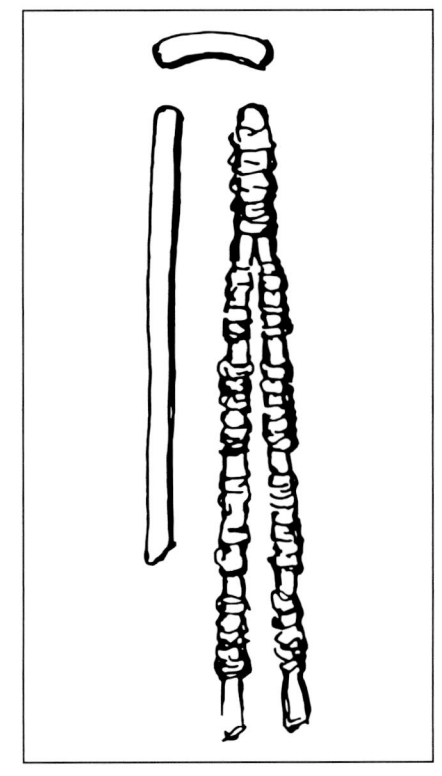

1.23 Method of making tags, commonly seen on Dena'ina tunics.
 Each tag is a thong which has been split for half its length and the unsplit end drawn through the skin of the garment. Split ends are decorated with quillwrapping as shown in Figure 1.22, and strung with silver willow seeds.

1.24 Method of making tags, commonly seen on Gwich'in tunics.
 A small skin rectangle is cut for most of its length into three segments. Each segment is decorated with porcupine quill wrapping as per Figure 1.22, and usually strung with a single silver willow seed. At the upper edge, the tag is sewn to the outside of the tunic.

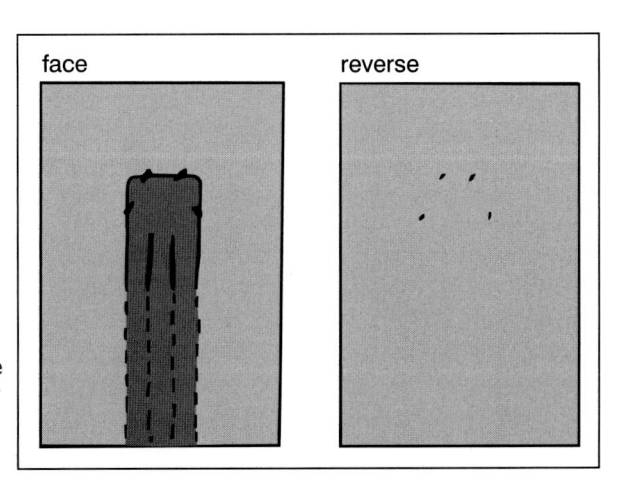

were attached at the sleeve ends of Dena'ina garments. No Gwich'in garments were found to have fur trim. The usual Gwich'in approach was to whip the neck edge with a fine thong (as seen on the tunic in Figure 1.2) or lace a thong through holes cut at regular intervals just below the edge. Both Dena'ina and Gwich'in methods of finishing the neck edge would serve dual purposes: they would prevent the soft skin from stretching as the tunic was pulled on and off; and they would provide an attractive edging to the garment.

Women's Tunics:

Many of the aspects of the decoration of men's tunics, described above, applied to women's garments as well. This discussion will highlight differences specific to women's garments. Dena'ina, Ahtena and Deg Hit'an women's tunics tended to be more extensively decorated than those of the Gwich'in. Examples attributed to the former groups had a broad band of woven quillwork attached across the breast. The longer, straight-cut dress had wide bands of woven quillwork at wrists as well. In technique, motifs and colours these bands were closely comparable to those seen on Dena'ina men's tunics. Fine, quill-wrapped fringing, similar to that on men's tunics, appears on these women's garments as well, bordering breastbands, crossing the back of the garment and finishing the bottom edge. Those dresses with a pointed lower edge had a line of tags attached down the centre line, as on men's tunics.

The long loose style of Dena'ina woman's dress had a slightly different decoration. Most of the examples studied had broad, undecorated skin fringing inserted in side seams and, with the exception of a quill-wrapped self-fringe at the bottom edge, no decoration on the lower part of the garment. The style seen in Figure 1.7, which has shoulders formed from additional, rectangular, skin pieces, was decorated with a single, horizontally placed, quillworked band across the upper front, and two bands across the upper back. The front and upper back bands are, in fact, one continuous piece, worked as a rectangle and then attached to the dress. The skin base to the quillwork is seamed at the corners, and the quill weaving tightens at the turns. This rectangle of woven quillwork is positioned high on the dress; its lines echo the upper front, back and shoulder seams of the garment, although they do not correspond exactly to these. The second quillworked band on the back of the garment is applied below the first, and crosses the garment horizontally, at underarm level. Broad, undecorated skin fringing borders these quill-woven bands.

The Gwich'in women's dresses were, by comparison, minimally decorated. The garment shown in Figure 1.9, for example, has no quillworked breast or back band. Decoration of the upper front is limited to a narrow lane of folded, sewn quillwork worked from the centre neck edge, down to where a breast band would be attached on a man's garment. The diagonal upper front seams and the top of the sleeve seam are covered with similar quillwork. A single lane of quillwork is worked at the wrists. On the lower half of the garment, skin tags are attached at the sides and over vertical dark brown painted lines at mid-front and mid-back. Fringed bands are attached across the lower front and back of the garment and at the bottom edge. Fringe and tag strands are wrapped with porcupine quills. Decoration of the little girl's garment illustrated in Figure 1.11 is very similar. The Gwich'in women's garments in the Smithsonian Institution are similar in their overall approach to decoration. On these examples, however, glass beads are used instead of porcupine quills and decoration is more elaborate, including bead-strung thongs which form fringes at neck front, and border upper front and sleeve seams.

Moccasin-Trousers:

The decoration of moccasin-trousers harmonized in materials and techniques with the tunics they were intended to be worn with. Typically, a band of porcupine quillwork was applied down the front of the leg, from mid-thigh to ankle. Lines of quillwork, often combined with red ochre, were worked on the upper foot and around the ankle. Garters made from quill-wrapped thongs usually encircled the leg just below knee level.

As was the case with upper garments, comparison of the decoration of Gwich'in and Dena'ina examples reveals both similarities and differences. A dominant feature of decoration, common to all, is the band of quillwork down the front of the leg. Different methods were used to apply the quills, however. On the Gwich'in moccasin-trousers (Figure 1.14) quills are applied using the same folded and sewn technique (straight, single quill) seen on the tunic of the outfit. On the Dena'ina example, the legging band is made from woven-in-place quillwork, the usual technique seen on upper garments from this group.

As noted on upper garments, quillwork colours and motifs worked on Gwich'in and Dena'ina moccasin-trousers differ. On the Dena'ina examples (including the one illustrated in Figure 1.13), quills typically are white, dark brown and ochre-orange. The pattern worked on the legging band of the garment in Figure 1.13 also is characteristic: two motifs, each built up from small rectangular units, repeat four times down the length, and checkerboard rectangles are worked at either end. The quillwork pattern on the Gwich'in legging bands is much simpler, consisting of blue and red crosses alternated against a background of white quills.

The second main area for decoration on the moccasin-trouser was the ankle area. On the Gwich'in garment illustrated in Figure 1.14, both red ochre and quillwork are applied to this part of the garment. A heavy line of red ochre is drawn down the centre foot to the toe and a similar line encircles the ankle and extends 10 cm (4") up the inner leg. The ankle line is bordered with double lines of bird quill, blue and white, each line worked over running stitch, as seen in Figure 1.25. A similar decorative line (4 lines of quills, alternated blue and red, over an ochre line) forms an inverted V at the ankle front. These lines echo, but do not coincide with, seam lines.

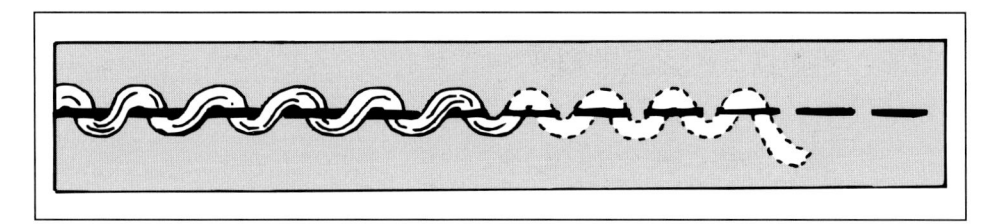

1.25 Line technique using porcupine or bird quills and sinew. The quill passes over and under a line of sinew running stitches. (DB)

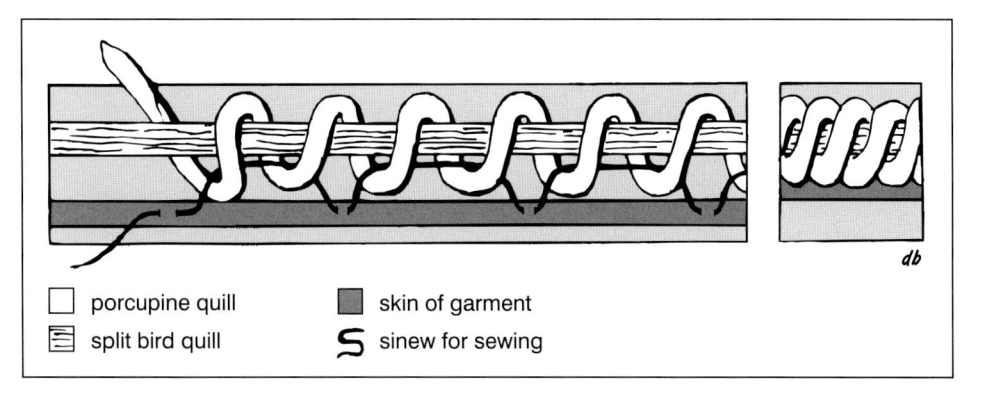

1.26 Line technique using bird and porcupine quills. The sinew provides firm and completely hidden attachment. (DB)

Definition of the ankle, and of an inverted V at the ankle front, with wrapped lines involving sinew and porcupine quills was a common feature on Gwich'in examples. Often, split bird quills were used in combination with, or instead of, porcupine quills in this work. Figure 1.26 illustrates a technique commonly employed in making such lines. Some Dena'ina moccasin-trousers had similar line-work in the ankle area. More often, however, they had a band of woven quillwork comparable to that seen on the legs of the garment sewn around the ankle. This can be seen, for example, on the garment illustrated in Figure 1.13. Sometimes, although not invariably, these Dena'ina moccasin-trousers had additional woven quillwork at the ankle front, delineating an inverted V between the base of the legging band and the strip which encircled the ankle.

Red ochre was also a frequent component of the decoration of the Gwich'in moccasin-trousers. Sometimes, as seen on the example provided here, it marked a line down the centre of the foot. More often, it was applied around the ankle, under and on either side of the quillworked lines. Outlining of the seam on the inside of the leg was also common: usually a painted line extended to knee level, sometimes it was drawn almost to the crotch. In contrast, ochre is notably absent on most Dena'ina moccasin-trousers dating to the 1840s.

A third element of the decoration of moccasin-trousers consisted of garters attached at knee level. The usual method of making these garters is illustrated in Figure 1.27. As the drawing shows, a weaving technique is employed, in which two thongs with a line of sinew between them form the warp, and porcupine quills, the weft. On the Gwich'in moccasin-trouser seen in Figure 1.14, the garter is formed from a 1cm (3/8") wide length of tanned caribou hide which has been split into four thongs. Paired thongs are wrapped with porcupine quills – mainly white, with small rectangular blocks of blue and red. The technique is essentially the same as that illustrated in Figure 1.27, except that in this instance the two segments are not interwoven at intervals. At the end of the garter, one unwrapped portion of each thong pair is drawn under the band of folded quillwork, and on the opposite side, through the unsplit end of the skin. The result is a garter which could be tightened and was, therefore, functional as well as decorative. Dorothy Burnham's drawing and accompanying detailed written analysis (Figure 1.28) elucidate this ingenious technique.

Garters on the Dena'ina garment resemble those of this Gwich'in moccasin-trouser insofar as they are also made from two pairs of thongs interwoven with porcupine quills. In this case (Figure 1.13), however, the garters are purely decorative: they are stitched to the legging on either side of the quill-woven band.

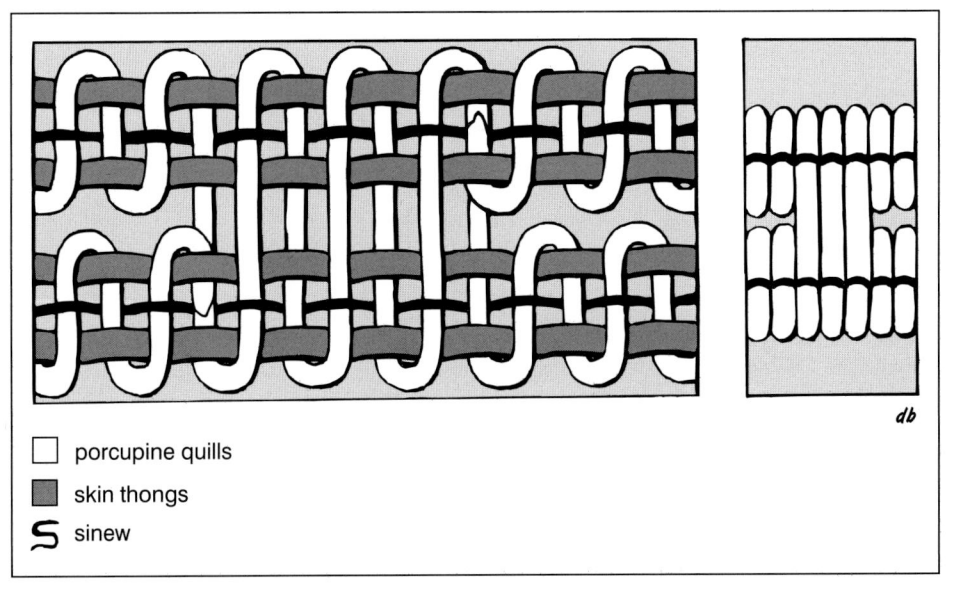

1.27 Technique used in making garters for moccasin-trousers. Two thongs with a line of sinew between them form the warp and porcupine quills, the weft. On some examples, three thongs are interwoven in the same way. Not all examples are linked by interweaving of the two segments, as shown here.

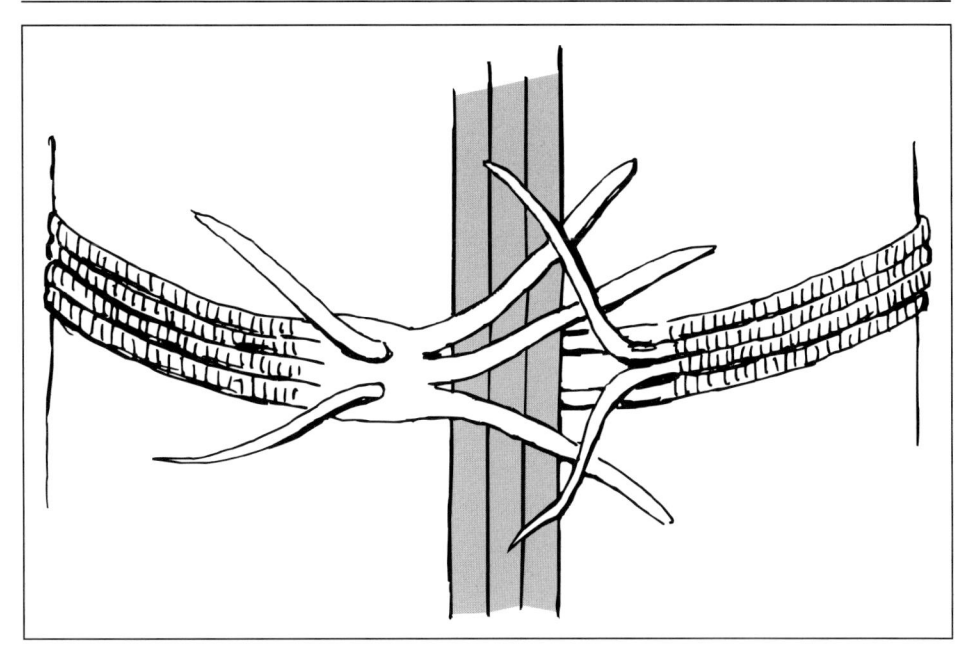

1.28 Method of attaching garter on the Gwich'in moccasin-trouser illlustrated in Figure 1.15. The garter is made from a strip of skin about 2 cm (5/8") wide and long enough to encircle the leg with extra length at either end. At one end the strip is split in three for about 6 cm (2 3/8"). Then there is a section of about 2 cm (5/8") length, left unsplit but with two holes pierced through it. On the other side of this section, the entire length of skin has been split into four thongs. These four thongs have been woven in separate pairs with porcupine quills (as in Figure 1.27) to within 8 to 10 cm (3" to 4") of the length. The unwoven lengths of thong are left free, providing one from each pair to be carried under the quill band on the leg front and then threaded through the two holes in the unsplit section of garter band. This adjustable joining of the two ends of the garter strip would make it possible to loosen or tighten the garter by pulling the ends. All dimensions are rough estimates. (DB)

Discussion

The most obvious point of difference in the decoration of Dena'ina and Gwich'in tunics and moccasin-trousers is in the quillwork techniques employed. The majority of Dena'ina garments are decorated with woven-in-place quillwork; those attributed to Gwich'in, with folded quillwork. Other differences include the use of fur trim at the neck and wrists of many Dena'ina tunics, and its absence on Gwich'in garments. The two or three-pronged "fork" motif drawn in red ochre at the top of the central line down the mid-point of the tunic was common to garments from southern and western Alaskan Athabaskans, but was not seen on any Gwich'in garments.

A number of factors may have influenced the development of regional approaches to decoration. The fact that woven-in-place quillwork appears on some Gwich'in items and folded, sewn quillwork on an Ahtena example suggests that Athabaskan women across the broader region were proficient in a variety of quillwork techniques. The dominant use of one or another technique in a given region probably reflects local convention and aesthetics. Contact with other Aboriginal groups may also have affected clothing decoration. For example, seamstresses in the eastern part of Gwich'in territory may have been influenced by the folded and loom-woven quillwork produced by other Mackenzie valley Athabaskans. Slavey women in particular were noted for their proficiency in this work.

Historical developments also had a significant impact on clothing decoration across the region. The fur trade brought new materials and foreigners from a variety of cultural backgrounds into Athabaskan territories. Cree and Metis, in particular, were important participants in the northern fur trade. They brought with them well-developed decorative art traditions involving folded and loom-woven quillwork, which may have influenced the work of Gwich'in seamstresses in the Mackenzie Delta and Peel River area. The most dramatic impact on clothing decoration was the introduction of a new media, glass beads. A detailed analysis of this aspect of clothing decoration is beyond the scope of this paper,[61] but a few observations based on comparison of Gwich'in and Dena'ina collections can be made. The decoration of Dena'ina garments reflects a decisive shift from indigenous to imported materials in the third quarter of the nineteenth century. Clothing dating to the 1840s and earlier is decorated with porcupine quills and silver willow seeds; that collected in the 1880s, with glass beads and dentalium shells. The Gwich'in collections suggest a more complicated situation. Many of the earliest, documented, Gwich'in garments – for example, those collected in the 1860s by Bernard Ross and others for the Royal Scottish Museum and the Smithsonian Institution – already reflect a preference for glass beads over porcupine quills in the decoration of traditionally styled caribou hide clothing. Ross and his colleagues collected eight multi-piece Gwich'in summer outfits. Only one outfit is decorated exclusively with porcupine quills. Another (Figure 1.1) is mainly quillworked, but has fringe strands strung with glass beads, instead of silver willow seeds. The remaining six outfits show no, or very minimal, use of porcupine quills. Instead, they are heavily decorated with imported glass and dentalium shell beads. Paradoxically, Gwich'in garments dating later in the nineteenth century are decorated largely with porcupine quills and silver willow seeds. As has been argued elsewhere, the late nineteenth century production, by the Gwich'in, of quillwork decorated, traditionally styled skin garments was probably influenced by a demand for such work by white collectors and tourists.[62] Although extant collections suggest a different situation with respect to the Dena'ina and other groups on the western periphery of Athabaskan territory, market demands may well have influenced decorative work on these garments as well. More research is required in this area.

The Proof of the Pudding...

Detailed study of a large number of Athabaskan tunics and moccasin-trousers and comparison of cuts and techniques of sewing and decoration has revealed different Gwich'in and Dena'ina approaches to garment styling and decoration. It is hoped that identification of these "variations on a (clothing) theme" will assist museum curators and researchers in the attribution of poorly documented clothing artifacts, of which there are many.

On a personal level, the fact that progress had indeed been made in this area was brought home to me during a visit to the Bata Shoe Museum (BSM) in Toronto in 1999. The ethnographic collections of this institution include two nineteenth century Athabaskan clothing outfits which are classic examples of the genre (Figures 1.29 and 1.30). Both are made from white caribou hide in a typically Athabaskan style: upper garments are pullover tunics with pointed lower edges, lower garments are a combination of trouser and footwear. The most obvious difference between the two outfits is that one (Figure 1.29) is decorated with porcupine quills, the other (Figure 1.30) with glass beads.

Both outfits were acquired by the BSM in the 1980s, from Canadian dealers. Their earlier collection histories are not known. A tenuous link between the outfit in Figure 1.29 and the Gwich'in of the lower Mackenzie River and Peel River regions is suggested by a notation, "Locheux [sic] Canada", written in black ink on the inside of the trousers of this outfit. (Loucheux is the name by which easternmost bands of Canadian Gwich'in were known in the late nineteenth and early twentieth centuries.) For this reason, and because in materials and general appearance, these outfits resembled Gwich'in clothing described and illustrated in the ethnohistorical literature and exhibition catalogues, the Shoe Museum catalogued both outfits as Kutchin (that is, Gwich'in) artifacts.

I first encountered the two outfits in 1987, while researching Northern Athabaskan footwear. At that time, although well aware that clothing of this style was common to a number of Athabaskan peoples in the nineteenth century, I saw no reason to dispute a Gwich'in attribution for these garments. The quillwork technique seen on the example in Figure 1.29 was comparable to that on other, better documented Gwich'in garments. As well, while there was no way of knowing when, or why, someone had written "Locheux" on the trousers of this outfit, there was always the possibility that the inscription was the work of someone knowledgeable about its origin. I subsequently published both garments as "Kutchin [Gwich'in] type", and suggested late nineteenth century dates of manufacture for both.[63]

Revisiting the collection twelve years later, it took me only a short while with each outfit to feel certain that I had been correct in suggesting a Gwich'in attribution for the outfit seen in Figure 1.29, but wrong in suggesting the same culture of origin for the one pictured in Figure 1.30. I now felt a Dena'ina

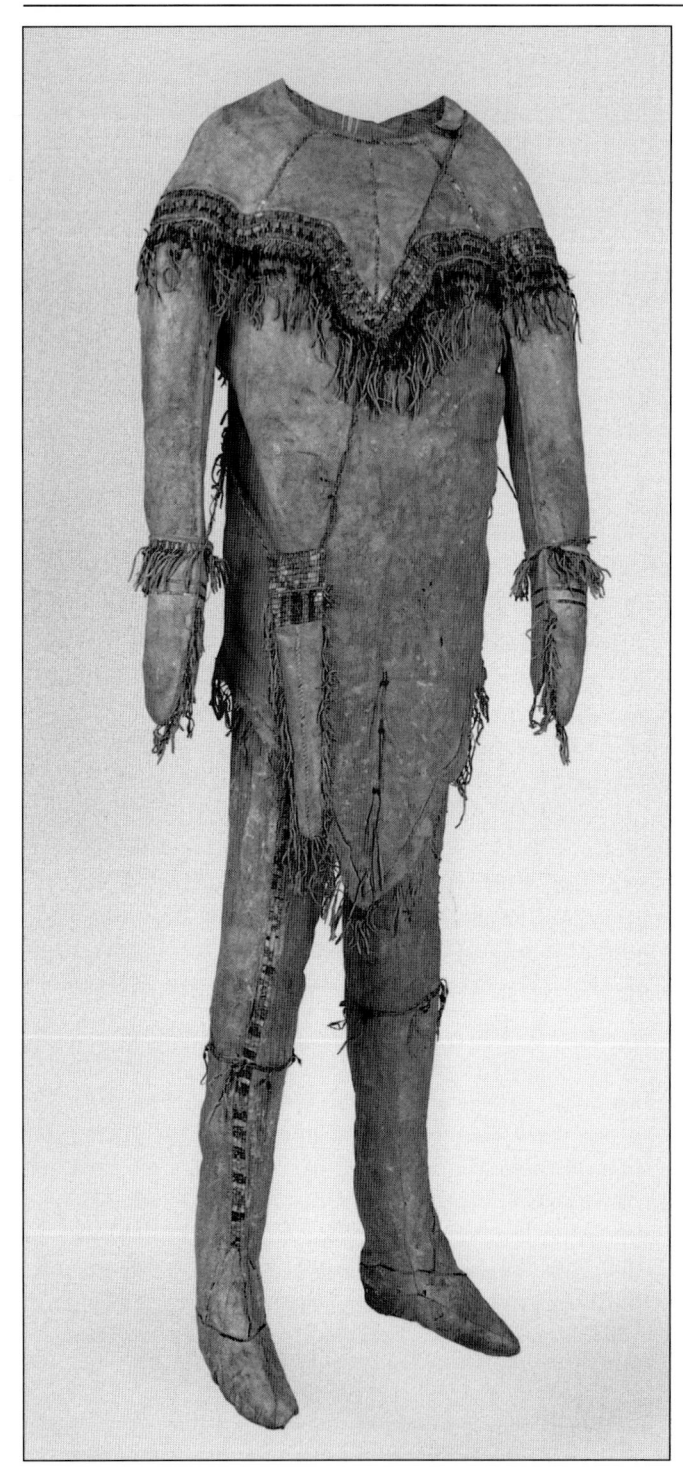

Traditional Summer Clothing of the Dena'ina and the Gwich'in

1.29 Gwich'in style outfit, late nineteenth century. Courtesy Bata Shoe Museum, Toronto 87.74.

attribution would be more appropriate in the latter case. My assessment was based not on new information about the history of these artifacts, but on observation of subtle differences in the way they were constructed and decorated - differences of whose significance I had been unaware twelve years earlier, and which I now recognized as indicators of culture of origin. These differences can be summarized as follows.

Typically Gwich'in features of the outfit shown in Figure 1.29 include:

1. Use of two relatively small caribou hides to form the body of the tunic, with seaming at the sides and diagonally on the upper front;

2. A sleeve construction like that seen in Figure 1.4;

3. Folded quillwork (straight single quill) on the breastband and on the upper front (at neck front, and in three lines from neck to breastband) of the tunic, and down the centre of each leg;

4. A thong laced around the neck;

5. Definition of seam and centre lines at the ankle front with lines of bird quill wrapped with bird quill (technique illustrated in Figure 1.26), and similar lines around the ankle.

Typically Dena'ina features of the outfit illustrated in Figure 1.30 include:

1. Use of a large, undivided, moose hide for back and front of the tunic. This is seamed up the centre front of the garment; the back extends over the shoulders to the front and is seamed at the centre front for 3 cm (1 1/4"), then joins with the piece which wraps around the sides, in diagonal seams extending to the armhole;

2. A pleat or dart taken on each side of the upper front, just to the front of the shoulder;

3. Neck opening and sleeve ends finished with narrow bands of (originally) furred hide, the inner surface of which is stained with red ochre;

4. Tags on the lower centre front and back of the tunic formed from a thong split for half its length and the unsplit end drawn to the inside, then back to the outside of the garment, as illustrated in Figure 1.23;

5. Decoration of breastband, sleeve ends and the bottom edge of the tunic. Glass beads rather than porcupine quills are used, but motifs – small rectangles of contrasting colours - are reminiscent of those seen on many Dena'ina quillworked garments.

This re-assessment of two outfits from the Bata Shoe Museum crystallized, for me, how much I had learned through a decade of working with Dorothy Burnham. Our careful analysis of a large number of traditional clothing items

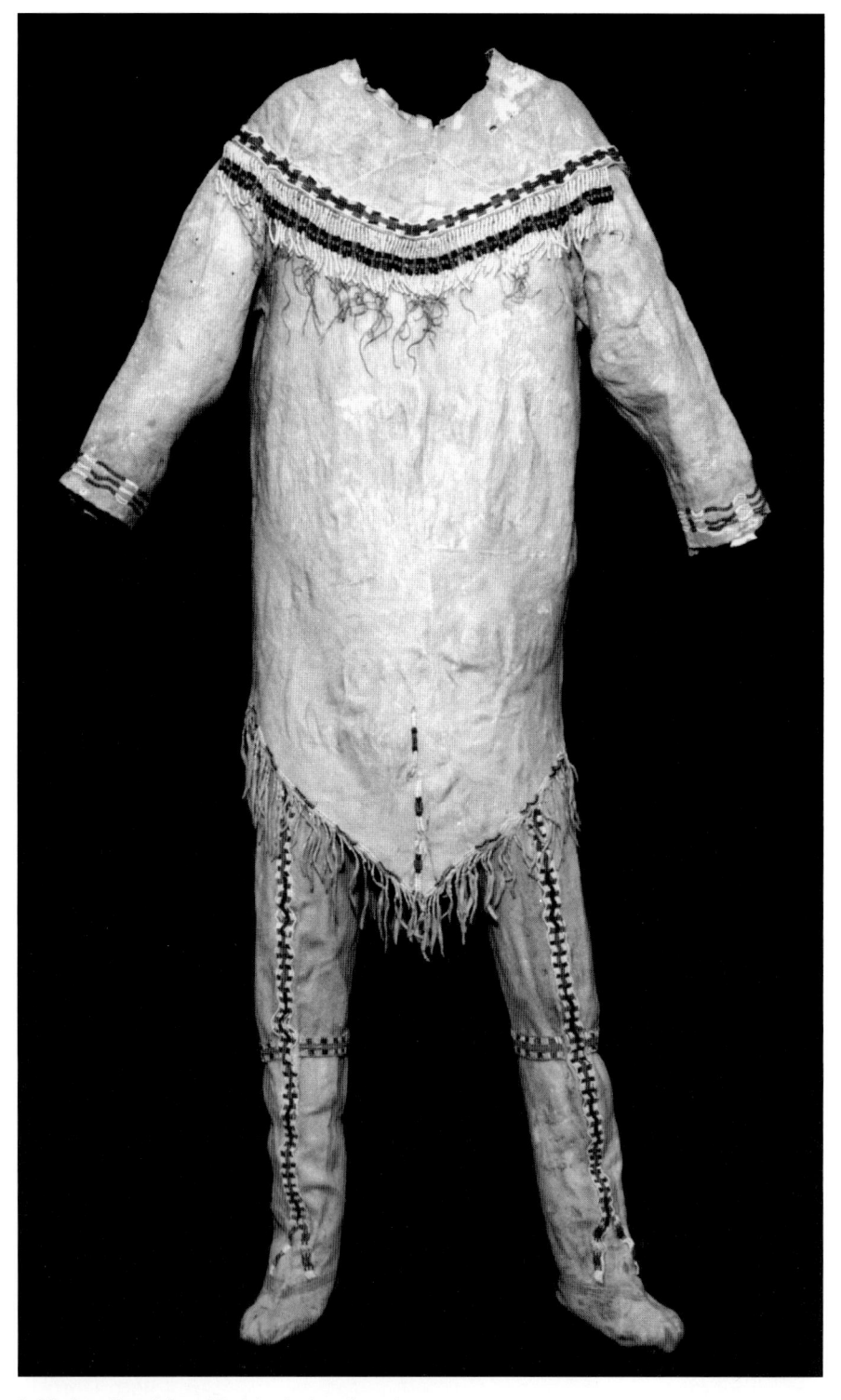

Traditional Summer Clothing of the Dena'ina and the Gwich'in

1.30 Dena'ina style outfit, late nineteenth century.
Courtesy Bata Shoe Museum, Toronto 83.161.2.

and the comparison of details of cut, construction and decoration (made possible through Dorothy's drawings) had led to the identification of regional approaches to materials, technologies, styles and decoration, within the broader Athabaskan clothing tradition. This information could, in turn, be applied to the attribution and dating of undocumented clothing artifacts.

The traditional clothing of Northern Athabaskan peoples is a compelling subject for research. This is not only because the garments are intriguing and often beautiful objects in themselves, but because they have the potential to tell us a great deal about the people who made and wore them. Clothing has utilitarian, social and ritual functions; it reflects a society's environmental resources, technical developments and cultural standards for what is fine or beautiful. However, in order for individual clothing artifacts to be useful to us as documents revealing of the history and culture of a given group of people, we have to be reasonably confident that we, in fact, do know who made them and when. In the case of old and rare artifacts, even this most basic information often is only come by through a lengthy research process. Careful study of extant examples and, in particular, the drawing out and comparing of garment cuts and techniques has an important role to play in this process.

Endnotes

1. Until recently, the Dena'ina have been referred to in museum records and ethnohistorical literature as the Tanaina; and the Gwich'in as Kutchin or Loucheux.
2. Nineteenth century sources include Zagoskin (1967), Murray (1910), Mackenzie (1970), Kirkby 1865; and Dall 1870. Osgood (1936, 1937, 1940) is the main twentieth century ethnographic source on this subject, but see also McClellan (1975) and McKennan (1959).
3. For discussion of post-contact developments in clothing of Northwest Territories' Athabaskans, see Thompson 1994.
4. Until recently, the Deg Hit'an have been referred to in museum records and ethnohistorical literature as the Ingalik.
5. Varjola 1990:27
6. Alekseev 1987:33
7. Siebert 1980; Dzeniskevich and Pavlinskaia 1988
8. Siebert 1980
9. Zagoskin 1967
10. Pierce 1990:213
11. Jacobsen 1977
12. VanStone 1981
13. Idiens 1979; Lindsay 1993
14. For a discussion of late nineteenth century Gwich'in summer clothing outfits in museums see Thompson 1999.
15. The tunic illustrated in Figure 1.3 was published by Siebert (1980) as Tanaina (Dena'ina). The *Crossroads of Continents* catalogue (Fitzhugh and Crowell

1988:225) lists it as Holikachuk. The latter attribution appears to be an error resulting from a mix-up of the documentation associated with this garment, with that of another, very similar, tunic (MAE 593.11). Personal communication, James VanStone to author, May 2000.

16. See also Conn 1974: 82; Conn 1991:90
17. Museum für Völkerkunde, Vienna 5085, 5086; illustrated in Thompson 1990:109; child's shirt is SI 49150
18. Dena'ina examples with this feature include MAE 2667.3; NMF VK168 and VK 173
19. Dena'ina examples with darts include MAE 518.3; MAE 2667.3; NMF VK 167, VK 169 and VK 176
20. Petroff 1900:85
21. MAE 593.10
22. MAE 518.2; MAE 2667.3
23. MAE 537.22
24. SMV IV-A-6147. On this garment, however, lower edge points are much shallower than is typical for men's garments.
25. Zagoskin 1980: 244
26. An example in the Berlin Museum (IV-A-9088) differs in having the hide forming the back wrap around to form side fronts as well.
27. Examples made in this way include MAE 593.13 (Kolchan)
28. Examples made in this way include MAE 620.41a; NMF VK174; SMV IV-A-9088
29. Mackenzie 1970:193
30. Petitot 1889:182 (translation by author)
31. Murray's description is corroborated by that of Rev. Kirkby: "The dress of the women is the same as that of the men, with the exception of the tunic being round instead of pointed in front. (Kirkby 1865:418)
32. SI 884 and SI 1855
33. Another example, descended through the family of Donald Smith, Lord Strathcona, recently surfaced at Christies Auction, May 17, 2000. I would like to thank Joanne Bird, Curator, Prince of Wales Northern Heritage Centre, Yellowknife, for bringing this to my attention.
34. Banfield 1974:385
35. Based on CMC VI-E-61 and 62.
36. Karen Wright Fraser noted that she worked with five hides measuring approximately 1m30cm (4'2") in length and 80cm (31 ½") in width, in reconstructing the tunic pictured in Figures 1.40 and 1.41. She used one each for front, back and sleeves. Personal communication to author.
37. Alexander Mackenzie purchased tanned moose hides from the Gwich'in he encountered on the lower Mackenzie River, but was told that these animals were scarce in their country. Mackenzie 1970:193
38. Banfield 1974:395
39. LH 996.64.4, tanned by Jane Dragon, Fort Smith, N.W.T.

40. Other Gwich'in moosehide garments are RSM 848.10 and SI 2029. Undocumented but "Gwich'in style" garments made from hide which is probably moosehide include a woman's dress in the McCord Museum, Montreal (ME938.12) and another in the Royal Ontario Museum (953.160.5)
41. Townsend 1981:626
42. Townsend 1981:627
43. Townsend 1981:626
44. Banfield 1961
45. Skoog 1968:43
46. Banfield 1961:76
47. Petroff 1900:86
48. VanStone 1981:3; Zagoskin 1967:3
49. A tunic in the Field Museum (14934) has back and part of a sleeve cut from one piece. See VanStone 1981:4
50. Thomas Burke Washington State Museum 145. Conn (1991) has described and illustrated the cut of this tunic.
51. VanStone 1982:57, Figure 7; Conn (1974: 83) illustrates another example with this cut.
52. The beaded legging bands on this garment are very similar to a pair which originated in southwest Yukon and are now in the George Johnston Museum in Teslin, Yukon.
53. MAE 2667-6; NMF VK175
54. VanStone 1981:13
55. British Museum 1982.28.16
56. CMC VI-Z-10; SI 328766
57. Dorothy Burnham has produced drawings of 11 different tag constructions.
58. Fitzhugh and Kaplan 1982:84; see also Thompson 1987:152
59. Reiss-Museum, Mannheim, FRG V-Am-3219; see Thompson 1987:152
60. Varjola 1990:107-116
61. Duncan (1989) has treated this subject comprehensively.
62. Thompson 1999
63. Thompson 1990

Works Cited

Alekseev, A.I.
> 1987 *The Odyssey of a Russian Scientist: I.G. Voznesenskii in Alaska, California and Siberia 1839-1849.* Alaska History 30. Ed. Richard A. Pierce, trans. Wilma C. Follette. Kingston: Limestone Press.

Banfield, Alexander
> 1961 *A Revision of the reindeer and caribou, genus Rangifer.* Biology Series 66, National Museums of Canada Bulletin 177. Ottawa.
> 1974 *The Mammals of Canada.* Toronto: University of Toronto Press.

Conn, Richard
- 1974 *Robes of White Shell and Sunrise.* Denver: Denver Art Museum.
- 1991 Some Design Concepts of Traditional Subarctic Clothing. *Arctic Anthropology* 28(1) 84-91.

Dall, William H.
- 1870 *Alaska and Its Resources.* Boston: Lee and Shepard.

Duncan, Kate
- 1989 *Northern Athapaskan Art: A Beadwork Tradition.* Seattle: University of Washington Press.

Dzeniskevich, G.I. and L.P. Pavlinskaia
- 1988 Treasures by the Neva: The Russian Collections. In *Crossroads of Continents: Cultures of Siberia and Alaska.* Washington: Smithsonian Institution.

Fitzhugh, William and Susan Kaplan
- 1982 *Inua: Spirit World of the Bering Sea Eskimo.* Washington: Smithsonian Institution.

Fitzhugh, William and Aron Crowell
- 1988 *Crossroads of Continents: Cultures of Siberia and Alaska.* Washington: Smithsonian Institution.

Idiens, Dale
- 1979 *A Catalogue of Northern Athapaskan Indian Artefacts in the Collection of the Royal Scottish Museum, Edinburgh.* Art and Archaeology 3. Royal Scottish Museum.

Jacobsen, Johan A.
- 1977 *Alaskan Voyage, 1881-1883: An Expedition to the Northwest Coast of America* [1884]. Erna Gunther, trans. Chicago: University of Chicago Press.

Kirkby, William W.
- 1865 A Journey to the Youcan, Russian America. Pp. 416-420 in *Annual Report of the Smithsonian Institution for the Year 1864.* Washington.

Lindsay, Debra
- 1993 *Science in the Subarctic: Trappers, Traders and the Smithsonian Institution.* Washington: Smithsonian Institution.

Mackenzie, Alexander
- 1970 *The Journals and Letters of Sir Alexander Mackenzie* [1789-1819]. Ed. W.Kaye Lamb. Toronto: Macmillan of Canada.

McClellan, Catharine
- 1975 *My Old People Say. An Ethnographic Survey of the Southern Yukon Territory.* Publications in Ethnology 6. Ottawa: National Museum of Man.

McKennan, Robert
- 1959 *The Upper Tanana Indians.* Yale University Publications in Anthropology 59. New Haven.

Murray, Alexander Hunter
- 1910 *Journal of the Yukon, 1847-48.* Ed. K.H. Burpee. Publications of the Public Archives of Canada 4. Ottawa.

Osgood, Cornelius
    1936 *Contributions to the Ethnography of the Kutchin*. Yale University Publications in Anthropology 14. New Haven.
    1937 *The Ethnography of the Tanaina*. Yale University Publications in Anthropology 16. New Haven.
    1940 *Ingalik Material Culture*. Yale University Publications in Anthropology 22. New Haven.

Petroff, Ivan
    1900 The Population and Resources of Alaska, 1880. In *Compilation of Narratives of Explorations in Alaska*. Washington: U.S. Government Printing Office.

Petitot, Emile
    1889 *Quinze Ans sous le cercle polaire*. Paris: Librairie de la Société des gens de Lettres.

Pierce, Richard
    1990 *Russian America: A Biographical Dictionary*. Kingston: Limestone Press.

Siebert [Zibert], Erna
    1980 Northern Athapaskan Collections of the First Half of the Nineteenth Century. *Arctic Anthropology* 17(1). Madison, Wisconsin.

Skoog, Ronald
    1968 *Ecology of the Caribou* (Rangifer tarandus granti) *in Alaska*. Ph.D. diss., University of California, Berkeley.

Thompson, Judy
    1987 "No Little Variety of Ornament": Northern Athapaskan Artistic Traditions. In *The Spirit Sings: Artistic Traditions of Canada's First Peoples*, 133-68. Toronto: McClelland and Stewart.
    1990 *Pride of the Indian Wardrobe: Northern Athapaskan Footwear*. Toronto: University of Toronto Press.
    1994 *From the Land: Two Hundred Years of Dene Clothing*. Hull: Canadian Museum of Civilization.
    1999 Marketing Tradition: Late Nineteenth-Century Gwich'in Clothing Ensembles. *American Indian Art Magazine* 24(4): 48-59.

Townsend, Joan
    1981 Tanaina. Vol. 6 of *Handbook of North American Indians*. Washington: Smithsonian Institution.

VanStone, James
    1981 *Athapaskan Clothing and Related Objects in Field Museum of Natural History*. Fieldiana Anthropology, n.s. no.10. Chicago: Field Museum of Natural History.
    1982 Southern Tutchone Clothing and Tlingit Trade. *Arctic Anthropology* 19(1): 51-61.

Varjola, Pirjo
    1990 *The Etholén Collection: The ethnographic Alaskan collection of Adolf Etholén and his contemporaries in the National Museum of Finland*. Helsinki: National Board of Antiquities of Finland.

Varjola, Pirjo and Joyce Herold
    1991 Early Ethnographic Collections from Alaska: An Exhibition from the National Museum of Finland. *American Indian Art* 17(3): 74-87.

Zagoskin, Lavrentii A.
    1967 *Lieutenant Zagoskin's Travels in Russian America, 1842-1844.* Ed. Henry N. Michael. Anthropology of the North: Translations from Russian Sources 7. Toronto: University of Toronto Press.

The Oldest Athabaskan Garment?

Judy Thompson

Introduction

Documentation of early Athabaskan clothing artifacts varies considerably in extent and reliability. Basic information, including name of field collector, date of collection, and culture of origin exists for some important early material, but collection histories for many fine examples are questionable, incomplete, or non-existent. Items in this latter category often have reached museums via circuitous routes, losing information as to provenance along the way. These "orphaned" garments are scattered today among institutions in Canada, the United States and Europe. Lacking even the context of a larger collection, they are often simply labelled "Athabaskan" or, without obvious justification, attributed to one Athabaskan group or another.

A garment of this type, a caribou hide tunic said to be "Kenai, circa 1800", was accessioned into the Canadian Museum of Civilization in 1973 (Figures 1.31 and 1.32). It came to the Museum as part of the Speyer collection, a large, privately owned collection of North American ethnographic materials that was "repatriated" to Canada from Germany.[1] The collection had been built up during the preceding half-century through purchases and exchanges within Europe. It was renowned for the quality, rarity and great age of its components.

The "Kenai, circa 1800" attribution for the tunic commands attention, particularly in the context of Northern Athabaskan clothing and decorative arts studies. "Kenai" suggests an Athabaskan origin. It was the term used by Russians and Germans in the nineteenth century, in reference to the Athabaskan inhabitants of the Cook Inlet region in Alaska, a people today known as the Dena'ina. "Kenai" survives as the name of the peninsula which forms the south shore of Cook Inlet (Figure 1.33). Within Athabaskan clothing collections, however, a date of 1800 is very early. The oldest, reliably documented,

The Oldest Athabaskan Garment?

1.31 Tunic (front view), "Kenai, circa 1800", Canadian Museum of Civilization VI-Y-5.

1.32 Tunic (back view), "Kenai, circa 1800", Canadian Museum of Civilization VI-Y-5.

Athabaskan garments are considerably later in date, mostly collected in the 1840s. Thus, if the suggested provenance for the Speyer tunic is accurate, this garment is arguably the oldest example of Athabaskan clothing in existence.

Its supposed great age alone would make the Speyer tunic a compelling subject for research. But it is an intriguing artifact for other reasons as well, embodying in its construction and decoration both features which are characteristic of Athabaskan clothing, and elements which are atypical or unique. A thorough study of the tunic, aimed at testing the veracity of the cultural attribution and date associated with it, and of reconstructing a plausible cultural and historical context for it, was, therefore, undertaken. As presented in this paper, there have been three main facets to the research of this artifact: a search for information about its European history; in collaboration with Dorothy Burnham, an analysis of the garment itself, and its comparison with other, related items in museum collections; and a study of ethnohistorical sources of information about the region, peoples and time period encompassed by a "Kenai, circa 1800" provenance.

European History

Attempts to verify and expand the collection history of the tunic by tracing its European background have been unsuccessful to date. The Speyer collection of North American ethnographic materials was built up in Europe between about 1926 and 1970, through the efforts of two Arthur Speyers, father and son.[2] Many items in the collection were over 200 years old when they were acquired by the Canadian Museum of Civilization in 1973. Among other hazards, they had survived wars, physical dislocation, changes of ownership and a variety of storage conditions. The Speyers were unusually painstaking in seeking out and preserving information related to the provenance and prior history of the artifacts they acquired.[3] Nevertheless, by the time they were assembling their collection, the histories of many fine items had already been lost, and where "documentation" was present or retrievable, it was often fragmentary and unsubstantiated. The tunic is a case in point: it is not known at what moment in its history it was ascribed a "Kenai, circa 1800" provenance, or who was the source of this attribution.

The Speyer collection was exhibited at the Deutsches Ledermuseum, Offenbach am Main, Germany, in 1968. A catalogue was published at this time, which supplied the above-mentioned provenance for the tunic, but no other information concerning its background was recorded.[4] Following acquisition of the tunic by the Canadian Museum of Civilization in 1973, Arthur Speyer noted in correspondence with a curator in the Museum's Canadian Ethnology Service that he had obtained this item from the Museum für Völkerkunde in Gottingen, Germany, and that it had been in the "Blumenbach" collection in that institution.[5] If correct, the connection to Blumenbach could be significant for, at the very least, it would support a late eighteenth century date for the tunic. Johann Friederich Blumenbach (1752-1840) was a German naturalist and anthropologist who acquired materials from Captain James Cook's voyages and others of this period.[6] Unfortunately, an inquiry to the Museum für Völkerkunde regarding a link between the Museum, Blumenbach and the Speyer tunic received a negative response. Although Blumenbach was identified as an early curator of ethnographic collections in that institution,

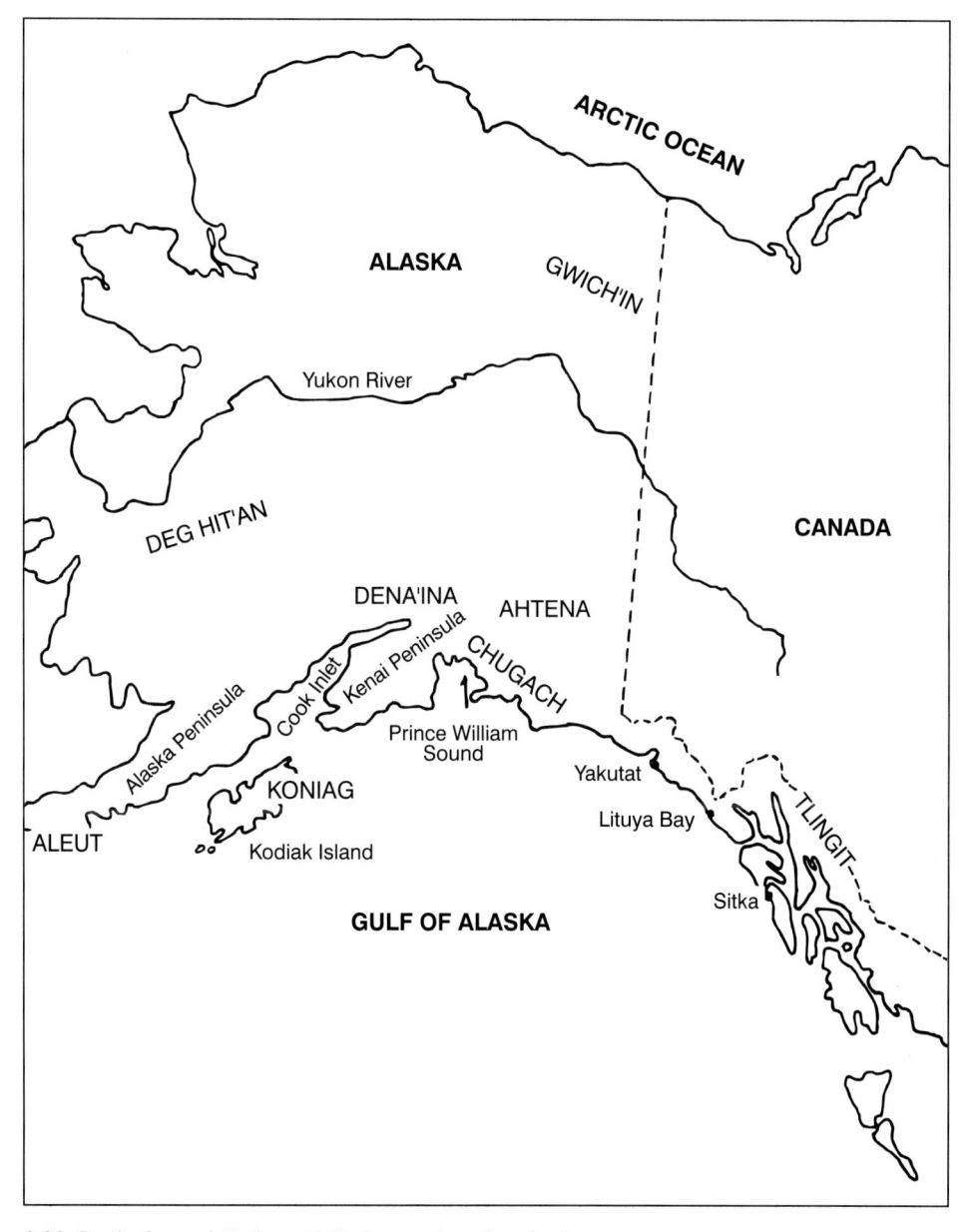

1.33 Pacific Coast of Alaska, with Native peoples referred to in text.
Map drawn by Peter Thompson.

no record was found of the tunic being part of the collection, either during his tenure or at any other time.[7]

Where written history is absent or unverifiable, the artifact itself may yield information about its origins and age. The tunic was examined carefully and the details of its construction, design and decoration recorded. It was then compared to analogous material in the Canadian Museum of Civilization and other collections.

Garment Description

The tunic is made from tanned, de-haired caribou hide which has been lightly smoked and used flesh side out. As Figure 1.34 illustrates, the body of the garment is formed from two basically rectangular skin pieces, a larger segment which forms the back and wraps around the left side to the centre front, and a smaller one which forms the right front. At the single side seam, the piece forming the back is cut obliquely into a broad fringe; this fringed section is folded to the outside, and the front and back sections are seamed on the inside. Sewing is with sinew thread in an overcast stitch on the inside of the garment. Shoulders are formed from additional skin pieces, roughly trapezoidal in shape, which join the front and back of the tunic in horizontal seams below the shoulder. Sleeves are simple tubes set into straight armholes. The underarms are left open. At the centre back, the tunic is 1m 16cm (3'9 ¾") in length: it would fall to about mid-calf on an individual approximately 1m 65cm (5'5") in height. The bottom edge of the garment is cut more-or-less straight, and slashed vertically into a fringe about 5cm (2") long.

The tunic is decorated with a fringed band of porcupine quillwork on the upper front, and with painting with red ochre on the shoulders and upper back. The quillworked band curves across the breast, carries around the upper arms, and ends on either side of the upper back. It is worked in a checkerboard pattern of zigzag stepped lines in white and dyed brown and orange quills. The band narrows as it goes around the upper arms, and the motif changes to a series of parallel, diagonal stepped lines.

Porcupine quills are applied to the breastband using a folded quillwork technique which in this paper will be called "reinforced, straight, single quill" (Figure 1.35). Superficially, this quillwork resembles that seen on many nineteenth century Gwich'in garments (see, for example, Figures 1.2 and 1.19), except that larger quills are used and the lanes are broader. The technique differs, however, from that used on Gwich'in garments in one important respect: the work has been reinforced by the enclosure within the folded quills of thin strips of a translucent, milky white material (Figure 1.36). Through microscopic analysis, this filler has been identified as whale baleen.[8]

Fascinating Challenges

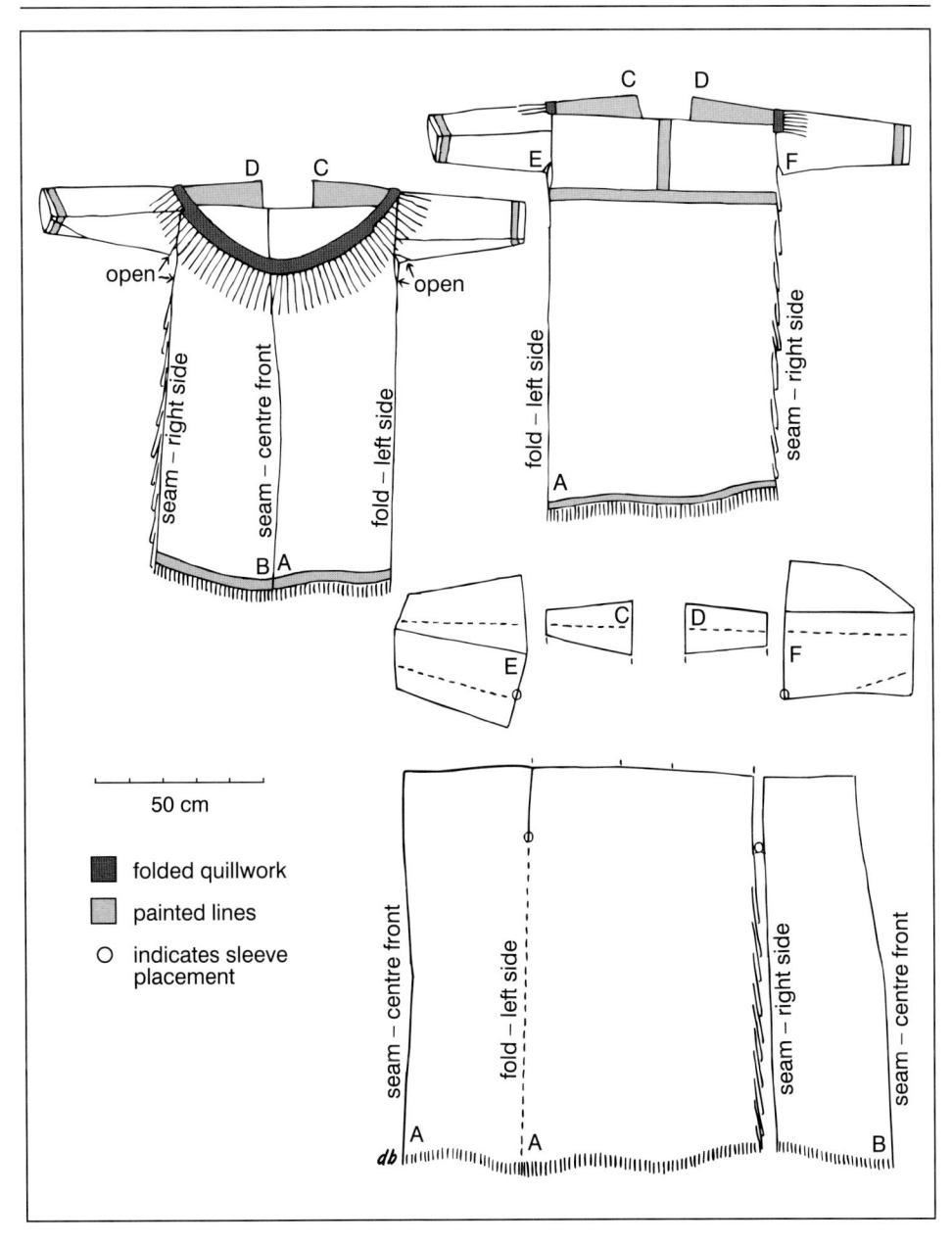

1.34 Cut of tunic illustrated in Figures 1.31 and 1.32.

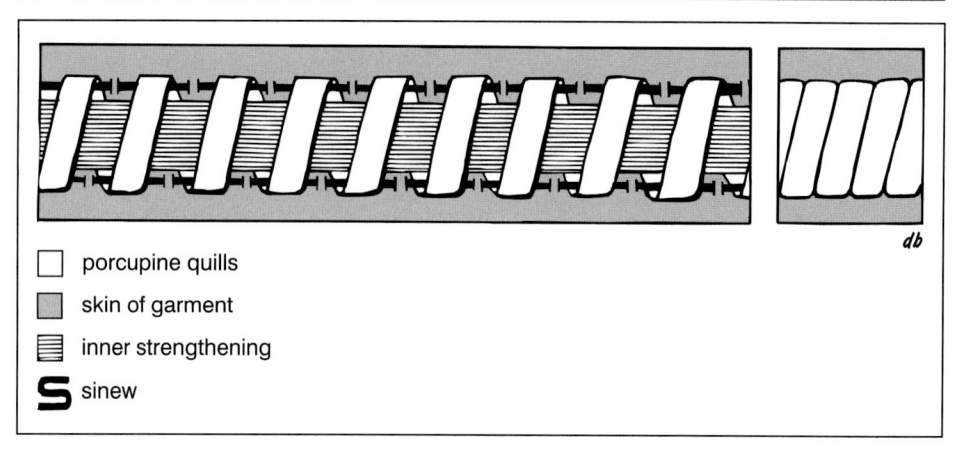

1.35 Folded quillwork technique: reinforced, straight, single quill.

The skin backing to the quillworked breastband extends slightly above and below it. At the top, the backing is sewn to the garment. At the lower edge of the backing, an additional skin band, unevenly smudged with red ochre and slashed vertically to form a fringe, is attached. Individual fringe strands are 15 cm (6") long and 5 mm (1/4") wide; each is wrapped with white porcupine quills for approximately half its length. The quillwrapping technique is the same as that illustrated in Figure 1.22 (previous paper). The self-fringe at the bottom of the tunic is similarly decorated with white quills.

The second important component to the decoration of this garment is painting with red ochre. Parallel, vertical lines cover the hide pieces forming the shoulders, and four parallel lines are drawn around the sleeve ends and the bottom of the garment (Figure 1.31). Two geometric-patterned bands, each about 4 cm (1 ½") wide, are painted on the upper back (Figure 1.32). One band extends from side to side at the level of the underarms: it is painted with a pattern of triangles alternated with groupings of five to nine vertical lines. The other painted band extends vertically from the centre neck to meet with the horizontal band. On this band, a simple cross motif alternates with horizontal lines in sets of three.

Athabaskan Origins?

The Kenai Region

The coast of south central Alaska curves westward along the Gulf of Alaska to the tip of the Alaska Peninsula. This shoreline is broken by two large indentations - Prince William Sound and, just to the north, Cook Inlet – separated by a

Fascinating Challenges

1.36 Detail, reinforced folded quillwork on breastband of tunic illustrated in Figure 1.31. Where the quillwork is damaged (as, for example, in the upper lane of work), the reinforcing element (in this case, whale baleen) can be seen underlying the surface layer of folded quills. The narrow diagonal strand extending from the top lane of the quillwork is a shred of baleen that has come loose from the body of the work.

landmass known as the Kenai Peninsula. Partially protected from cold arctic air by the high mountains of the Alaska Range, this region enjoys a relatively mild climate. It is a land of spectacular physical beauty. In the words of one nineteenth century visitor:

> *The country...is enchanting. The mountains have high, sharp peaks and are close to the sea...The snow that cover[s] the highest peaks form[s] several glaciers, while the shoreline [is] covered with the lushest green. A lovely odor fill[s] the air and seem[s] to come from the clusters of birch trees. The rocky coast [is] irregular ... and [falls] into ravines, coves, and pillars – a painter's paradise.[9]*

The same traveller remarked upon the rich animal resources of the area:

> *The landscape, the volcanic outcroppings, glaciers, fantastic rock structures, waterfalls, grottoes, and caves combine with a wealth of animal life such as I have seldom seen. The rivers swarm with salmon and other fish, the sea offers seal hunting, bears and caribou are there in quantity, [and] the rocks are covered with gulls' nests...[10]*

In the late eighteenth century, around the time when the Speyer tunic is reputed to have been collected, a number of different Aboriginal peoples either lived in the region of the Kenai Peninsula or visited it for purposes of hunting, trading, or warfare.[11] It was the homeland of Alutiiq (Pacific Eskimo peoples), principally the Chugach Eskimo who had villages on the shores of Prince William Sound and the Koniag, who lived on Kodiak Island, at the entrance to Cook Inlet. A people related to the Chugach had villages along the south coast of the Kenai Peninsula and partway up the coast of Cook Inlet. The remainder of this coast and the region around the head of Cook Inlet, as well as adjacent inland areas, were the territory of the Dena'ina, an Athabaskan people. Other Athabaskans, the Ahtena, lived inland from Prince William Sound, in the valley of the Copper River. Tlingit, the most northern of Northwest Coast peoples, visited Prince William Sound on trading expeditions and on raids. Large parties of Aleut hunters employed by Russian fur traders were often in the region as well.

If the Speyer tunic originated in the Kenai Peninsula region, it could, in theory, have been collected from any one of these Aboriginal peoples. Non-Athabaskan as well as Athabaskan attributions must be considered. Of the possible non-Athabaskan sources for this garment, an Aleut or Alutiiq origin seems unlikely: these people wore clothing of a different style, made from different materials. Contemporary descriptions of Aleut clothing, for example, mention parkas made from bird and sea mammal skins or from animal intestines, rather than from dehaired caribou hide:

> *The [Aleut] woman's frock is made of sealskin and that of the men, of the skin of birds; both reaching below the knee. This is the whole dress of the women. But over the frock, the men wear another made of gut, which resists water and has a hood to it, which draws over the head.*[12]

Aleut clothing was, furthermore, decorated with "embroidery of feathers, human hair, and ocher-colored skin strips"[13], rather than with porcupine quillwork and fringes. Alutiiq (Chugach and Koniag Eskimo) clothing was similar, in that upper garments consisted of "long, usually hoodless, fur and bird-skin parkas and hooded rain parkas sewn from strips of [seal, sea lion or bear] intestine."[14] These Eskimo garments "were often richly ornamented with hair, skin, and feather tassels and colourful embroidery."[15]

A stronger case can be made for a Tlingit source for the Speyer tunic. From their home territories immediately south of the region under discussion here, this Northwest Coast people traded with Athabaskan neighbours in the interior for tanned moose and caribou hides and porcupine quillwork, as well as for finished garments made from these materials. Tlingit also made long sea voyages north to trade and conduct raids, and in this way could have acquired Athabaskan clothing from the Kenai Peninsula region. Decorated Athabaskan clothing was particularly coveted by well-to-do Tlingit for ceremonial wear and can be seen worn in combination with classic Northwest Coast garments in several early illustrations.[16]

Tlingit also produced skin clothing themselves. Robes of furred skins (sea otter, wolf, bear), worn by both men and women, are mentioned in early accounts as well as depicted in contemporary illustrations.[17] The French explorer La Perouse noted in 1786 that some of the Tlingit he encountered at Lituya Bay wore "complete shirts of otter skins".[18] The Spanish at Yakutat in 1791, undoubtedly struck by the near nudity of Tlingit men, commented that women were "decently clothed" in a long, sleeved tunic of tanned skin.[19] Twentieth century Tlingit recalled the manufacture of men's pants and women's dresses of sealskin.[20] Today, little is known about the style and decoration of Tlingit skin clothing. The impression given by the historic accounts and illustrations is that, for everyday activities, clothing was minimal and garments were simple in design. Clothing was not essential for survival, as it was for people living inland or further to the north.

Although the most plausible of non-Athabaskan sources for the Speyer tunic, a Tlingit origin is, nevertheless, far less likely than an Athabaskan origin. In materials, design and decoration, this garment can be linked to better documented Athabaskan artifacts. For example, tanned, de-haired caribou hide was used by virtually all Athabaskan peoples in the manufacture of summer garments. Porcupine quills, hide fringes and red ochre also were commonly used by Athabaskans in the decoration of clothing. Only the presence of whale baleen in the quillwork of the Speyer tunic is unusual in a general Athabaskan context. In this instance, however, it supports a Dena'ina origin. Among Athabaskans, the Dena'ina were unique in inhabiting a seacoast and in hunting whales and other sea mammals.

The Speyer tunic can be correlated as well, on the basis of shared design features, to some documented Athabaskan garments collected in the Kenai Peninsula region. For example, the way in which a single hide piece forms not only the back of this tunic but a part of the front as well, is often seen on Dena'ina garments collected in the 1840s (see Figure 1.5, previous paper). A simple sleeve construction and straight armhole are also common to these Dena'ina garments and the Speyer tunic. Some Dena'ina women's dresses from mid-nineteenth century collections further resemble the Speyer tunic in having shoulders formed from separate skin pieces joined to the front and the back of the tunic in horizontal seams below the shoulder (see Figure 1.7, previous paper).[21] These Dena'ina women's dresses are also like the Speyer tunic with respect to the finish of the lower edge (cut straight with self fringes) and in having a broad, diagonally slashed, fringe in the side seam.

The Speyer tunic has, however, a rather meagre shape, and looks distinctly skimpy in comparison with the Dena'ina garments referred to above. Possibly, the woman who made it had to cope with an insufficiency of good quality, tanned caribou hide. A lack of adequate sewing material may also explain the unsewn underarms of this tunic, an extraordinary feature not observed on any other Athabaskan garments. Perhaps, working with hides sufficient to cover the body of the person for whom the garment was intended but not large enough to provide the fullness through the upper back that would enable arms to move freely, the seamstress solved the problem by simply leaving the underarms unseamed. She could have achieved the same results by constructing Gwich'in style sleeves as seen in Figure 1.4 (previous paper): the option she chose required less work and skill, and retained a basically Dena'ina design for the garment.

The decoration of this garment combines features characteristic of nineteenth century Athabaskan clothing, with elements which are unusual or anomalous. The quillworked breastband is typically Athabaskan in its shape and placement on the garment. Quill colours and motifs are also consistent with Athabaskan tradition. However, the rather coarse appearance and simple patterning of the quillwork and, in particular, the use of a reinforced folded technique distinguish this breastband from the majority of mid-nineteenth century Athabaskan garments. Dena'ina, Ahtena, and Deg Hit'an garments, for example, usually are decorated with quite different quillwork, achieved through weaving the quills according to the method illustrated in Figure 1.18 (previous paper). This woven work was done with very slender quills and produced intricately patterned motifs. Nineteenth century Gwich'in quillwork more closely resembles that seen on the Speyer tunic, in that a folded technique is used. However, Gwich'in work lacks a reinforcing element and the lanes are narrower.

The use of reinforced folded quillwork in the decoration of the Speyer tunic may be an important indicator of both the date and region of origin of this garment. The technique is associated in particular with late eighteenth and early nineteenth century artifacts, and appears to have been known to both Northwest Coast and Athabaskan seamstresses. It is found, for example, on two early nineteenth century tunics which today are housed in the Museum of Anthropology and Ethnography, St. Petersburg.[22] Figure 1.37 illustrates one of these tunics, a garment probably acquired in 1804-05 by a Russian sea captain, Iurii Lisianskii. Another, very similar, tunic is in the collection of the British Museum, London: this example may have been collected by Captain George Vancouver on the North Pacific coast in 1794.[23] The fronts of each of these tunics are decorated with multiple, parallel, fringed bands of reinforced folded quillwork.

None of these tunics is well-documented, but they can be linked, through ethnohistorical sources and pictorial and artifactual evidence, to the Tlingit of the Northwest Coast.[24] For example, a Tlingit chief, "Tzachey" was painted in 1793 wearing a tunic of this type.[25] Another tunic, said to be over 200 years old and in appearance very like the museum examples, has been passed down through successive generations of the Auk clan of the Tlingit and survives in private, Aboriginal ownership in Juneau, Alaska.[26]

A variety of other artifacts attributed to the Tlingit, as well as some collected among the Tsimshian, their neighbours to the south, are decorated with reinforced folded quillwork similar in technique and patterning to that of the Speyer tunic. These Northwest Coast items include Tlingit hide armour collected at Sitka in 1884[27], a shaman's hat collected by Louis Shotridge in 1927[28], and a dance apron collected in Wrangell, Alaska in 1931.[29] The Northwest Coast collections of the Canadian Museum of Civilization include two pairs of Tsimshian leggings decorated with reinforced folded quillwork: one pair was collected late in the nineteenth century, the other early in the twentieth century.[30] Most of these artifacts appear to have been already old when collected, and their quillworked bands even older. Presumably, such quillwork was highly prized by coastal peoples, and was saved when the article to which it was attached was no longer useable, so that it could then be applied to a new item.[31]

The fact that reinforced folded quillwork is seen on a range of artifacts attributed to Northwest Coast peoples does not, however, preclude an Athabaskan origin for the Speyer tunic. As has already been demonstrated, several aspects of the cut of this garment link it to Athabaskan tunics of a somewhat later date. In addition, the fact that quillwork on the Speyer tunic consists of a single, curving breastband as opposed to multiple, parallel bands also suggests an Athabaskan origin. Furthermore, at least one documented

The Oldest Athabaskan Garment?

1.37 Tunic, possibly collected by Iurii Lisianskii, 1805.
Courtesy Peter the Great Museum of Anthropology and Ethnography, St Petersburg 633-31.

Athabaskan tunic, an Ahtena woman's dress collected in 1841 (Figure 1.38) has a breastband similar to that of the Speyer tunic, in that it is composed of relatively broad lanes of folded quillwork, with checkerboard patterning in dark brown, ochre and white.

A quillworked breastband (Figure 1.39) remarkably similar to that adorning the Speyer tunic is in the British Museum. Not only is the quillwork technique used on the two bands the same (reinforced, folded), but motifs and colour combinations are closely comparable. The shapes of the two bands are alike

1.38 Ahtena woman's dress, collected by I.G. Voznesenski in 1841.
Courtesy Peter the Great Museum of Anthropology and Ethnography 593.10.

The Oldest Athabaskan Garment?

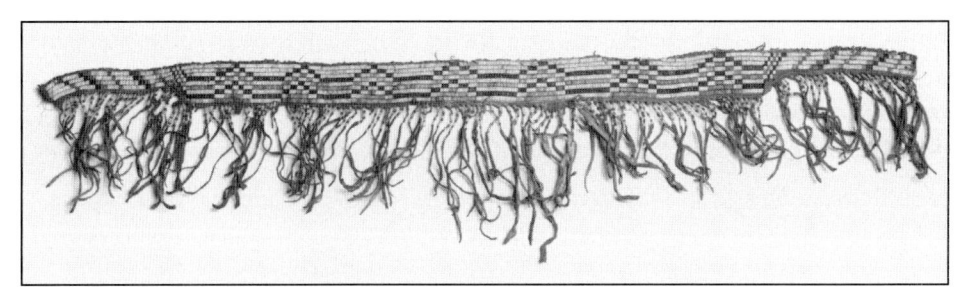

1.39 Quillworked breastband, collected by George Hewett, Cook Inlet, 1794. Courtesy British Museum, London Van.206

as well – each narrows at either end, at the point where the band would go around the upper arm. The British Museum example is of particular significance to the attribution and dating of the Speyer tunic, for it is solidly documented as to date and place of collection. It was collected by George Hewett, surgeon's mate on Captain George Vancouver's expedition to the North Pacific coast in 1794. In Hewett's catalogue, this item is listed as an "ornament for leather slop."[32] "Slop" is defined in the Oxford Dictionary as "a workman's loose outer garment",[33] a description that could well apply to a garment like the Speyer tunic. Hewett's apparent knowledge of the function of the "ornament" he collected suggests that he saw garments decorated with work of this type while he was in Cook Inlet.

Another aspect of the decoration of the Speyer tunic which may assist in attribution is the fringing along the lower edge of the breastband and at the bottom of the garment. Both the presence of fringes and the technique involved in their decoration support an Athabaskan attribution. Athabaskan fringes invariably were decorated by wrapping individual strands with porcupine quills for part of their length. The technique employed in this work, illustrated in Figure 1.22 (previous paper), was used by all Athabaskan seamstresses. Normally, however, silver willow (eleagnus) seeds would also be included in the decoration of breast and back fringes: a single seed bead would be threaded on each fringe strand, between segments of quillwrapping. Silver willow seeds can be seen, for example, on the breastband fringe of the Ahtena woman's tunic illustrated in Figure 1.38. They are, however, not present on the fringes of the Speyer tunic. Rather than casting doubt on an Athabaskan origin for this garment, the absence of silver willow seeds may further support an early date of manufacture and a Dena'ina attribution for it. The quillwrapped fringing of the Hewett breastband (Figure 1.39), for example, also lacks silver willow seeds, as does the fringing on another Cook Inlet item, a "Dagger Case", collected by Hewett in 1794.[34]

Painting with red ochre is perhaps the most enigmatic feature of this intriguing garment. Red ochre frequently appears on Athabaskan upper garments, but it usually takes the form of lines defining seams and edges and more generalized smudging of fringes and other areas. No other garments with painting as extensive and detailed as that seen on the Speyer tunic have been located. In particular, decorative work covering shoulder areas and defining a mid-line on the upper back of the garment is very unusual in an Athabaskan context. The horizontal placement of the painted band crossing the upper back is, on the other hand, strongly reminiscent of bands executed in woven quills attached across the backs of Dena'ina and Ahtena women's dresses of the 1840s (see, for example, Figure 1.6, previous paper). Furthermore, the motif of this horizontal painted band - a pattern of triangles alternated by vertical bars – brings to mind similar patterning executed in quills on Dena'ina, Ahtena and Deg Hit'an garments. The impression created by this painted band on the Speyer tunic is of an artist's sketch, a mock-up of work which normally and/or ideally would have been done in quills.

In summary, comparative analysis of the Speyer tunic supports a Dena'ina attribution and a date of circa 1800 for this artifact. How would a garment like this have functioned in late eighteenth century Dena'ina society? Clues as to its intended function are found within the garment itself. The use of dehaired hide identifies it as an item of summer clothing, and the straight-cut bottom edge implies it was a woman's garment. (Athabaskan men's tunics normally had a distinctive pointed bottom edge, front and back.) It may have been intended for everyday wear: some aspects of its design and construction suggest it was put together rather quickly from materials that were on hand. It is made from relatively poor-quality hides, ones scarred and riddled with holes as a result of warble fly infestation when the animal was alive. It is constructed from unusually small sections of hide. (Note, in particular, the make-up of the sleeves and the size of the shoulder segments.) The breastband, worked in relatively durable reinforced quillwork technique, could well have been re-cycled from another, no longer wearable, tunic. The painted decoration has the appearance of being quickly executed: in the case of the geometric patterned bands on the upper back, the painting perhaps was done in lieu of more time-consuming porcupine quillwork.

Whatever the reason for and circumstances surrounding its manufacture, this garment reflects considerable skill and experience in Athabaskan skills associated with clothing manufacture. The caribou hides, albeit scarred and with holes, are tanned to a thin, smooth finish, seams are sewn with tiny, regular stitches using fine sinew thread, fringes are individually and carefully wrapped with porcupine quills, and the quillworked breastband is handsome and technically well-executed.

The European Connection

If we assume a Dena'ina origin, and a circa 1800 date of manufacture for the Speyer tunic, how would it have come into European hands?

White people were part of the cultural mix in the Kenai Peninsula region from the mid-eighteenth century onwards. An expedition led by Vitus Bering, a Dane in the service of the Russian navy, is the first recorded visit by Europeans to the region. Bering was in the Gulf of Alaska in 1741. He perished later on the voyage, but surviving members of his crew returned to Russia with tales of the rich animal resources of the region. Within a few years, Siberian fur hunters were extending their search for pelts to the Aleutian Islands, then to Kodiak Island, and finally to the mainland of Alaska. By the 1780s, permanent Russian trading posts were established in Cook Inlet and Prince William Sound.[35]

During the same period, other nations – England, Spain, and France, among others - became interested in the region. Captain James Cook's third voyage, in 1778, and the subsequent publication of his journal, brought the rich sea otter herds of the North Pacific coast to world attention.[36] During the final quarter of the eighteenth century, numerous maritime expeditions reached Prince William Sound and Cook Inlet. Many were commercial enterprises, interested solely in fur. Others were government-sponsored, intent on exploration, establishing sovereignty or finding a northwest passage which would link the Pacific and Atlantic Oceans. Of the official expeditions, two in particular were significant with respect to the contacts they made with people in the Kenai Peninsula area, the ethnographic information they recorded, and the collections they assembled. These were the above-mentioned voyage of Captain James Cook in 1778, and that of Captain George Vancouver in 1794.[37]

Both the Cook and the Vancouver expeditions encountered Aboriginal peoples on several occasions while they were in Prince William Sound and Cook Inlet. Usually, these meetings were accompanied by reciprocal gift-giving and by barter. The Indigenous peoples were skillful traders and keen to acquire European goods; in return they offered food supplies, fur pelts and material culture items - "garments, weapons, fishing-tackle and ornaments in great variety".[38] Many examples of Native clothing probably came into the possession of European seamen in this way.

A few contemporary accounts provide tantalizing glimpses of the role clothing played in encounters between Aboriginal people and White men in this early post-contact period. For example, in Cook Inlet in 1778, people who were either Dena'ina or Alutiiq approached Captain Cook's vessels holding up "a leather frock on a long pole" as a sign of their peaceful intentions. They offered in trade "a few of their fur dresses, made of the Skins of Sea Beaver [otter], Martins, Hares".[39] In 1794, as George Vancouver's expedition sailed south from the Kenai Peninsula region, his ships were visited by a party of sea otter hunters from Kodiak Island. They were eager to trade and well-supplied for that purpose, with "bows, arrows, darts, spears, fish-gigs, whale-gut shirts, and specimens of their very neat and curious needle-work."[40]

These documented transactions are exceptional: the majority of such exchanges went unrecorded. Where records were kept, often they were subsequently lost, or disassociated from the collections to which they referred. Artifacts were equally vulnerable: following acquisition, many were dispersed, lost or destroyed. Hide clothing was highly susceptible to insect damage, and many a moth-eaten garment was probably simply thrown away within a few years of collection. Surviving inventories make for frustrating reading, as they tell us of ethnographic collections that are no more. At the same time, these inventories are valuable sources of information about the kinds of artifacts that were collected in the early post-contact period. For example, clothing items acquired in Cook Inlet appear on two inventories of collections made by members of Captain Vancouver's crew.[41] A "Catalogue of Curiosities" compiled by Archibald Menzies, naturalist and official collector for the expedition, includes, under the heading "From Cook's Inlet":

> *A pair of Boots & Garters curiously ornamented – a present of a Chief at the head of the Inlet;*
> *Ornamented fringes for the Chiefs' War Dress,*
> *Two Skin Dresses – animal unknown;*
> *Camlico or Frocks made from the finer Membranes of the Intestines of Marine Animals.*[42]

As already noted, George Goodman Hewett, surgeon's mate, also formed a collection: his catalogue refers to the following items from "Cooks River":

> *Stockings;*
> *Ornament for Leather Slop;*
> *[Ornament] for stockings*[43]

Of the above items collected on Vancouver's voyage, only the "ornaments" (quillworked bands of the type used to decorate Athabaskan garments) are known to have survived to the present day. Both are in the British Museum collection.[44] As has already been discussed, the "Ornament for Leather Slop" (Figure 1.39) is of particular importance to the present study.

The precise circumstances surrounding the collection of the Speyer tunic will probably never be known. However, if the circa 1800 date and Kenai location are accurate, as comparative analysis of the garment suggests they are, this artifact probably was acquired in a transaction such as those described above. Received by a European seaman or Russian trader in exchange for beads, iron or possibly an article of European clothing, it would have been added to a private or official collection of ethnographic "curiosities" and transported to Europe, via a long sea voyage, soon after collection.

Conclusion

In some respects, the Speyer tunic will always remain an enigma. Researchers may forever puzzle over why the seamstress left the underarms unsewn and painted the shoulders and upper back of this garment with red ochre, over who she was and for whom she made this garment. Nevertheless, research on this early ethnographic artifact has generated a considerable amount of information pertinent to our understanding of it. Specifically, information derived from historical accounts, ethnographic research and, in particular, the study of a broad range of material in museum collections has enabled us to reconstruct a plausible, defensible, ethnographic and historical context for this unique early garment. It has also substantiated the slight and unverifiable information which was associated with this artifact when the Canadian Museum of Civilization acquired it in 1973. There appears to be no reason to dispute, and considerable evidence to support, a "Kenai, circa 1800" attribution for the Speyer tunic. It may, therefore, with justification be considered the oldest Athabaskan garment in existence.

Endnotes

1. Brasser 1976:12
2. ibid.
3. ibid.:11
4. Benndorf and Speyer 1968
5. correspondence, Arthur Speyer to Ted Brasser, March 3, 1974. CMC Library, Archives and Documentation Division, I-A-194M: Box 18, Folder 5.
6. Jonathan King, personal communication, October 30, 2000.
7. correspondence, Dr. Gundolf Krüger to author, July 22, 1999
8. Identified through microscopic analysis. Identification by Dr. Henry Ouellet, Zoological Division, Canadian Museum of Nature. Bokman 1990.
9. Jacobsen 1977:191
10. ibid.:192
11. de Laguna 1972:182
12. Cook 1785:509
13. Black and Liapunova 1988:56
14. Clark 1984:194
15. Fitzhugh 1988: 51
16. For example, in a group of Tlingit drawn by the French artist Gaspard Duche de Vancy at Lituya Bay in 1786 (reproduced in Henry 1984:146-7), one man wears an Athabaskan-style sleeved shirt and moccasin-trousers of dehaired skins decorated with fringes.
17. for example, Dixon 1789:169, quoted in de Laguna 1972:36; drawing by Cardero in Henry 1984:164.
18. La Perouse, quoted in de Laguna 1972:433

19. Malaspina, quoted in de Laguna 1972:434-435
20. de Laguna 1972:435
21. Museum of Anthropology and Ethnography 620.41; National Museum of Finland VK17
22. Museum of Anthropology and Ethnography 633.31 and 561.3
23. British Museum 1982 Am28.21; King 1994:55
24. Thompson 1991
25. ibid:72; see also Cole 1980:209-210
26. In the early 1970s, this garment was on loan to the Alaska State Museum in Juneau Alaska. (Steve Henrikson, personal communication). Following its return to its owners, it appeared in a photograph in a local newspaper, the Juneau Empire, April 11, 1991.
27. Smithsonian Institution 74440
28. University of Pennsylvania Museum NA11758
29. Portland Art Museum 48.3.557
30. VII-C-2095 and VII-C-1187
31. Several artifacts were examined on which both regular folded and reinforced folded techniques were present. In every case, bands made without the reinforcing element were more damaged than those with it.
32. King 1994: 48
33. Allen 1990:1145
34. British Museum Van 99
35. Townsend 1981:635-636
36. Cook and King 1785
37. Beaglehole 1967; Lamb 1984
38. Lamb 1984:1247-8
39. Beaglehole 1967:364
40. Lamb 1984: 171
41. King 1994
42. ibid.:43
43. ibid.:48
44. British Museum Van 206 and Van 207

Works Cited

Allen, R.E., ed.
    1990 *The Concise Oxford Dictionary of Current English*. Oxford: Clarendon Press.

Beaglehole, J.C., ed.
    1967 *The journals of Captain James Cook on his voyages of discovery. The voyage of the "Resolution" and "Discovery", 1776-1780*. Published for the Hakluyt Society. Cambridge: At the University Press.

Benndorf, Helga, and Arthur Speyer
    1968 *Indianer Nordamerikas, 1760-1860*. Offenbach am Main, West Germany: Deutsches Ledermuseum, Shuhmuseum.

Black, Lydia, and R.G. Liapunova
> 1988 Aleut: Islanders of the North Pacific. In *Crossroads of Continents*, ed. W. Fitzhugh and A. Crowell, 52-57. Washington: Smithsonian Institution.

Bokman, Wilf
> 1990 Unpublished report identifying materials on Canadian Museum of Civilization artifacts: VI-Y-5, VII-C-2120, VII-C-2095. Conservation Services Division, Canadian Museum of Civilization, Ottawa, Ontario.

Brasser, Ted
> 1976 *"Bo'jou Neejee!": Profiles of Canadian Indian Art*. Ottawa: National Museum of Man.

Clark, Donald
> 1984 Pacific Eskimo: Historical Ethnography. In *Arctic*. Vol.5 of *Handbook of North American Indians*. Washington: Smithsonian Institution.

Cole, Douglas
> 1980 Sigismund Bacstrom's Northwest Coast drawings and an account of his curious career. *British Columbia Studies* 46: 61-86.
>
> 1985 *Captured Heritage: The Scramble for Northwest Coast Artifacts*. Vancouver: Douglas and McIntyre.

Cook, James, and J. King
> 1785 *A Voyage to the Pacific Ocean Undertaken, by the Command of His Majesty, for Making Discoveries in the Northern Hemisphere. Performed Under the Direction of Captains Cook, Clarke, and Gore, in His Majesty's Ships the Resolution and Discovery; in the Years 1776, 1777, 1778, 1779, and 1780*. 3 vols. London: G. Nicol and T.Cadell.

de Laguna, Frederica
> 1972 Under Mount St. Elias: the history and culture of the Yakutat Tlingit. *Smithsonian Contributions to Anthropology*. Vol 6. Washington: Smithsonian Institution.

Fitzhugh, William
> 1988 Eskimos: Hunters of the Frozen Coasts. In *Crossroads of Continents*, ed. W. Fitzhugh and A. Crowell, 42-52. Washington: Smithsonian Institution.

Fitzhugh, William and Aron Crowell, eds.
> 1988 *Crossroads of Continents: Cultures of Siberia and Alaska*. Washington: Smithsonian Institution.

Henry, John Frazier
> 1984 *Early Maritime Artists of the Pacific Northwest Coast, 1741-1841*. Seattle: University of Washington Press.

Jacobsen, Johan A.
> 1977 *Alaskan Voyage, 1881-1883: An Expedition to the Northwest Coast of America (1884)*. Trans. Erna Gunther. Chicago: University of Chicago Press.

King, J.C.H.
> 1994 "Vancouver's Ethnography: A Preliminary Description of Five Inventories from the Voyage of 1791-95." *Journal of the History of Collections* 6(1): 33-58.

Lamb, W.Kaye, ed.
> 1984 *George Vancouver: A Voyage of Discovery to the North Pacific Ocean and Round the World 1791-1795*. 4 vols. London: The Hakluyt Society.

Thompson, Judy
    1991 "Some Curious Dresses of the Natives": A re-examination of some early garments from the Alaska coast. *American Indian Art Magazine* (16)3: 66-76.

Townsend, Joan
    1981 Tanaina. In *Subarctic*. Vol. 6 *Handbook of North American Indians*. Washington: Smithsonian Institution.

Acknowledgements

The research described in the preceding two papers would not have been possible without the assistance of colleagues in other museums. My thanks to all who over the course of a 30 year research project have provided access to collections and helped in numerous other ways. In particular, Dorothy Burnham and I would like to acknowledge the following individuals, who ensured that both artifacts and work space were available to her, so that she could produce drawings of garments from their collections: Dale Idiens, National Museums of Scotland, Jonathan King, British Museum, Moira McCaffrey, McCord Museum, Ken Lister, Royal Ontario Museum, and Pirjo Varjola, National Museum of Finland.

The contributions by Karen Wright Fraser and Ingrid Kritsch to the Athabaskan section of the book are also gratefully acknowledged. Finally, I would like to thank Judy Hall, Leslie Tepper, Dorothy Burnham, and Melanie Thompson for reading and providing critical commentary on the preceding two papers.

The Gwich'in Solution

1.40 Gwich'in style tunic (front view), late 19th century.
Canadian Museum of Civilization VI-Z-10.

The Gwich'in Solution

Dorothy K. Burnham

About 10 years ago, my first Gwich'in caribou skin tunic (Figures 1.40 and 1.41) was spread out before me, and I started to take the accurate measurements needed to make a scale diagram of exactly how its parts were cut and joined together. Doing such an analysis of any rare and old garment is not easy. Most are fragile, and often they are stiff with age.

I approached this unfamiliar garment with admiration and some trepidation. During many years of research I had made similar diagrams of a wide variety of garments. This one looked fairly simple. I should have known better. It wasn't! I drew length, width and outline of the back to 1/10 scale[1], then the front, traced off these pieces and tried joining them. When I joined them, I found that the back came far forward, creating a very strangely shaped armhole – was this right? I repeated the measuring and joining. It was right. The sleeve head had to fit that angular space. As it was undoubtedly going to be a bit tricky to plot, I tackled the simpler lower part of the sleeve first, measuring seam length and circumference at wrist, elbow and top of seam. This produced a normal tapered sleeve shape. It had a single seam, the top of which met the body of the garment close to the point where back joined the front. By laying the garment flat, it was possible to measure each side fold of the sleeve. The upper fold was a little longer than the seam length and the lower fold was considerably longer (as illustrated in Figure 1.42).

The head of the sleeve was then delineated by plotting a line from the top of the sleeve seam to the point where the upper fold of the sleeve met the garment at the turn of the shoulder, then down the back to the armpit and the top of the lower sleeve fold, and then with an abrupt turn back up to the sleeve seam completing the round. The resulting sleeve head was angular and an unusual shape, but it fitted the armhole accurately.

The Gwich'in Solution

1.41 Gwich'in style tunic (back view), late 19th century.
Canadian Museum of Civilization VI-Z-10.

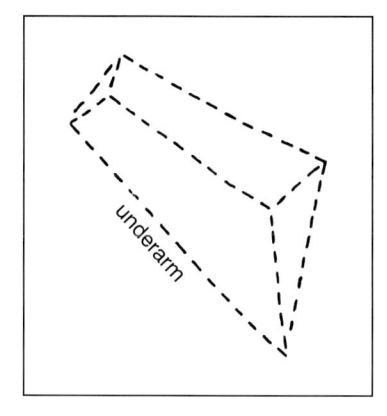

1.42 Gwich'in sleeve design.

We now had a scale diagram of one Gwich'in tunic (Figure 1.43). This garment was an excellent example of the high standard of craftsmanship expected in the Gwich'in community. It was beautifully made and decorated. It had one intriguing peculiarity. It did not want to lie flat on the table, but had a strong feeling of forward movement. With the pattern draft before me the reason for this was very clear. The large back, folding forward over the small front, placed the armholes very far forward, and the sleeve shapes gave plenty of room for arm movement forward and upward. It seemed unlikely that this particular cut of body and sleeve parts was unique to this one garment - and it wasn't.

As I continued working with Judy Thompson on her research concerning the clothing of a vast and varied northern area, we had the opportunity to analyze and make diagrams of many more skin garments and among them there were a number of tunics similar to this Gwich'in one. It was fascinating to find how consistent was the use of that particular cut. Sizes and proportions varied but a large skin for the back and a smaller one for the front, forwardly placed and angular armholes, and similarly shaped sleeves remained constant. The cut was repeated for man, and somewhat longer for woman, small for a child, furred for winter and dehaired for warmer weather. It suited the nomadic way of life and made excellent use of the available raw material, caribou skin. The neck opening was well fitted and when worn with either attached or separate hood was comfortably snug. The back shoulders, with all decoration placed low, were ready for carrying a heavy pack or a baby. The cut of the sleeves gave ample leeway for the movements required for paddling or portaging a canoe, pitching a tent, or dragging a sled. The garment could be made fairly generously and worn layered if more warmth was needed. The shoulder and sleeve seams were well positioned to withstand strain. The pointed length, longer at back and front, gave warmth, while the shorter sides allowed ease of movement. This tunic, when worn with a pair of moccasin trousers, as they always were by both men and women, provided a unique, Gwich'in, solution to the designing of a body covering, made of readily available materials that could protect from swarms of mosquitoes in summer and harsh cold in winter. It was not

The Gwich'in Solution

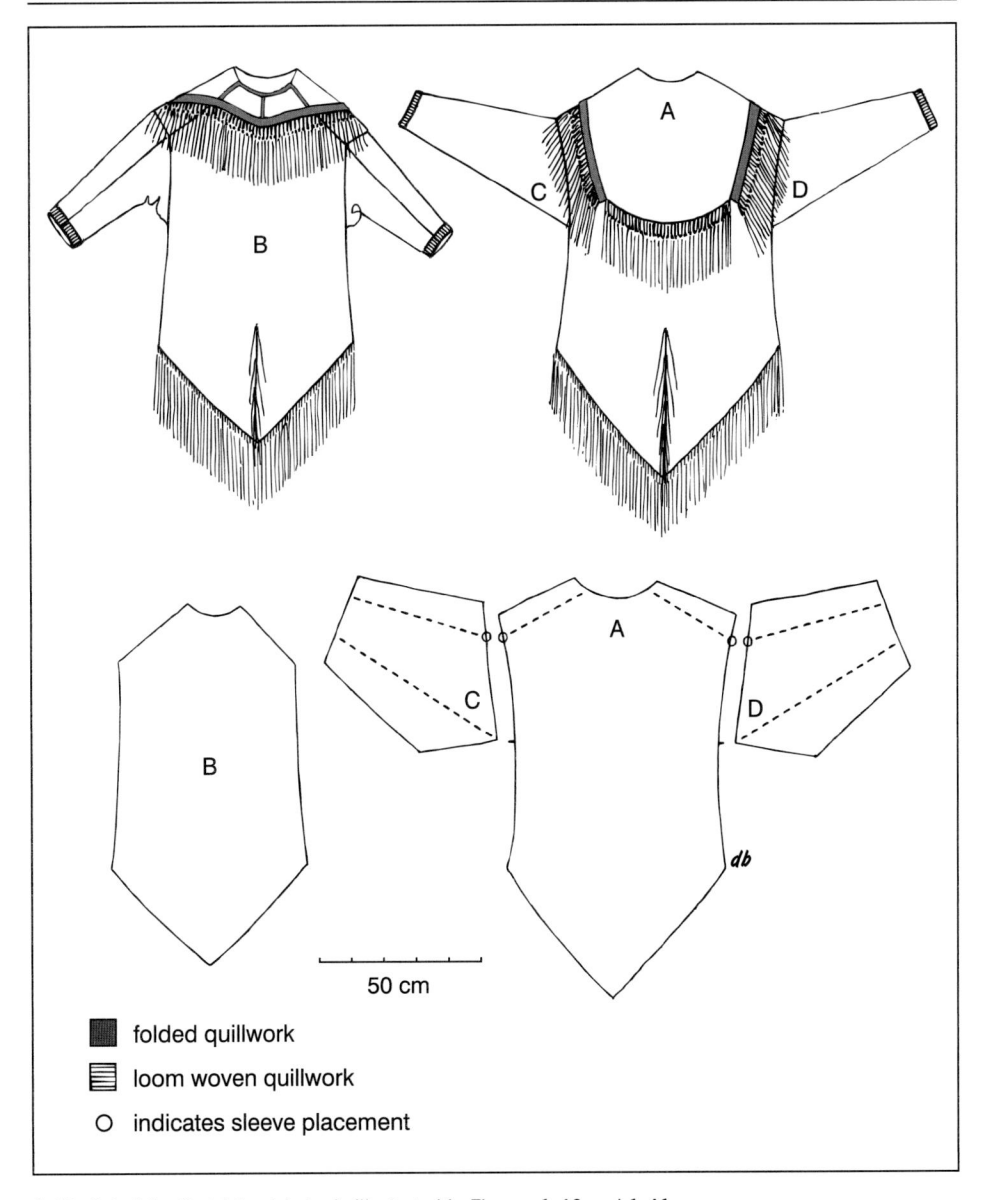

1.43 Cut of the Gwich'in style tunic illustrated in Figures 1.40 and 1.41.

only practical and comfortable, but with the skill of a Gwich'in woman could be stunningly handsome.

Endnote

1. For full sized garments I usually choose to work on a 1/10 scale. It is easy to reckon all the measurements with no mathematics when 1cm=1mm and it produces a drawing large enough for clarity and small enough to fit on a reasonably sized sheet of paper. It is also easy to enlarge even to full size because in reverse 1mm=1cm.

Revitalization

1.44 Karen Wright Fraser, at the Canadian Museum of Civilization, Hull, June 1999. Photograph by Steven Darby.

Revitalization

Judy Thompson

Although I have not had the pleasure of meeting Dorothy Burnham, I have heard a lot about her and I have the utmost respect for the work she has done. If not for this work, I would only be able to admire this clothing from afar and not even know where to begin to attempt to make a replica. Her beautiful work of figuring out how these techniques were applied has paved a path for the future generations to continue this work that was almost lost forever. Mah'si Cho Dorothy, for breaking trail. You have given us a chance to make a connection to our Grandmothers and Grandfathers and for that our hearts are no longer heavy.

Karen Wright Fraser, November 3, 2000

Garments of the type illustrated in this chapter have not been made in Athabaskan communities for over a century. Research on nineteenth century clothing in museum collections has produced detailed information about how these early garments were cut, sewn and decorated. Increasingly, this information is being utilized by contemporary Athabaskan individuals and community organizations seeking to revive traditional skills and re-create clothing true to their particular cultural heritage.

The two accounts which follow describe very special projects of this type. The first, by a young Gwich'in seamstress, Karen Wright Fraser, tells the story of her decision to make an old-style garment using an example from the Canadian Museum of Civilization collection as a model. Dorothy Burnham's drawings of the cut of the garment, and detailed information that had been compiled in the course of research on a large number of comparable specimens were important resources for this project. By chance, Karen Wright Fraser's independently conceived and organized plan dovetailed with a similar, but larger-scale enterprise initiated by the Gwich'in Social and Cultural Institute (GSCI). As Ingrid

Kritsch, Research Director of the Institute, describes in her contribution to this volume, a plan to "repatriate" traditional skills to four Gwich'in communities through re-creating items of traditional clothing is now underway.

> *While growing up in Inuvik I did not have the opportunity to experience much tradition or heritage of my people...As a youngster I often wondered about my great grandparents and how they lived – I was so sure it must have been better than how we were living (sort of lost). I knew they had a purpose and lived a good life and I often would dream about that life...When [in 1998] I saw pictures of the Gwich'in outfits from 1870 and 1875 and saw how absolutely beautiful they were I had to fight off the biggest lump in my throat because it was so overwhelming for me. I was experiencing a grieving feeling of something that was lost and at the same time I was experiencing happiness and excitement and a very, very proud feeling that I wished I could have felt when I was so young and needed to feel that...*
>
> *I have an idea that I think would be a big challenge and hard work but so very worth it. I would like to make a replica of a Gwich'in summer tunic. I would like to get the whole process documented by video and then show it in the schools in the Mackenzie Delta. I really believe that if the youth see something from the past that is positive, it would help some of the children feel better about themselves and maybe even encourage them to become seamstresses or fashion designers...*
>
> From a letter written by Karen Wright Fraser to Judy Thompson, January 27, 1999.

My People Did This:
The Re-Making of a Gwich'in Garment[1]

Karen Wright Fraser

The Idea

The first time I got the idea to make a traditional garment was when I saw the Gwich'in tunic in *From the Land: Two Hundred Years of Dene Clothing*.[2] It was the first time I ever saw an outfit that my ancestors might have worn, or that they made. I had never even heard of anything like that. When I was growing up, if I saw Native Americans on television and they were wearing hide outfits, I always thought that was just television, it wasn't real, because from my people I'd never even heard anything about it...So when I saw this dress and I read that it was Gwich'in, it just took my breath away and I must have cried. I'm sure I cried. It was so overwhelming. I thought, how beautiful, our people did this. I felt so proud, just to see this, that our people had such skill and did such beautiful work. I couldn't believe it took me so long to see this outfit in this book - it took me 32 years to see this! So, I thought, why did I not see this before, and how important it is for others to see it.

After I got the idea, then I didn't know if it was legal, if I would be allowed to make a copy of this dress because the Museum had it and I didn't know if I would be allowed to make a copy. So I wrote a letter to Judy Thompson and I was just hoping. I had my fingers crossed that she would say, "Yes, you can do it!" She wrote back and said that she was very excited and yes for sure and that she was always hoping that someone would do it. And so, I was really happy.

Then, I had to figure out where I was going to get funding for all this. So, I called a meeting and I asked Dennis Allen to help me out because he's a camera man, he's trained in film-making, and I asked Ingrid Kritsch from the Gwich'in Social and Cultural Institute. Ingrid was very excited about the idea because in their long-term plans, they wanted to do the same thing... So we had a meeting, a little planning session, and it was all really exciting. We helped each other out and started writing letters.

I travelled to Ottawa to the Canadian Museum of Civilization, and brought along Dennis Allen and an elder, Mary Kendi, to see the real outfit. That was really worth it – it was a good trip. I can still remember the first time we saw it [the garment illustrated in Figure 1.40]. It was really impressive. Mary Kendi was 84, and when she saw the traditional Gwich'in outfits for the first time, they started bringing memories back to her that she hadn't thought of for years and years. That was really special - she started telling us stories and we documented that.

Making the Garment

Materials

To make the tunic, I needed white caribou hides, porcupine quills, silver willow seeds, sinew, and dyes from plants.

Caribou Hides

What would have been ideal would have been to go and get some Gwich'in ladies to prepare the caribou hides. There are only a few Gwich'in ladies from the Mackenzie Delta that I know who prepare these hides, so that was difficult. Also, as I'm living in Yellowknife, it would have been too costly for me and a camera person to go up and watch this being done and help out, and film it. So, I asked people in Lutsel Ke'e [a Chipewyan community on the East Arm of Great Slave Lake]. There, everybody tans, so I just bought my hides from there.

The white hides are bleached from the wind and the sun. They tan them and scrape them, soak and scrape. Then they hang them outside and the wind and the sun bleaches them white.

Porcupine Quills

The porcupine quills were harder to get! It was really hard to get these. For this project I wanted to get everything I could from the land, but I didn't know anyone who hunts porcupine. So I thought, well, I'll just get them the way I get them for my crafts, I'll just order them from the craft store. But the time came for me to start getting all my supplies and I phoned every craft store I knew. No one had quills and they said they hadn't had any for a long time and they didn't anticipate getting any. So I thought, oh no, what am I going to do? Now my whole project is in jeopardy, because it was time to do the quillwork.

My husband said, "Don't worry, something will come up". And so, one day we were on our way, we were driving down the road to Hay River to watch a jigging competition, and I was worrying about it all the way, thinking, how am I going to do this? We had our weekend in Hay River, and on the drive back, we were driving along, talking, and there was something big on the road. I was looking as we got closer, and as we drove by I looked. It was a porcupine dead on the road! I looked at Roger and he said, "What was that?" and I said, "A porcupine!" and he said, "Do you want it?" and I said, "Yes!" So we put the brakes on. I couldn't believe it; it was as though it was just placed there, just waiting for me. We brought it home and I was thinking what am I going to do with this? I had no idea how to prepare it or anything! But it was really good, a good experience.

So, at my house, I skinned it, and threw out the body. I started plucking [the carcass] and it was really easy…If you leave that hide to decompose a bit, it is easy. If you tried to do it when it was freshly killed it would be hard to take the quills out, and when you took them out, most of them would break. So it's better if you leave it for a day or two, or maybe even three days. The quills are all facing downward from the head, so you stand behind the head. You pick a bunch between your thumb and your pointer finger and pull away from yourself (like plucking a duck).

It's a long process to clean and sort the quills. When you're plucking the quills…all the hair is with it too, so when you're ready to clean the quills you have to take all the hair out. Then you have to wash the quills very well, in hot soapy water, not boiling. You put the quills in there, in a sink or basin, and you have to just keep moving them through the suds and keep doing that. Then you drain that and rinse the quills – you have to do it two or three times because there's so much oil on the quills that if you don't wash it properly the dye won't take. You let them dry and afterwards you can start the dyeing process.

Dyes for Quillwork

I tried using natural dyes from the land such as red willow, black lichen and blueberries, but the colour was far too faint. So I ended up using Rit commercial dyes. You just get a small pan and put water in and pour the dye powder in until the colour is very rich. Then you put a few handfuls of quills in. Use a wooden spoon to swoosh them around. Do not leave the pan on the stove after it has started to boil. Take it off the heat and it will only take a few more minutes, then rinse the quills. Repeat, if the colour isn't dark enough.

Silver Willow Seeds

The silver willow seeds, that's another story…The seed is from inside a berry, and there's a hole poked through the centre of it. On each fringe strand there's going to be a little section of wrapped porcupine quills and then this seed is going to be strung through the fringe, and then after the seed, again there'll be another little band of porcupine quills wrapped on the fringes... it looks really beautiful.

I searched all the books I could find in the library to try and find out what plant the silver willow seeds came from. Then Judy Thompson sent me some information and it explained they were found beside riverbeds and on mountain slopes and what kinds of other plants would be around it. My husband and I went searching by boat down the Yellowknife River, and ... nothing! We drove the highways all over Yellowknife and down to Rae, and ... nothing! I had my cousin Randall Tetlichi looking in Old Crow. I asked my sister in Inuvik and she had people looking in Inuvik. She had a whole class from Aurora College looking for this plant, she had the research staff searching, and no one could find it. Oh, I was getting worried! I was thinking again that my whole project was in jeopardy. This was not working out!

Then, I thought about this lady in Yellowknife named Alexandra Melbourne. She writes an article in the paper once a week and it's about northern plants, so I called her and explained my dilemma and told her that I had been searching far and wide right across the Northwest Territories ... and I couldn't find this plant. She said, "I know where a bush is!" ... I just about fainted, you know, but I was still thinking, it's probably the wrong one. She said, "Could you meet me at the Museum[3] in 10 minutes?" ... She took me outside the Museum and she showed me this bush. There were about a thousand berries on this big bush. I was so happy! And the fragrance coming from that bush was just amazing, strong and nice. And it was a beautiful colour, silvery green. The berries are not very big, they come in clusters. She said, "You can't pick them. The Legislative Assembly, the government of the Northwest Territories, re-planted all these plants and they got them from all over the Northwest Territories and no one's allowed to touch them."... But I met with John Anderson, the man who looks after it, and explained to him, and he said, "No problem, go ahead and pick whatever you need."... So I picked as many as I could.

At home, I boiled the berries. I had to clean all the meaty, fleshy part of the berry off, and then the seed was there. Then, while they were still wet, I stuck a darning needle through each seed, made a little hole and strung it on this big string of sinew, so it could dry like that. And that hole is still so small that I'm thinking, "How am I ever going to get it on the fringe?" I thought it couldn't be done. But when I saw the garments at the Museum I saw it could be done. The fringes are cut very thin. The end of the fringe is moistened and twisted between your thumb and forefinger, then threaded through the seed.

Red Ochre

Then, there is the red ochre. I didn't know where I was going to get the red ochre. I had never heard of anybody using it. So I was asking people that I knew, again, and they didn't know where to get it. Then, I was talking to my brother Dennis in Fort McPherson and he said his mother-in-law talked about ochre. So he said he would talk to her and get back to me. I waited for that call. Then he called and said, "Jane Charlie (that's the late Johnny Charlie's wife), Jane Charlie knows where to get it and if you come up to Fort MacPherson, she'll take you there." I said, "Yes, I'll be there in June!" So I travelled up there and my brother Dennis guided us. Jane Charlie brought her grandson who was about 19, and we travelled out there. It was really exciting. They said it was a very spiritual place. People around Fort McPherson, the Tetlit Gwich'in, they know about this place, they know the story of this place. But being from Inuvik, I never did hear about it... The older ladies know about it...they'll dye shoelaces for mukluks, they'll dye them red, some of them. So, they said years ago they used to travel to this place to get Ts'aii [red ochre]. "It's a special place and if you go there, you're only allowed to take one cup", they said, "you mustn't be greedy, and you have to leave something behind, pay an offering, matches, tea, or something. If you don't leave anything behind, then a big storm will come."

The day I got to McPherson, it was raining a little, and Jane Charlie almost wouldn't take me. She said her brother-in-law and another guy, when she told them earlier in the day where she was going to take me, they said, "Well, you can't go in bad weather, it's going to get really bad." So she was saying, "I don't know if we should go", and I was saying, "Let's go!" I was saying, "It's only drizzling, right?" But the closer we got [to going], then I started getting scared too! So we were kind of worried about that.

But we went. We had to walk through brush for half an hour or so just to get there from the highway. We got to this place and we had to tie a rope around a tree and rappel back down a slope. And all the red ochre was there on the slope. I couldn't believe [that] I made it there. It was really nice. So, I took my ochre and I left my tobacco and matches. I brought a yoghurt container and kind of scooped some up. Some of it is powdery and some of it is sort of rock...you could crush it.

There's a little river down below; it must be Rock River. It was far down ... there's the slope, and then a drop off ... so way down there, Dennis told me to take a look. Right in the soft wet sand on the side of the river were big grizzly bear tracks. That was kind of exciting, too, because it seemed really powerful - this big grizzly bear was walking down there and it was another sign of some sort.

When we finally got back to the road it was overcast, dreary and drizzly. I was so happy, I was so thankful, I was so grateful - I had come so far and it was so important to the project. We started driving down the highway ... we went over a little hill, around a corner, up another hill, and then you could look over the hill, and it was like a new day. The sun was shining, you could see green grass and hills - it was just beautiful! We all just drove in silence; we couldn't believe how beautiful it was. And it all seemed so special.

I dropped Jane Charlie off in Fort McPherson and I started back to Inuvik. I got to the ferry and drove on to the ferry and I looked in my rear view mirror, and all I could see in my mirror was this big eagle feather. I looked back and a girl was holding it. It was so beautiful; I've never seen so beautiful an eagle feather before. So, I got out of the vehicle and went up to her and I said, "I just had to come and see your eagle feather, it's so beautiful". She said, "Do you want it?" And I said, "oh no", but she kept offering it to me, so, I took it. I just about started crying because if you're ever given an eagle feather, it's really special. We had just come from Rock River and I'd just had that experience of getting the red ochre, and getting this feather just finished the whole day off. It was like a good sign, that this feather was meant for this dress. It was meant to be. So I explained to her about the dress, that she was just there to give that feather for the dress. So I told her I would put her name in the credits and I would have that feather with the dress.

Techniques

Quillwork

There are no Gwich'in people that I know that still do quillwork. I know some people who say they remember their mum doing it, or they remember doing it a bit when they were young, but nobody does it anymore. It's lost. So I had to travel to the Dehcho, to Fort Simpson, and learn the techniques from Slavey ladies. They shared those techniques with us in a workshop. They were teaching us a slightly different technique, not the one I needed to do the band for the dress. I went off by myself to a table in the back and tried over and over until I got it. I figured out how to do the one that I needed.

When I was ready to use my quills, I stuck them into a washed Styrofoam meat tray and then cut the tips off.

I cut the band that decorates the front of the tunic out of hide and then sewed the porcupine quills on it using a folded technique (Figure 1.19) and cotton thread.

Fringes

The fringes were cut from caribou skin (19cm (7 ½") long and 2 mm (1/8" wide). The technique used to wrap quills on the fringe is amazing. The drawing by Dorothy Burnham was very easy to follow, it worked really well (Figure 1.22). First, you take a fringe and loop a piece of sinew from the top to part-ways down the middle of the fringe, then you moisten a quill and flatten it between your front teeth. You hold the end of the quill to the fringe and begin wrapping, making sure that you cover the end so it cannot pop back up and come undone. When you get to the end of the quill you put the end of it into the sinew loop and pull the sinew from the top of the fringe. This pulls the end of the quill up and under the rest of the quill and keeps it all together. You must do this a few times before you get into the right rhythm and get a good tension going.

I wrapped each fringe with one blue and three red porcupine quills. Then I wet the end of the fringe, twisted it to a fine point and threaded it through a silver willow seed, then wrapped it with three more red porcupine quills. After all the fringes are wrapped and smudged with red ochre, they will be attached to the garment using a hemming stitch.

Construction

I didn't want to cut the pattern out of the hides until I was really sure. The hide is so precious…there are so few people who tan hides and prepare them today. So, when we were at the Museum [CMC],[4] I cut out a pattern in brown paper, and the sleeve, that was <u>hard</u>! Even when you look at Dorothy Burnham's drawing (Figure 1.40) it doesn't look simple, because that sleeve, you look at it and think, what is that? It's so sophisticated, and nobody has seen it before in our day, even in our parent's day, on any clothing. It's lost. But it was really smart how they did that; they really understood how the body works! I think we had professors of anatomy, and they didn't even know it!

So, that sleeve is really different. It was hard to figure out, even though the drawing was there. We tried it, and couldn't get it for the longest time. Finally when we got the right angles, the way Dorothy drew it, then it did really work. The ladies [elders Rosie Stewart. Renie Martin and Rosie Firth] were really interested in seeing that too. They were really looking forward to putting a tunic together later.

Next, I cut the outfit out in muslin. Finally, I cut it out in hide according to Dorothy's drawing. Everything fit just great. The sleeves are so very interesting. Dorothy has a beautiful gift to be able to figure out these sleeves just by looking at them.

I used caribou sinew and an overcast stitch to sew the tunic together. In October 2000, I am still working on this tunic and I hope to be done in the next few months.

Acknowledgements

I would like to thank the following for contributing to this project: Canada Council of the Arts; Parks Canada (Inuvik region); Economic, Culture and Employment (Yellowknife region); Canadian North Airlines; Gwich'in' Tribal Council; Gwich'in' Social and Cultural Institute; Prince of Wales Northern

Heritage Centre; Judy Thompson, Canadian Museum of Civilization; Jane Charlie; Alexandra Melbourne; Jennifer Bowen and Dennis Allen.

Mah'si Cho to everyone who showed a genuine interest in this project and who shared with me the importance of reviving the techniques of our Gwich'in clothing. It is my dream to one day see our people walking proud wearing jackets and dresses adorned with porcupine quill-wrapped fringes and silver willow seeds dangling.

Endnotes

1. An interview Judy Thompson recorded with Karen Wright Fraser in February 2000 provided the body of the text; this was subsequently added to and revised by Karen Wright Fraser.
2. Thompson Judy, From the Land: *Two Hundred Years of Dene Clothing*. Hull: Canadian Museum of Civilization; 1994.
3. Prince of Wales Northern Heritage Centre
4. Karen is referring here to a second visit made to the CMC, in February 2000, in connection with the Gwich'in Social and Cultural Institute's plan to revive the skill of making traditional clothing. Karen visited the CMC in company with Gwich'in elders Rosie Firth, Rosie Stewart, and Renie Martin

The Gwich'in Traditional Clothing Project

Ingrid Kritsch

It is a snowy morning in February in Hull, Quebec. A research team of eight from the Northwest Territories excitedly enters the Canadian Museum of Civilization, and is signed in by the Curator of Ethnology, Judy Thompson. The group has travelled over 3,000 miles to meet with Ms. Thompson and to examine and film Gwich'in clothing. Dennis Allen, a Gwich'in and Inuvialuit filmmaker who is part of the team, leads the way down the corridor with Judy, followed by a line of women ranging in age from 35 to 70. He is teasingly called Shahnuut'iee by the women, after a legendary Gwich'in chief in the 1800s who had many wives.

The group enters the Ethnology Division storeroom and sits down. Moments later, a trolley is wheeled in, and a man's caribou skin outfit, heavily decorated with porcupine quills, silver willow seeds and fringes, is carefully laid out on a table in the store room. A hush falls on the room. The three Gwich'in elders' eyes open wide and a collective sigh is expressed – "Ahhhh!!" Others in the room exclaim, "How beautiful!" as they admire the elegant lines of the clothing, the vibrant colours of the quillwork, and the small, neat stitching - stitching so neat and fine, that you can barely see it. The garments are over a hundred years old and this is the first time the elders have seen this type of clothing. It makes them feel close to their ancestors. They feel honoured to be able to see it and touch it, and they are grateful that the museum has taken such good care of it over the years.

The Gwich'in Traditional Clothing Project

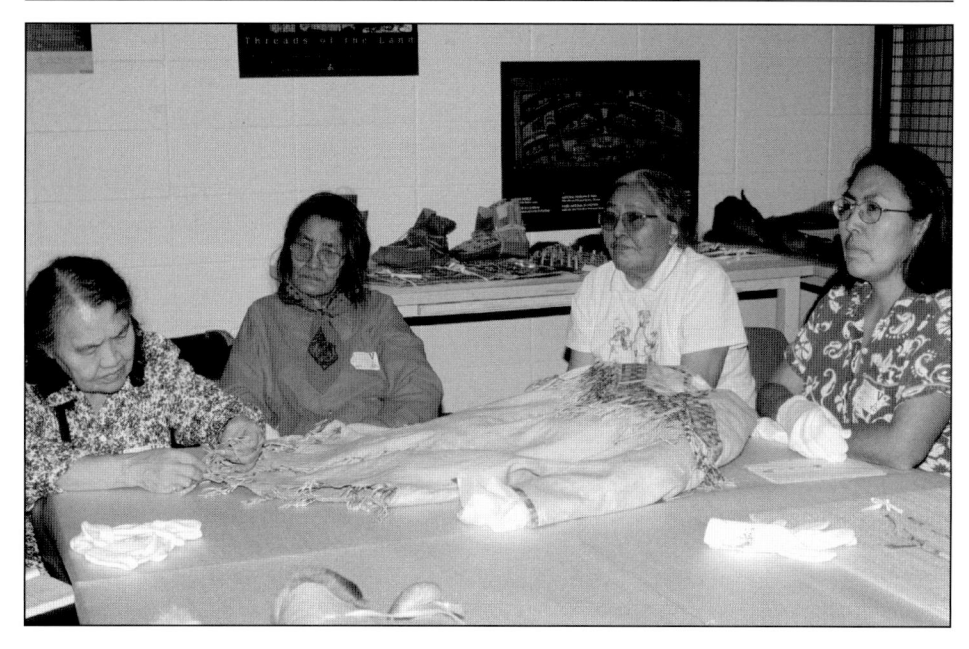

1.45 Members of the Gwich'in Traditional Clothing Project Team, at the Canadian Museum of Civilization, February 2000. Left to right: Renie Martin, elder, Inuvik; Rosie Stewart, elder, Ft McPherson, Rosie Firth, elder, Ft. McPherson, Alestine André, Director, Gwich'in Cultural Institute. Photograph by Judy Thompson.

Introduction

We are very excited about a repatriation project that we are carrying out in partnership with the Prince of Wales Northern Heritage Centre (PWNHC).[1] The objective of the project is to replicate traditional Gwich'in caribou hide garments from the 1800s, which are currently housed in the Canadian Museum of Civilization (CMC) in Hull and the Smithsonian Institution in Washington, D.C. At the present time, clothing of this type is no longer made by the Gwich'in of the Northwest Territories, nor is any example of this clothing available in this region.

The repatriation project evolved from the 1992 signing of the Gwich'in Comprehensive Land Claim Agreement between the Gwich'in, the Canadian Government and the Government of the Northwest Territories. More specifically, it developed out of a repatriation clause in the claim and a desire by the Gwich'in to reclaim control of their heritage, cultural self-esteem and identity.

Recognizing that the repatriation of specific items may take many years of negotiation, the Gwich'in, through the Gwich'in Social and Cultural Institute (GSCI),[2] decided in 1996 to initiate a series of cultural enhancement projects. Traditional material culture items housed in a variety of museums would be studied with the intent of replicating these objects and, thereby, repatriating the skills and knowledge needed to produce these items in the Gwich'in

Settlement Area.[3] The Board of Directors of the Gwich'in Social and Cultural Institute, representing all four Gwich'in communities (Aklavik, Inuvik, Fort McPherson and Tsiigehtchic), decided that traditional clothing from the nineteenth century would be an ideal place to start. In their view, the clothing reflects not only a very beautiful and personal link to the past but also a visible expression of the intimate relationship that the Gwich'in have with the land, and their knowledge of it. The clothing is made entirely from caribou skins, sewn with sinew and decorated with indigenous materials - porcupine quills, silver willow seeds, and red ochre. To produce such clothing requires a high degree of skill and knowledge.

The GSCI Board felt that replicating the clothing would have important cultural and educational benefits and possible economic spin-offs as well. For example, replicating the clothing would provide an opportunity for all four Gwich'in communities to be involved in a hands-on project. It would enable local people to not only document the knowledge and skills related to making this clothing, but also help them use these old skills and knowledge, inspiring current and future generations of Gwich'in to learn more about their past, and take pride in their culture. It would also give the Gwich'in an opportunity to work with a variety of museum staff from the PWNHC, CMC and possibly other museums with expertise in the area of traditional clothing, education and exhibit design.

Methodology

The clothing project is being carried out in three phases over the course of approximately two to three years, depending upon funding. Coordinated by GSCI, and drawing upon the expertise of PWNHC and CMC staff, Gwich'in elders and seamstresses from all four Gwich'in communities will replicate eight sets of clothing – of which four will remain in the Gwich'in Settlement Area, and four will be accessioned into the PWNHC collection. Having a visual record of this project for both archival and educational purposes was deemed important, so the entire project will be recorded on video camera.

Phase I began in February 2000. At this time, the Government of the Northwest Territories Department of Education, Culture and Employment provided funding for an eight member research team to examine and film Gwich'in clothing housed at the Canadian Museum of Civilization (Figure 1.45) and the Smithsonian Institution. The research team included: three Gwich'in elders/seamstresses, Rosie Firth and Rosie Stewart of Fort McPherson and Renie Martin of Inuvik; Gwich'in seamstress Karen Wright Fraser of Yellowknife; two GSCI staff, Alestine Andre and Ingrid Kritsch; one PWNHC staff, Joanne Bird, Curator of Collections; and a Gwich'in/Inuvialuit filmmaker, Dennis Allen of Yellowknife. Judy Thompson, Curator of Western Subarctic Ethnology at the CMC worked with the team at the CMC and then joined us to travel to the Smithsonian Institution later in February. The purpose of the travel was to select items for replication from these collections.

Both the Canadian Museum of Civilization and the Smithsonian welcomed the team warmly, providing access to their collections and advice and information about the clothing. For example, during the course of examining the clothing at the CMC, the elders and Karen Wright Fraser[4] were puzzled about how the sleeves were attached to the body of the tunic. Judy Thompson had one of the patterns drawn by Dorothy Burnham enlarged to the proper scale, and in this way we were able to understand how the garment was constructed. Mrs. Burnham's detailed patterns showing the cut of the garments and the sewing and decorative techniques used on the clothing will continue to prove invaluable when it comes time to make the clothing.

After viewing the Gwich'in clothing at the Canadian Museum of Civilization and the Smithsonian, the team decided to replicate four outfits representing a family group - a man's summer outfit and a young boy's winter outfit from the CMC collection, a woman's summer outfit from the Smithsonian Institution, and a young girl's summer outfit. The latter outfit may be based on an outfit in the Royal Ontario Museum collections, for which Dorothy Burnham has drawn a pattern. With the exception of the young boy's winter outfit (made in the twentieth century from furred caribou hide), the clothing dates to the second half of the nineteenth century and is made of tanned caribou skin. Producing four outfits will entail much work, but will result in each Gwich'in community having an example for display and use.

Phase II of the project will begin in the fall of 2000, when we will carry out additional oral history research about traditional Gwich'in clothing and put together a team of seamstresses from the Gwich'in communities to replicate the clothing. A film crew will videotape Gwich'in men hunting caribou during the fall hunt, a time when hides are at their prime. Ochre will be collected from a location long renowned for its sacred importance. Finally, workshops for tanning hides, porcupine quillwork, beading and sinew thread making will be held at a camp outside Fort McPherson.

Later in the year, once the hides have been tanned, the seamstresses will begin cutting out and sewing the garments, using the patterns drawn by Dorothy Burnham. We also hope that the seamstresses will have access to at least one of the original garments at this time, by way of a loan to the PWNHC.[5] During the course of the winter and spring, the seamstresses will complete all eight outfits for both the GSCI and PWNHC using traditional materials and methods of construction and decoration as much as possible. Participants and activities will be recorded and filmed during both phases. When all the work is finished, at the end of Phase II, a celebration consisting of a fashion show and feast will be held.

Phase III will likely take an additional year. In this phase we intend to produce a 30-minute documentary video on the clothing replication project. As well, we hope to work with the PWNHC on exhibits, educational kits and interpretive materials for use by the schools, museum and GSCI.

Conclusion

The Gwich'in elders appreciated the fact that the clothing and other items had been safely stored by the museums so that they and others could see and enjoy them today and learn from them. They recognized that if they had not been collected and stored carefully they most likely would not have survived. They are very excited about the prospects of this project and believe that it has not only great educational benefits for the Gwich'in but also for the Canadian public. It is a wonderful example of what can be accomplished when Aboriginal people and museums work together, each bringing their respective strengths and skills to a project, each benefiting in their own way.

This project is important to the Gwich'in. The clothing stored in museums is no longer seen in the communities. It provides a visual link to their ancestors and their history, and provides them with an opportunity to reintroduce skills and knowledge lost within the past century. It also brings forth stories that have not been heard for a generation. Carrying these stories and knowledge into the future will raise an awareness, understanding and appreciation of Gwich'in culture.

This project is important to the museums involved as well. It will improve their understanding and knowledge of how the clothing was manufactured, and thereby enhance the story that they tell to their visiting public and ensure that the public becomes more informed about Aboriginal people within Canada.

Endnotes

1. The PWNHC is located in Yellowknife and it is the territorial museum for the Northwest Territories.
2. The GSCI was established in 1992 by the Gwich'in Tribal Council which is responsible for implementing the land claim on behalf of Gwich'in beneficiaries. The Institute is a non-profit charitable organization whose mandate is to document, preserve and promote the practice of Gwich'in culture, language, traditions and values. It is also responsible for carrying out the heritage and cultural aspects of the claim.
3. The Gwich'in Settlement Area was created with the signing of the Gwich'in Comprehensive Land Claim Agreement in 1992 and encompasses the four communities of Aklavik, Fort McPherson, Inuvik, and Tsiigehchic (formerly called Arctic Red River).
4. Karen Wright Fraser is currently replicating one of the tunics in the CMC collection on her own initiative. She will coordinate the GSCI project over the next two to three years once funding is in place.
5. The PWNHC has found that having an original one hand has been invaluable during the course of another replication project they are carrying out in collaboration with the Dogrib Nation – a Dogrib caribou skin lodge from the late 1800s originally collected by Frank Russell for the Museum of Natural History at the University of Iowa.

Section 2
Arctic Studies

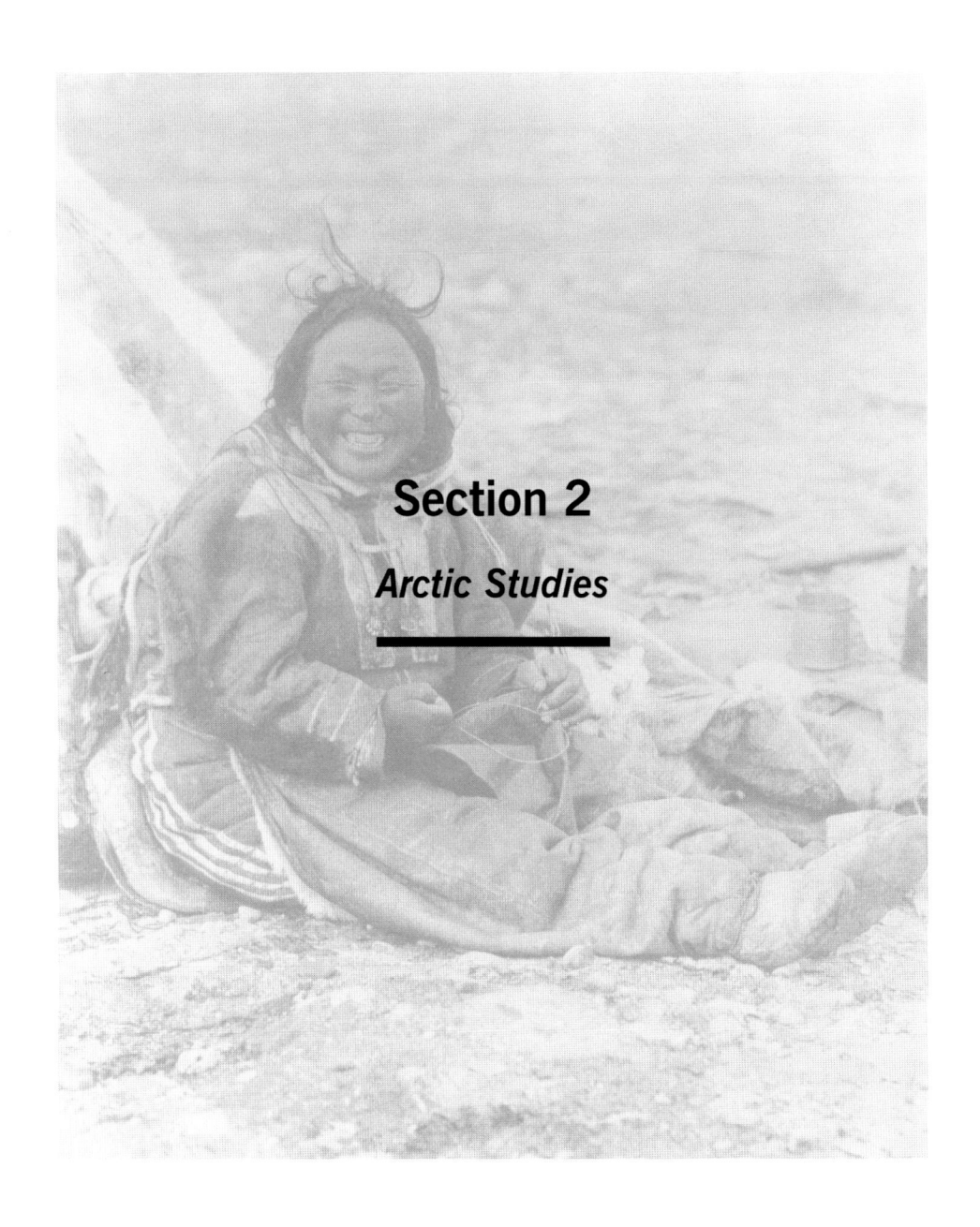

Higilaq, a Copper Inuit woman, sewing with sinew.
Photograph by George H. Wilkins, near Bernard Harbour, 1915.
Canadian Museum of Civilization 51570

Northern Canada showing places and names referred to in text.

COPPER INUIT
1. Ulukhaqtuuq *(Holman)*
2. Prince Albert Sound
3. Bernard Harbour
4. Qurluqtuuq *(Coppermine)*
5. Coronation Gulf
6. Iqaluktuuttiaq *(Cambridge Bay)*

IGLULINGMIUT
7. Iglulik
8. Naujaat/Aivilik *(Repulse Bay)*
9. Wager Bay
10. Fullerton Harbour

CARIBOU INUIT
11. Qamanittuaq *(Baker Lake)*
12. Igluligaarjuk *(Chesterfield Inlet)*
13. Kangiqliniq *(Rankin Inlet)*
14. Arviat
15. Lake Ennadai

"Following The Traditions of Our Ancestors": Inuit Clothing Designs

Judy Hall

We still follow our grandmothers, and their grandmothers. It's the way we pass it on. It is the traditional way of doing it. We are following the traditions of our ancestors.

Lizzie Ittinuar, Kangiqliniq (Rankin Inlet), Nunavut, 1992

Introduction

The Canadian Arctic, extending from the Alaska/Yukon border in the west to Baffin Island and the Labrador coast in the east, is the homeland of the Inuit. Mostly above the tree line, the land is a vast expanse of tundra blanketed with snow during the long, intensely cold winter and with low-growing plants in the cool spring and short summer. Survival in this northern land has depended on the invention of effective technologies that have provided food, shelter, and protection from the climate. Clothing is one of the adaptations that has enabled Inuit to live in this demanding environment. Clothing reveals Inuit cultural expression, ingenuity, adaptation and technical expertise. The study of Inuit clothing can also lead us to a greater understanding of Inuit history and Canadian exploration in the north.

This paper discusses five garments made by Inuit seamstresses early in the twentieth century, which today are stored at the Canadian Museum of Civilization. The first section presents each garment in its cultural context, with information drawn from historical accounts, archival photographs, the knowledge and skill of Inuit seamstresses, and detailed drawings by Dorothy Burnham. The second section examines the collection history of the garments, placing them in the broader context of Canadian exploration and presence in the north at the beginning of the twentieth century.

Protection, Identity and Regional Style: Inuit Clothing Designs

The five garments described in this paper were made by women of three Inuit groups in Arctic Canada: the Copper Inuit, Caribou Inuit and Iglulingmiut (see Map). The Copper Inuit occupy the north-central region of the Canadian mainland around Coronation Gulf and on Victoria and Banks Islands. The Caribou Inuit live west of Hudson Bay along the coast and inland to Lake Ennadai. The territory of the Iglulingmiut extends from north-west Baffin Island to Devon Island and the Melville Peninsula on the mainland. Each of these populations is composed of smaller groups. Today, these Inuit live on the land and in the modern communities of Ulukhaqtuuq (Holman), Iqaluktuuttiaq (Cambridge Bay), Qurluqtuuq (Coppermine), Iglulik, Naujaat/Aivilik (Repulse Bay), Qamanittuaq (Baker Lake), Kangiqliniq (Rankin Inlet), Igluligaarjuk (Chesterfield Inlet) and Arviat, as well as in southern cities.

The garments are all made of barren-ground caribou (*Rangifer tarandus*), one of the principle sources of clothing material. As Rhoda Karetak of Arviat recalls: "The caribou had an important place in the lifestyle of the Inuit of the past. It was very important for survival."[1] The pursuit of caribou determined the seasonal round of activities. Rene Taipana of Ulukhaqtuuq (Holman) explains:

> *We would travel to the lake and stay there until late spring waiting for the land to dry up so we could hunt caribou. We would fish and get an occasional caribou for meat, while waiting for the hair of the caribou to become good for clothing. That's how people lived back then. And when the land was good, we travelled inland hunting for caribou - for clothing and food... We used to live that way throughout the summer. And when it was around the end of August or September, we would start our gradual trip back to the coast. When the caribou hair is thick, we would hunt for those caribou with the thick hair for the outer parka called* **qullitaq**.[2]

Preparing caribou skins for clothing is a highly technical skill that is mainly the responsibility of women. The skin is scraped to remove the fat and tissues, dried, and re-scraped until the surface becomes pliable and soft. The fur is left on the garment to provide warmth and insulation. In the past, all parts of the caribou were used in clothing preparation. The tendon along the backbone became sinew thread, and bones and antlers were fashioned into scrapers, needles and needlecases. As Lucy Tasseor Tutsweetok of Arviat notes:

> *Every part of the caribou was utilized, even the muscles in the shoulder blade ... were used for thread. Our ancestors had a way of making use of every available scrap.*[3]

the shoulder blades (as seen in Figure 2.2, upper right) – often this piece came from the tail of the caribou and was a symbolic reference to the animal.[14] Further details on this parka can be found in the following paper, *Masters of Design*.

Certain aspects of this parka illustrate that factors other than protection were involved in its design. The hood left the forehead and cheeks exposed, the short front provided inadequate coverage of the body, and the sleeves left the wrists bare.[15] In fact, this type of decorated parka was usually worn when people gathered for a drum dance or when visiting. Drum dances were held in large snowhouses or tents when people met to celebrate a successful hunt and to welcome friends. On these occasions, warmth was not the primary consideration; it was more important to wear beautifully made and decorated garments. For hunting and travelling during the winter, men wore a longer parka that provided greater protection.[16]

The outer parka worn by Copper Inuit women (Figure 2.3) was different in design to the man's parka. It had an enlarged, elongated hood, broad, pointed shoulders and angular chest panels. Usually, this garment had a rectangular or triangular extension at the centre of the short front edge as seen in Figure 2.4. On the parka illustrated in Figure 2.3, however, the extension is absent, but implied by the insertion of white fur. A triangular piece of caribou fur sewn to the upper back between the shoulders (Figures 2.5 and 2.6) creates the extra fullness required to accommodate an infant. As the child grew, the triangular gusset was replaced with a larger piece of skin.[17] Like the man's parka, the woman's parka was cut in a complex pattern incorporating many seams and decorative inserts of white caribou belly fur (Figure 2.6). Pairs of fine dehaired skin fringes are attached to the front edge, on the tail and hood, and from the centre back. This style of woman's parka with fringes was called *nigyagalik* and was also worn when dancing.[18] The loon and ermine skin attached to the back of the shoulders, as seen in Figure 2.5, were amulets for the woman's spiritual protection and transferred the animal's power to the wearer. The ermine made the woman "quick and lively, a person who can do things with a burst of energy"; the loon helped her become a "good singer and dancer."[19]

During the winter, women wore two layers of clothing. The inner layer had the fur against the body for warmth. In contrast to the intricate piecing of the outer parka, the undecorated inner parka was cut in a simpler pattern as illustrated in Figure 2.7. The front and back were made from a single caribou skin with a hole cut for the neck opening. The fur flowed upward on the front of the garment which prevented it from "riding-up" and flowed downward on the back for comfort. The hood and sleeves were added separately. The hood was made from two main pieces with triangular additions around the face opening. Large pieces and fewer seams on the inner garment ensured greater heat retention.

Fascinating Challenges

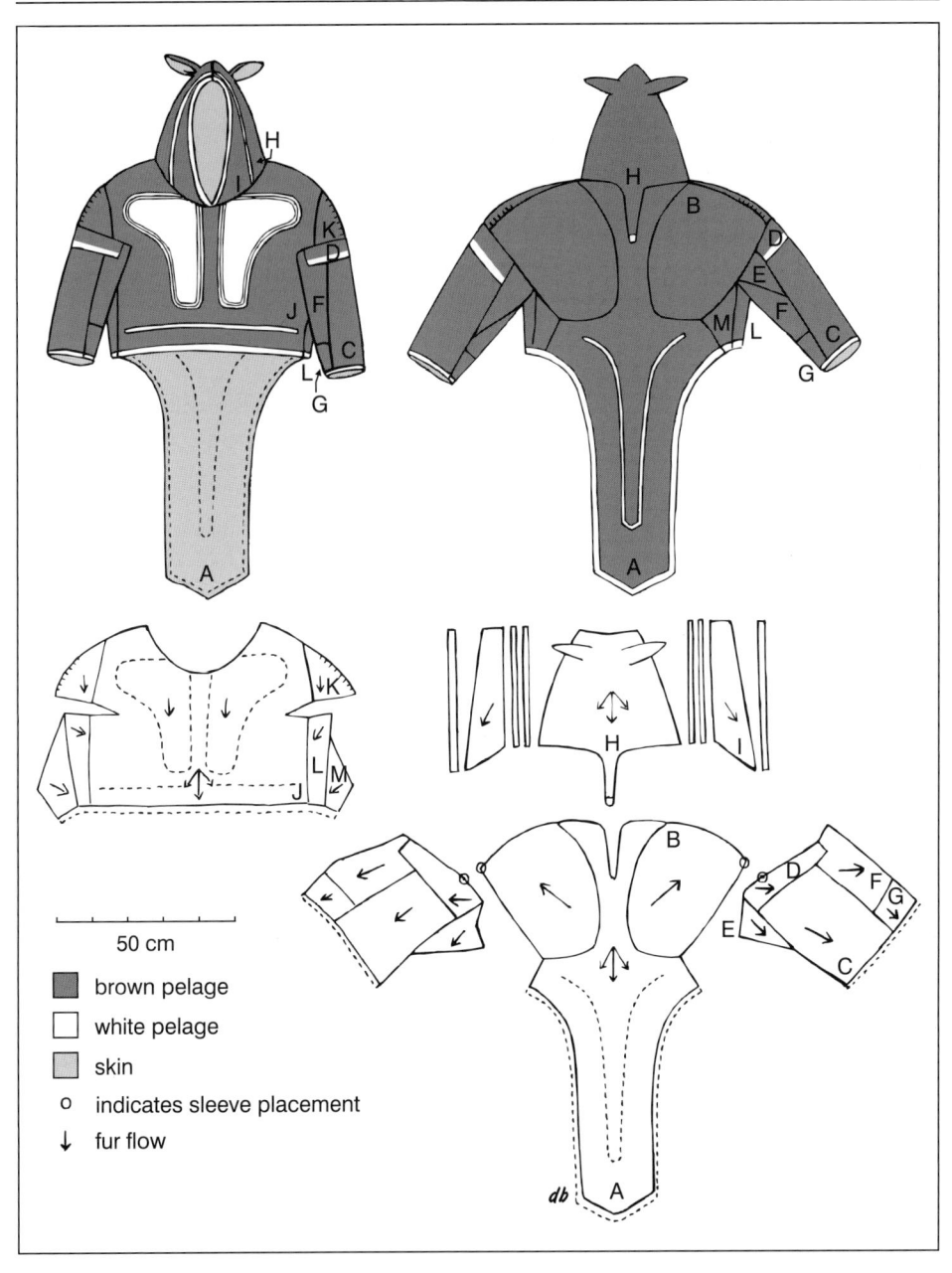

2.2 Cut of man's outer parka illustrated in Figure 2.1. Canadian Museum of Civilization IV-D-960.

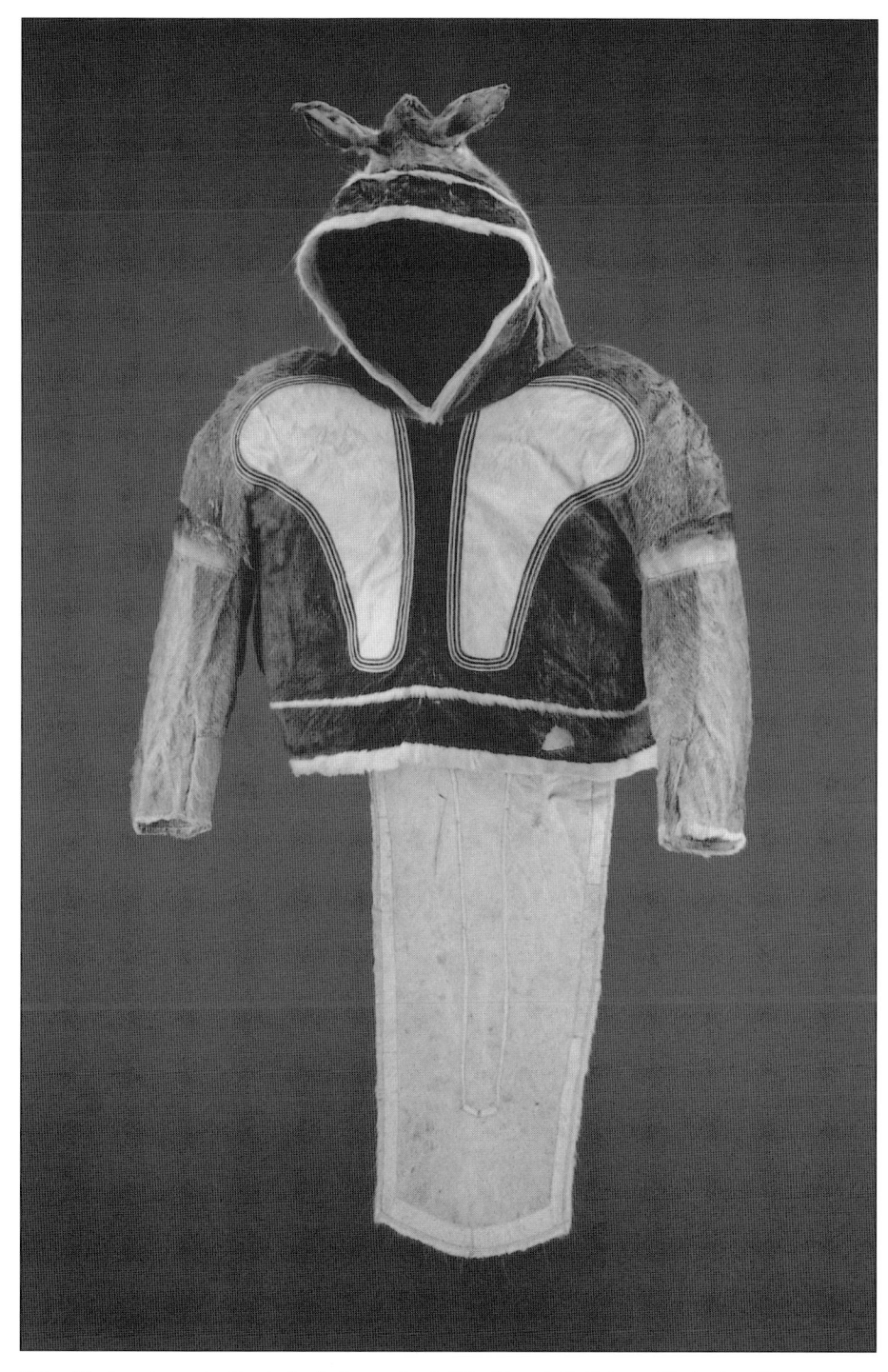

"Following The Traditions of Our Ancestors": Inuit Clothing Designs

2.1 Man's outer parka (front view). Copper Inuit (Kilusiktormiut). Belonged to Ilaciaq, "the greatest shaman in the country." Collected by Diamond Jenness, Bernard Harbour, 1916. Length 145.0 cm (57"); Width 71.0 (28") cm. Canadian Museum of Civilization IV-D-960.

Once the skin was prepared the seamstress cut out the garment freehand[4] and sewed the pieces together using fine sinew stitches. From their mothers and grandmothers, girls learned all the steps in clothing manufacture. They also learned that being an accomplished seamstress was a skill that ensured the survival of their family. Creating a well-made garment was a source of pride. Elisapee Kiliutak explains:

> *When a woman has her first child, her mother and her grandmother help her to make her amautik [woman's parka]. That's how we start to learn ... When we make an amautik, we have to do a lot of trying on to see how it will fit. Even if the amautik is completely finished, we have to take it apart if there is even one little mistake. We can't leave mistakes to spoil the amautik.*[5]

For both men and women, a complete clothing outfit consisted of a parka with attached hood, pants, and mittens, worn in one or two overlapping layers depending on the season, and several layers of footwear. The outer covering of clothing has the fur to the exterior, while the inner layer has the fur against the body for warmth.[6]

The clothing was designed for survival in a northern environment. However, beyond the practical function of protection, each garment discussed in this paper conveys implicit messages about the wearer. Variations in cut and decoration reflected the wearer's age, gender and occupation. Women's parkas (amautit), for example, symbolize the woman's maternal role in Inuit society.[7] The amautik has a pouch (amaut) on the back in which the mother carries an infant. Wide shoulders permit the child to be moved to the front for breast-feeding and the large hood allows air to circulate to the child. In contrast, men's parkas are designed to assist the hunter in the pursuit of game.[8] A close-fitting hood provides protection but does not obscure the hunter's vision. Ample shoulders ensure freedom of arm movement and permit the hunter to insert his arms inside the parka for warmth.[9]

Clothing also reveals the cultural affiliation of the wearer.[10] Distinct styles are indicated by the cut of the garment, the juxtaposition of brown and white fur decoration, and the thickness of the fur. The man's outer parka illustrated in Figure 2.1 is an example. It was made by a Copper Inuit (Kilusiktormiut) seamstress in the Coronation Gulf region at the beginning of the twentieth century. The parka is characterized by a straight-cut front edge, a close-fitting hood, a long straight tail reaching to the calf, and rounded chest panels. Using two caribou skins[11], the Copper Inuit seamstress produced a complex pattern with intricate piecing of the hood, sleeves and back with inserts of white caribou fur and dehaired and dyed sealskin (Figure 2.2). The chest panels are made from white caribou belly fur, the stripes around the upper arm from the caribou's rump, and the hood from caribou headskin.[12] Because the ears have been left on and form part of the finished hood, Elsie Nilgak of Ulukhaqtuuq (Holman) calls this style *hiutitalik*.[13] A tuft of white fur is inserted between

2.3 Woman's outer and inner parka (front view). Copper Inuit (Kilusiktormiut). The inner parka forms a double layer with the fur against the body. It is visible around the face opening on the hood and as the furred extension on the back tail. Collected by Diamond Jenness, Coronation Gulf region, 1913-16. Length 107.0 cm (42 1/8"); Width 78.5 cm (31").
Canadian Museum of Civilization IV-D-944 a,b.

"Following The Traditions of Our Ancestors": Inuit Clothing Designs

Regional styles of men's and women's garments evolved in response to available resources, local and individual preferences and environmental factors.[20] Figure 2.8 illustrates a man's parka style common to the Caribou Inuit who live on the west of Hudson Bay. It was made by a Caribou Inuit (Qairnirmiut) seamstress near Igluligaarjuk (Chesterfield Inlet) at the turn of the twentieth century. Like the Copper Inuit man's parka in Figure 2.1, this parka has a short front edge, broad shoulders, close-fitting hood, and a long back tail. It differs from the Copper Inuit example, however, in the selection of thicker caribou skin taken later in the year and in certain design elements, which can be seen in the drawing in Figure 2.9. Bands of white caribou belly fur lengthen the front edge and widen the back tail. The front of the parka is made of brown caribou fur; white chest panels are not commonly found on Caribou Inuit (Qairnirmiut) men's parkas.[21] Three divided rectangular blocks of brown and white caribou fur were often inserted on the back of men's parkas from this region. These blocks may have served as abstract references to amulets for the spiritual protection of the wearer[22] or added to the

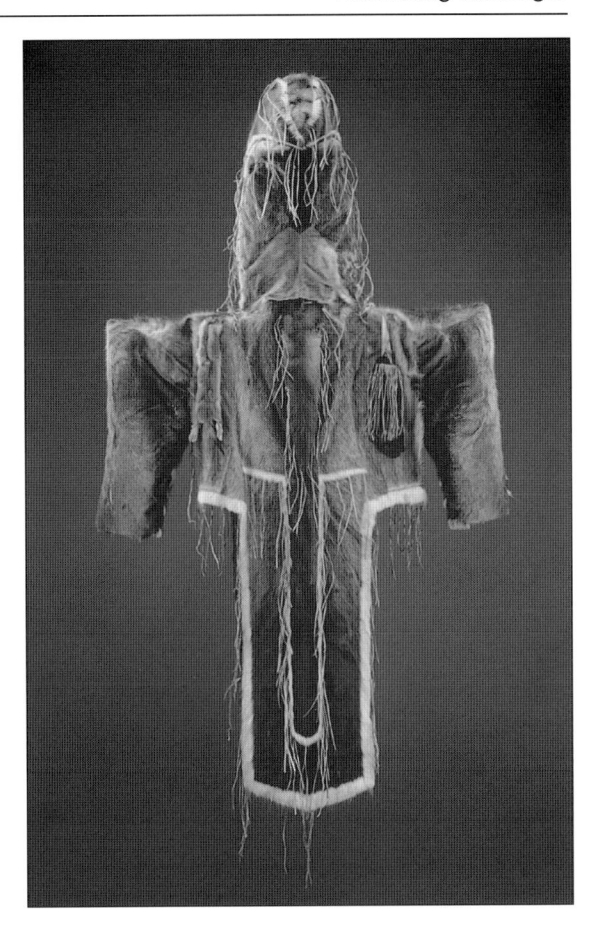

2.5 Woman's outer parka (back view). Copper Inuit (Kilusiktormiut). Canadian Museum of Civilization IV-D-944 b.

appearance and cut of the garment.[23] Closely spaced, partially-dehaired skin fringes in a double layer around the front and back tail provide additional protection from the cold and prevent the edges from curling.[24]

The woman's outer parka (amautik) illustrated in Figure 2.10 was also made by a Caribou Inuit (Qairnirmiut) seamstress from the west of Hudson Bay at the beginning of the twentieth century. It forms a stylistic pair with the man's parka in Figure 2.8. This parka exhibits characteristics common to Inuit women's parkas throughout the Arctic: enlarged hood, broad shoulders, elongated front and back panels, and a pouch (amaut) on the back to carry a baby. However, the overall fullness of the design, the wide bands of white caribou fur, the fringes on the chest panels, around the shoulders and the bottom edge, and the use of thick caribou fur reflect the preferences of seamstresses on the west side of Hudson Bay. Complex piecing of narrow and wide bands of white and brown caribou fur around the hood opening and sleeves (Figure 2.11), sewn with fine sinew stitches, attest to the exceptional skill of the seamstress. The construction of the pouch is, as Dorothy Burnham has remarked, an "engineering feat." The bottom of the pouch is an extension of the back of the garment and three additional pieces at the base of the hood create the fullness that accommodates

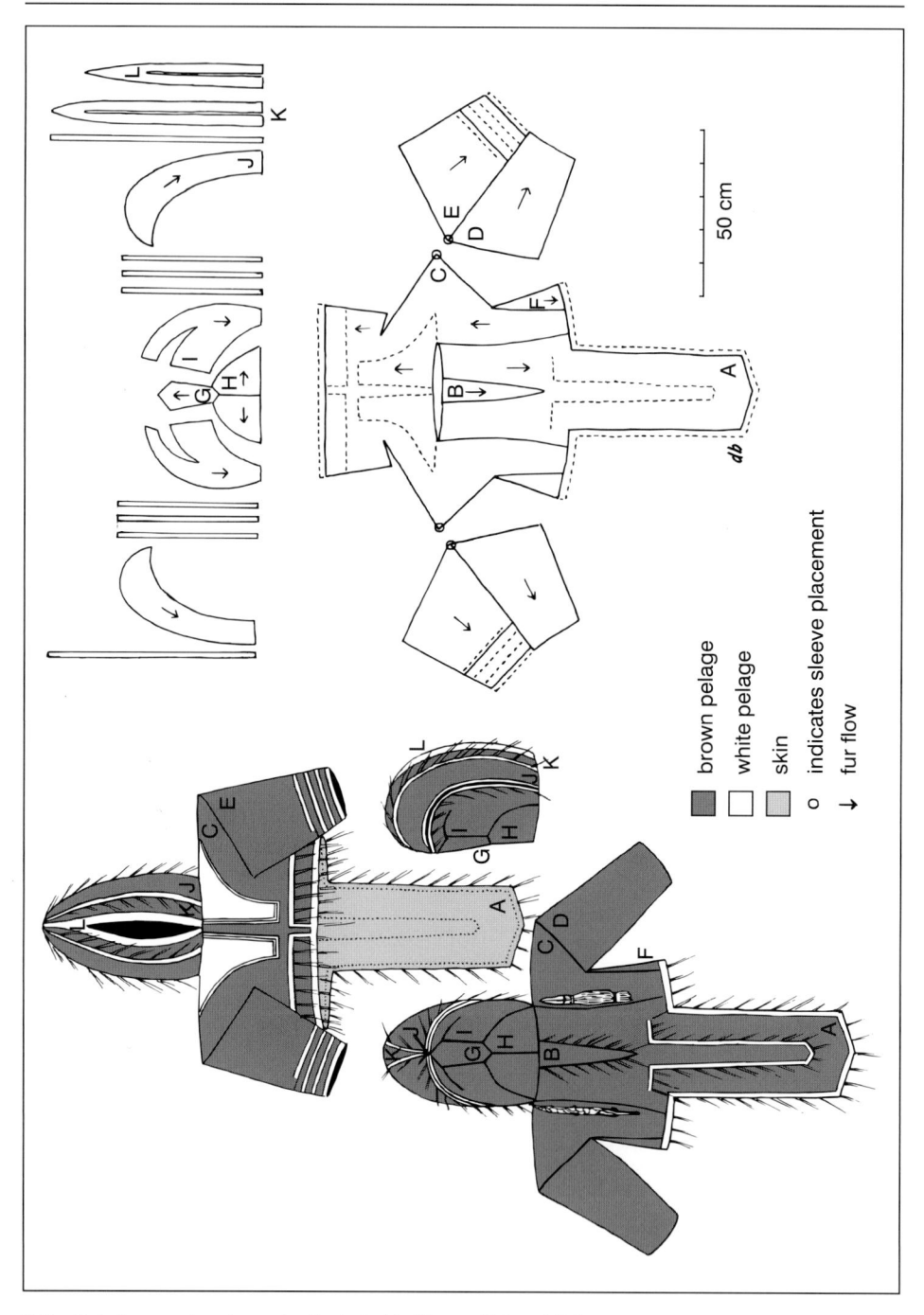

2.6 Cut of woman's outer parka illustrated in Figures 2.3 and 2.5. Canadian Museum of Civilization IV-D-944 b.

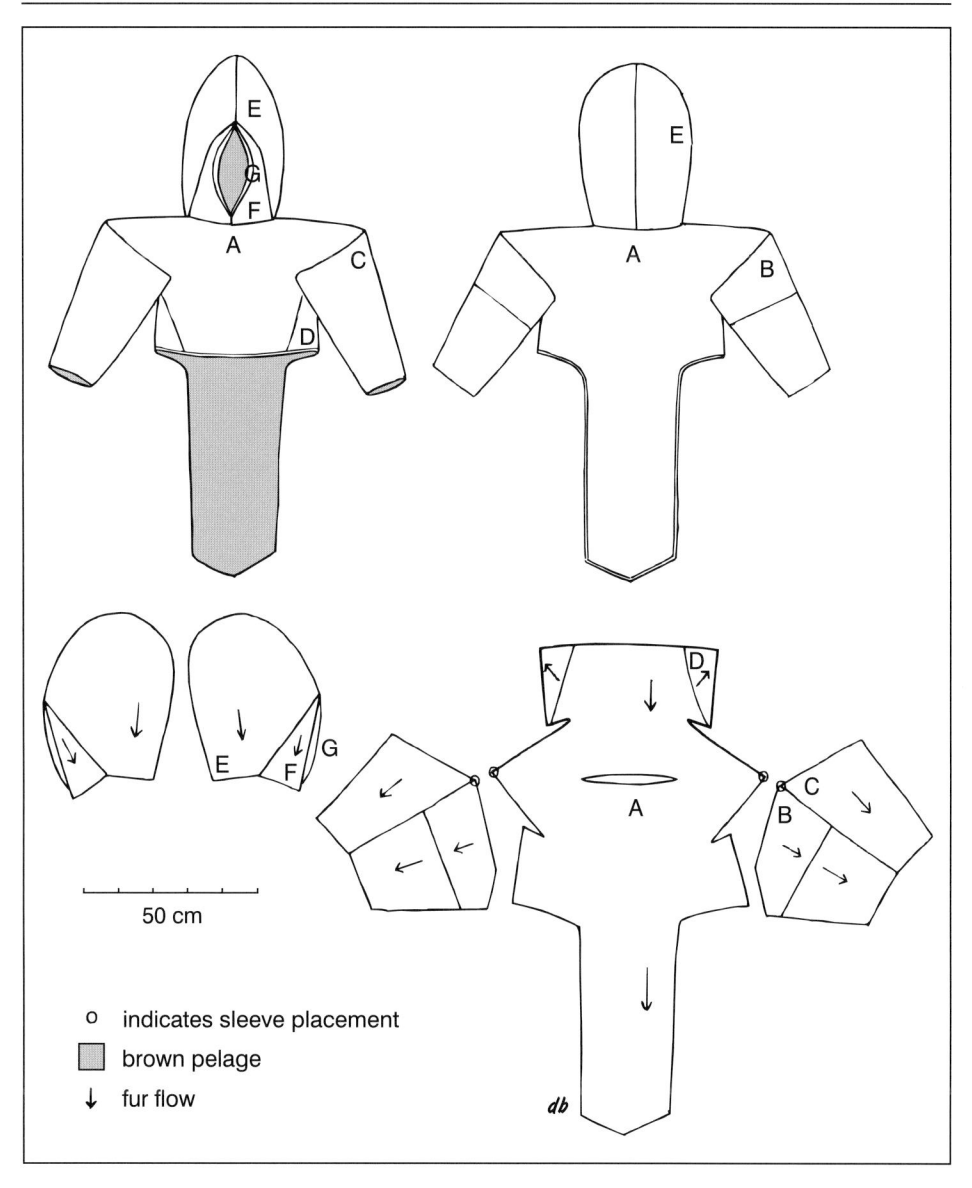

Fascinating Challenges

2.7 Cut of woman's inner parka illustrated in Figure 2.3.
Canadian Museum of Civilization IV-D-944 a.

"Following The Traditions of Our Ancestors": Inuit Clothing Designs

the baby (Figure 2.11, side insert). Further details on the construction of the pouch can be found in the following paper, *Masters of Design*. A skin belt was positioned under the pouch to secure the infant. To distribute the weight, a button at each end of the belt was threaded through skin loops at the neck as shown in Figures 2.10 and 2.11.

The woman's inner stockings illustrated in Figure 2.12 exemplify how functionality, symbolic references to identity and regional differences converge in the design and construction of Inuit garments. The stockings were made by an Iglulingmiut seamstress near Wager Bay at the turn of the twentieth century and represent one regional style worn by Inuit women. The stockings are

2.8 Man's outer parka (back view). Caribou Inuit (Qairnirmiut). Collected by Arsène Turquetil, Igluligaarjuk (Chesterfield Inlet), 1912-18. Donated by Les Soeurs de l'Esperance, 1918. Length 145.0 cm (57"); Width 61.0 cm (24").
Canadian Museum of Civilization IV-C-924.

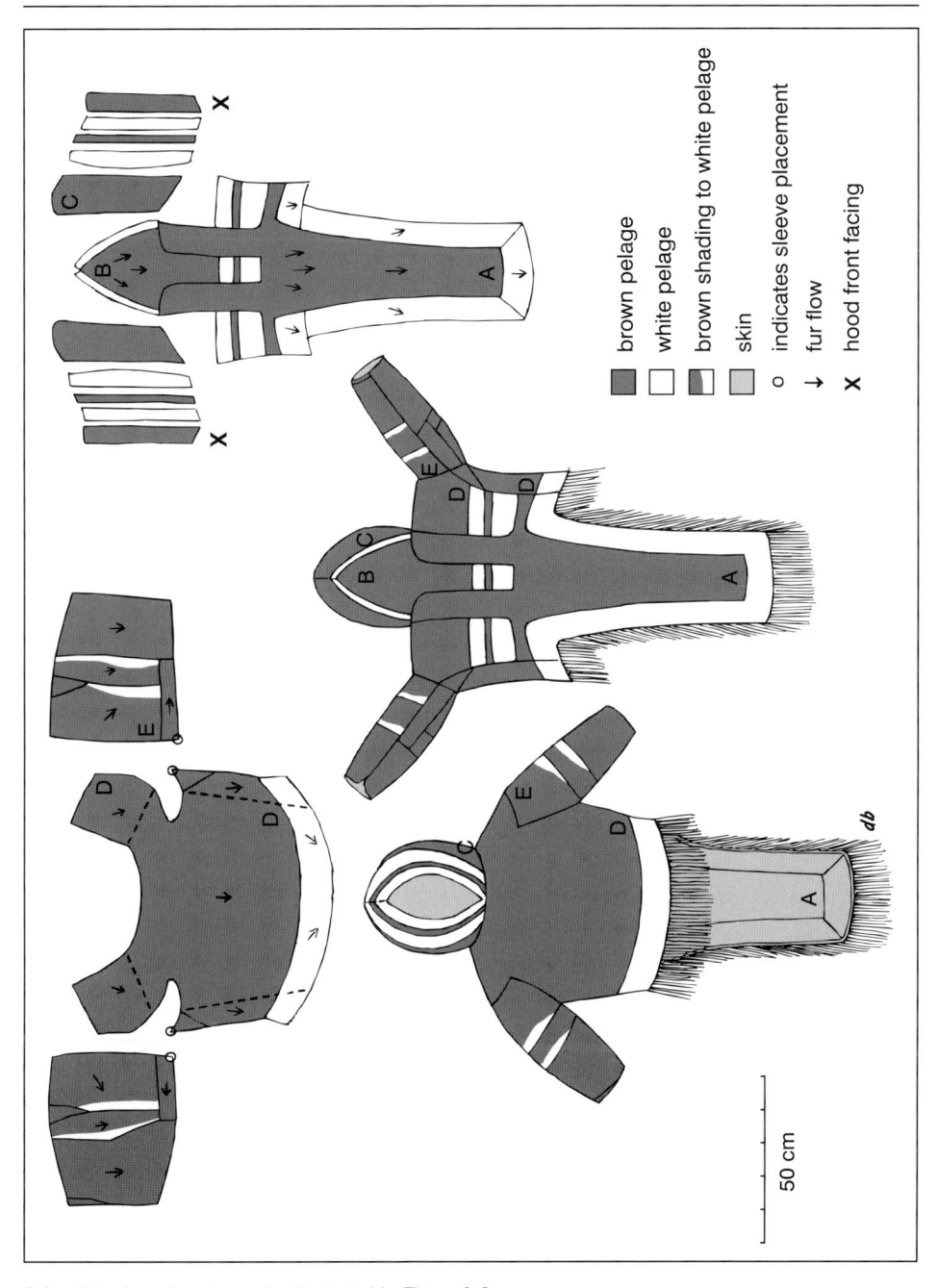

Fascinating Challenges

2.9 Cut of man's outer parka illustrated in Figure 2.8.
Canadian Museum of Civilization IV-C-924.

"Following The Traditions of Our Ancestors": Inuit Clothing Designs

2.10 Woman's outer parka, *amautik* (front view). Caribou Inuit (Qairnirmiut). Collected by Albert P. Low, Fullerton Harbour, 1903-04. Length 180.0 cm (70 ¾"); Width 75.0 cm (29 ½"). Canadian Museum of Civilization IV-C-628.

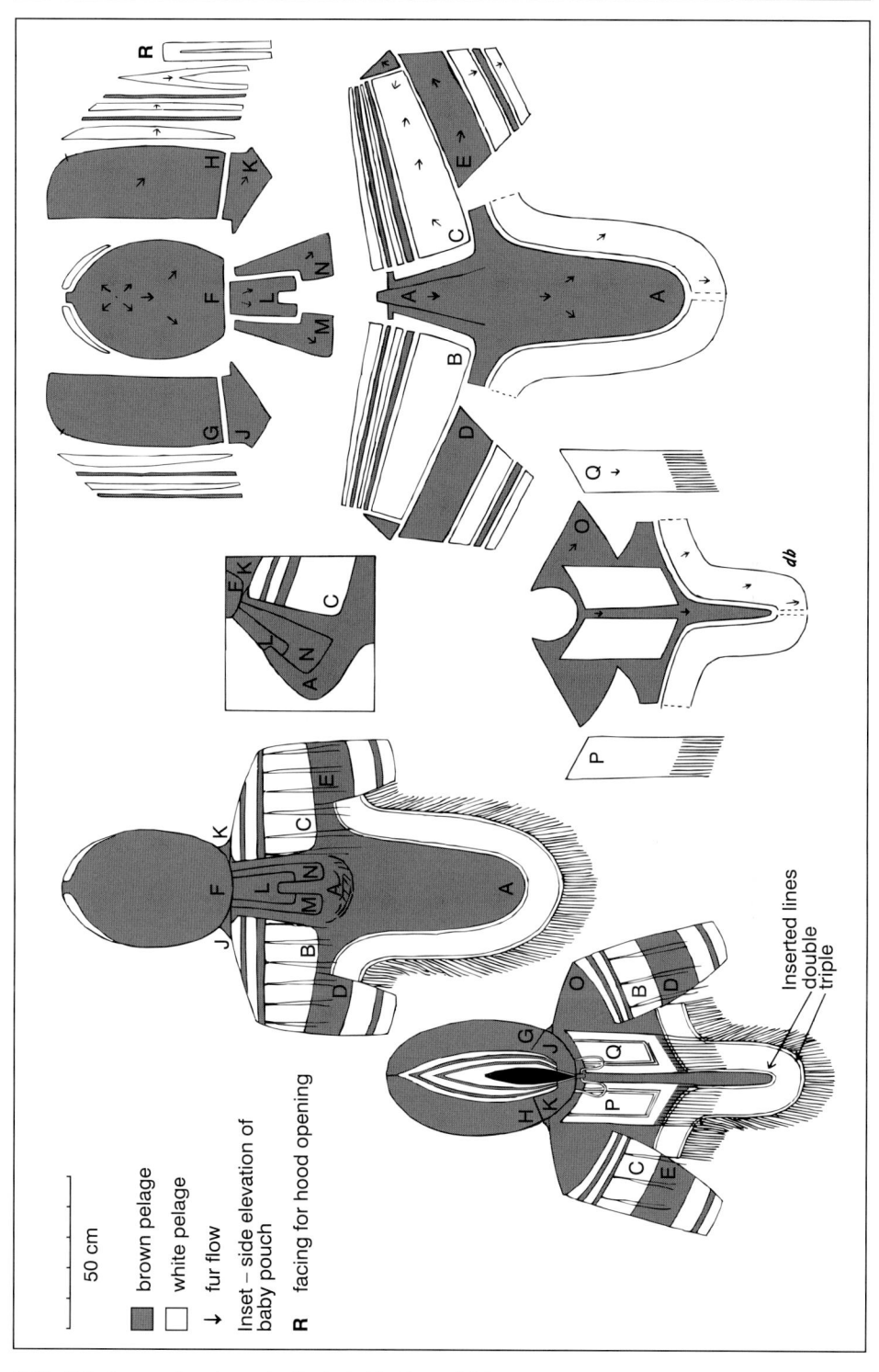

Fascinating Challenges

2.11 Cut of woman's outer parka illustrated in Figure 2.10. Canadian Museum of Civilization IV-C-628.

"Following The Traditions of Our Ancestors": Inuit Clothing Designs

made of caribou skin with the fur to the interior for warmth. Additional pieces of fur are sewn to the exterior of the sole to provide traction on the snow and ice. Each stocking incorporates a complex pattern of multiple pieces (Figure 2.13) that produce the extra width and side pouch below the knee and the tapered upper extension that was secured around the waist. European materials, such as wool stroud, printed cotton cloth and glass beads, used on these stockings as decoration had been available from whalers, traders and explorers since the early eighteenth century. This particular style of women's stocking was made

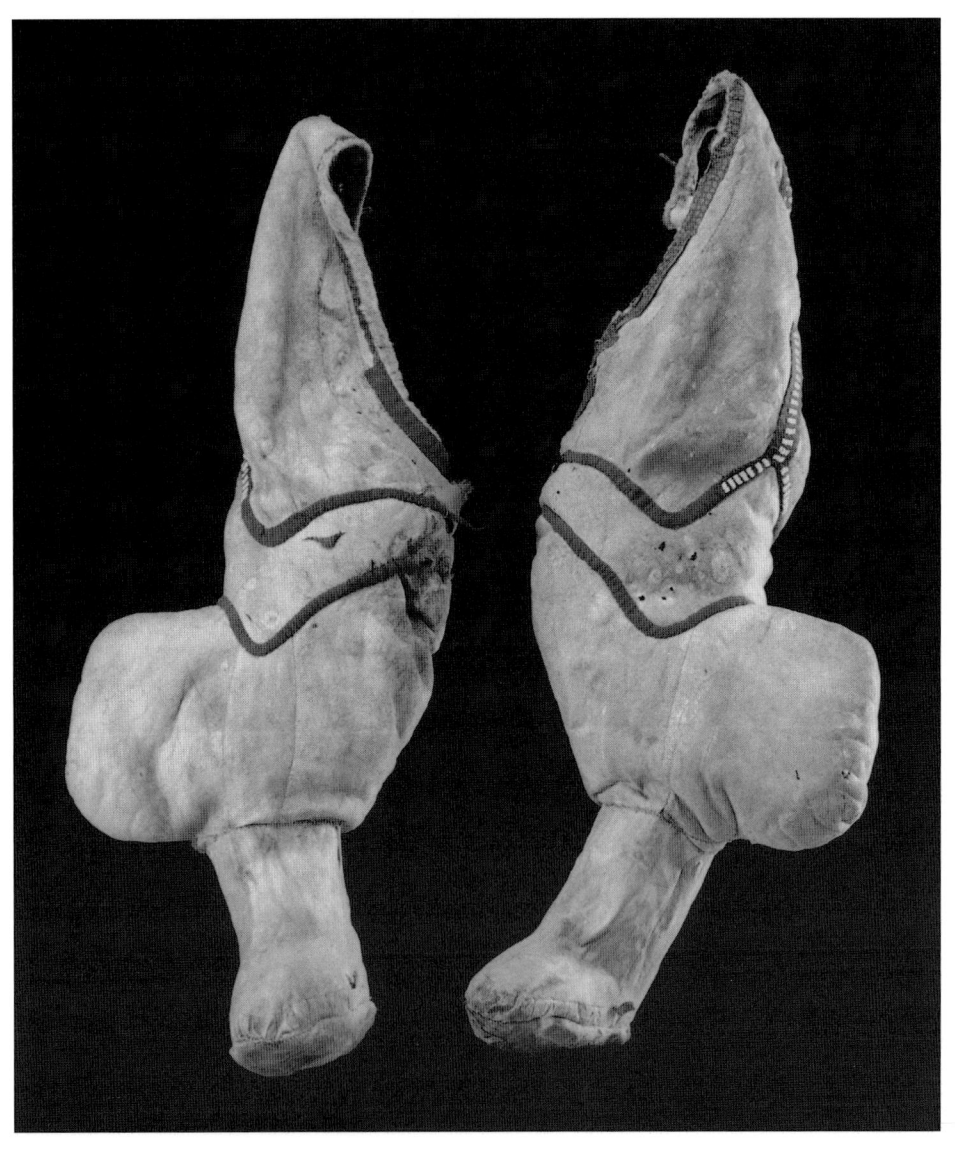

2.12 Woman's inner stockings. Iglulingmiut. Collected by T.D. Caldwell, Wager Bay, before 1911. Length 108.0 cm (42 ½"); Width 39.0 cm (15 3/8"); Height of pouch 25.0 cm (9 7/8"). Canadian Museum of Civilization IV-C-665 a,b.

Fascinating Challenges

by Iglulingmiut and Caribou Inuit (Paatlirmiut[25] and Qairnirmiut[26]) women and was worn with the caribou-skin parka (Figure 2.14). In contrast, the style of stockings worn by Copper Inuit women can be seen in Figure 2.4.

The ingenious cut of the Iglulingmiut stockings intrigued many early explorers to the north. George Lyon, a British explorer on an expedition to discover a Northwest Passage, noted the cut of Iglulingmiut women's stockings and boots in 1824. In his journal, Lyon remarked that:

> *The boots of the [women] are, without dispute, the most extraordinary part of their equipment, and are of such an immense size as to resemble leather sacks... the bulky part being at the knee, the upper end is formed into a pointed flap, which, covering the front of the thigh, is secured by a button or knot within the waistband of the breeches.*[27]

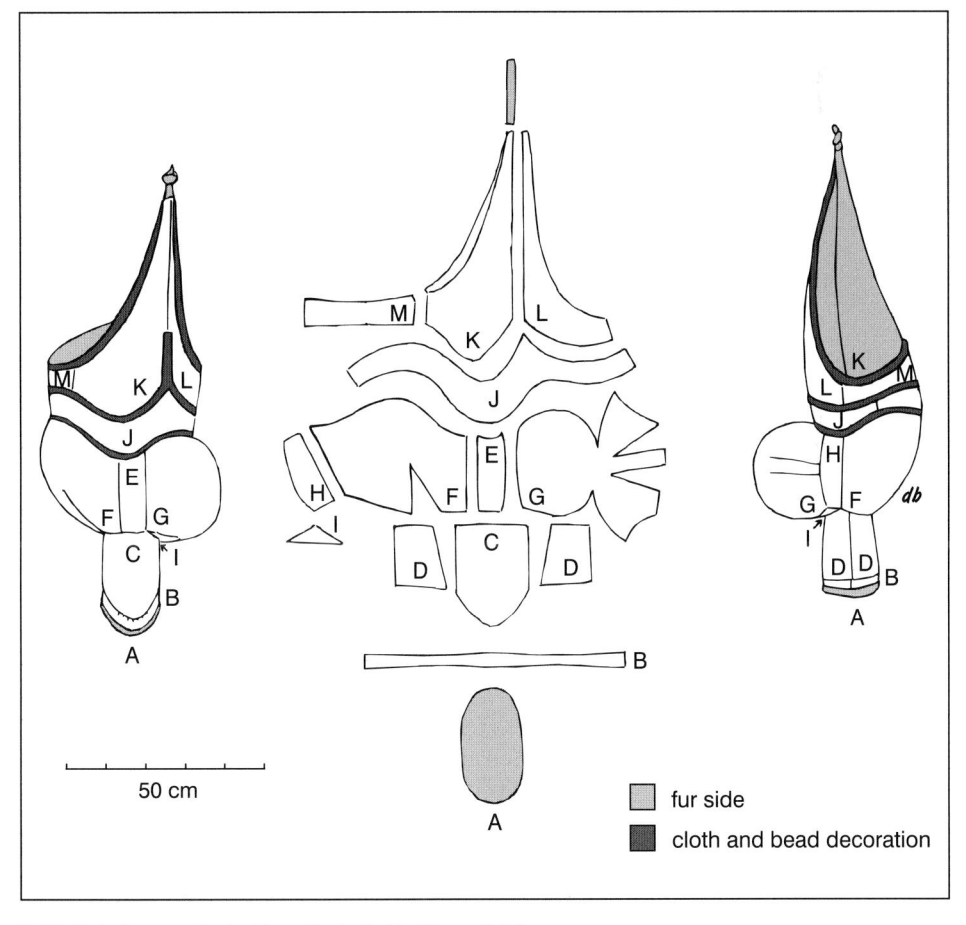

2.13 Cut of woman's stockings illustrated in Figure 2.12.
Canadian Museum of Civilization IV-C-665 a,b.

The stockings were also admired by American anthropologist Franz Boas who observed in 1907 that "by far the most remarkable of the women's garments are their stockings, which bulge out enormously just below the knee."[28]

The function of the pouch has also been the subject of much speculation. William Parry, commander of an expedition to discover a Northwest Passage between 1821 and 1823, noted that the stockings "form their principle pocket."[29] Later, in 1924, Danish anthropologist Kaj Birket-Smith remarked that "the extension on the boot has no practical purpose whatever beyond that the women now and then may use them for storing small objects."[30] Elders today suggest similar uses. According to Emily Alerk of Qamanittuaq (Baker Lake), the pouch was used for storing mittens when travelling and functioned "as a purse to put everything in."[31] Sally Webster, also of Qamanittuaq, remembers that: "My mother told me that the pouches were used to hold mittens and other things when carrying a baby in the mother's arms."[32] The pouch could also be for "carrying sewing supplies and children's treats,"[33] "to store and dry spare caribou-skin diapers,"[34] or for carrying caribou fat.[35] Elders in the community of Iglulik[36] have not confirmed the suggestion that the pouch was used for warming the feet.[37]

By the 1940s, this style of stocking was no longer made partly due to a shortage of caribou skins.[38] As well, by the turn of the century some women were replacing caribou-skin stockings with cotton skirts for summer wear (Figure 2.14). Today, a few seamstresses like Elizabeth Alariaq of Iglulik are once again making this style of caribou-skin stocking.[39]

Whalers, Scientists and Missionaries: Northern Exploration in Canada

The first part of this paper placed each garment in its cultural context in Inuit society. This section discusses the clothing in the broader historical framework of northern exploration. The story of how these garments came to the Canadian Museum of Civilization reflects European, American and Canadian presence in the north in the early twentieth century and the relationships that developed between the newcomers and the Inuit. Since the sixteenth century, Europeans had been exploring the Arctic in search of a Northwest Passage. By the eighteenth century, whalers and fur traders were harvesting the rich natural resources of the region. Early contact with the Inuit was limited. However, this changed in the nineteenth and twentieth centuries when whalers, traders, explorers, missionaries, anthropologists, and government officials spent extended periods in the north. Prolonged contact had a profound effect on Inuit culture and life.

The woman's parka illustrated in Figure 2.10, for example, was obtained by Albert P. Low at Fullerton Harbour in north-west Hudson Bay between 1903 and 1904. Low was in command of the ship *Neptune* on a Canadian government expedition to Hudson Bay and the Arctic islands. The purpose of the expedition was to enforce Canada's authority over Arctic territories that had been transferred from Britain in 1870 and 1880.[40] Canada had done little to assert its sovereignty over these regions and, by the turn of the century, European and American whalers, miners, explorers, and private citizens were increasingly present in the Canadian north. Norwegian explorers were mapping and claiming Arctic islands and American whaling vessels had been operating around Baffin Island and in Cumberland Sound and north-west Hudson Bay.[41]

In August 1903, the *Neptune* headed north from Halifax. The expedition included Northwest Mounted Police to enforce Canadian law and customs regulations[42] and scientists to collect information on the geology and natural resources of the area. The *Neptune* visited the whaling stations around Cumberland Sound and over-wintered in Fullerton Harbour beside the New England whaling schooner *Era*.

At Fullerton Harbour, Low and George Comer, the captain of the *Era*, hired Iglulingmiut (Aivilingmiut) and Caribou Inuit (Qairnirmiut) men to hunt whales, drive the sleds, haul ice and provide fresh caribou meat for the ships' crew.[43] Inuit women were employed as seamstresses to make and repair the crew's caribou-skin winter clothing. During the winter, Low and his crew took a census of the Inuit population and observed their "habits, manners, customs and religion,"[44] a study which included clothing. For example, in his account of the voyage of the *Neptune*, Low describes women's attire as:

> similar to those worn by the men, but they are cut differently. The coat, in the body, is much looser, and the hood is larger and more open, being prolonged into the back to form a receptacle for the baby, who is carried naked there, the weight being supported by two thongs sewn to the shoulders in front and which, crossing the breast are attached under the arms. Unlike the men's coats, those of the women have an apron, reaching nearly to the knee in front, and a longer tail behind. The ... outer garment is decorated with strips and patches of white deerskin, all very neatly appliquéd.[45]

Low also took photographs (Figure 2.14) which were developed in the makeshift darkroom on the *Neptune*.[46] The following summer of 1904, the *Neptune* sailed to Ellesmere Island, visited the whaling stations at Cumberland Sound and again in Hudson Bay, before returning to Halifax.[47]

Association with whalers, traders and government officials had a profound impact on Inuit life that affected their distribution, economy and material culture. Seasonal hunting patterns changed as populations congregated around the whaling ships for employment. In return for supplying meat, trapping fox and hunting whales and other fur-bearing animals, the Inuit received guns,

"Following The Traditions of Our Ancestors": Inuit Clothing Designs

2.14 Women on board ship at Fullerton Harbour. The woman seated at front right is wearing caribou-skin stockings. Photograph by Albert P. Low, Fullerton Harbour, 1903-04. Courtesy National Archives of Canada, Ottawa C51.

ammunition, tobacco, metal tools such as knives and needles, and European food and clothing[48] (Figure 2.14). The acquisition of imported materials influenced all aspects of traditional culture.

Once Canada had established its presence in Hudson Bay and the eastern Arctic, the government looked to the western Arctic where Europeans and Americans were encroaching on its jurisdiction. Sweden and Norway had claimed part of the area and negotiations had taken place with the American government concerning the boundary with Alaska. In 1913, the Canadian government sponsored a major scientific expedition to the western Arctic, called the Canadian Arctic Expedition. Geographical exploration and the discovery of new land were priorities, but the expedition members were also instructed to gather scientific information and collections.[49] The man's parka illustrated in Figure 2.1 and the woman's parka in Figure 2.3 were acquired at that time.

The Canadian Arctic Expedition left Victoria, British Columbia in June 1913, on board the flagship whaler *Karluk* and included geologists, cartographers, oceanographers, biologists, meteorologists, and anthropologists. The story of the expedition is one of tragedy, conflict, adversity and, ultimately, considerable scientific accomplishment. To achieve its objectives, the expedition was divided into two parties. The northern party, based on Banks Island, was responsible for exploring and collecting scientific data in the Beaufort Sea and north of Coronation Gulf. The party mapped and claimed many Arctic islands for Canada. The southern party, which was primarily responsible for scientific work, travelled along the northern coast mapping the geological formations. They established their winter headquarters at Bernard Harbour in August 1914. Diamond Jenness, the anthropologist for the southern party, spent two years among the Copper Inuit studying language, music, social organization, and material culture. From May to November 1915, Jenness travelled with the Inuit on south-west Victoria Island.[50] Along with expedition cinematographer, George Wilkins, Jenness and others made photographic records of Copper Inuit culture and life, including clothing (Figure 2.4).

Jenness also assembled an extensive collection of Copper Inuit material that was deposited in the Museum in Ottawa. Although we don't know the specific transactions that took place for the acquisition of individual objects, Jenness' diary contains many entries referring to "another day spent buying."[51] On Monday September 28, 1914, for example, Jenness wrote: "The Eskimos [Inuit] came down again this morning to trade, and I bought a considerable number of specimens from them."[52] Jenness' list of items traded illustrates the value placed on European goods by the Inuit at the turn of the century. A canister of gunpowder, for example, was traded for a man's parka; a lard can for a pair of sealskin overshoes; a box of cartridges for a hat, a pair of shoes and woman's boots; and cotton trousers for sealskin boots.[53]

Some information on the acquisition of the man's parka in Figure 2.1 can be gleaned from Jenness' diary. The parka belonged to Ilaciaq whom Jenness met at Bernard Harbour between March 19 and April 4, 1916. In his diary, Jenness recounts meeting Ilaciaq and trading for collections.

> *Number of Eskimos [Inuit] settled round the station [Bernard Harbour]; many eastern people – Kilusiktok. Amongst them was the celebrated shaman Ilaciaq, who has the repute of being the best shaman anywhere in the country…I traded a good deal with the Kilusiktok natives, especially for clothes and skins – their clothes on the whole were very much more elaborately adorned with insertions of red and white and black than those of the Eskimos [Inuit] around here.*[54]

When Jenness started his field study in 1914, he observed that the Copper Inuit "had preserved their old culture virtually unimpaired."[55] However, during the time the Canadian Arctic Expedition was in the north, changes in the material culture and economy had already started to occur.[56] The clothing Jenness and others collected for the Museum represents a style that was soon to be displaced. Alaskan Eskimo, Inuvialuit and American whalers and traders brought a longer style of caribou-skin parka from Alaska, which quickly replaced the existing Copper Inuit design.[57] In addition, by the 1920s, fabric had become readily available from trading posts and had become popular as summer wear.[58] The cloth tape sewn around the front edge and back tail of the woman's inner parka in Figure 2.7 illustrates that even earlier fabric was being incorporated into traditional Copper Inuit clothing.[59] The prodigious collecting of members of the Canadian Arctic Expedition and others may also have contributed to the rapid displacement of traditional Copper Inuit clothing.[60]

The man's parka in Figure 2.8 illustrates another aspect of European and Canadian presence in the Arctic at the turn of the century. Arsène Turquetil, a missionary of the Oblats de Marie Immaculée, acquired the parka between 1912 and 1918. After many years as a missionary in northern Manitoba, Turquetil travelled among the Caribou Inuit (Ahiarmiut) near Lake Ennadai in 1901 and 1906. He used his experience living with the Inuit to establish the first mission in the Keewatin Diocese at Igluligaarjuk (Chesterfield Inlet) in 1912.[61] In addition to his missionary work, Turquetil developed the first prayer book and grammar[62] and made notes on Inuit customs, including clothing.[63] He also made ethnographic collections that were eventually deposited in the Canadian Museum of Civilization and the Musée d'Ethnographie in Neuchâtel, Switzerland.[64] In July 1925, he became the first Apostolic Prefect of Hudson Bay responsible for over one and a half million square miles. At the time of his retirement in 1942, he had established 12 missions in the north.[65]

Conclusion

Inuit clothing from all areas of the Arctic collected by whalers, missionaries, explorers, government officials and anthropologists is preserved at the Canadian Museum of Civilization and other museums. A part of this remarkable collection was displayed at the Museum in the exhibition *Threads of the Land: Clothing Traditions from Three Indigenous Cultures*.[66] The sharing of knowledge between the Inuit community and the Museum was integral to this exhibition. Information on the clothing, including the drawings by Dorothy Burnham which illustrate this paper, archival photographs and photographs of the garments at the Canadian Museum of Civilization have been sent to Inuit communities, seamstresses, and to northern museums so that they can contribute to the historical and cultural records in the north. Loans of objects to museums in the Northwest Territories and Nunavut and circulation of a travelling exhibition of Inuit clothing to many communities have ensured that the information reaches a northern audience.

In 1992, the Canadian Museum of Civilization sponsored a visit by Lizzie Ittinuar from Kangiqliniq (Rankin Inlet) and Emily Alerk and Sally Webster from Qamanittuaq (Baker Lake). They spent a week at the Museum studying the Caribou Inuit clothing collected by Low, Turquetil and others. Later the same year, Elsie Nilgak, Alice Omigmak, and Julia Ogina from Ulukhaqtuuq (Holman) spent a week looking at the Copper Inuit clothing collected on the

Canadian Arctic Expedition. The seamstresses examined each garment, noting the overall composition and decoration as well as details of patterns and stitching. It was the first time since the 1930s that Inuit from Ulukhaqtuuq (Holman) had studied traditional Copper Inuit caribou-skin clothing. Elsie Nilgak arrived each day wearing a black and white fabric parka based on the Copper Inuit style (Figure 2.15).

Inuit clothing, studied in its cultural context, reveals a wealth of information about Inuit society. Placed within a broader historical framework, the clothing documents cultural change and adaptation to external influences. The knowledge and expertise of Inuit elders and seamstresses, analysis of the clothing preserved at the Canadian Museum of Civilization and other museums in the United States and Europe, and the patterns of the garments meticulously drawn by Dorothy Burnham will all contribute to the continuation of this remarkable northern clothing tradition by future generations of Inuit women.

2.15 Elsie Nilgak of Ulukhaqtuuq (Holman), Northwest Territories, wearing fabric parka at Canadian Museum of Civilization, November 1992. Photograph by Judy Hall.

Epilogue

The Inuit Women's Association (Pauktuutit) in Ottawa is preparing a proposal for the protection of intellectual property rights related to the woman's parka (amautik) in the context of the United Nation's Biological Diversity Convention.[67] Respecting the concern of Inuit women regarding the commercialization and marketing of Inuit clothing designs, the drawings in this paper are not to be reproduced in any format without permission from the Canadian Museum of Civilization.

Acknowledgements

My research on Inuit clothing at the Canadian Museum of Civilization was greatly enhanced by the visit to the Museum of Lizzie Ittinuar, Emily Alerk, and Sally Webster, and Elsie Nilgak, Alice Omingmak and Julia Ogina with Jill Oakes and Bernadette Driscoll respectively. I would also like to acknowledge the Inuit Women's Association (Pauktuutit) for agreeing to review the paper and for their support over many years. I would also like to thank Judy Thompson, Dorothy Burnham and Peter Hall for reading the paper and providing critical commentary.

Endnotes

1. Karetak 1982:62
2. Condon 1996:63-64
3. Kalluak 1993:34
4. Oakes 1991:119-21
5. Hill and Hill 1994:75
6. Jenness 1946:11; Stefansson 1914:115
7. Driscoll 1980, 1983, 1987a:182
8. Driscoll 1987a:176
9. Stefansson 1913:77
10. Driscoll 1980:15
11. Elsie Nilgak, personal communication, 1992; Jenness 1946:11
12. Elsie Nilgak and Alice Omingmak, personal communication, 1992
13. personal communication, 1992
14. Jenness 1946:12
15. Stefansson 1914:115,119; Jenness 1946:17; Oakes 1991:14,24
16. Jenness 1946:17
17. ibid.:34
18. Elsie Nilgak and Alice Omingmak, personal communication, 1992
19. Elsie Nilgak, personal communication, 1992
20. Driscoll 1980:15

21. Birket-Smith 1929,1:204
22. Driscoll 1987a:181
23. Marsh 1987:172; Emily Alerk, personal communication, 1992
24. Birket-Smith 1929,1:200
25. Manitoba Museum of Man and Nature, Winnipeg H5.21.123, collected by Donald B. Marsh, Arviat, 1938. Illustrated in Hall et al 1994:44
26. Royal Ontario Museum, Toronto HC2404, collected by Luta Munday, Qamanittuaq (Baker Lake), 1920. Illustrated in Driscoll 1987b:A13
27. Lyon 1824:316
28. Boas 1901:105
29. Parry 1824:496
30. Birket-Smith 1929,1:221
31. personal communication, 1992
32. personal communication, 1991
33. Driscoll 1987b:113
34. Ulayok Kaviok in Oakes 1991:78
35. Annie Majurtuq in Pharand 1975:38
36. Elizabeth Alariaq and Rose Iqallijuq in Pharand 1975:38
37. According to Low (1906:180): "Between the knee and ankle they have a curious bag on the outer side of the leg, which is used for their feet when seated within the snow-houses, the footwear being removed and the feet withdrawn inside the breeches and thrust into these bags – a very comfortable plan."
38. Lizzie Ittinuar, personal communication, 1992
39. Issenman 1997:131
40. Smith 1961:53,63
41. Ross 1975
42. Low 1906:3
43. ibid.:27
44. Low 1904:128A
45. Low 1906:179-80
46. Burant 1998:84
47. Zaslow 1975:172-173
48. Low 1904:127A; Ross 1975:69-70; Ross 1976:98-99
49. Diubaldo 1978:66-68
50. Jenness 1922:10
51. Jenness 1991:400
52. ibid.:301
53. ibid.:Appendix 3
54. ibid.:581
55. Jenness 1946:1
56. Jenness 1928:249-50
57. Stefansson in VanStone 1994:6; Jenness 1946:1; Oakes 1991:24

58. Fabric clothing was not collected on the Canadian Arctic Expedition, however, photographs were taken of men and women wearing fabric shirts and trousers. Canadian Museum of Civilization 36997, 50992, 51002, 51003.

59. The tape was added to prevent the edge from curling; originally, a strip of skin would have served this purpose.

60. Driscoll 1995:6-7. The Canadian Ethnology Service of the Canadian Museum of Civilization has over 3000 Copper Inuit objects collected by Diamond Jenness, Vilhjalmur Stefansson, C.D. Melvill and J. Hornby, Joseph Bernard and W. Hoare between 1911 and 1925. The collection includes over 150 parkas (6 parkas were subsequently transferred to Cambridge University Museum of Archaeology and Anthropology, Cambridge, England and 2 parkas to the Royal Ontario Museum, Toronto). Other collections of Copper Inuit material acquired at the turn of the century are at the Field Museum of Natural History, Chicago (VanStone 1994); Royal Ontario Museum, Toronto; Smithsonian Institution, Washington; American Museum of Natural History, New York; Burke Museum of Natural History and Culture, Seattle; University of Pennsylvania Museum, Philadelphia; Pitt Rivers Museum, Oxford, England; National Museum of Denmark, Copenhagen.

61. Turquetil 1954-5,32:7

62. Clabaut 1955:8

63. Turquetil 1926:427-428

64. Csonka 1988:33-97

65. Clabaut 1955:6

66. This exhibition included clothing from the Copper and Caribou Inuit, the Dene of the Northwest Territories, and the Nlaka'pamux of interior British Columbia and was on display from February 3, 1995 to September 14, 1997. Hall et al 1994.

67. For further information and to request a copy of the proposal, contact Tracey O'Hearn, Executive Director, Inuit Women's Association (Pauktuutit), 192 Bank Street, Ottawa, Ontario K2P 1W8.

Works Cited

Birket-Smith, Kaj
    1929 The Caribou Eskimos: Material and Social Life and Their Cultural Position. Vol. 5, Pt. 1 of *Report of the Fifth Thule Expedition, 1921-24*. Trans. W.E. Calvert. Copenhagen.

Boas, Franz
    1901 The Eskimo of Baffin Land and Hudson Bay. *Bulletin of the American Museum of Natural History* 15(1):1-370. New York.

Burant, Jim
    1998 Using Photography to Assert Canadian Sovereignty in the Arctic: The A.P. Low Expedition of 1903-4 aboard the CGS *Neptune*. In *Imaging the Arctic*, ed. J.C.H. King and Henrietta Lidchi, 76-87. London: British Museum Press.

Clabaut, Armand
    1955 Bishop Turquetil: First Bishop of the Eskimos. *Eskimo*, 38 (December): 3-11.

Condon, Richard G.
- 1996 *The Northern Copper Inuit: A History*. Toronto: University of Toronto Press.

Csonka, Yvon
- 1988 *Collections Arctiques*. Neuchâtel, Switzerland: Musée d'ethnographie.

Diubaldo, Richard J.
- 1978 *Stefansson and the Canadian Arctic*. Montreal: McGill-Queen's University Press.

Driscoll, Bernadette
- 1980 *The Inuit Amautik: I Like My Hood to Be Full*. Winnipeg: The Winnipeg Art Gallery.
- 1983 *The Inuit Parka: A Preliminary Study*. Master's thesis, Carleton University, Ottawa.
- 1987a "Pretending to Be Caribou": The Inuit Parka as an Artistic Tradition. In *The Spirit Sings: Artistic Traditions of Canada's First Peoples*, 169-200. Toronto: McClelland and Stewart.
- 1987b Arctic. In *The Spirit Sings: Artistic Traditions of Canada's First Peoples*, exhibition catalogue, 109-31. Toronto: McClelland and Stewart.
- 1995 "Silent Echoes: The Displacement and Reappearance of Copper Inuit Clothing." Paper presented to the annual meeting of the American Anthropological Association, Washington.

Hall, Judy, Jill Oakes, and Sally Qimmiu'naaq Webster
- 1994 *Sanatujut: Pride in Women's Work. Copper and Caribou Inuit Clothing Traditions*. Hull: Canadian Museum of Civilization.

Hill, Tom, and Richard Hill, eds.
- 1994 *Creation's Journey: Native American Identity and Belief*. Washington: National Museum of the American Indian, Smithsonian Institution Press.

Issenman, Betty Kobayashi
- 1997 *Sinews of Survival: The Living Legacy of Inuit Clothing*. Vancouver: University of British Columbia Press.

Jenness, Diamond
- 1922 The Life of the Copper Eskimos. *Report of the Canadian Arctic Expedition, 1913-18*. 12(A). Ottawa.
- 1928 *The People of the Twilight*. Chicago: University of Chicago Press.
- 1946 Material Culture of the Copper Eskimos. *Report of the Canadian Arctic Expedition, 1913-1918*. 16. Ottawa.
- 1991 *Arctic Odyssey: The Diary of Diamond Jenness, Ethnologist with the Canadian Arctic Expedition in North Alaska and Canada, 1913-1916*. Ed. Stuart Jenness. Hull: Canadian Museum of Civilization.

Kalluak, Mark
- 1993 *Pelts to Stone: A History of Arts & Crafts Production in Arviat*. Ottawa: Indian and Northern Affairs Canada.

Karetak, Rhoda
- 1982 Preparing Wildlife for Use. *Inuktitut* 50 (May): 58-66.

Low, Albert P.

    1904 *The Government Expedition to Hudson Bay and Northward by the S.S. 'Neptune' 1903-04*, Geological Survey of Canada, Summary Report for 1904. Annual report (n.s.), 16(A): 122-143.

    1906 The Cruise of the *Neptune, 1903-04. Report on the Dominion Government Expedition to Hudson Bay and the Arctic Islands on Board the D.G.S. Neptune, 1903-04*. Ottawa: Government Printing Bureau.

Lyon, Captain George F.

    1824 *The Private Journal of Captain G. F. Lyon of H.M.S.* Hecla, *During the Recent Voyage of Discovery under Captain Parry*. London: John Murray.

Marsh, Donald B.

    1987 *Echoes from a Frozen Land*. Edmonton: Hurtig.

Oakes, Jill

    1991 *Copper and Caribou Inuit Skin Clothing Production*. Mercury Series Paper 118. Canadian Ethnology Service. Hull: Canadian Museum of Civilization.

Parry, William E.

    1824 *Journal of a Second Voyage for the Discovery of a North-west Passage from the Atlantic to the Pacific: Performed in the Years 1821-22-23, in his Majesty's Ships* Fury *and* Hecla. London: John Murray.

Pharand, Sylvie

    1975 Clothing of the Iglulik Inuit. Manuscript. Canadian Museum of Civilization Archives.

Ross, W. Gillies

    1975 *Whaling and Eskimos: Hudson Bay, 1860-1915*. Publications in Ethnology 10. Ottawa: National Museums of Canada.

    1976 Canadian Sovereignty in the Arctic: The Neptune Expedition of 1903-04. *Arctic* 29(2): 87-104.

Smith, Gordon W.

    1961 The Transfer of Arctic Territories from Great Britain to Canada in 1880, and some related matters, as seen in official correspondence. *Arctic* 14(1): 53-73.

Stefansson, Vilhjalmur

    1913 *My Life with the Eskimo*. New York: The Macmillan Company.

    1914 The Stefansson-Anderson Arctic Expedition of the American Museum of Natural History: Preliminary Ethnological Report. *Anthropological Papers of the American Museum of Natural History* 14(1). New York.

Turquetil, Arsène

    1926 Notes sur les Esquimaux de Baie Hudson. *Anthropos* XX1: 419-434.

    1954-5 How the Hudson's Bay Mission was founded. *Eskimo*: 33-37.

VanStone, James W.

    1994 *The Noice Collection of Copper Inuit Material Culture*. Fieldiana Anthropology, n.s., no. 22. Chicago: Field Museum of Natural History.

Zaslow, Morris

    1975 *Reading the Rocks: The Story of the Geological Survey of Canada, 1842-1972*. Ottawa: The Macmillan Company of Canada Limited.

Masters of Design

Dorothy K. Burnham

I had been working with Judy Thompson on Athabaskan material for some time, when the exhibition *Threads of the Land: Clothing Traditions from Three Indigenous Cultures* was proposed. It was to be made up of three areas of Native clothing and an important section would be drawn from the Canadian Museum of Civilization's two particularly excellent areas of Inuit materials: garments from the Copper and from the Caribou Inuit. Judy Hall was the curator of that part of the exhibit and she asked me if I would do some drawings of that material for her. Of course, I couldn't resist and said "Yes", but without fully realizing just what I was getting myself into. I did know that the garments were complex, but really had no idea just how complex.

In all museums, large and small, it seems difficult to find a safe uncluttered space where an extra body can work. Up to that time, I had been doing a lot of my work on a table in the storeroom, but the light wasn't good and it was lonely. So, I was delighted when the Conservation Division cleared space for me and welcomed me in. The daylight was good and the company excellent. I started my work on Inuit clothing in comfort.

The volunteer division of the museum keeps careful records of when and how long their volunteers work, but I could give them no idea of what time I put in. I was living in Ottawa, a short bus ride to the Museum, and I just kept turning up to work. Usually I stayed about 3 to 5 hours, or until I could no longer see straight and then I finalized the rough drawings at home. It was fascinating material and I was enjoying myself.

The three garments described in this paper have all been well placed in their cultural and historic context in the previous paper by Judy Hall. It is there that photographs and diagrams of them are to be found. I simply give some additional details that cannot be easily seen, but are arrestingly obvious with the careful scrutiny required for the making of a measured drawing. They seem to demand sharing.

One of the first garments that Judy Hall produced for me to draw was the elegant man's outer parka from the Copper Inuit (Figures 2.1 and 2.2). It was made of very beautiful furred caribou skin with the natural colours of the fur carefully placed to enhance the decorative effect of the garment. As I worked on it I realized that, more subtle than the use of colour, was the careful selection of the direction of the fur flow. On the diagram, as I always do in my drawings, I have indicated the fur flow with arrows, up at the sides and down in the centre. But not from drawing or photograph can the way this subtlety adds to the light, shade and beauty of the parka be conveyed. The cleverly engineered hood was cut from the head of the caribou, ears and all. The beautifully shaped white fur chest panels with the three surrounding lines of piping, fine strips of caribou and seal skin, are typical from this area. This woman created a personal masterpiece, a credit to herself and to the mother who had taught her.

This was the first time that I had been able to handle an Inuit garment such as this and I was very impressed with my close up view of the details. But, as I turned it over to measure it, and saw the inside, I just sat down and gasped. Row on row of fine even sinew stitches were so closely packed that they almost covered the 2 mm (1/8") wide pipings, as they held them in place. It made me dizzy to think of the skill and time consuming work lavished on this garment. I am not a great one for statistics, but a few hard facts seemed the best way to convince both others and myself just how impressive this work was. I decided to count, measure and multiply. Three pipings surround each chest panel. It requires 4 rows of stitches to join these to each other and to the chest panel and the garment. There are 4 stitches to each centimeter of sewing. It was difficult to measure the length of each row of stitches as they wound their way around the curved outline of the panel, but a length of 85 cm (33 ½") is about right. We have 85 multiplied by the 4 rows and that multiplied by the 4 stitches per centimeter resulting in the seamstress making nearly 1400 stitches on that chest panel. Add to that a second chest panel, numerous decorative bands and a long, fine, inserted white line centering the elegantly shaped parka tail.

As I continued to analyze and draw a wide variety of garments of similar quality and complexity, men's and women's, I came to realize that impressive as it was, this was not an unusual amount of effort for an Inuit woman to expend to have her husband suitably dressed for gatherings and drum dances. I became somewhat accustomed to this expenditure of Inuit women's skill and time. Nevertheless, when a magnificent woman's parka (Figures 2.10 and 2.11) of furred caribou skin with large hood and pouch for her baby was put in front of me, I almost chickened out and fled. I didn't think I could draw this garment, but I couldn't help feeling that, in some way, my honour was at stake. If an Inuit woman of almost one hundred years ago could make it, surely I could draw it. I had, at least, to try. I took my courage firmly in hand and with what seemed like a thousand pieces, managed to bring it all together into a neat drawing (Figure 2.11). It was certainly the most time consuming drawing I have ever done, and I am happy to say that I think it is the best one.

The challenge of this work is to take a three-dimensional object, render it accurately in a two-dimensional diagram, in such a way that another person can understand it and, if required, use the diagram to produce a three-dimensional object. The construction of the baby pouch and determining how to show it in the diagram was difficult. I hope that, with the addition of the inset side view and all the pieces, identified by letter, anyone who is really interested will be able to understand the way the centre back, A, has been shaped and slashed to slot neatly into place joining the three pieces, L, M, N, that extend down from the hood, creating a safe comfortable place for the mother's baby.

The skill of basic sewing and the adding of complex bands of different colours, fine pipings similar to those on the man's parka, and loose fringes of skin spaced across the shoulders all add to the lavish beauty of this garment. But to me, the most impressive work was the making of the fringe. It consists of two layers of fine white caribou skin slashed into slender segments, some of them 21 cm (8 ¼") long and all only 2 mm (1/8") wide. I always marvel at the skill and concentration shown in the slashed skin fringes I have examined, but this one seems to me to verge on the impossible. It may not be magic, but it comes very close.

Anything would have been an anticlimax after that superb parka, but I almost laughed when along came a pair of women's inner stockings (Figures 2.12 and 2.13). The contrast was extreme and they brought me down to the reality of ordinary everyday living in a cold climate. They were made for comfort and warmth with the fur side of the skin on the inside next to the wearer. The skin was of poor quality, possibly all the maker could spare for herself and they were much worn. Even the soles seemed to have been replaced. But, they were cleverly designed to be pulled over short fur pants. The making, sewing and trimming were carefully and well done, with an ingenious cutting and shaping of small pieces of skin to provide a pocket on the side of the leg. The making of that bulge must have been a considerable challenge. I know it took me a long time and much muttering to analyze it, but all the time I was working on it I kept thinking what a wonderfully convenient and safe place for a woman to stow away small important necessities like her sewing kit, while travelling.

When doing this work, time and space seem to drop away and I have a strong feeling of closeness to both seamstresses and wearers. There is nothing like careful and close scrutiny of garments, such as these, to make one realize the amazing mastery of design and craftsmanship of Inuit wives and mothers on whom rested the task of clothing their families. I have been privileged and my life has been much enriched.

This text has been adapted and enlarged from videotape made at the Canadian Museum of Civilization in October, 1999.

Section 3

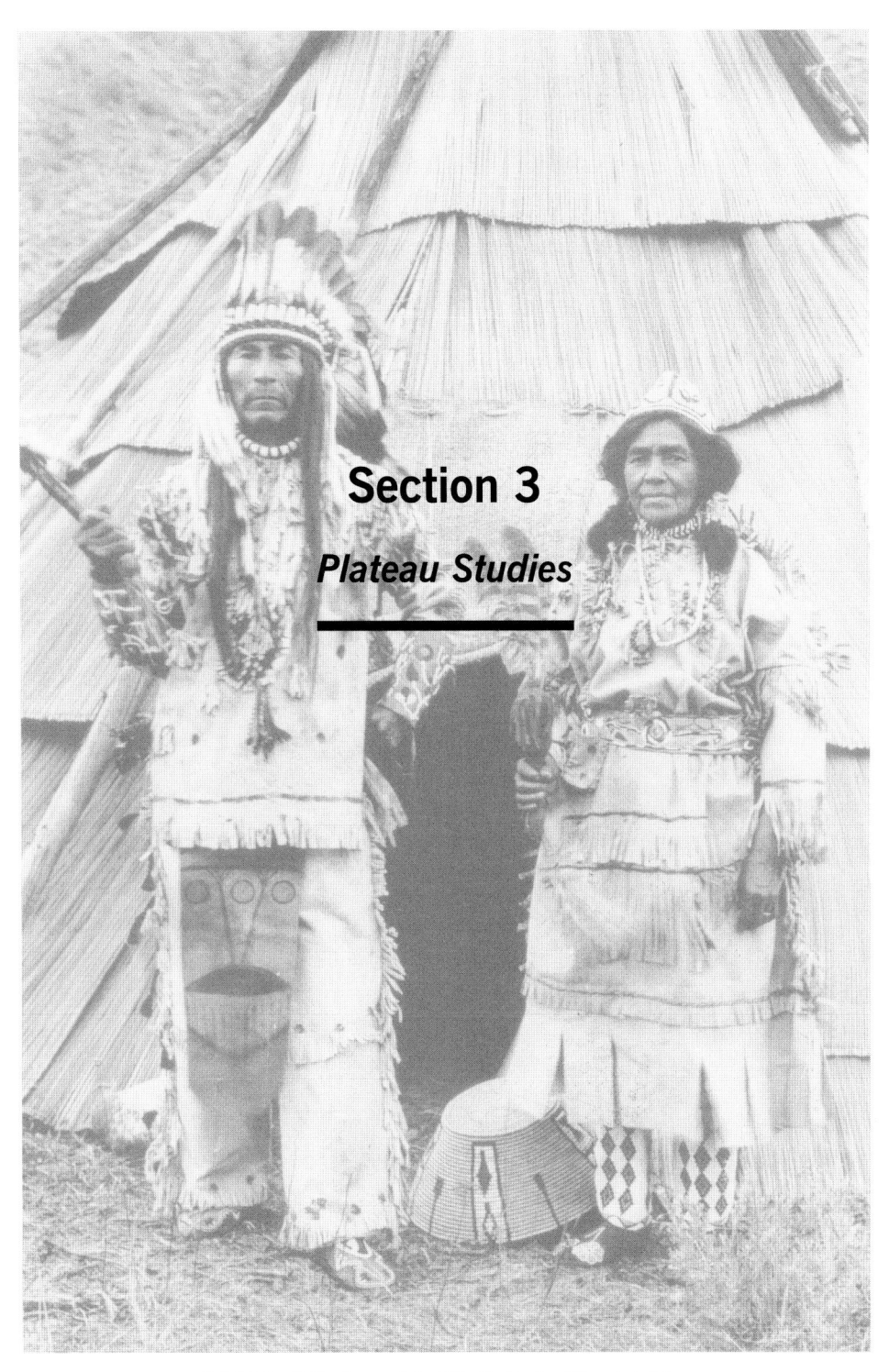

Plateau Studies

Chief John Tetlenitsa and KwElEmákst in traditional clothing.
Photograph by James A. Teit 1914. Canadian Museum of Civilization 26997.

Nlaka'pamux Traditional Territory.

The Old Made New Again: James Teit and the Revitalization of Cultural Knowledge

Leslie Tepper

Introduction

In 1994, the Nlaka'pamux[1] community and the Canadian Museum of Civilization joined together in a collaborative effort to re-create the first woven garments made by Nlaka'pamux weavers in almost fifty years. These newly made capes became part of a rebirth of interest in traditional spinning and weaving by members of the Nlaka'pamux Nation living near the towns of Spences Bridge, Merritt and Lytton, British Columbia.

The success of this project and the subsequent renewal of interest in traditional material culture were made possible by two resources. First, the information needed to recreate these garments was available through extensive, well-documented collections. At the end of the nineteenth century, the ethnographer James A. Teit, with the assistance of people in the Nlaka'pamux community, compiled a rich resource of ethnographic data, myths, songs, and artifacts. His collections provide invaluable information regarding traditional Nlaka'pamux material culture. The second resource was the partnership forged between the Nlaka'pamux community and the Canadian Museum of Civilization. Although such alliances between First Nations and Museums are becoming more commonplace,[2] few collaborations have a similar history of shared co-operation. Almost a hundred years after James Teit and the Nlaka'pamux first recorded traditional knowledge and recreated traditional objects for the Canadian Museum of Civilization, the community and the museum began the process once again. This paper presents the history of an important museum collection and describes a museum-community collaboration that renewed traditional knowledge.

The Old Made New Again: James Teit and the Revitalization of Cultural Knowledge

3.1 James Teit and his wife, Susannah Lucy Antko outside their home.
American Museum of Natural History Library, New York 11686.

The Old Made New – 1894-1922

The Nlaka'pamux Collections

Between the years of 1894 and 1922, James Alexander Teit systematically bought or commissioned objects, models and reproductions from members of the Nlaka'pamux Nation. His goal was to record the traditional culture of the Interior Salish of British Columbia. The result was the creation of one of the finest documented collections of North American Indian material culture in the world. The early twentieth century efforts of Teit and the Nlaka'pamux people who worked closely with him rekindled the community's interest in their traditional culture and left a legacy of museum and community co-operation which has continued to this day.

James Teit

Teit was born in 1864, a son of a shopkeeper in a small village in the Shetland Islands. At the age of nineteen, he emigrated to Spences Bridge, British Columbia to work for his uncle, John Murray, who owned a general store, fruit orchard, and other local enterprises. A memoir by Mrs. Smith, a neighbour, recalls,

> *At that time (1894) there was no one else living on the north side of the river, except James Teit who was living in his uncle's little cottage. He had helped his uncle run the store, but his heart was not in such work. Instead he loved to travel through the country with the Indians and study the country and the native tribes.*[3]

In 1892, Teit married Susannah Lucy Antko, a member of the Cooks Ferry Band living near Spences Bridge. He lived with her family and became familiar with the history and traditions of the Interior Salish community. Teit enjoyed hunting and fishing with the Native people who traded at his uncle's store. He "learned from them the location of the best hunting grounds and this led to his becoming a guide to hunting parties which came to British Columbia from all over the world".[4] Mrs. Smith remembered:

> *Starting out from Spence's Bridge, he would take them by pack train into the Cariboo and Chilcotin. My children were always greatly excited when the pack trains returned, usually with fine trophies of the hunt. He also made trips to the Skeena and Bulkley areas as well as trips into the Cassiar country, going by steamer to Wrangell and then up the Stikine River.*[5]

A new career began for James Teit after he met Franz Boas, a young anthropologist who was conducting a survey of Native tribes. Boas was recording linguistic information, identifying the traditional territories and taking anthropomorphic measurements of the different tribal groups living in the northwestern areas of British Columbia and the United States.[6] He had been engaged in this work since 1888, moving from one area to the next, using missionaries, Indian agents, and schoolteachers as his contacts with Native communities. In September 1894, Boas, hot, dusty and tired, arrived at Spences Bridge, and spent a disagreeable night at the local hotel.

> *In the morning everything looked quite hopeless. I took a ferry across the river because the bridge had been washed away in the spring. On the other side I went to see a man, a Salvation Army warrior and a big farmer who raises...fruit and is supposed to know the Indians very well. He sent me to another young man who lives three miles away up the mountain and who is married to an Indian. So I started up the mountain in the great heat and finally found the house, where he lives with a number of Indians. He was not at home, I waited, entertained by his wife and an old man and after an hour he came. The young man James Teit is a treasure! He knows a great deal about the tribes. I engaged him right away.*[7]

Before leaving Spences Bridge, Boas asked Teit to write a paper on the "customs and legends of the tribe." Although there is no record of other requests, Boas apparently asked Teit to collect artifacts, since later that fall Teit wrote, "I will see shortly what I can do in the way of geting (sic) some costumes, weapons &c made as you desire, but the Indians are even more scattered now than they were when you were here, it will be difficult for me to make arrangements for some little time".[8]

Thus James Teit began a collection of almost three thousand Nlaka'pamux artifacts, models, replicas and samples which he gathered over a 28 year period. The collections, now housed in five museums,[9] are supported by detailed documentation, photographs, and recordings. These collections represent more than an archival record of a particular time and place. They reflect the newly developing role of ethnographer.

Unlike other museum collectors, Teit did not depend on his anthropological work for his livelihood. During the years he worked for Boas and Sapir, he was also a rancher, a guide for big game hunters and occasionally was employed by local road building companies and laid railroad track near his home. Teit, however, had an advantage over the anthropologists who made only seasonal visits to Native communities, or those who made only one extended period of research in a community. Such scholars could gather only data from informants who happened to be available within those time frames. In contrast, Teit's activities span a lifetime of involvement in the Native community.[10]

Teit's work should be considered as an important contribution to the beginning of Canadian anthropology and a reflection of a new approach to anthropological research. When Boas first requested Teit to write a paper on the "customs and legends of the tribe", the methodology of collecting information was in its infancy. Many of the early nineteenth century amateur ethnologists had been armchair anthropologists, who developed theory from written works, travel accounts and questionnaires completed by colonial administrators, missionaries or other travellers. Fieldwork experience became an established practice only in the latter half of the nineteenth century. The employment of Boas by the British North American Anthropology Association to study the Northwest marks the beginning of "the collection of data by academically trained natural scientists defining themselves as anthropologists, and involved also in the formulation and evaluation of anthropological theory."[11] The requirements of fieldwork as outlined by Boas included systematic collecting, knowledge of the language, and involvement of the Native people as informants.[12] James Teit's ethnographic methodology met all of these criteria.

Under Boas' tutelage Teit became one of Canada's first ethnographers.[13] He collected information to define the cultural boundaries of the Plateau communities; obtained information on kinship organization, and compiled vocabulary lists. He collected myths, stories, and information on material culture, ethnobotany, and traditional activities. In his correspondence with Boas and Sapir, James Teit served as a witness as well as a participant in testing new approaches in methodology and theory. Teit, probably prompted by Boas, developed a series of questions in an effort to collect specific data. Such techniques were particularly important in his fieldtrips to the Southern Plateau, where opportunities for research could not be readily repeated. Testing, evaluating, and revising his fieldwork skills, Teit helped to shape a methodology for this emerging academic discipline. Years later, Sapir asked Teit to draw up ethnological interview questions in an effort to establish cultural boundaries between Athabaskan peoples. He wrote, "If you can let me have a list of the twenty test questions that you used in determining Salish boundaries in Washington, a serviceable list of a parallel nature could perhaps be made out."[14]

In addition to his growth as an interviewer, Teit developed expertise as a photographer, a recorder of songs, a linguist, and as a physical anthropologist. Boas and Sapir supplied Teit with up-to-date ethnographic publications and discussed problems of theory and methodology with him. Teit corresponded with experts in physical anthropology, met with anthropologists such as

3.2 Sinsimtko, Kwolalp, Roi.pellst, TekwitlixkEn and XaxalExkEn worked with James Teit to record Nlaka'pamux traditions. Photograph by James A. Teit, 1914
Canadian Museum of Civilization 27000.

Diamond Jenness, and assisted archaeologists and other ethnologists who came to work in the British Columbia Interior.

Teit purchased artifacts to illustrate his ethnographic research. These objects stimulated discussion with members of the community, and served as tools to educate scientists as well as visitors to museum exhibitions. Moreover, Teit, unlike many collectors of his time, collected artifacts as only one component of a vast resource of information. One of the first acquisitions he sent to the American Museum of Natural History for identification was a set of botanical specimens.

> *I send herewith to you the first part of the collection of native plants &c used by the Indians for different purposes. I hope you will be able to get them recognized by some reliable person. It will be to your advantage as well as mine to obtain the proper names of these plants...I will be able to send you quite a number of these for recognizing during the coming summer.*[15]

This shipment was followed in later years by samples of paint and food, face casts, physical anthropology measurements and wooden carvings of heads showing hairstyles and face paintings. What emerges most clearly from Teit's correspondence is his desire to procure a body of material to record and demonstrate every aspect of Nlaka'pamux traditional life. Indeed, his entire life was a commitment to the documentation, understanding, and defence of the Native people of British Columbia.

The Process of Collecting

Museum collections often reflect a particular time span in the life of a specific cultural group. The presence and absence of certain objects, the processes used in their manufacture and the methods and patterns of decoration often indicate the continuity and changes in the history of that society. The community in which Teit was collecting was moving away from its traditional way of life. For almost 100 years, European goods had enhanced, decorated, and gradually replaced objects of Native manufacture. People lived in single family homes, cooked on stoves with store-bought pots and slept on beds covered with Hudson Bay blankets. Although seasonal harvesting of traditional foods such as fish, berries and Indian potatoes remained, these items often supplemented store bought provisions. The Native style of clothing reflected the general European fashion of the day, modified by the demands of special occupations such as the clothes worn by cowboys or miners. Although daily life appeared to the casual observer to be almost completely European, extensive cultural knowledge remained among the middle-aged and elderly members of the community. Traditional technological expertise, stories, myths, and beliefs as to the nature of the world were available to Teit, who systematically and meticulously collected this information.

Teit also gathered census data. The high mortality among the Native population suggested to him that this community and its traditional customs were in danger of disappearing. He believed that as much information as possible should be collected before such knowledge disappeared with the death of the older generation. In 1897 Teit wrote to Boas:

> *A very few more years, and most things will be very hard to obtain, as many of these old fashioned articles at present possessed by the old people will be buried with them thus many valuable things – always the best because they were used formerly by the people that own them - are lost every year, whilst the young people are incapable (by themselves) of making most of the old articles correctly as they have never seen them made.* [16]

At first the collecting of material culture was slow and Teit had difficulty gaining the community's interest in the project. He purchased small objects from his wife, such as gambling bags and dice, a bone awl and a mat. At the end of the first year, Teit submitted an invoice for root diggers, a few baskets, and bags and commissioned items of clothing. Teit's greatest difficulty was obtaining materials for reproductions:

> *It would really require 12 months to make a complete collection as certain things needed for the complete manufacture of some articles can only be obtained in their respective seasons.*[17]

3.3 James Teit holding a shield now in the collection of the Peabody Harvard Museum, Cambridge.
Photograph courtesy of Sigurd Teit.

He also notes:

> *Another difficulty is in the procuring of buckskin of which so many of the articles formerly worn by or used by the tribe were made. I went up river to a village where the people used to dress a large number of skins for sale, but was told by them that they did not now dress many skins as there was no sale for them. Therefore each family only dressed enough skins for moccasins and gloves but no more. I have since written to Spalleeumcheen for some but although promised, they have not yet arrived. I suppose there is nothing for it but to be patient.[18]*

Obtaining information was at times difficult. Teit visited one Native man who was reluctant to share his extensive knowledge despite Teit's use of "different kinds of tactics" including the purchase of a bow and arrow at twice the usual price. Other trips were successful mainly as opportunities to meet people in neighbouring communities. By the end of 1896, however, Teit was offered more artifacts than he was able to purchase. Word had spread that he was buying old objects and contemporary items made in the traditional style and the Nlaka'pamux began to bring items to his home. However, his collecting began to arouse some controversy in the community.

> *It is a pity there is no more money to procure other articles of importance, as the Indians are just commencing to take an interest in the matter, and are now anxious to make or to sell anything that I wish to get, and this notwithstanding that some of the chiefs and others on council, talked strongly against the people selling any of their former articles.[19]*

Teit appears to have been sensitive to the emotions surrounding the sale of older materials, but was driven by his perception of imminent loss of artifacts and related knowledge. Years later, when he was collecting Athabaskan material for Edward Sapir at the Canadian Museum of Civilization, this issue was again raised. Sapir had written inquiring about the small number of artifacts collected during Teit's summer fieldwork.

> *I presume that you were so much occupied with purely ethnological work that you did not care to devote much energy to more specimen collection which would account for the rather small number of museum specimens that you have collected. As we are very poorly off, however, in regard to Athapaskan (sic) museum material I hope that on the next trip you will be able to make a more substantial collection.[20]*

Teit acknowledges the small collection and explains:

> *Regarding the specimens I collected I will submit data with them. I made no great effort to obtain specimens because I knew from the first the tribe as a whole were against the sale of old things to collectors, and several individuals stated they were sorry they had sold what they did to Lieut. Emmons. There appears to be a growing tendency in some tribes in BC to preserve what they retain of old stuff, and pass it on to their children. Also to educate their children in old tribal traditions and lore. There is also a revival (probably a reaction from the too rapid adoption of the white man's methods) of old dances, certain games, music and songs and costumes taking place in certain tribes of both Coast and Interior and this movement seems to be spreading. The tribes of the Interior most affected at present are the Kootenay, Lillooet and Tahltan and Shuswap.[21]*

The Collections

Teit compiled several large collections of Nlaka'pamux material[22] one of which was for Franz Boas at the American Museum of Natural History in New York and another for Edward Sapir at the Geological Survey of Canada, (now the Canadian Museum of Civilization in Hull). A third collection was sold to the Peabody Harvard Museum in Cambridge. A smaller collection, (now housed at the Field Museum of Natural History in Chicago), was gathered by Teit with funding provided by Homer Sargent, a big game hunter who had an interest in Native culture. A few Interior Salish artifacts, probably collected by Teit, were sold by Charles Newcombe to the Smithsonian Institution at the turn of the century. The Provincial Museum of British Columbia, (now the Royal British Columbia Museum), received several collections from Teit, who believed that the Interior Salish cultures should be represented in the provincial museum.

The American Museum of Natural History houses Teit's finest research collection of northern Plateau material culture. Teit and Boas, working together, selected materials not only to illustrate every aspect of Nlaka'pamux traditional life, but also to represent all the known variations. As the only collector working systematically in the region, Teit was able to find the most diverse and representative objects of traditional Nlaka'pamux culture. The pieces he purchased were intended to provide data on a "vanishing" community. Early on Teit suggested an acquisitions plan to Boas:

> *You will find descriptions of a good many articles &c in use here in the paper I have written. Perhaps it might be well for you to single out what are the most important of these, so as to expend the money at your disposal on them first, and let me know, leaving*

> *the rest to some future time when you are able to get some additional money.*[23]

During the next decade, the Teit-Boas correspondence frequently referred to the need to fill gaps in the collection's representation of technology, art forms, and illustrative material in an effort to complete their ethnographic overview. Models and commissioned artifacts supplied missing pieces of the material culture puzzle. To show hunting technology for example, Teit purchased or had made five different types of bow, seven different types of arrows and a variety of quivers, clubs and knives. In May of 1898, he wrote: "It will require about three more pairs of moccasins and about seven or eight more pipes to make a complete collection of these for the museum – showing all their varieties or rather types."[24] The various tools and materials needed for the preparation of skins or for weaving baskets were purchased to illustrate traditional as well as contemporary techniques. Clothing represented a particularly rich area for collecting. A wide variety of traditional clothing styles was purchased in an effort to illustrate the changes of fashion in Nlaka'pamux history.

Teit's diverse assemblage of some 900 Nlaka'pamux artifacts, models and specimens collected at the turn of the century has never been duplicated. The amount of time and sums of money expended has never again been invested in such concentrated, systematic collecting. Yet the desire to compile another "scientific collection", this time for a Canadian museum, occupied Teit for two decades in the new century.

Edward Sapir, the newly appointed Director of the Anthropology Division of the Geological Survey of Canada, employed Teit following a recommendation by Boas. Sapir created the position of field researcher with a mandate to conduct research among the Athabaskan groups.[25] Teit, however, was occupied with never-ending demands from Boas, and felt obligated to refuse full time employment. He did, however, accept a series of assignments and made several fieldtrips to the north. One of his early tasks was building up the collections. Lists of artifacts and collecting requirements were issued to the staff working in the Anthropology Department. For the Plateau, the amount of available funds never matched the need. Older objects became increasingly expensive or were no longer available. Moreover, the death of knowledgeable elders meant that fewer people knew how to make reproductions of traditional objects. Nevertheless, in 1912, Teit notes in a postscript to Sapir "I am acquiring some specimens every week for your museum and for the Victoria Provincial Museum and I will soon have quite a lot on hand".[26] Teit also had a personal collection he had slowly been buying.

> *I have quite a collection of my own gathered up during the last five years whenever I had a chance. I hated to see good rare things ... go by, at times when I had no funds for collecting from the Museums, so I bought them with my own money*

> *although sometimes not very convenient for me. A few of these things can hardly be duplicated now, so I am glad I got them.*[27]

This collection was offered to Sapir, but the Canadian Government's wartime economy had reduced the museum's acquisition budget. Sapir made a special plea for the purchase of the collection, arguing that the value lay in the "detailed catalogue of sixty closely written pages ... in which each specimen is carefully described, much valuable ethnological material being given in connection with each entry".[28] Sapir's request was refused. Teit, who was unable to work during a lengthy period of illness, needed to recover the personal funds he had expended to acquire the objects. He approached a wealthy collector, George Heye, whose collections are now the core of the Smithsonian's Museum of the American Indian.

> *I tried to sell my collection to Mr. Heye in New York but he is willing only to buy those things in it which have actually been in use no matter how good the others are and he proposes to have them sent to him for inspection first. I don't mind sending them for inspection so much, but think that his buying only things which have seen actual service is not on the whole the best method of showing the old culture of an area.*[29]

Sapir was not surprised. "You understand of course, that Mr. Heye is far from being what we call a scientific collector. He is after all is said and done, a curio collector on a vast scale. He would be the last man that I should care to dispose of scientific material to."[30] Teit eventually found a buyer, the Peabody Harvard Museum. In a letter to the Director, Teit explains "... I need the money I have expended on it and therefore am anxious to sell it to any museum that is really scientific."[31]

Teit collected objects for the Canadian Museum of Civilization between 1912 and 1920. Some were acquired during his Tahltan fieldwork, but the major portion were Nlaka'pamux artifacts collected from communities near his home. These objects, like those in the collection of the American Museum of Natural History, were shipped with detailed descriptions such as an explanation of the imagery or of the techniques of manufacture or of use. Here again Teit attempted to provide a wide and complete range of Nlaka'pamux material culture. Samples of food in various stages of preparation - raw, ready for cooking or cooked - and fungi, mosses and barks used for paints and dyes were carefully identified by their Latin names and traditional use. Teit also attempted to acquire a range of hunting and fishing equipment, clothing and objects for adornment. He sent, for example, "samples of three old gloves showing styles of making gloves" (Acquisition list #53, 1920). The Canadian Museum of Civilization collection is particularly strong in baskets and woven bags, mats, capes, and clothing made from hemp, cedar or willow bark. All of these objects were meticulously catalogued with the names of basketry or painted designs.

Information on the maker of the object is usually missing in Teit's documentation. Only a few of the remaining notes or invoices list the sources of the artifacts and some of these are vague. For example, a basket was purchased in 1915 from "Paddy's wife" (VII-M-407) and another from "Henry George's wife" (VII-M-408). The absence of names in the documentation of artifacts is all the more surprising when compared to the information supplied with Teit's wax cylinder recordings of traditional songs. These wax recordings typically provided the singer's name, tribal affiliation, and often some life history. The individuals in the photographs are, of course, clearly identified, but many prints included information on birth dates, Native as well as English names, tribal affiliation and occasionally family relationships. Why would Teit omit from the detailed documentation of the artifacts the names of the tanners, seamstresses, carvers, and weavers who created or supplied the various objects? One reason may be Teit's perception of artifacts as products of communal memory, rather than the work of individual artists or craftsmen. The artifacts he collected for the museum were generally considered in three categories: archaeological materials, models of early material culture, and objects still in use (but altered to meet contemporary needs). Since most of this material was generally outside of daily use or personal ownership, it may have been viewed as representative of a generalized past and not the work of a skilled individual artist or crafts person. The approach also reflects the anthropological writing and research of the period, in which the individual became the anonymous contributor of information to an ethnographic history.[32] Unlike photographic portraits or songs which were, and continue to be, considered personal property, artifacts were a form of ethnographic information which could be separated from the individual's craftsmanship and applied to an overall group.

Recreating Traditional Material Culture- Early Twentieth Century

Although Teit was able to purchase some older artifact material, he depended on the community's memory and skills to attain his goal of acquiring a complete range of traditional material culture. His work for Boas had begun during a period when only a few people in the community could recall the traditional technology. The need to make bows and arrows, stone tools, traditional paints, and woven or tanned clothing began to disappear early in the nineteenth century, when trading posts were established in the Interior. However by interviewing elderly people who remembered the teachings of their grandparents, Teit learned about a way of life which predated European contact and at the same time obtained models of traditional objects. In a letter to the Director of the Peabody Harvard Museum, he justified the large amount of newly made materials in his collection.

> *Specimens in use now a days are generally more or less modified and not true types of the old culture although of course they have their values. It would be impossible to get a clear and full idea of the old material culture of this area (or I suppose now a days any*

> *area except the Eskimo) by purchasing specimen only of the things now in use. The only way to do is to obtain from the Indians who have the knowledge, specimens made by them which are true copies of the things formerly in use. Most of my collection consists of this kind of materials the specimens having been used only to the extent to show they were actually serviceable such as some kinds of tools, and games &c and clothes worn a time or two at a dance or a gathering or for the taking of pictures and then sold to me.[33]*

And again,

> *No collection of any account can be made in this country now nor anywhere else where I have been without models. There is hardly anything used by the Indians anywhere now that is not modified more or less and if you want to have specimens of the old things you must have good models.[34]*

In a few cases, the techniques of traditional manufacture were still well known and some objects continued to be made for everyday use.

> *Almost all the old men of the Upper Makyapamux (sic), for instance, have seen stone arrow-heads made, or have manufactured them themselves; and many of them can make them today without any difficulty. Some of the stone arrow-heads sent to the American Museum in New York, were made by an old Indian at Spence's Bridge...Stone scrapers used in tanning skins are also still made and used here; stone spear-heads and tomahawk blades have also been made here by Indians within the last couple of years as specimens; and stone pipes are made almost every day by someone or another throughout the tribe.[35]*

In regard to other items, such as clothing, European styles and materials had largely replaced the use of tanned skins. Teit's portrait photographs show men dressed in cotton and wool shirts and pants and, on more formal occasions, in suits and vests. Headwear included bowlers or cowboy hats, reflecting the fashion at the turn of the century. Women's clothing included skirts and blouses with a shawl over the shoulders, or Victorian style dresses with puffed sleeves, high neck collars and floor length skirts. Buckskin shirts, jackets and chaps continued to be made for men working on cattle ranches. Fur coats and jackets were sewn for men tending the winter trap lines. These items had changed from the old Nlaka'pamux styles by the addition of collars, pockets, buttons, and often extra fringing.[36] However, pre-contact styles of shirts were still occasionally seen at ceremonial dances or festive gatherings.[37] Decorated leather moccasins and gloves continued to be made for family use and for sale to tourists. Traditional knowledge of tanning and sewing buckskin had not disappeared completely, but was in serious decline.

European goods also reduced the need to make fibre garments. Traditionally, woven skirts, vests, leggings and capes were worn in hot weather, or when animal hides were scarce. With the establishment of trading posts in the British Columbia Interior, cotton and wool fabrics began to replace twined willow, cedar and sagebrush textiles. Fibre garments were retained for certain ceremonial activities, such as sweat bathing. They were also adapted for use in more contemporary religious practices. Figure 3.4 shows Nlaka'pamux actors dressed in woven garments for a Passion play early in the twentieth century. Nlaka'pamux elders recall their grandmothers making willow bark garments.[38] Like skin tanning and other traditional activities, the knowledge of fibre preparation and weaving was disappearing. Teit's purchases of hats, long and short leggings, capes, skirts and shirts, many of them apparently unworn, helped to maintain weaving skills for another generation.

3.4 People wearing woven garments, Nicola Valley, British Columbia, early 20th century. Princeton and District Pioneer Museum Collection, Princeton.

The Legacy

James Teit and the many Nlaka'pamux people who supported and worked with him created an extraordinary resource for the Native as well as the non-Native community. The wealth of this resource lies in the range and diversity of the objects collected and in the detailed information that accompanied them. Associated with the artifacts are records of songs, myths, ethnographic information, and photographs. Teit's activities served as a warning call as well as an opportunity for the renewal of traditional knowledge. Communities became aware that objects of value and important cultural knowledge were being lost. Teit's activities provided an opportunity, particularly for the younger generation, to see traditional objects and learn traditional information.

Teit's contributions can perhaps be summarized by one of his own reports. The words reflect his careful scholarship, fears for the present and hopes for the future.

> *I have taken considerable trouble to obtain as much information as possible re. these songs and my notes on them will cover some 50 pp. of foolscap. Some of the records are of considerable value as they represent songs not now used and with the death of a very few more of the oldest people they would be lost forever. This winter I have been encouraging some of the young men here to learn the songs of some of the old time dances &c and also to learn the dances. At last two or three of them took the matter up and have been practicing off and on during the last month or more.*[39]

The Old Made New Again – 1994

From the time of James Teit's death in 1922 to the early 1990s, the potential for research and public exhibitions of these collections remained largely untapped. At the American Museum of Natural History, a representative sample was placed on exhibit as part of a general overview of Northwest Coast Native cultural traditions. At the Canadian Museum of Civilization, the ethnographic staff focused their efforts on presenting exhibits of the Pacific Coast, the Plains, the Arctic, and the Eastern Woodlands. In 1991, I was appointed as a full-time curator of Plateau ethnology, and began work on an exhibit of Teit's collections, to be called *Earthline and Morning Star*.[40]

Early in the project, the Nlaka'pamux Tribal Council in Lytton and the Nicola Valley Tribal Council in Merritt were asked if their communities would help develop an exhibit on traditional and contemporary clothing. The leadership in both councils welcomed a museum/community partnership and assigned local co-ordinators. Meetings were arranged between the curator and the elders as well as with seamstresses, jewellery makers and tanners who had a special interest in the exhibit. During the next four years members of the community and I worked together throughout every stage of the process, from initial research and selection of objects for display, to planning and celebrating the opening of the exhibit.

An important element of the process was to bring the community and the museum closer together by sharing information. Three elders, Mabel Joe, Mandy Brown and Theresa Albert, visited the museum to study the collections and to make the initial selections for the exhibit. These women, experienced basket makers, deer hide tanners and seamstresses, reviewed the collections

3.5 Mandy Brown, Mabel Joe and Theresa Albert working with the collections. Photograph by Steve Darby, Canadian Museum of Civilization.

and shared their knowledge of their culture and community history. The discussions were videotaped and copies of the tapes were made available to the Nlaka'pamux communities. Copies of the documentation of artifacts and slides illustrating the objects were sent to the communities' tribal offices.

Meetings were held with the elders, tribal council staff, and the general community in British Columbia where I presented slide shows to provide background information on the Museum and objects in the collection. As the exhibit developed, the storyline and ideas for the exhibit's design were discussed with the community. The final design was presented at a public gathering in Lytton where the curator and the elders, who had worked as members of the advisory committee, responded to questions and concerns about the content, display, and representation.

At different stages of the development of the exhibition, community representatives visited the Museum to view the collections and talk with the staff. Two Nlaka'pamux educators, Jean York and Trudy Dunstan, met with members of the Muscum's educational department. Nathan and Rhoda Spinks, elders from Lytton, Jean York, a teacher and member of the Cook's Ferry Tribal Council and Mandy Jimmie, cultural officer with the Nicola Valley Tribal Association, served on the exhibit planning team for the overall show and in particular for the Nlaka'pamux component.

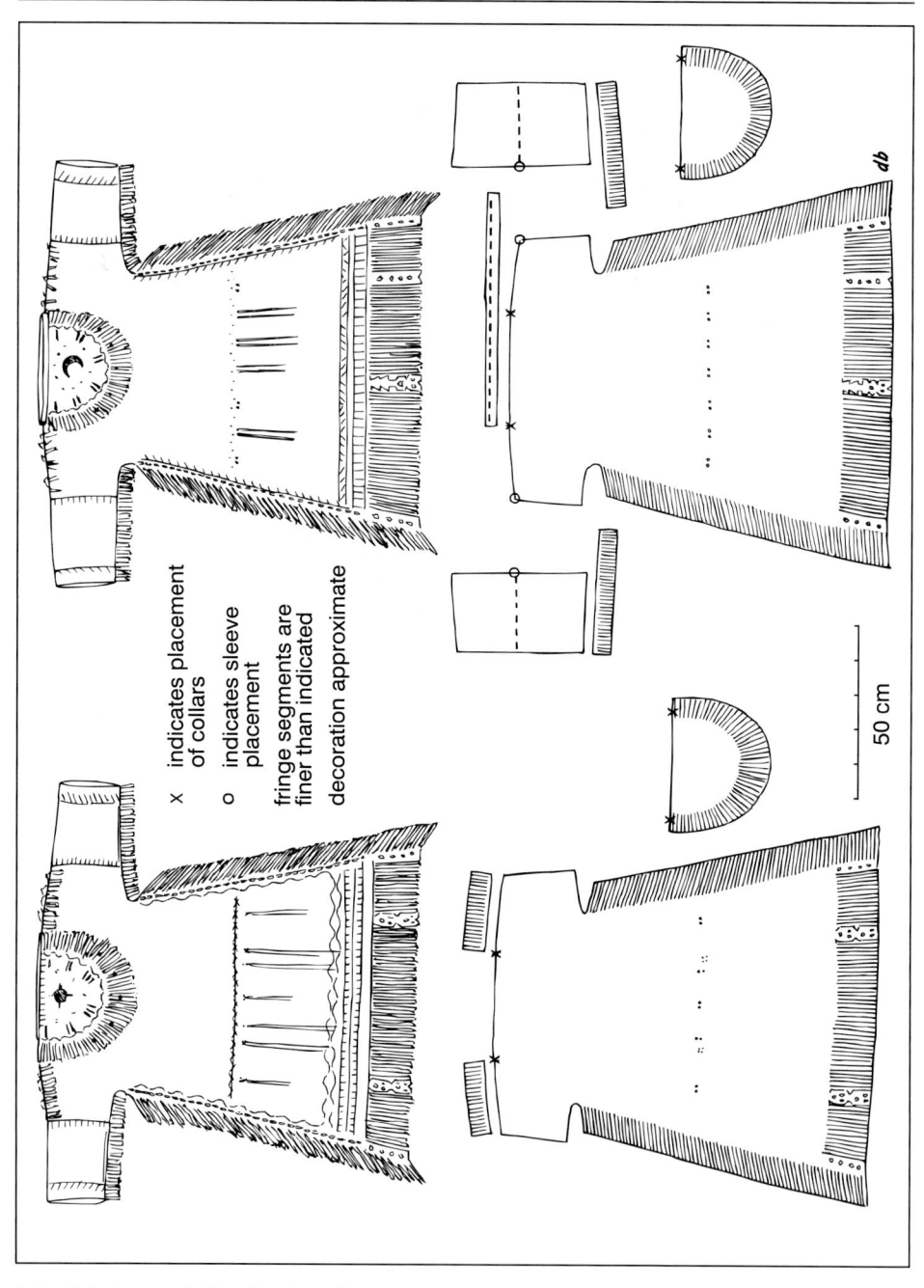

3.6 Cut of woman's deerskin dress. Canadian Museum of Civilization II-C-626.

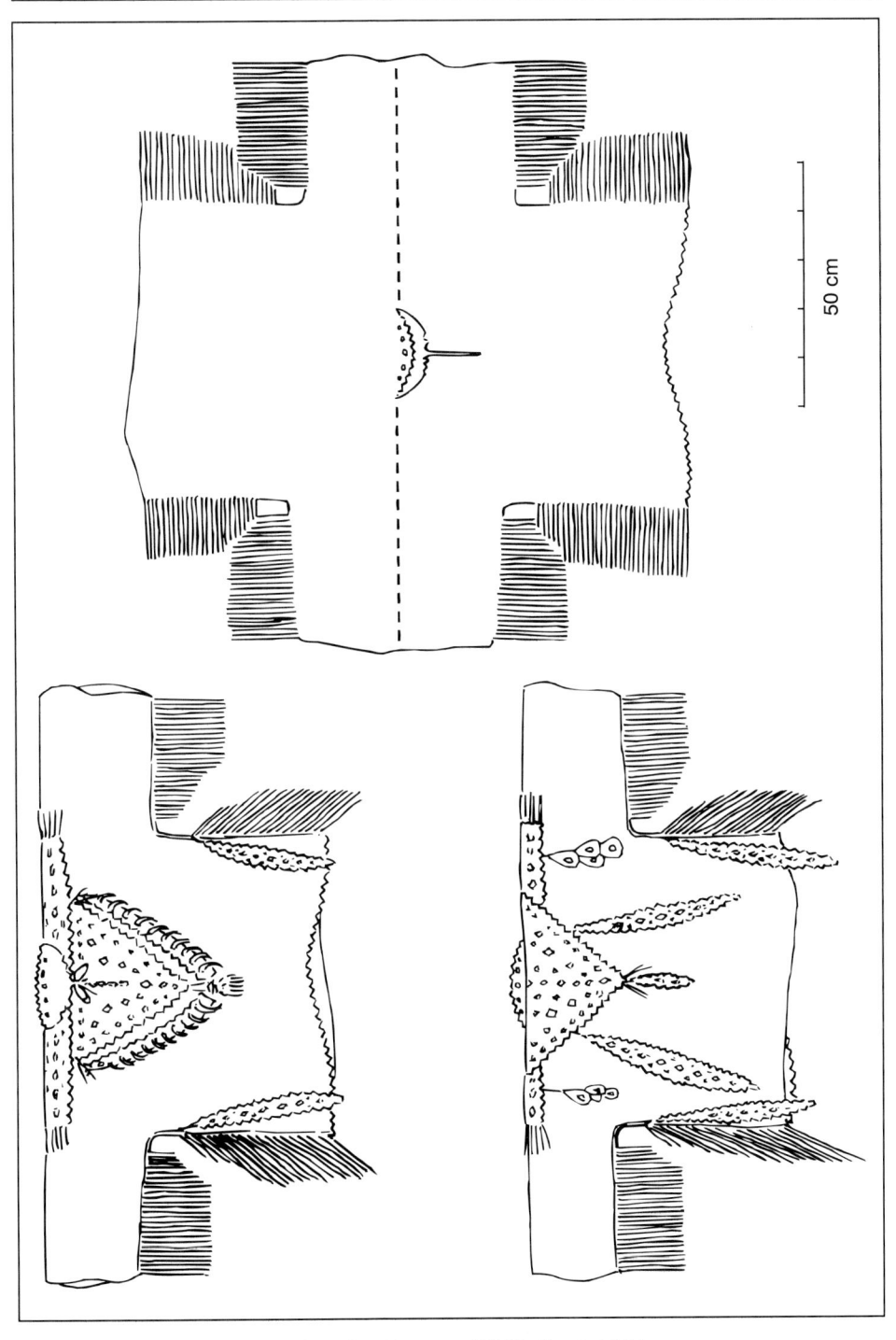

Fascinating Challenges

3.7 Cut of man's deerskin shirt. Canadian Museum of Civilization II-C-354.

Concerns were raised, during the discussions, about the handling and display of certain artifacts. Some items of clothing were considered to be sacred, and needed special treatment. These included objects associated with shamans or with puberty rituals. Clothing painted with images seen during vision experiences was also considered to be objects of power. The elders requested that women's material be handled and conserved by the Museum's female staff and men's material be treated by male conservators and preparators. The elders also requested that men's and women's clothing be displayed in separate cases, and in different exhibit areas. Objects associated with puberty or shamans needed to be shown in areas slightly removed or sheltered from a rapid flow of visitors. Together, the curator and the Native advisors developed procedures and a storyline that provided solutions to these concerns.

The Nlaka'pamux leadership applied for funds to bring elders, young people and the advisors to celebrate the opening of the exhibit. A small stipend from the Canadian Museum of Civilization helped to make the trip to the museum affordable for many people. In a private ceremony before the opening, Mabel Joe asked her family and friends to sing her song to honour everyone's work. Chief Byron Spinks, the Chief for the Lytton Band, and Chief David Walkem of the Cooks Ferry Band spoke at a formal public opening. The years of shared effort came to fruition in a public forum that was a source of pride for members of the Nlaka'pamux community as well as for the Museum staff.

The work for the exhibit stimulated a number of other projects during this period. Shannon Kilroy, a Nlaka'pamux seamstress, used Dorothy Burnham's drawings of the construction and ornamentation of traditional buckskin clothing to incorporate elements of Plateau materials and style into her contemporary clothing designs. The museum and the community worked together to design a small travelling exhibit of Nlaka'pamux clothing. Sturdy boxes were constructed with pullout units, to display objects from the Canadian Museum of Civilization as well as local Nlaka'pamux collections. These boxes were exhibited at the Siska and Cooks Ferry First Nations communities.

Recreating Traditional Material Culture- Late Twentieth Century

New artifacts were needed to exhibit the themes of continuity and change in Nlaka'pamux clothing. Examples of contemporary buckskin dresses, shirts, moccasins, and gloves were purchased or commissioned from skin tanners and seamstresses living in Lytton, Spences Bridge, and Merritt. However, a similar effort to acquire examples of contemporary fibre garments was unsuccessful. Although several elders continue to spin hemp threads and remembered how to prepare willow for weaving, the knowledge needed to weave willow and hemp threads and shape the fabric for woven clothing appeared to have been lost.

Fascinating Challenges

3.8 Silver-willow bark cape and headdress.
Canadian Museum of Civilization 94-60.

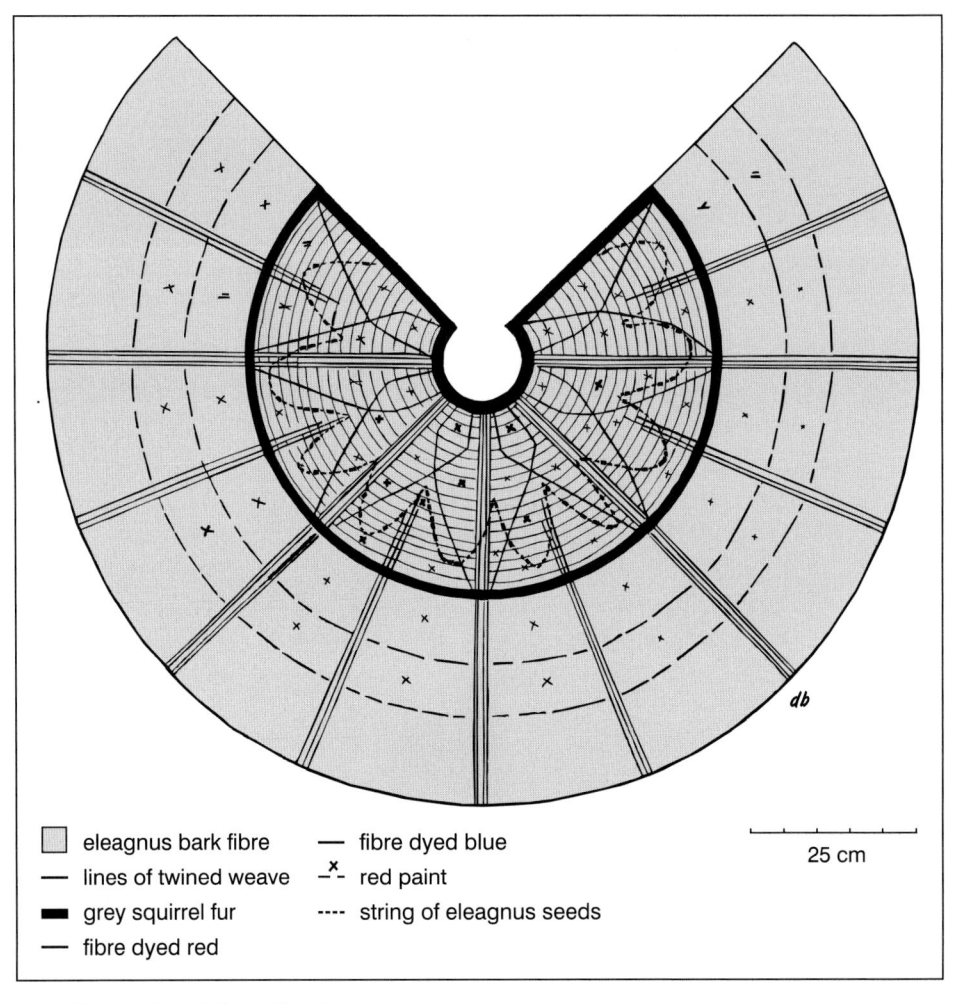

- eleagnus bark fibre
- lines of twined weave
- grey squirrel fur
- fibre dyed red
- fibre dyed blue
- red paint
- string of eleagnus seeds

25 cm

3.9 Construction of silver-willow bark cape.
Canadian Museum of Civilization II-C-604.

To regain the missing information, Dorothy Burnham analyzed several Nlaka'pamux willow and cedar bark garments in the Canadian Museum of Civilization collection. She produced detailed drawings illustrating the techniques of twined weaving, along with methods of adding new warp threads, and weft turning at the selvages. A woman's decorated willow bark cape served as the model for the reproduction project.

To find a weaver to recreate the cape, the curator asked David Walkem, Chief of the Cooks Ferry Band Council at Spences Bridge, for assistance. He recommended Mary Anderson, an elder in his community, who knew how to spin hemp and prepare the willow, along with Pearl Hewitt who was interested in learning these techniques. The detailed drawings of the decorated willow bark cape prepared by Dorothy Burnham, served as a guide for the weaving and decoration. Mary Anderson wove a small replica of the cape.

Fascinating Challenges

3.10 Mary Anderson presenting model silver-willow bark cape to community, Lytton. Photograph by Leslie Tepper.

Pearl Hewitt wove a full size cape and recorded the various stages of gathering, preparing and weaving the materials. Her report of this project, illustrated with selected photographs, is an important contribution to this volume. These weavings were formally presented to the Canadian Museum of Civilization at two celebrations, one at Spences Bridge and the other at Lytton, in honour of the artists and their work. Both capes were displayed in the exhibit, *Earthline and Morningstar*.

The willow bark cape project stimulated interest in traditional weaving among other Nlaka'pamux communities. The Canadian Museum of Civilization and the Lytton Band Council co-sponsored a well-attended cedar bark-weaving workshop organized by Nathan and Rhoda Spinks. Mandy Brown wove a cedar bark cape that was also included in the exhibit. Shortly after the opening of the exhibit, Mandy Jimmie obtained a number of government grants to teach weaving and spinning to people living on the different reserves in the Nicola Valley. The workshop participants researched museum collections, and also used published materials, photographs, and Dorothy Burnham's drawings. This group has revitalized the skills of fabric construction and produced capes, hats, mat tipis, and wall hangings for a new generation. Today's weavers are offering items for use or sale that are equal to, and in some cases exceed, the craftsmanship of objects purchased by Teit a hundred years ago. The artists have also expanded the traditional forms by making painted mat wall hangings for the church and band offices and constructing summer hats from tule reeds. Willow bark capes have been made for graduation ceremonies and weddings.

3.11 Summer hats made from tule reeds. Hat with tall crown made by Maggie Shuter. Hat with low crown made by Sarah McLeod.
Canadian Museum of Civilization II-C-921 and II-C-922.

Conclusion

At the end of the nineteenth century, James Teit with the assistance of people in the Nlaka'pamux community recorded ethnographic information, songs, and stories. Teit's commissions recreated objects that had almost faded from the community's cultural memory. His intent was to preserve the knowledge of a way of life that seemed to be disappearing with the passing of the elders. However, as young people viewed the making of traditional objects and listened to old stories and songs, the cultural knowledge of a community was transferred to a new generation.

At the end of the twentieth century, the Museum and the Native community came together once again to view these wondrous collections and build a way to remember and celebrate Nlaka'pamux culture. Just as Teit's work helped to renew and preserve traditional knowledge into the twentieth century, so the Nlaka'pamux people, by drawing on the knowledge of the elders as well as the resources of the Museum, have renewed and preserved their knowledge for the new millennium.

Endnotes

1. The Nlaka'pamux Nation is also known as the Thompson Indians.
2. See for example Ames 1990; Winter 1995.
3. Smith 1989:71.
4. Banks 1970:48.
5. Smith 1989:71
6. Boas' fieldwork was funded by the British North American Anthropology Association (BNAAA), by the American Museum of Natural History, and by the Canadian Government.
7. Rohner 1969:139.
8. Teit to Boas, Oct 6, 1894 American Museum of Natural History.
9. These museums are: the American Museum of Natural History, New York; The Field Museum, Chicago; The Peabody Harvard Museum, Cambridge; The Canadian Museum of Civilization, Ottawa; and the Royal British Columbia Museum, Victoria. A smaller collection, probably put together by Teit, was sold by C.F. Newcombe to the Smithsonian in Washington. This latter collection lacks the documentation and support material usually provided by Teit.
10. For a study of Teit's other activities see Wickwire 1979, 1993 and Campbell 1994.
11. Stocking 1983:74.
12. Rohner 1969: xxix.
13. Teit's status has variously been defined as a "valuable assistant" (Boas 1898:112), a field technician (Smith 1959), and an "anthropologist in the most meaningful sense of the term" (Campbell 1994:footnote 4). Correspondence between Sapir and Boas and particularly between Sapir and Teit suggests that Teit was considered a researcher of equal standing with other museum staff. Indeed, Sapir's initial offer

of employment was for a full time position similar to that held by Harlan Smith and C. Marius Barbeau.

14. Sapir to Teit, Dec. 21, 1912 Canadian Museum of Civilization.
15. Teit to Boas, April 3, 1895 American Museum of Natural History.
16. Teit to Boas, Feb 20, 1897 American Museum of Natural History.
17. Teit to Boas, Oct. 29, 1894 American Museum of Natural History.
18. Teit to Boas Dec. 6, 1894 American Museum of Natural History.
19. Teit to Boas, Feb 1, 1897 American Museum of Natural History.
20. Sapir to Teit Nov 12, 1912 Canadian Museum of Civilization.
21. Teit to Sapir, Dec 4, 1912 Canadian Museum of Civilization.
22. The collection of the American Museum of Natural History is approximately 900 objects; the Canadian Museum of Civilization collection is approximately 800; Peabody Harvard collection is approximately 500; and the Royal British Columbia Provincial Museum has approximately 200 pieces.
23. Teit to Boas, Feb. 28, 1895 American Museum of Natural History.
24. Teit to Boas, 1898 American Museum of Natural History.
25. For a review of Teit's work in the north among the Tahtlan see Fenn, (1997).
26. Teit to Sapir, May 17, 1912 Canadian Museum of Civilization.
27. Teit to Sapir, Feb 17, 1913 Canadian Museum of Civilization.
28. Sapir to McConnell, Oct 13, 1914 Canadian Museum of Civilization.
29. Teit to Sapir Feb. 2, 1915 Canadian Museum of Civilization.
30. Sapir to Teit, Feb 9, 1915 Canadian Museum of Civilization.
31. Teit to Willoughby, March 2, 1915 Canadian Museum of Civilization.
32. Wickwire also notes a similar lack of names of the Teit's informants for the ethnographic record. She suggests this anonymity and the use of the past tense throughout the text was Boas' preference (1998:207). For a discussion of Boas' thinking on the role of the individual artist see Jacknis 1992.
33. Teit to Willoughby, April 18, 1915 Canadian Museum of Civilization.
34. Teit to Willoughby, April 18, 1915 Canadian Museum of Civilization.
35. Teit 1898:271.
36. Tepper 1994.
37. Teit to Sapir Feb 2, 1915 Canadian Museum of Civilization.
38. See Amaron 2000.
39. Teit to Sapir Feb 24, 1917, Canadian Museum of Civilization.
40. The exhibit, on Nlaka'pamux clothing was part of a larger exhibition titled *Threads of the Land: Clothing Traditions from Three Indigenous Cultures* co-curated by Judy Thompson, Judy Hall and Leslie Tepper.

Works Cited

Amaron, Beryl
    2000 More than Useable Tools: Towards an Appreciation of Nle'kemx Fibre Technology as a Significant Expression of Culture. Masters Thesis University of Northern British Columbia.

Ames, Michael M.
> 1990 Cultural Empowerment and Museums: Opening Up Anthropology through Collaboration. In *Objects of Knowledge,* ed. Susan Pearce, 158-173 London: The Athlone Press.

Banks, Judith, Judd
> 1970 Comparative Biographies of Two British Columbia Anthropologists: Charles Hill-Tout and James A. Teit. Masters Thesis, University of British Columbia.

Boas, Franz
> 1898 The Jesup North Pacific Expedition. In *A Franz Boas Reader: The Shaping of American Anthropology 1883-1911,* ed. George W. Stocking Jr., 107-116 Chicago: University of Chicago Press.

Boas, Franz
> 1923 Obituary of James Teit. *Journal of American Folklore* 36:102-103.

Campbell, Peter
> 1994 'Not as a White Man, Not as a Sojouner' James A. Teit and the Fight for Native Rights in British Columbia, 1884-1922. *left history* 2(2): 37-57.

Fenn, Catherine J.
> 1997 Life History of a Collection: The Tahltan Materials Collected by James A. Teit. *Museum Anthropology* 20(3):72-91.

Jacknis, Ira
> 1992 'The Artist Himself': The Salish Basketry Monograph and the Beginnings of a Boasian Pradigm. In *The Early Years of Native American Art History,* ed. Janet Catherine Berlo, Seattle: 134-161 University of Washington Press.

Rohner, Ronald
> 1969 *The Ethnography of Franz Boas.* Chicago:University of Chicago Press.

Smith, Marion W.
> 1959 Boas' Natural History Approach to Field Methods. In *The Anthropology of Franz Boas,* ed. Walter Goldschmidt, Memoirs #89, American Anthropology Association, vol. 61, no. 5, pt. 2.

Smith, Jessie Ann
> 1989 W*idow Smith of Spences Bridge.* As told to J. Meryl Campbell and Audrey Ward, Sonotek Publishing.

Stocking, George W. Jr.
> 1983 "The Ethnographer's Magic: Fieldwork in British Anthropology from Tylor to Malinowski." In *Observers Observed: Essays on Ethnographic Fieldwork. History of Anthropology,* ed. George W. Stocking, Jr. vol. 1, 70-120. Madison: University of Wisconsin Press.

Teit, James A.
> 1898 Letter to the Editor. *American Archaeologist* 2(10): 271.

Tepper, Leslie
> 1994 *Earthline and Morning Star: Nlaka'pamux Clothing Traditions.* Hull: Canadian Museum of Civilization.

Wickwire, Wendy
> 1979 'Jimmy Teit': Anthropologist of the People. *Nicola Valley Historical Quarterly* 2(2):4. Merritt, British Columbia.

1993 "Women in Ethnography: the Research of James A. Teit. *Ethnohistory* 40(4): 539-562.

1998 'We Shall Drink from the Stream and So Shall You': James A. Teit and Native Resistance in British Columbia, 1908-22. *The Canadian Historical Review* 79(2):199-236.

Winter, Barbara J.

1995 New Futures for the Past: Cooperation Between First Nations and Museums in Canada. *U.B.C. Law Review* 29-36.

The Making of a Traditional Nlaka'pamux Silver-Willow Cape

Pearl Hewitt
Project Co-ordinator And Crafts Person

Acknowledgements

I would like to think the following people for their assistance in the competing of this cape project

Project Director (Canadian Museum of Civilization)
Leslie Tepper

Elders: (My Advisors)
Theresa Albert
Mary Anderson
Phyllis Orr

Helpers: (Gathering of Materials)
Oliver Hewitt
Vincent Wilson
Craig Sturdivant
Donna Charlie
Edith Frye
Rose Marie Charlie   (3 years old)
Morris Wilson Jr.   (4 years old)
Donovan Charlie   (5 years old)

Chiefs & Council and Staff of Cook's Ferry Band
(Encouragement & Support]
Chief David Walkem
Councillor Jean York

Councillor Rose Spence
Bunnie Billy
Hazel Billy
Esther Darlington
John Jones
Jack Miller
Clarence Walkem

Table of Contents

1. Acknowledgements
2. Materials Used
3. Gathering of Materials
4. Preparation of Materials
5. Gathering of Preparation Time
6. Making of the Cape

Materials Used

1. Silver-willow Bark (/q'wu'ys::)
2. Silver-willow Seeds
3. Indian Hemp (s/p'ec'-n)
4. Buckskin ('es/k' l::)
5 Dyes

Gathering of Materials

Silver-willow Bark

The silver-willow bark was gathered between Spences Bridge and Merritt in the interior of British Columbia alongside the Nicola River in September and October of 1993.

The largest and longest silver-willow bushes were selected. One or two stems were cut from each bush. Side branches were cut off, the bark stripped off in strips as long as possible, then set aside until they are ready to prepare.

Silver-willow Seeds

The seeds were gathered in the same locations and at the same time as a silver-willow bark.

3.12 Pearl Hewitt presenting the finished cape to the community, Spences Bridge. Photograph by Chief David Walkem.

Indian Hemp

Indian hemp was also gathered between Spences Bridge and Merritt in the interior British Columbia alongside the banks of the Nicola River. It was gathered in November 1993.

The longest possible stems were selected and cut. The top part of each stem was removed and the remainder of the stem was trimmed. They were then bundled up until they were to be used.

3.13 Gathering the materials. Rose Marie Charlie stripping silver-willow bark near Spences Bridge. Photograph by Chief David Walkem.

Buckskin

Prepared buckskin [deer hide] was purchased from a Native Elder at the Kamloops Annual Pow-wow.

Dyes

Commercial dyes were used - red and blue Dylon dry dye.

Preparation of Materials

Silver-willow Bark

Using the silver-willow bark collected, the outer bark was stripped off, leaving the inner bark in strips in the longest possible lengths. Using a kitchen paring knife, pass the inner bark over the knife to separate the bark into four or more layers. The layers of bark are then stored until ready to use or cut into desired lengths.

Making of the Cape

It was with great honour that I accepted the task of making this Nlaka'pamux silver-willow cape. The materials used in this project are silver-willow bark and Indian Hemp.

When I went to gather the silver-willow bark, silver-willow seeds and Indian Hemp, I had the help of three adults and three young children.

Most of the materials were gathered and prepared before I actually started making the cape.

Before undertaking the making of the adult size cape, I made a doll-sized cape and skirt using similar materials and procedures. The doll model was 12 inches in height.

I started to work on making the skirt for the doll and it took me six hours to complete it. The over-all size of the skirt was 8 inches in circumference and 6 and 1/2 inches in length. The woven part of the skirt measured 3 and 1/4 inches from the waist down.

I worked on the miniature cape and it took 6 and 1/2 hours to complete. The over-all size of the cape was 13 inches wide and 4 inches in length. The woven part of the cape measured 2 and 3/4 inches from the neck down. As a finishing touch to the cape, I added silver-willow seeds as decor around the neck area and down the front of it.

Measurements of the Actual Cape

Neck area: 25 and 1/2 inches in circumference

Bottom Hem: 75 inches in circumference

Length: From the top hem to edge of fringe - 30 inches

Woven portion - 16 inches from top down

Fringe portion - 14 inches

Weaving: Distance between stitched rows - approximately 1 inch or two fingers apart

Details: The construction started with 10 vertical rows of red coloured silver-willow with 6 groups of strands to each one and 9 vertical rows of natural colour silver-willow with 5 groups of strands to each one.

The top part of the cape was then woven with two lengths of buckskin measuring 80 inches by 1/8 inch, another 70 inches by 1/8 inch of lacing was used as an inside support to hang the cape. Another buckskin lacing was used below the top one to secure the top hem.

Buckskin

From the prepared buckskin, cut lacing 1/8 to 1/4 inch wide to desired lengths.

Dyes

Dye the desired amount of silver-willow blue and red. It is easier to use prepared dye rather than soaking the material for three weeks or more.

Gathering and Preparation Time

Silver-willow Bark – approximately 7 days to gather and prepare for use.

Silver-willow Seeds – approximately 3 days to gather and prepare for use.

Indian Hemp – approximately 2 weeks to gather and prepare for use.

Cape – the cape was completed between November 23, 1993 and January 24, 1994. The work took place on 25 separate days totalling 200 hours.

3.16 Pearl Hewitt and Carolyn Lytton preparing the silver-willow warp threads. Photograph by Chief David Walkem.

Indian hemp [prepared damp]

The raw material was spray-soaked or soaked in a large container until the raw material was soaked through. It was then split in half lengthwise. The outer fibrous part is peeled off by putting the end of the stem in the mouth and peeling back the outer part in strips as long as possible in length. The strips are then hung in a cool dry place until they are ready to use. To make into thread, prepare the fibre by using a knife and passing it over it until the outer layer breaks away, leaving a soft fibrous thread. Dampen the fibre and rub it down along the leg. Several pieces are prepared in this manner to have on hand later. Two-ply hemp is made by joining two single strands together and rubbing them down along the leg. Repeat the process and join other strands to make it longer. The hemp is then set aside until needed.

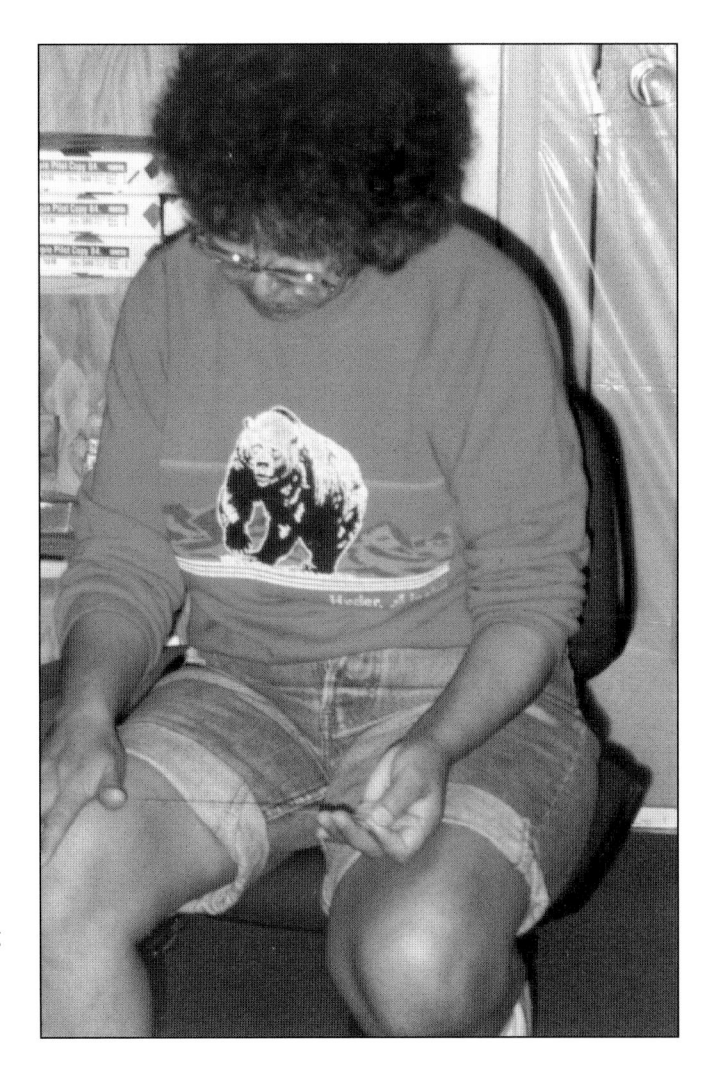

3.15 Pearl Hewitt spinning hemp thread. Photograph by Chief David Walkem.

Silver-willow Seeds

The seeds were put into a plastic or cloth bag. The seeds in the bag were rubbed around by hand or rolled back and forth on the table until the outer coating is crushed. The seeds were then removed from the bag and washed in a soapy water mix until clean. They were then dried and stored until ready to use or soaked and strung on to thread and stored until needed.

Indian hemp [prepared dry]

The hemp was split in half lengthwise. It was then stepped on until the inner stem was crushed. The inner part of the stem was then peeled off. The outer fibrous part is either stored or prepared by using a knife and passing the fibre over it until the outer layer breaks away, leaving a soft fibrous thread. To make into thread, the fibre is dampened and rubbed among the skin of the leg. This same process is done to several pieces to have on hand to use later. Two-ply hemp is made by joining two single strands together and rubbing down along the leg. The process is repeated and other stands are joined to make it longer.

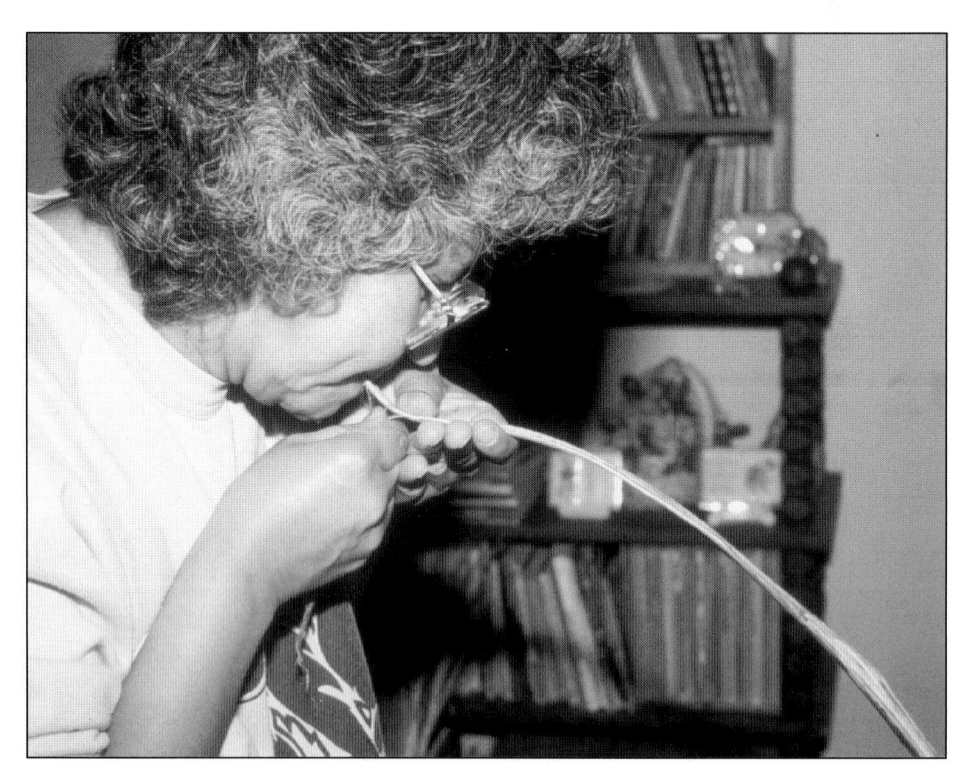

3.14 Hemp preparation. Pearl Hewitt removing the outer bark of the hemp stem. Photograph by Chief David Walkem.

Fascinating Challenges

The third row of stitching was started with twine Indian Hemp and it was woven straight across the cape.

To the next row of stitching 2 groups of natural silver-willow strands were added to each vertical row of natural colour in order to start a flare to the cape.

To the fifth row of stitching a vertical row of red was added to the centre part of the natural silver-willow and two groups of natural colour were also added.

To the next row of stitching, red was added and it was turned into two vertical rows. The following stitched row was done without adding any more material.

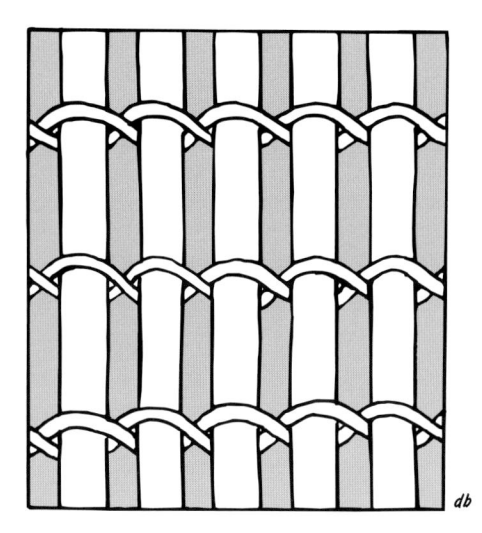

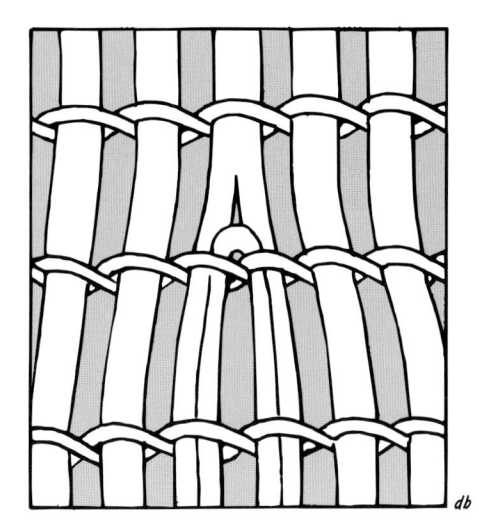

3.17 Twined weave.

3.18 Twined weave with one added warp.

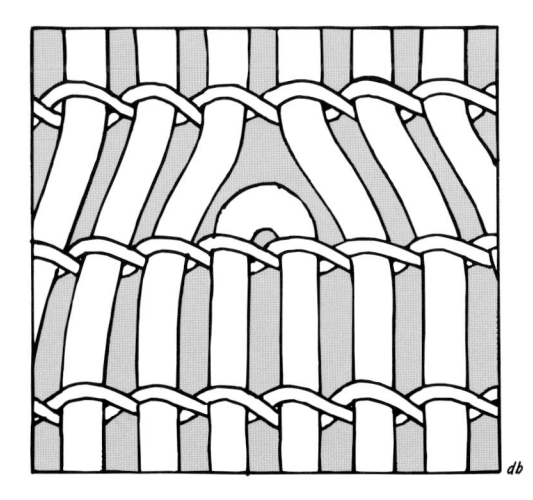

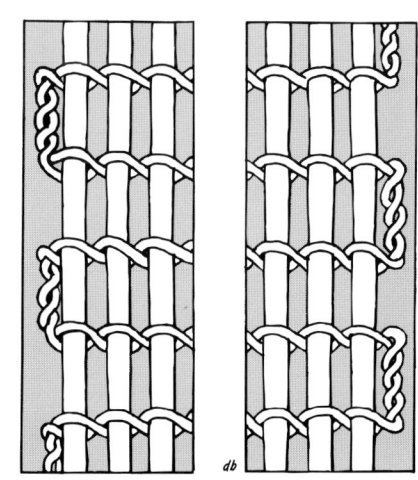

3.19 Twined weave with two added warps.

3.20 Twined weave, weft turning.

The Making of a Traditional Nlaka'pamux Silver-Willow Cape

To the seventh row of stitching blue coloured silver-willow was added to the centre part of the natural silver-willow. From here the design on the cape is starting to take shape into a floral pattern and the flare of the cape is widening.

To the next two rows, Indian Hemp was again added and vertical rows were added as needed.

In the tenth row, buckskin lacing was used instead of hemp to add more character to the cape.

For the next three rows, Indian Hemp was again used and vertical rows were added as needed.

For the finishing touch to the bottom hem, two rows of buckskin lacing were woven in. Also added was a string of silver-willow seeds as decor to the top part of the cape.

The overall size of the cape is 30 inches in length and measures 70 inches in width at the hem.

3.21 Children's capes made by Pearl Hewitt. Left to right: Chief David Walkem, Mandy Jimmie, Pearl Hewitt and Vincent Wilson. Photograph by Leslie Tepper.

The Observant Eye:
Analyzing Nlaka'pamux Woven Mats

Leslie Tepper

With this project I have not been making things. There are other people doing the fine quillwork, or weaving. I am purely an observer...But it has been a joy to observe.

Dorothy K. Burnham[1]

It is often said that museums contain treasures of the past. Their storeroom shelves are filled with objects of human ingenuity and artistic imagination. Only a small percentage of a museum's holdings, however, are selected for exhibition, highlighted in catalogues or analyzed in professional publications. This paper presents a group of objects in the collection of the Canadian Museum of Civilization that have not yet been exhibited, nor attracted scholarly interest. To the observant eye, however, these objects provide interesting information about Aboriginal weaving at the end of the nineteenth century.

The museum treasure under study is a group of fibre mats made by Nlaka'pamux weavers living on the British Columbia Plateau between 1885 and 1922. In appearance they are plain or woven with colours that are now muted. The designs are uncomplicated, but attractive. Like many simple objects, woven mats performed multiple functions in a variety of settings. Mat covered tipis provided shelter from rain or hot sun during summer months. Rain capes and women's skirts were woven mats with strings added to tie the garment around the shoulder or waist. Twined mats placed on the floor of houses or on the ground offered clean sleeping surfaces, eating areas or workspaces. When folded and sewn along the base and one side, the mats could be transformed into utilitarian bags.

The Observant Eye: Analyzing Nlaka'pamux Woven Mats

3.22 Floor mat made of rushes and silver-willow bark. Woven using tabby and twine techniques. Canadian Museum of Civilization II-C-333.

By the late nineteenth and early twentieth centuries, mats and mat making technology were in decline. Bark and hemp mats were being replaced by other textiles, such as wool and cotton cloth and rag rugs. In contrast to the popular decorated basketry from this region, fibre mats did not attract the interest of tourists and collectors. As a result, few examples of Nlaka'pamux mats are held in museum collections or are found in people's homes today. The Canadian Museum of Civilization is fortunate to have more than 50 examples of Nlaka'pamux rush, reed, and silver-willow[2] bark mats. The majority of these are tipi mats that were used for traditional summer housing. The remaining mats may have been purchased to illustrate a variety of uses, weaves, and decorative elements.[3]

This paper presents an overview of the Canadian Museum of Civilization mat collection. It also offers a detailed analysis of the weaving techniques by incorporating several worksheets prepared by Dorothy Burnham. These worksheets are valuable examples of her meticulous and systematic analysis of material culture. Researchers may find them to be a useful template for recording the specific structures of woven objects. In presenting the detailed artifact analysis, it is hoped that scholars will supplement this report with studies of woven mats in other collections.

The Project

Analysis of Nlaka'pamux mats began in 1994, shortly before the opening of an exhibit on Nlaka'pamux clothing traditions.[4] An important component of this exhibit and its associated publication[5] was the study of garments woven from silver-willow bark, cedar, and hemp. The collection holds several capes that James Teit documented as rain capes and as mats. He noted:

> *Few people had rain capes excepting amongst the Utamkt (people living below Lytton). Among the Upper Ntlak, (people living above Lytton) usually ordinary mats of various kinds were thrown over the head and shoulders by people who had to go abroad in very wet weather. These were held in position with the hands or fastened with strings or pins of wood, etc. However some people of both sexes (some say only a few) had real rain capes woven of bark, well shaped and trimmed with fur. Some of them had long fringes and they varied in length from mere coverings for the shoulders to cloaks reaching below the waist.*[6]

I was interested in this dual-purpose clothing and household object, and extended the analysis of weft-twined garments to mats.

At the same time the research project was getting underway at the museum, the Nlaka'pamux community was also beginning to study traditional woven materials. Mandy Jimmie, the Cultural Officer at the Nicola Valley Tribal

Association, had obtained a grant to recreate a mat tipi. During the production process, people in the community would become skilled in identifying, gathering and preparing the raw materials, and in spinning, weaving, and constructing a summer dwelling. The participants in this project thus became researchers, ethnobotanists, spinners, weavers, and architects.[7]

The Canadian Museum of Civilization researchers and people involved in the community project found opportunities to work together. Mandy Jimmie and I visited elders living on several reserves near Merritt to discuss their memories of mat makers and mat types. Information on woven material in the museum's collection and copies of Dorothy's drawings were sent to the project participants. Mandy spent time at the museum studying and photographing the hemp and fibre artifacts. Chief Gordon Antoine from Coldwater also visited the museum and discussed mats and materials. While working on the weaving analysis and on the Athabaskan and Woodlands quillwork projects, Dorothy responded to requests for information on tumplines and twined baskets and drafted the construction of a small twined basket.

The primary focus of the Canadian Museum of Civilization project, however, was to analyze Nlaka'pamux mats, made of rush, reed, silver-willow bark, and hemp fibres. Dorothy studied a number of mats and drew the starting and finishing edges, selvages, and designs. These drawings were a continuation of an earlier study that illustrated twining techniques used for several clothing items (see Figures 3.17-20). Sixteen new drawings are published here for the first time.

Nlaka'pamux Mats in Context

The Nlaka'pamux mats in the Canadian Museum of Civilization collection are part of an extensive material culture tradition of sewn and twined rush, reed and bark fabrics found throughout North America. As Holmes noted in his 1896 study of prehistoric textiles in eastern North America:

> *No class of articles of textile nature were more universally employed by the aborigines than mats... Mats are not so varied in form and characters as are baskets, but their uses were greatly diversified; they served for carpeting, seats, hangings, coverings, and wrappings, and they were extensively employed in permanent house construction, and for temporary or movable shelters.*[8]

Archaeological and historical data show an ancient and continuous use of twined weaving in western North America.[9] The people living in the Great Basin, south east of traditional Nlaka'pamux territory, used reeds and rushes to construct houses and boats. Their clothing, containers, and fishing nets were made from twined fibres.[10] To the north west of the British Columbia Plateau, the cultures of the Pacific Coast produced twined Chilkat and Raven's Tail blankets, basketry, hats, and cedar bark clothing.[11] Other Plateau communities (in what are now British Columbia, Washington, Oregon and Idaho) used sewn and twined fabrics to make mat tipis or tents, silver-willow clothing and a wide variety of bags, baskets, and mats.[12] Although the making of household mats and tule tipis has almost disappeared, twining technology has been revitalized in British Columbia with the resurgence of Coast Salish, Chilkat and Raven's Tail weaving.

Ethnographic and technical studies of weaving in British Columbia have focused primarily on basketry[13] and blankets.[14] While Nlaka'pamux ethnobotanical research on materials used in weaving has been fairly extensive,[15] there is little detailed information on the construction and use of mats.

3.23 Mat tipi. Photograph by James A. Teit, 1914.
Canadian Museum of Civilization 26628.

3.24 Taking down mat tipi. Photograph by James A.Teit, 1914. Canadian Museum of Civilization 27038.

The Collection

The majority of the Plateau artifacts in the Canadian Museum of Civilization were collected by James Teit. Edward Sapir, Director of the Anthropology Division of the Geological Survey of Canada, (now the Canadian Museum of Civilization), hired Teit in 1913 primarily to conduct fieldwork among British Columbia's Athabaskan communities. However, Teit continued to collect Nlaka'pamux artifacts, photographs[16] and wax cylinder recordings[17] until his death in 1922.[18] The artifact collection comprises approximately 700 objects which were commissioned or purchased primarily from communities near Lytton, Spences Bridge, and Merritt, British Columbia. Some of the objects may have been acquired prior to Teit's contract with the Survey, others were purchased during his period of museum employment, and a few were sent to the museum by his widow in 1925. The collection contains a broad range of styles of basketry, skin and fibre clothing, fishing and hunting equipment, stone, bone, and wood tools. It also includes samples of plants used for food, dyes and basketry. Table One shows the type and number of woven objects in the Canadian Museum of Civilization Nlaka'pamux collection.

Table One: Woven Objects in the Nlaka'pamux Collection

Type	No. in Collection
Baskets	234
Bags	61
Mats	51
Woven clothing[19]	18

Teit's documentation describes the materials, techniques of manufacture, and intended use of many of the objects. However, information about the people who made or owned the mats is lacking. It is not known whether they were young or old, men or women, or whether they were also basket makers.[20] Two references suggest that mats were still being woven at the end of the last century when Teit was collecting. In his ethnographic publication, *The Thompson Indians*, Teit generally described traditional activities in the past tense. His discussion of mat weaving, however, was couched in the present tense, suggesting that mats were still being woven.[21] A second indication is found in the documentation and invoices he submitted to the American Museum of Natural History for 1894 and 1895, where he provides the names of people from whom he purchased the mats, including his wife Antko.

> *No.11 - 996*
> *A tent-mat ... used for tenting purposes. They are called tule mats by the whites from the name of the material of which they are made. The sticks at each end are made of rose-brush wood, and the tules are sewn together with bark twine. This mat is of average length and height. Bought from Antko Dec. 26,1894.*
>
> *No. 23 - 1018*
> *A seip or ceip mat made of a grass called lauts or koutelt. This kind of mat was used as a floor or bed-mat by the Indians for covering the floors of their houses or lodges especially in those places where they sat down or slept. The grass is woven over thread. Paid Waxaninik May 15, 1895 $3.00.*
>
> *No.24 - 1019*
> *A seip mat made of young likelt of tule, the same material of which the tent mats like No.11 are made of (No.s 22 [a bag], 23 and 24 are still in common enough use among the tribe). Paid Wazinik June 2, 1895 $2.00.*

> *No.28 - 1023*
> *A sagebrush bark cloak or small blanket ... This kind was worn by the poorer Indians as a cloak around the shoulders. Ones made exactly the same but larger were used as blankets ... These cloaks were said to withstand rain very well and keep a person tolerably dry. The string used in binding the sagebrush bark is the usual varieties of bark twine ... Paid Waxamimik June 7, 1895 $2.50.*
>
> *No.31 - 1026*
> *A zalt or tablemat on which food was spread at mealtime ... Paid Naukawilix, Waxamimik and Kweltko June 7, 1895 ($5.25 for 29-31).[22]*

It is unclear whether these mats were owned or made by the people named. Teit commissioned objects for the American Museum of Natural History collection and these mats may have been woven for him. Some of the people listed on this invoice also may have made the mats in the Canadian Museum of Civilization collection.[23]

Nlaka'pamux Mats in the Canadian Museum of Civilization

As noted above, the Canadian Museum of Civilization's collection holds tent or tipi mats and other household or special use mats. They are woven using various combinations of rush, reed, or silver-willow bark strands as warp, and weft threads of silver-willow or hemp. Several mats are twined, some are woven, and others combine sewing and twining, or weaving and twining. This section of the paper gives an overview of the mats in the collection. It is followed by detailed discussion of the construction of tent mats and other household mats in the collection.

Mats in the Collection

Table Two lists the types of Nlaka'pamux mats in the Canadian Museum of Civilization collection and their sizes. Thirty-five mats were made for a summer tipi with two more used for the door coverings. The remaining thirteen mats are identified as floor or bed mats, one table or food mat, and several as general purpose or simply rush mats. The vagueness of the documentation suggests that these mats were interchangeable.

Table Two: Mat Sizes

Cat. No.	Object	Length m (ft)	With m (ft)
II-C-285	Tent Door	.80 (2.62)	1.52 (4.98)
II-C-299	Tent Door	.79 (2.59)	1.09 (3.57)
II-C-321	Shaman's Mat	.80 (2.62)	1.29 (4.23)
II-C-322	Rush mat	.96 (3.14)	1.27 (4.16)
II-C-323	Rush Mat	.82 (2.69)	1.77 (5.80)
II-C-324[24]	Bed Mat	.74 (2.42)	1.42 (4.65)
II-C-325	Table or Food Mat	.84 (2.75)	1.00 (3.28)
II-C-333	Bed or Floor Mat	.56 (1.83)	1.24 (4.06)
II-C-326	General Purpose	.62 (2.03)	.65 (2.13)
II-C-327	Floor mat	.63 (2.06)	.93 (3.05)
II-C-328	Mat	.72 (2.36)	.96 (3.14)
II-C-358	Skirt or Bag	.85 (2.78)	*
II-C-334	General purpose	.73 (2.39)	.89 (2.91)
See table 5	Tent mats	See table 5	See table 5

* width at waist .85m (2.78ft); width at hip 1.20m (3.93ft); width at knee .83m (2.7)

Materials

The Nlaka'pamux used tule (*Scirpus acutus*) and cattails (*Typha latifolia*) for mats to cover tipis, for household use, and even to make canoes or rafts.[25] Turner identifies Common Reed Grass (*Phragmites australis*) as another material used for mat making.[26] These plants grow in marshy areas and along the edges of lakes. They are particularly plentiful in the southern interior of British Columbia, and are found in Nlaka'pamux traditional territory near Douglas and Nicola lakes.

Rush mats were well adapted for housing, room dividers and mattresses. Peterson notes:

> *Rush may be rolled, folded, or crushed into a compact bundle without adverse effects. It seems likely that rush mats were preferred... because they were better adapted to survive the rigors of a semi-nomadic existence.*[27]

Ethel Isaac, a Nlaka'pamux elder, stated that cattail leaf mats were more suitable as plates for food, for sitting on, or for sleeping than tule mats. According to Mrs. Isaac, tule mats were made for drying berries or for tipi mats.[28] Mabel Joe, another Nlaka'pamux elder, noted that "thread made from q'wuys (silver-willow) fibres was often used instead of sp'ec'n (hemp) to sew cattail mats.[29] Table Three identifies the materials used in the mats under study.

Table Three: Mats by Material

Catalogue no.	Documented Use	Materials (Identified by Teit)
II-C-283-284; 286-298; 300-319	Tent Mats	Rushes; silver-willow or hemp twine
II-C-285	Tent Door	Rushes, silver-willow bark twine
II-C-299	Tent Door	Rushes, silver-willow bark twine
II-C-321	Shaman's Mat	Rushes
II-C-322	Rush mat	Rushes
II-C-323	Rush Mat	Rushes, grasses,
II-C-324	Bed Mat	Rushes
II-C-325	Table or Food Mat	Rushes, silver-willow bark twine
II-C-333	Bed or Floor Mat	Rushes; silver-willow bark twine
II-C-334	General purpose	Rushes; silver-willow bark twine
II-C-326	No identified purpose	Silver-willow bark, hemp twine, overlay of dyed silver-willow bark
II-C-327	Floor mat	Silver-willow bark; hemp twine
II-C-328	Mat	Silver-willow bark; hemp twine
II-C-358	Skirt or Bag	Silver-willow bark; hemp twine

Construction

A limited number of construction techniques are used on aboriginal mats across North America. In their study of mats woven near the Great Lakes, for example, Whiteford and Rogers note:

> *There are three basic types of mats, and the techniques of manufacture that distinguish them are the same as those recognized in basketry: sewing, weaving and twining.*[30]

Teit uses a similar division of sewn, woven and twined techniques in discussing Nlaka'pamux mat construction.

Sewing
*The Upper Thompson Indians make a variety of mats of tule
(Scirpus sp.) and bulrushes (Typha latifolia L.) which are woven
or sewed with twine made of the bark of Apocynum cannabinum L
… The end of the mat is made of rosewood. The reeds are strung
on bark strings, and held in place by other bark strings which
pass around them near their ends.*[31] *(See Figure 3.25)*

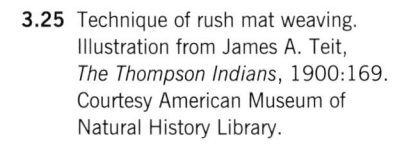

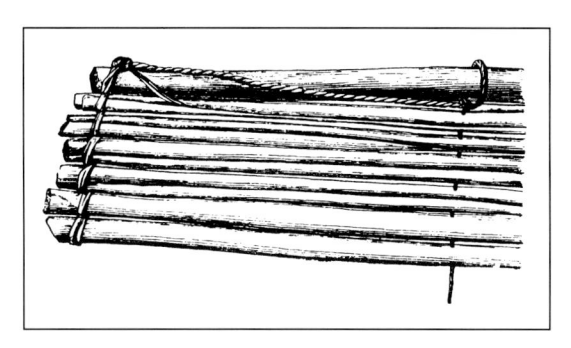

3.25 Technique of rush mat weaving. Illustration from James A. Teit, *The Thompson Indians*, 1900:169. Courtesy American Museum of Natural History Library.

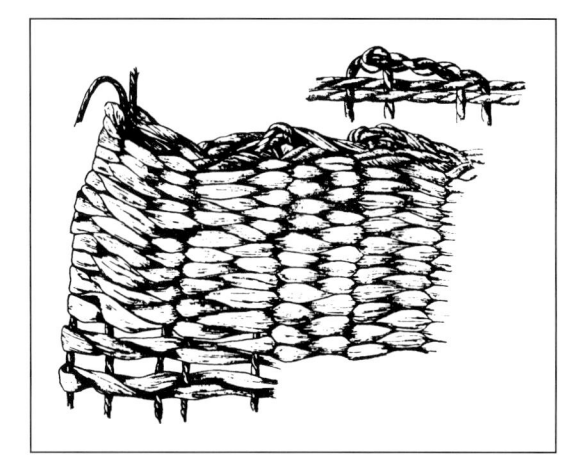

3.26 Technique of grass mat weaving. Illustration from James A. Teit, *The Thompson Indians*, 1900:169. Courtesy American Museum of Natural History Library.

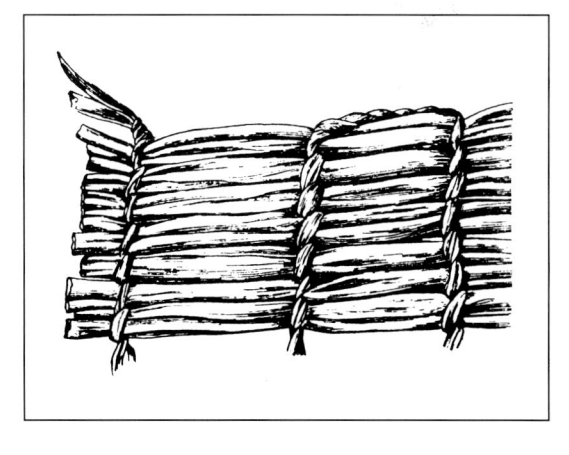

3.27 Technique of small rush mat weaving. Illustration from James A. Teit, *The Thompson Indians*, 1900:169. Courtesy American Museum of Natural History Library.

The Observant Eye: Analyzing Nlaka'pamux Woven Mats

Weaving
Mats made of young reeds and bulrushes, which are used to cover the floor of the lodge and as tablemats, are woven in a different manner. The selvage consists of a two-stranded bark string, which holds the warp. The latter is of a lighter two-stranded bark string, which is passed through the selvage string ... (see Figure 3.26). The grasses are woven into this groundwork as indicated in the same Figure. By using grass of different colors, (sic) patterns are obtained. Sometimes strands of wool are woven into the mat in place of grass. At the lower end the rushes are generally cut off. This kind of matting is also used for making pouches.[32]

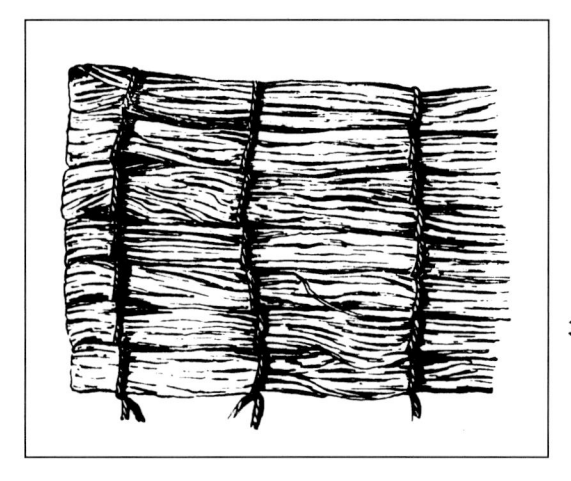

3.28 Technique of rush mat weaving. Illustration from James A. Teit, *The Thompson Indians*, 1900:169. Courtesy American Museum of Natural History Library.

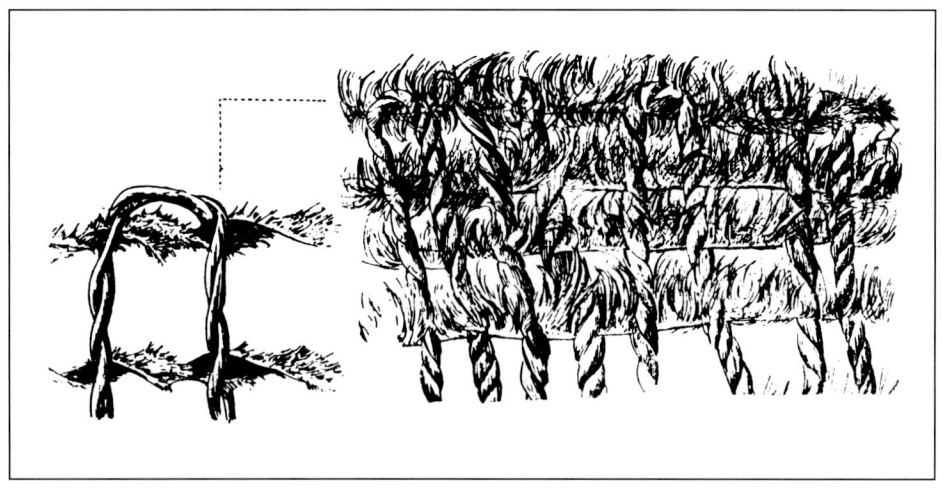

3.29 Technique of twining used for skin blankets. Illustration from James A. Teit, *The Thompson Indians*, 1900:169. Courtesy American Museum of Natural History Library.

> *Twining*
> *Some tablemats are woven in a still different manner. They are made of young tule or bulrushes, and tied with twine made of Apocynum cannabinum L. or Elaeagnus argentea Pursh. (See Figure 3.27) This method of weaving is identical with that used by the Coast Indians in making cedar bark blankets. It is also used by the Thompson Indian in weaving matting for the manufacture of bags, and in weaving blankets of twisted strips of rabbit-skin, pouches and socks of sagebrush.[33] (See Figure 3.28)*

The mats in the Canadian Museum of Civilization collection reflect these techniques. All of the tent mats are sewn. A number of household mats are twined and others are woven as warp-faced tabby. Only one mat in the study mixes techniques. It is woven, but has several rows of twining at the start and finishing edges. Table Four identifies the weaving techniques used.

Table Four: Object by Use and Weave

Catalogue no.	Use	Technical Analysis
II-C-283-284; 286-298; 300-319	Tent Mats	Sewn/Twined
II-C-285	Tent Door	Warp-faced tabby
II-C-299	Tent Door	Warp-faced tabby
II-C-321	Shaman's Mat	Warp-faced tabby
II-C-322	Rush mat	Warp-faced tabby
II-C-323	Rush Mat	Warp-faced tabby
II-C-324	Bed Mat	Warp-faced tabby
II-C-325	Table or Food Mat	Twined Weave
II-C-333	Bed or Floor Mat	Tabby/Twined
II-C-334	General purpose	Twined Weave
II-C-326	No identified purpose	Twined Weave
II-C-327	Floor mat	Twined Weave
II-C-328	Mat	Twined Weave
II-C-358	Skirt or Bag	Twined Weave

Sewn Tent Mats

From December to March, Nlaka'pamux families lived in a circular semi-subterranean house which was roofed with wooden rafters and insulated with dirt and sod.[34] Their summer dwelling, occupied during the remaining eight months, consisted of a pole structure with a mat or bark covering. Teit provided detailed descriptions of the construction of both the round and square summer houses. He notes,

> *In building circular lodges, which were larger than the square ones, a dozen or more long poles were placed some distance apart, with their butts upon the ground, outside the cleared space, forming a complete circle from fifteen to twenty feet in diameter. The poles were placed with their small ends toward the centre of the space, where they met and supported one another without being fastened together.*[35]

The square and rectangular lodges were similarly constructed of poles, but laid out to create lower tent-like roofs. The tent poles were tied with withes and supported by cross beams.

3.30 Tent mat. Canadian Museum of Civilization II-C-288.

Both types of structures were covered with mats or bark.

> *Over the bottom of this framework around the circumference, were spread long reed mats, measuring about five by twelve feet. Another row of mats, slightly overlapping the lower ones, was laid above these. And so on to within about three feet of the point where the poles met. The space above was left open for the exit of smoke and the admittance of light.*[36]

For protection from the cold, additional mats were laid around the base of the lodge. Layers of buffalo, elk, moose, or caribou skins would also be added, if needed, for greater insulation. Two small mats helped control the temperature in the lodge. One was attached to a long pole and covered the opening at the top of the tipi at night or in inclement weather. The other mat covered the doorway. This "was a space, three feet by five feet or less, ... over which hung a piece of mat, skin or blanket, a little larger than the hole, and stiffened at the lower end by a thin piece of stick."[37]

Teit published a single size for tipi mats (3.66 meters x 1½ meters or 12 feet x 5 feet). However in the Museum's collection, the length ranges from about 4½ meters (15 feet) to about 1½ meters (5 feet). (See Table Five.) The longest mats would cover the lower portion of the tipi, and shorter mats would be needed as the tipi narrowed toward the top. The width of each mat remains relatively stable varying from less than a meter to almost a meter and a half (a difference of 3 to 5 feet).

The construction of tent mats is simple and has been described by several authors.[38] Tule stems (about .5cm to .75cm in diameter) are laid in rows. The base of one stem is aligned with the tip of the next, providing a uniform thickness of stems for the length of the mat. The stems are then sewn with a hemp or silver-willow thread (Z2S; diameter .1 to .2cm) using a thin needle with an eye at one end. The Canadian Museum of Civilization has only one example of a Nlaka'pamux mat making needle (II-C-652) which was collected by C.F.Newcombe in 1909 from the Nicola Valley. Teit collected both bone and metal mat making needles for the American Museum of Natural History.[39] The lines of sewing are approximately 10 cm apart. A mat may have between 9 to 12 lines of sewing, depending on the width. The ends of the mats have sticks of rose wood which hold the mat rigid. (See Figure 3.25.)

Table Five: Tent Mat Dimensions
(by Decreasing Length)

Catalogue No.	Length: m (ft)	Width: m (ft)
II-C-311	4.60 (15.09)	1.25 (4.10)
II-C-292	4.44 (14.56)	1.22 (4)
II-C-313	4.40 (14.43)	1.45 (4.75)
II-C-306	4.20 (13.77)	1.24 (4.06)
II-C-307	4.20 (13.77)	1.08 (3.54)
II-C-295	4.10 (13.45)	1.20 (3.94)
II-C-315	4.00 (13.12)	1.12 (3.67)
II-C-297	3.90 (12.79)	1.60 (5.25)
II-C-290	3.75 (12.30)	1.45 (4.75)
II-C-298	3.72 (12.20)	1.27 (4.16)
II-C-312	3.70 (12.14)	1.35 (4.42)
II-C-293	3.66 (12)	1.15 (3.77)
II-C-300	3.60 (11.81)	1.17 (3.83)
II-C-301	3.60 (11.81)	1.15 (3.77)
II-C-305	3.50 (11.48)	1.10 (3.6)
II-C-309	3.50 (11.48)	1.34 (4.39)
II-C-319	3.46 (11.35)	1.08 (3.54)
II-C-314	3.40 (11.48)	1.15 (3.77)
II-C-302	3.30 (10.82)	1.24 (4.06)
II-C-289	3.23 (10.59)	1.30 (4.26)
II-C-308	3.20 (10.49)	1.30 (4.26)
II-C-316	3.10 (10.17)	1.05 (3.44)
II-C-318	3.01 (9.87)	.90 (2.95)
II-C-291	2.90 (9.51)	1.40 (4.59)
II-C-304	2.66 (8.72)	1.26 (4.13)
II-C-296	2.60 (8.53)	.98 (3.2)
II-C-284	2.30 (7.5)	1.15 (3.77)
II-C-287	2.24 (7.3)	.98 (3.2)

Table Five: Tent Mat Dimensions (by Decreasing Length)

Catalogue No.	Length: m (ft)	Width: m (ft)
II-C-310	2.10 (6.88)	1.23 (4.03)
II-C-283	2.10 (6.88)	.98 (3.2)
II-C-317	2.00 (6.56)	1.25 (4.10)
II-C-294	1.95 (6.39)	1.37 (4.49)
II-C-303	1.65 (5.41)	1.26 (4.13)
II-C-286	1.50 (4.92)	1.19 (3.9)
II-C-288	1.50 (4.92)	1.10 (3.6)

A Finished Tipi

After the Nlaka'pamux mat project was completed in 1996 at Merritt, the participants erected a tipi and invited the community to celebrate. Standing inside the structure one could smell the fresh grassy scent from newly made mats rattling in the breeze. A soft, yellow light came through the translucent gold coloured reeds and through the spaces created by the twisted weft threads.

The interior of a furnished tipi can be envisioned from Teit's description of the traditional household setting.

> ... the Indians slept on a thick layer of brush or dry grass covered with skins or grass mats. The rolled-up ends of these, or skin bags filled with down of bulrushes or of birds, served as pillows... Other mats, spread on the ground at meal-times, served for tables. These measured about three feet by five feet. The people squatted round them helping themselves to the food. [40]

The interior insulating lining of painted hides[41] and decorated cedar root storage baskets would have added colour and design. Decorated floor and eating mats would have offered patterns and strong, bright colour, while the plain mats would give subtle tints and textures to the living space.

Woven and Twined Household Mats

Overview

Studies of rush, reed and silver-willow bark mats have described the collecting of the materials, preparing the threads and the process of weaving.[42] This study of Nlaka'pamux mats is an opportunity to look at the differences as well as the similarities in weaving. Each mat is an individual creation, reflecting the materials at hand and the weaver's choice of pattern, and technique. To identify the range of techniques Dorothy Burnham drew the following elements on a selected number of mats:

a) tabby and twined weaving

b) three selvage treatments

c) two methods of starting the warp

d) six ways of finishing the lower edge.

Her work indicated a general relationship between weaving techniques and the materials used, (see Table Six, parts A and B). The tabby weaves shown in diagrams A and B (Figures 3.31 and 3.32) were used with reed warps. Twining techniques shown in diagrams M and N (Figures 3.33 and 3.34) were used with composite warps. On one mat, both tabby and twined weaving are noted. This floor mat, II-C-333, is a warp-faced tabby with rows of twining at the start and finishing edges.

Table Six: Mats by Warp Material and Weave

A. Reed Warp

Cat. No.	Object	A	B	M	N
II-C-285	Tent Door (Warp-faced tabby)	X	X		
II-C-299	Tent Door (Warp-faced tabby)	X	X		
II-C-321	Shaman's Mat (Warp-faced tabby)	X	X		
II-C-322	Rush mat (Warp-faced tabby)	X	X		
II-C-323	Rush Mat (Warp-faced tabby)	X	X		
II-C-324	Bed Mat (Warp-faced tabby)	X	X		
II-C-325	Table or Food Mat (Twined Weave)			X	*
II-C-333	Bed or Floor Mat (Tabby/Twined Mix)	**	*		
II-C-334	General purpose (Twined Weave)			X	X

B. Composite Warp

Cat. No.	Object	A	B	M	N
II-C-326	General Purpose (Twined Weave)			X	X
II-C-327	Floor mat (Twined Weave)			X	X
II-C-328	Mat (Twined Weave)			X	X
II-C-358	Skirt or Bag (Twined Weave)			X	X

* Starting edge cut off ** Looser tabby weave

Fascinating Challenges

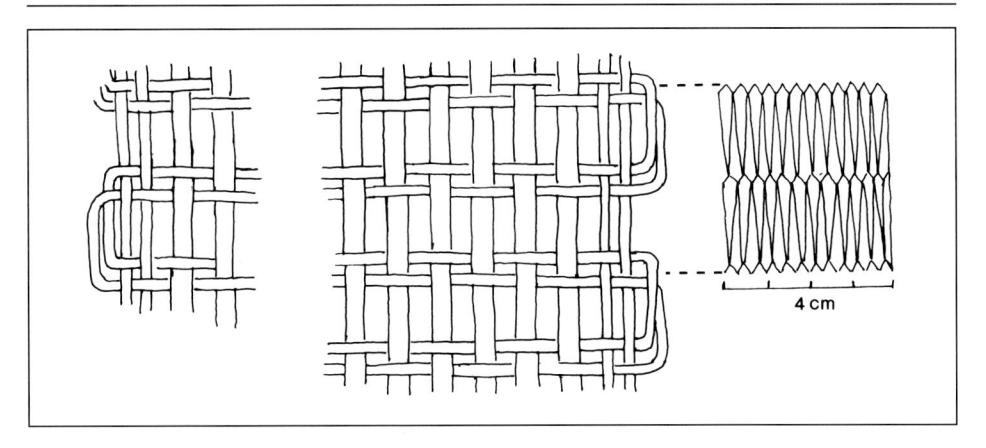

3.31 Construction A: plain weave.

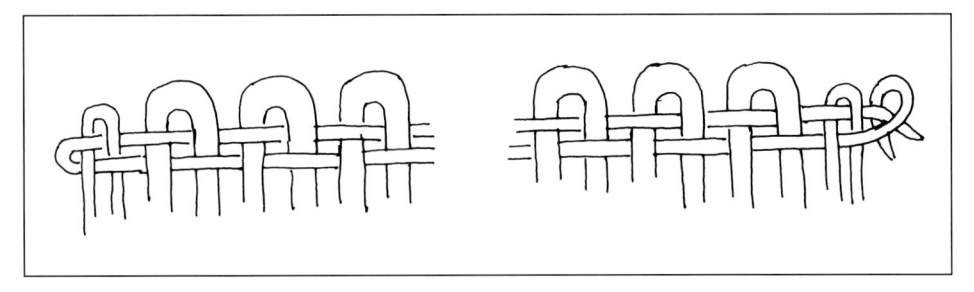

3.32 Construction B: plain weave, starting edge.

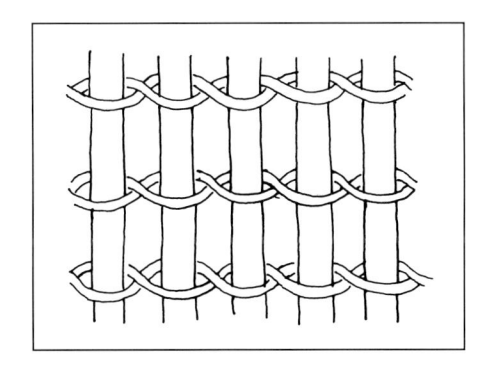

3.33 Construction M: twined weave.

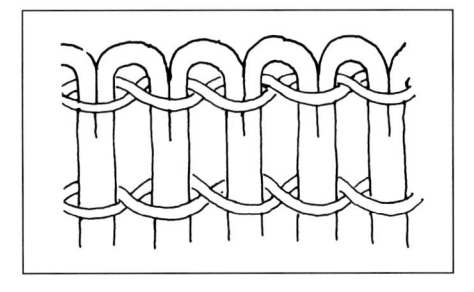

3.34 Construction N: twined weave, starting edge.

— 205 —

Selvage Treatments

Table Seven shows different selvage treatments for woven and twined mats of reed and composite materials. Similar to the findings on tabby and twining techniques, there is an apparent relationship between selvage treatment and type of material used. However the table does not show all the variations recorded on the worksheets. For example, II-C-322 has a coloured edge, and II-C-324 and II-C-333 have heavier weft threads in the selvage. The weaver of a rush mat, II-C-323, varied the weft turning along the selvages (Figure 3.38).

Table Seven: Selvage Treatments Identified by Diagram

A. Reed Warp

Cat. No.	Object	C	D	O
II-C-285	Tent Door (Warp-faced tabby)	X		
II-C-299	Tent Door (Warp-faced tabby)	X		
II-C-321	Shaman's Mat (Warp-faced tabby)	X		
II-C-322	Rush mat (Warp-faced tabby)		X	
II-C-323	Rush Mat (Warp-faced tabby)	X	X	
II-C-324	Bed Mat (Warp-faced tabby)	X		
II-C-325	Table or Food Mat (Twined Weave)			X
II-C-333	Bed or Floor Mat (Tabby/Twined Mix)	X		
II-C-334	General purpose (Twined Weave)			X

B. Composite Warp

Cat. No.	Object	C	D	O
II-C-326	General Purpose (Twined Weave)			X
II-C-327	Floor mat (Twined Weave)			
II-C-328	Mat (Twined Weave)			X
II-C-358	Skirt or Bag (Twined Weave)			X*

* II-C-358 is a modified form with only 2 twists in the space, rather than three

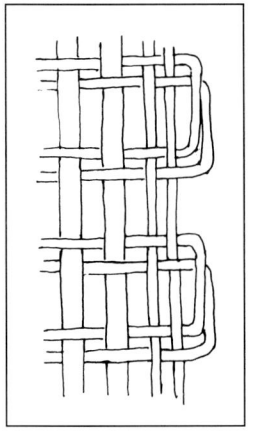

Fascinating Challenges

3.35 Construction C: plain weave, selvage treatment I.

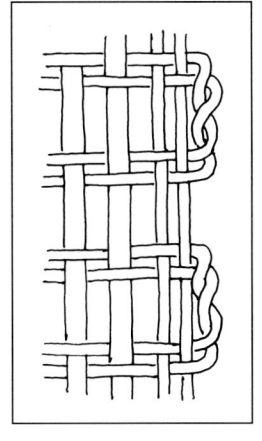

3.36 Construction D: plain weave, selvage treatment II.

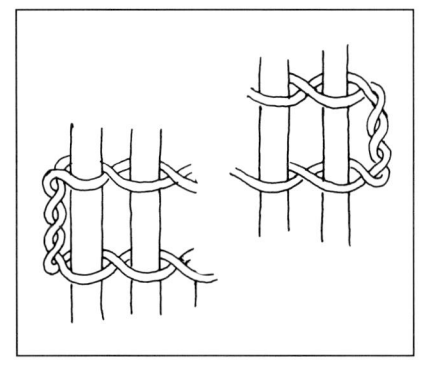

3.37 Construction O: twined weave, selvage treatment.

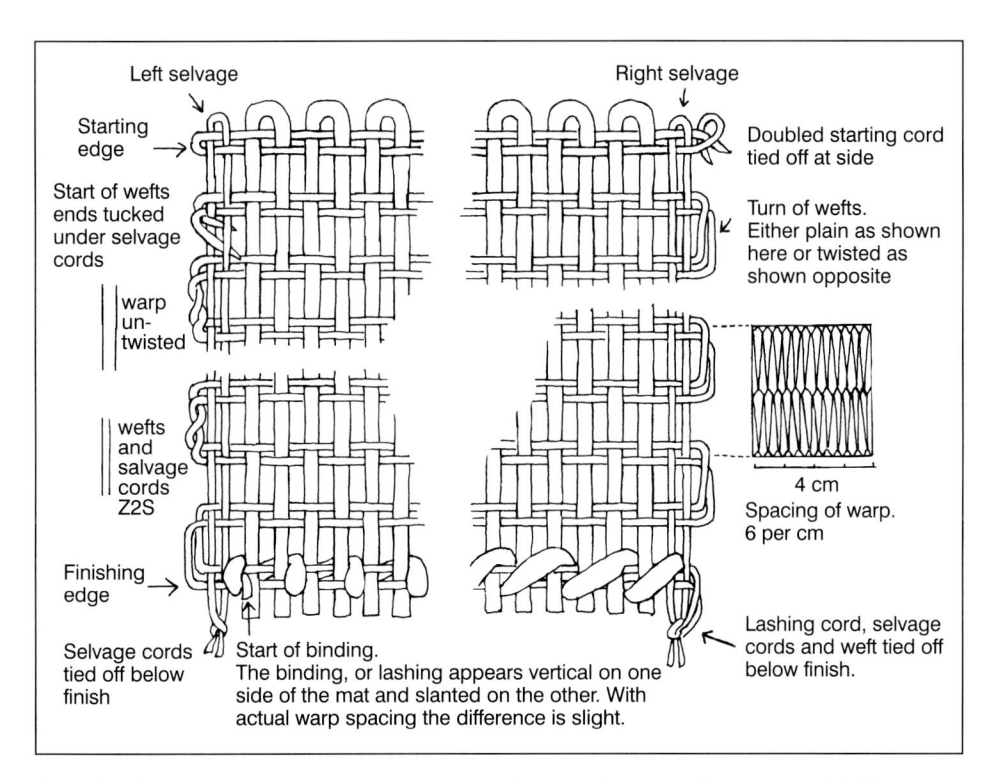

3.38 Variations of selvage treatment within one mat. Canadian Museum of Civilization II-C-323.

Left selvage
Right selvage

Starting edge
Doubled starting cord tied off at side

Start of wefts ends tucked under selvage cords

Turn of wefts. Either plain as shown here or twisted as shown opposite

warp un-twisted

wefts and salvage cords Z2S

4 cm
Spacing of warp. 6 per cm

Finishing edge

Selvage cords tied off below finish

Start of binding. The binding, or lashing appears vertical on one side of the mat and slanted on the other. With actual warp spacing the difference is slight.

Lashing cord, selvage cords and weft tied off below finish.

Finishing Techniques

Mats in the collection show several variations in finishing techniques, particularly among the tabby weave mats. (See Table Eight.) The choices vary from a simple wrapped binding stitch (diagram E, Figure 3.39) to a complex mixture of crossed warps held by a final two rows of weft and double wrapped binding stitch (diagram H, Figure 3.42).

Table Eight: Variations in Finishing Techniques by Diagram

A. Reed Warp

Cat. No.	Object	E	F	G	H	R	S
II-C-285	Tent Door (Warp-faced tabby)	X					
II-C-299	Tent Door (Warp-faced tabby)				X		
II-C-321	Shaman's Mat (Warp-faced tabby)			X			
II-C-322	Rush mat (Warp-faced tabby)	X					
II-C-323	Rush Mat (Warp-faced tabby)	X				X	
II-C-324	Bed Mat (Warp-faced tabby)		X*	X*			
II-C-325	Table or Food Mat (Twined Weave)		No special treatment
II-C-333	Bed or Floor Mat (Tabby/Twined Mix)		No special treatment
II-C-334	General purpose (Twined Weave)					X	

B. Composite Warp

Cat. No.	Object	E	F	G	H	R	S
II-C-326	General Purpose (Twined Weave)						X
II-C-327	Floor mat (Twined Weave)				X		
II-C-328	Mat (Twined Weave)				X		
II-C-358	Skirt or Bag (Twined Weave)				X		

* The finishing edge of this mat is not consistent.

Fascinating Challenges

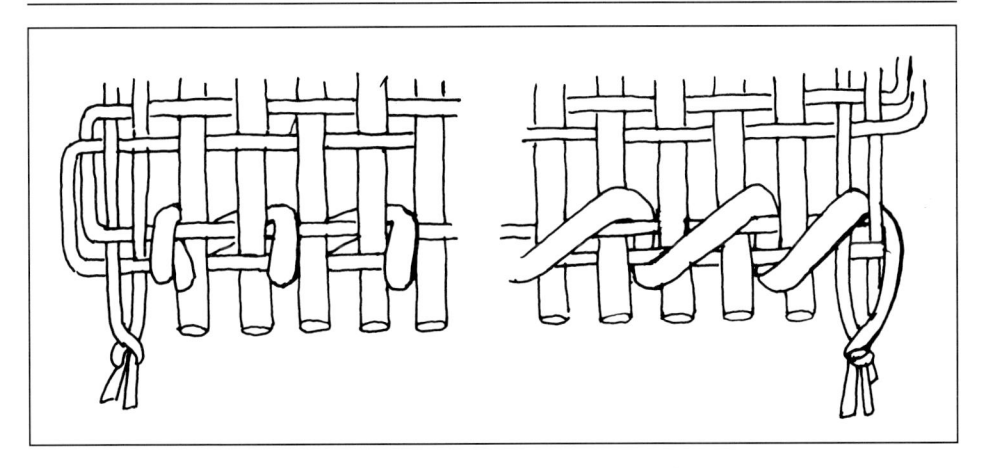

3.39 Construction E: plain weave, finishing treatment I, front and back views.

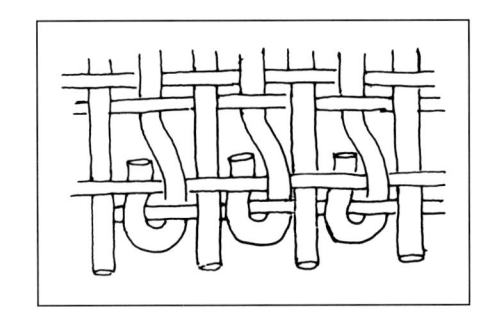

3.40 Construction F: plain weave, finishing treatment II.

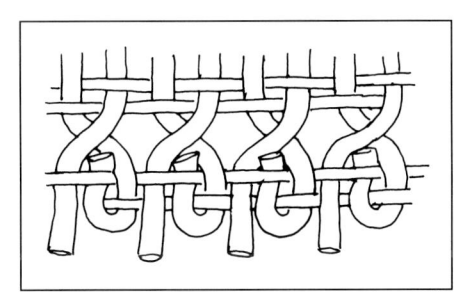

3.41 Construction G: plain weave, finishing treatment III.

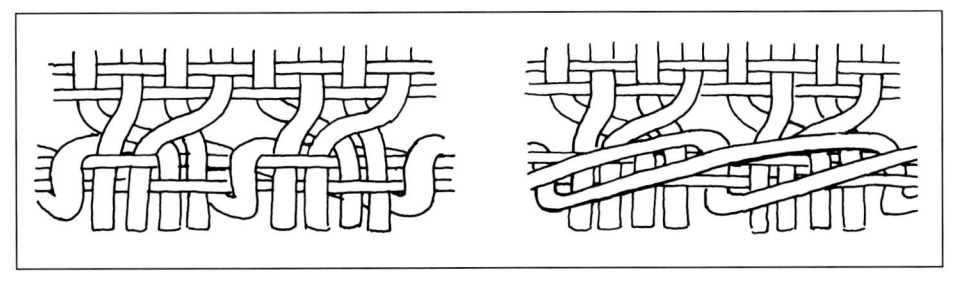

3.42 Construction H: plain weave, finishing treatment IV, front and back views.

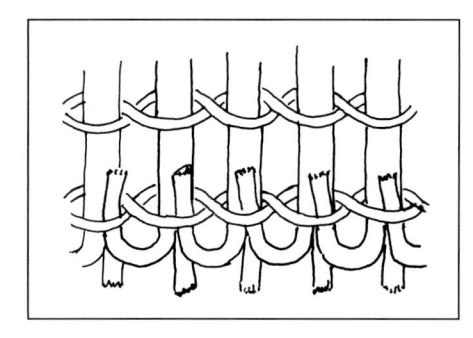

3.43 Construction R: twined weave, finishing treatment I.

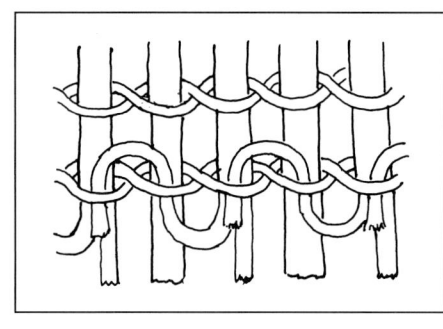

3.44 Construction S: twined weave, finishing treatment II.

Warp Additions

Skilled Nlaka'pamux weavers were able to change the shape of garments, bags and mats by using various weaving techniques. Adjustments were made by controlling the tension of the weave and by adding to or reducing the thickness of the warp threads. Composite materials such as silver-willow, sagebrush and softened reeds in particular, can be expanded or narrowed in diameter by controlling the tightness of the weft threads. The diameter can also be changed by adding or subtracting extra fibre in the warp strand. Another technique found on Nlaka'pamux bags is weaving the warp threads tightly together at the beginning and ending edges, but leaving a looser tension in the middle section. This allows a billowing out of the bag's centre to create a larger carrying capacity. Systematic additions of warp threads also change the shape of the fabric. Initially square fabrics can take on the circular shape needed for capes and cloaks by increasing the warp count every few weft passes across the garment. Adding extra warp threads in the centre of a bag makes it more capacious without adding bulk at the top and bottom edges. Dorothy Burnham diagrammed three examples of warp thread additions; the first two were drawn from a silver-willow bark cape, (II-C-604, Figures 3.18 and Figure 3.19[43]) and the third from a mat, (II-C-328, Figure 3.45).

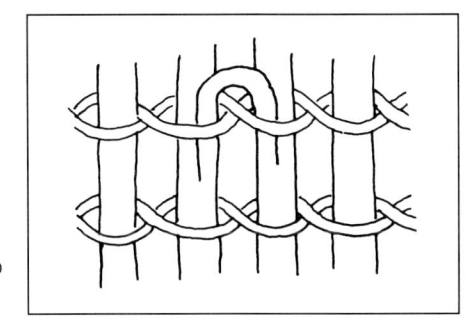

3.45 Construction P: twined weave, addition of warp thread.

Mat Design and Decoration

Table and floor mats were made more decorative by the use of simple weaves and colour combinations. Thick and thin reeds, tightly woven, gave an attractive textured surface. Striped patterns were made by arranging the subtle variations in the colour of the reeds. Some mats had brightly dyed warp or weft threads, or coloured materials were inserted into the weaving at regular intervals. Table Nine gives an overview of decorative techniques used in the mat sample. Three decorative techniques are discussed in greater detail in the final section of the paper.

Table Nine: Decorative Elements

A. Reed Warp

Cat. No.	Object	Decorative Elements
II-C-285	Tent Door (Warp-faced tabby)	Thick & thin warp
II-C-299	Tent Door (Warp-faced tabby)	Thick & thin warp
II-C-321	Shaman's Mat (Warp-faced tabby)	Paint, Coloured Warp
II-C-322	Rush mat (Warp-faced tabby)	No special treatment
II-C-323	Rush Mat (Warp-faced tabby)	Striped colour & weave
II-C-324	Bed Mat (Warp-faced tabby)	Texture only
II-C-325	Table or Food Mat (Twined Weave)	Diamond Lattice
II-C-333	Bed or Floor Mat (Tabby/Twined Mix)	No special treatment
II-C-334	General purpose (Twined Weave)	No special treatment

B. Composite Warp

Cat. No.	Object	Decorative Elements
II-C-326	General Purpose (Twined Weave)	Diamond Lattice
II-C-327	Floor mat (Twined Weave)	Paint, Coloured Warp/Weft
II-C-328	Mat (Twined Weave)	No special treatment
II-C-358	Skirt or Bag (Twined Weave)	Dyed Warps, Inset Motif

Worksheets

Dorothy Burnham's detailed analyses of five mats in the collection are provided in this section. One worksheet presents a typical warp-face tabby weave. Two others illustrate the variations of a lattice work decoration on twined mats. The fourth worksheet describes a skirt decorated with dyed warps and inset coloured threads, a form of decoration found on many twined bags in the collection. A final worksheet shows an unusual mat that was used as a shaman's headdress. As noted earlier, these worksheets provide data for comparative research on mats in other collections. The information can also be used by contemporary weavers for the reproduction of historic mats.

Warp-Face Tabby

Worksheet One:

1. **Location and Catalogue Number:** Canadian Museum of Civilization II-C-285.

2. **Object:** Woven reed mat. Warp-faced tabby with textural banding in the weft. Single colour. Peeled stick supports.

3. **Measurements:** Length – 80cm; Width – 152 cm.

4. **Culture:** Nlaka'pamux (Thompson Indians).

5. **Date:** Early 20th Century.

6. **Source:** Collected by James A. Teit.

7. **Visual Description:** Rectangular reed mat; beige colour; tabby weave with fairly heavy, unspun reed warps completely covering the lighter wefts, which are used in pairs. A regular textural banding at 2cm intervals in the weft direction (Figure 3.31) is created. Both faces are unpatterned.

    At either edge and in the centre, peeled sticks have been forced in and out through the fabric to provide support for the mat. The sticks are sharpened at the finishing edge of the mat. Tied to one of the sticks there are fairly long cords of Indian hemp. Z2S and unspun.

    Quality – Excellent.
    Condition – Good.

8. **Technical Description:**

    Warp:

    Material: Unspun reed; Diameter 3-4mm. Occasionally at irregular intervals the lengths are renewed by laying another length of reed in beside the first one.

3.46 Tent door mat showing variegated texture. Canadian Museum of Civilization II-C-285.

Count: 7-8 per cm.

Selvages: At either side of the mat a pair of warps, Z2S similar to the wefts, forms a simple selvage.

Order: Perfectly plain.

Weft:

Material: Indian hemp. Z2S with a strong twist in the plying
Count: 2 per 2cm. spaced Tabby A, 7mm, Tabby B, 13mm, and repeat.
Order: 2 wefts of identical colour and material are used alternately.

Construction:

Field: Plain warp-faced tabby. The combination of the heavy very closely set warp, which compresses and expands easily under pressure, with the lighter wefts which are widely spaced in pairs creates a strong repeating weft-wise textural banding (Figure 3.31).

Starting Edge: A weft yarn double the width of the mat provides the first two passes of the weft. This starting yarn is folded double at one side and the two ends are tied off in a knot at the other side. The reed warps, which are double the length of the mat, have been folded at the top to make two warp ends which are held in order by the pass of the two starting wefts (Figure 3.32).

Side Edges: A pair of warps similar to the wefts is woven in simple tabby down either side of the mat. Around them the wefts turn in pairs, always maintaining their order as Tabby A and Tabby B as they move down the side of the mat to the next pass of wefts (Figure 3.35).

Finishing Edge: Across the width of the mat a cord, similar to the warp reeds, binds the warp in pairs to the final two shots of weft. This binding appears vertical on one face and slightly diagonal as it moves from one pair to the next on the other face (Figure 3.39). Below this binding the warp reeds have been cut off closely and evenly.

9. **Decorative Techniques:** None other than texture.

10. **Comments:** Although the weave is perfectly plain tabby the effect obtained by the combination of heavy, squashable, closely spaced warps with harder, lighter weight wefts, widely spaced in pairs, is clever and very effective producing an interestingly textured mat with excellent insulating qualities.

    When Chief Gordon Antoine visited the Canadian Museum of Civilization and was shown these mats he commented that the reeds varied in smell. He thought it probable that this was due to the particular area of origin, whether bog or higher, dryer ground.

11. **Comparative Material:** Other similar mats collected by Teit: II-C-321, 322, 323, 324

Decorated Mats

Two twined mats are decorated with lattice work designs. One of them, (II-C-325), has undulating lines made by twining the weft in an up and down sequence. This pattern appears on both sides of the mat. A second design, (II-C-326), is made by adding a warp float on one side to create a pointed diamond design. A comparative piece, a rush mat in the American Museum of Natural History collection (AMNH 16/9193) creates the same technique of warp floats using red wool.

Decorative Style I – Use of weft threads as pattern

Worksheet Two:

1. **Location and Catalogue Number:** Canadian Museum of Civilization – II-C-325.

2. **Object:** Reed mat, twined weave with undulating lines.

3. **Measurements:**

   Length – 84cm.
   Width – 100cm.

4. **Culture:** Nlaka'pamux (Thompson Indians).

5. **Date:** Early 20th Century.

6. **Source:** Collected by James A. Teit.

7. **Visual Description:** Rectangular reed mat, beige colour with fairly heavy closely set reed warps; plain Z-twist twining over single warps, (Figure 3.33) moving in undulating lines to form an all-over diamond lattice pattern.

   Quality – Excellent.
   Condition – Good, with a few small breaks in the reed tips at start and finishing edges.

8. **Technical Description:**

   Warp:

   Material: Heavy, unspun reeds. (Diameter 4-6mm).

   Count: 2-2.5 per cm.

3.47 Food mat showing undulating weave pattern. Canadian Museum of Civilization II-C-325.

Selvages: None.

Order: Plain.

Weft:

Material: Beige, Indian hemp? 2-3mm diameter with a slight Z twist.

Count: 2 passes within 6cm, spacing variable according to pattern.

Order: Plain.

Construction:

Field: Simple Z-twist twining over single warps. 2 passes per 6cm, moving in undulating lines which creates a diamond pattern, each unit of which is approximately 4cm in height and 9cm wide (Figure 3.48).

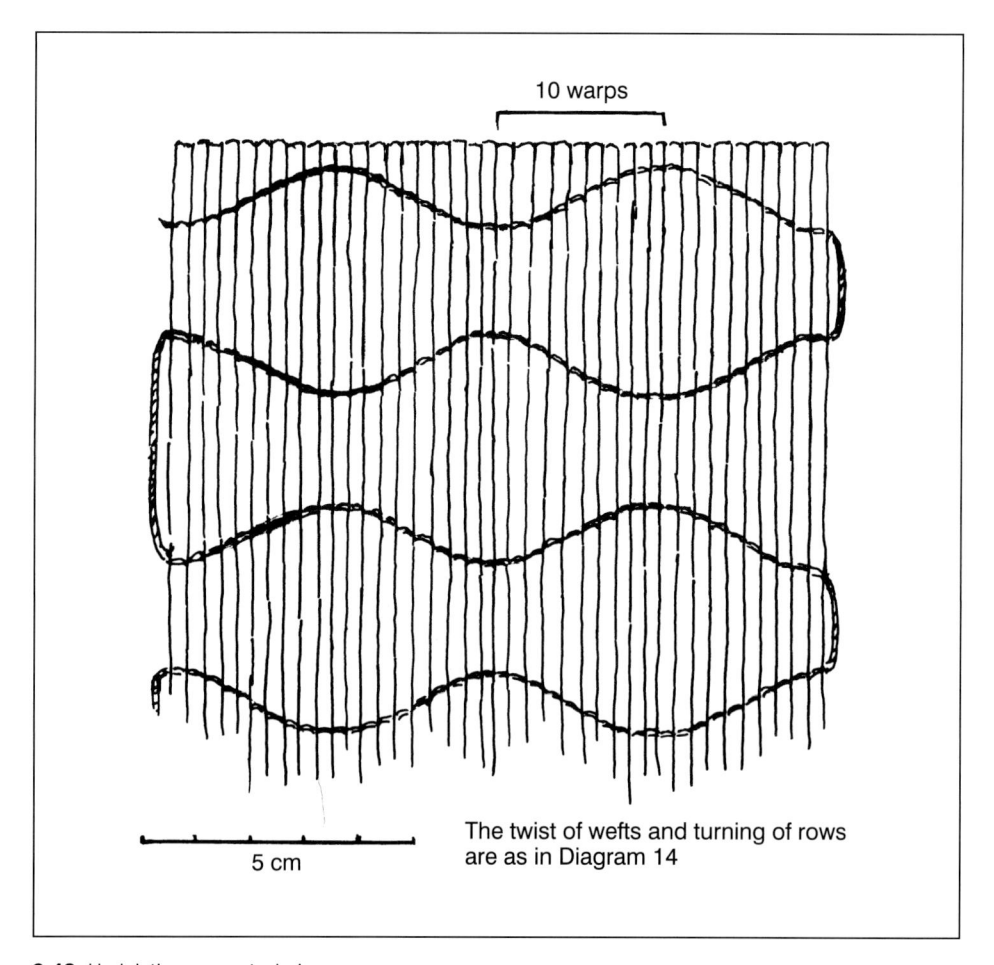

3.48 Undulating weave technique.

Starting Edge: Straight line of twining with the warp cut off just above it. The wefts at the starting point have been twisted together, carried down the side and secured by knotting them into next pass of weft.

Side Edges: As per Figure 3.37 with the length of the carry at the edge either quite short or longer, depending on the pattern.

Finishing Edge: Undulating line of twining similar to field with the warp cut off in a straight line just below it. The wefts are knotted together at the finish.

9. **Decorative Techniques:** None other than the very effective undulating pattern of the basic weave.

Decorative Style II – Use of additional pattern warps

Worksheet Three:

1. **Location and Catalogue Number:** Canadian Museum of Civilization – II-C-326.

2. **Object:** Rectangular twined weave mat with diamond lattice worked on one face with floating brown pattern warps.

3. **Measurements:**

   Length – 62cm.
   Width – 65 cm.

4. **Culture:** Nlaka'pamux (Thompson Indians).

5. **Date:** Early 20th Century.

6. **Source:** Collected by James A. Teit.

7. **Visual Description:** Rectangular mat with heavy, closely set, beige composite fibre warps held by spaced rows of simple twined weave. A diamond lattice pattern is created on the face of the fabric by brown pattern warps, (Figure 3.50).

   Quality – Excellent.
   Condition – Good.

8. **Technical Description:**

   Warp:

   Material: Beige, composite vegetal fibre forming a heavy rather soft warp: Diameter approximately 5mm.

   Count: 2 per cm.

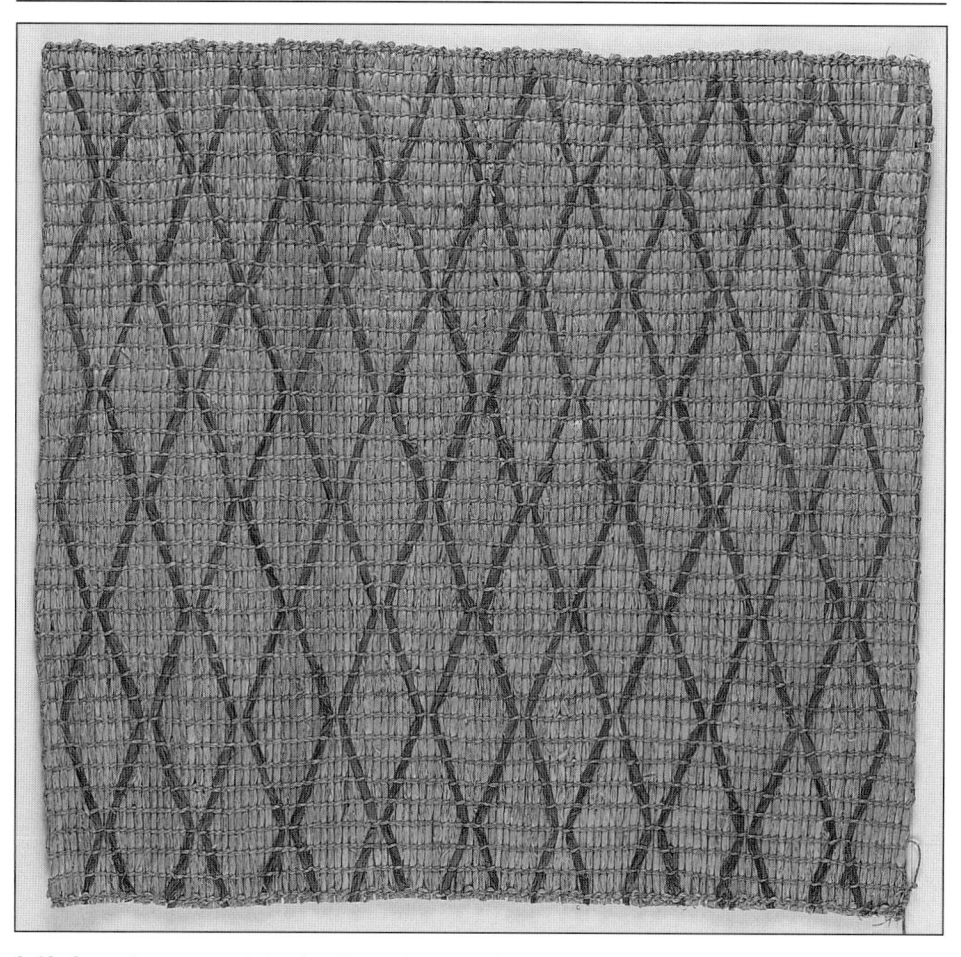

The Observant Eye: Analyzing Nlaka'pamux Woven Mats

3.49 General purpose mat showing diamond pattern. Canadian Museum of Civilization II-C-326.

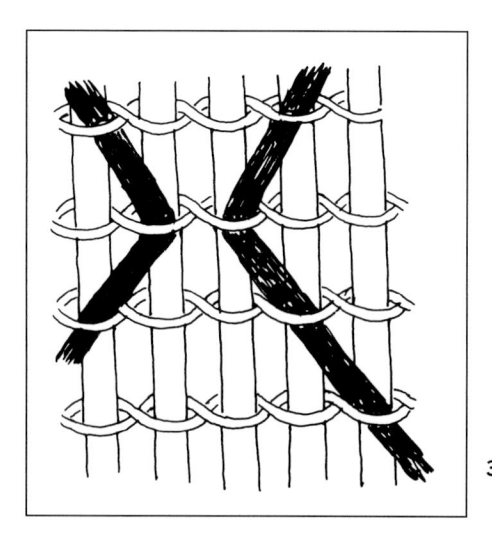

3.50 Construction T: decorative technique, diamond pattern. (top)

Selvages: None, but on the left side a section of brown pattern warp is woven in with the edge warp.

Order: At the start of pattern 9 beige, 2 beige with brown and repeat.

Weft:

Material: Indian hemp, Z2S, fairly coarse.

Count: 1 pass per 1.5cm

Order: Plain.

Construction:

Field: Twined weave, Z-twist, worked over single warps. 1 pass per 1.5 cm. (Figure3.32).

Starting Edge: As per Figure 3.34.

Side Edges: As per Figure 3.37.

Finishing Edge: As per Figure 3.44, with the turn up showing on the pattern side

9. **Decorative Techniques:** Extra brown pattern warps float to form a diamond lattice on the face of the mat (Figure 3.50). These brown pattern warps are worked in with every 10th and 11th basic warp and they move 1 space apart with each pass of weft. After the 5th pass they reverse direction and move together again, thus forming an all over lattice pattern.

Decorative Style III – Inset Colour Threads

Worksheet Four:

1. **Location and Catalogue Number:** Canadian Museum of Civilization – II-C-358.

2. **Object:** Wrap-around skirt; beige composite vegetal warp; twined weave with stripes and warp patterning in red, green and blue.

3. **Measurements:**

   Length – 85cm.
   Width at waist – 85cm.
   Width at hip – 120cm.
   Width at knee –83cm.

4. **Culture:** Nlaka'pamux (Thompson Indians).

5. **Date:** Early 20th Century.

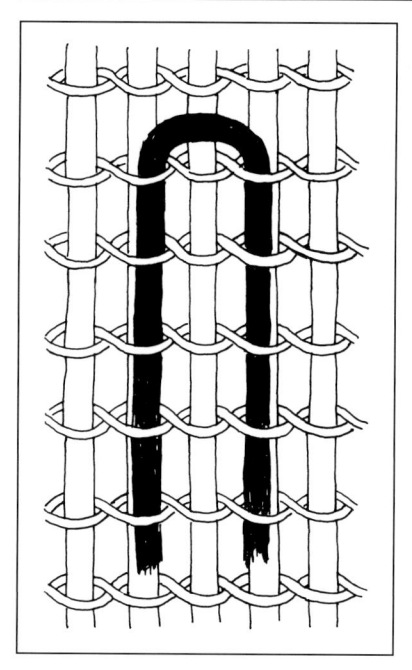

The Observant Eye: Analyzing Nlaka'pamux Woven Mats

3.51 Construction U: decorative technique, U-shape additions. (right)

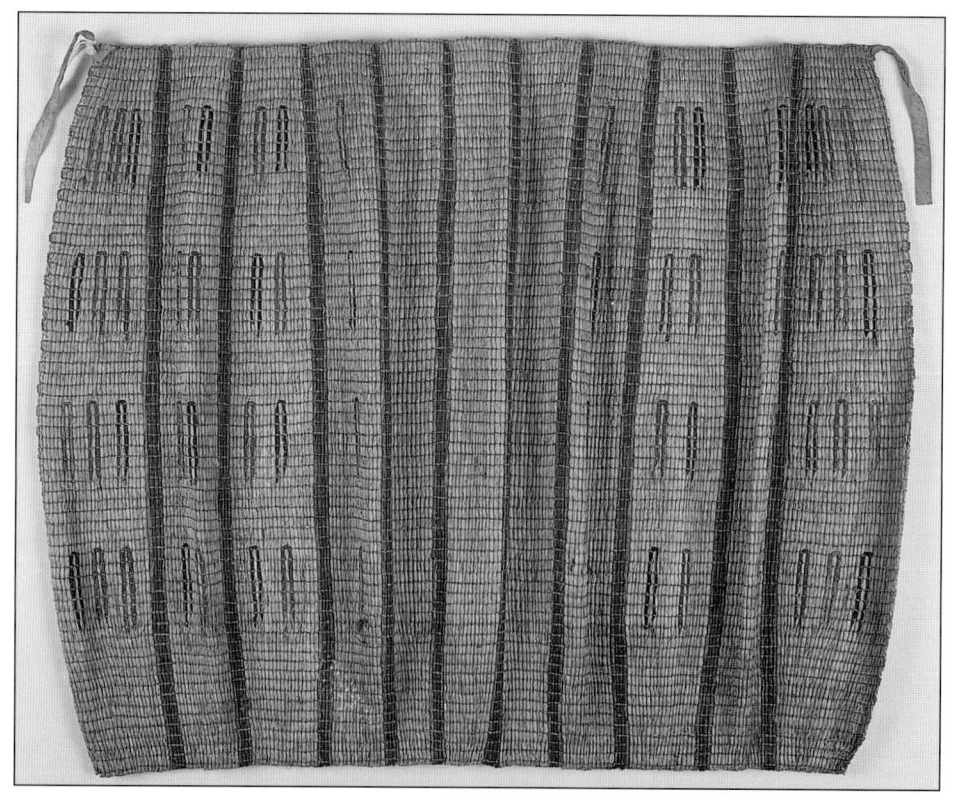

3.52 Wrap-around skirt showing dyed warps and inset decorations. Canadian Museum of Civilization II-C-358.

6. **Source:** Collected by James A. Teit.

7. **Visual Description:** Distorted rectangular shape with skin ties attached to either side at the top. Closely spaced beige, unspun, composite vegetal fibre warp; weft somewhat darker colour, probably Indian hemp; twined weave in spaced rows with vertical stripes and simple motifs inlaid with short lengths of pattern warps in red, green and blue.

   Quality – Excellent.
   Condition – Excellent.

8. **Technical Description:**

   Warp:

   Material: Composite of shredded plant fibre making a heavy, but soft and fairly pliable warp, diameter 3-6mm.

   Count: Towards the top and the bottom of the skirt the warps are spaced about 2.5 per cm., while in the central part 2 per cm.

   Selvages: At either side of the weave there are 2 warp ends, hard-spun Z2S, similar in colour to the main warp and woven as in the field.

   Order: Plain.

   Weft:

   Material: Probably Indian Hemp, darker in colour than the warp; Z2S, diameter 2-3mm.

   Count: One pass per 1.2cm

   Order: Plain.

   Construction:

   Field: Rows of Z-twist twining enclosing single warps, as per Figure 3.33, spaced 1.2cm apart.

   Starting Edge: Diagram N, Figure 3.34.

   Side Edges: As per Figure 3.37, but usually with only 2 twists in the space.

   Finishing Edge: As per Figure 3.43, with the turn up on the undecorated side of the weave.

9. **Decorative Techniques:** Dyed warps are used to make vertical stripes always in the order – green, red, red, green. These are fairly evenly spaced around the skirt making eleven panels. At the front of the skirt the first panel on either side has 4 ranks of 3 simple inverted U-shaped motifs

inlaid. Each motif extends vertically through 7-8 passes of weft. The next two panels have 4 ranks of similar motifs repeated twice, then a panel with 4 ranks of similar single motifs and at the back of the skirt 3 undecorated panels.

10. **Comments:** The shaping of the garment, expanding it to fit over the hips of the wearer, is achieved by condensing the warp spacing at top and bottom and by adding or subtracting warps as necessary. With composite warps this can be done in various ways by adding fibre and making two warps from one or by reducing fibre and combining warps. It appears that the actual diameter of many of the warps, at hip level, has been increased by the subtle addition of fibre.

11. **Comparative Material:** Similar mats collected by Teit: CMC II-C-326, 327, 328 and 334.

Shamanic Mat

Teit collected two mats which were used as a headdresses or facemasks by Nlaka'pamux shamans (American Museum of Natural History 48-8713a-e and Canadian Museum of Civilization II-C-321). Both mats are woven of reeds and painted. Only the technical description of the Canadian Museum of Civilization mat is provided here, but both mats are similar in construction. Dorothy Burnham notes that the material and techniques used in the Canadian Muscum of Civilization mat are the same as those used in other warp-face tabby reed mats.[44]

The two shamanic mats are painted with simple images similar to those used for pictographs, tattoos, face paint, and to decorate clothing and tools. Teit provided explanations of some of the pictographic images[45] and of the meaning of the designs used for tattoos and face paint.[46] Interpretations of the painted designs on clothing were often given in the artifact documentation. Symbols might have different meanings depending on the context. Thus, a wavy line could indicate water, a snake, or a path, depending on the surrounding signs. Only the creator of the images knew the story or references that were recorded. The meanings were often deliberately obscured for personal protection or privacy.

Groups of images sometimes told of a person's dream or vision. These stories described an encounter with a supernatural being, which could appear in animal or plant form, or as manifestations of the planets, the dawn, or other cosmic phenomenon. As a result of the encounter, the individual was often given special skills or abilities. Shamans could have one or more supernatural encounters and "accomplished their supernatural feats by the help of their guardian spirits, who gave them instruction by means of vision or dreams."[47]

While curing an illness the shaman wore strings of deer-hoofs around his knees and ankles, and a cape or pouch made from albino deer hide. He covered his head and face with a woven mat shaped into a conical form and secured with pins. The images painted on the mat in the American Museum of Natural History are described by Teit.

> *No. 418 - 8713 a-e Shaman's mat used as a mask when going after souls etc. The painting in red signifies success and protection from harm, (this is for the shaman in his mission) also the red painted trail. The black means death and the darkness of the trail also defeat to the spirits who oppose him. White means the ghosts and spirit land or the dead with whom he will come in contact. Designs? are of different colors viz. black or dark color. Red or blood color and yellow or green color. Some shamans therefore painted themselves with these colors. The sticks or pins represent the distance a shaman's spirit can travel. These are always two, four, six, and seven. The shaman who used this mat could only go as far as four sticks could take him. The shades pulled out these pins and if a shaman went too far or stayed too long all the pins might be pulled out and his mask thus fall off leaving him open to harm or death at the hands of the shades who resented his intrusion after departing souls. When a shaman returned from his journey only one pin was left in his mask as a rule. A shaman who used seven pins could generally reach the land of souls and return safely leaving 6 pins in the hands of the shades.*[48]

The mat in the Canadian Museum of Civilization collection has only one wooden pin or skewer. The designs are described as follows.

> *The central cross probably means 'crossing of trails' or 'of influences'. The small half circles near the ends of the spokes are probably 'hills'. This is probably a mystic place or kind of shrine between hills. The four radiating lines are probably trails leading in or out of their place from opposing directions, or possibly the four directions or quarters. The tracks of a grizzly bear mother and cub leads towards the place, and tracks of other creatures from the other three directions. The elongated tracks may be human tracks or trail... The small tracks close together may possibly be weasel, and the other Coyote.*[49]

Worksheet Five:

1. **Location and Catalogue Number:** Canadian Museum of Civilization – II-C-321.

2. **Object:** Woven reed mat. Warp-faced tabby with textural banding in the weft. Warp variegated, beige to very pale grey-green. On one face there is a cross design in rough red paint.

3. **Measurements:**

    Length – 80cm.
    Width –129cm.

4. **Culture:** Nlaka'pamux (Thompson Indians).

5. **Date:** Early 20th Century.

6. **Source:** Collected by James A. Teit.

7. **Visual Description:** Rectangular reed mat; variegated beige to grey-green colours; tabby weave with fairly coarse, unspun reed warps completely covering the lighter wefts, which are used in pairs. A regular textural banding at 2cm intervals in the weft direction is created (Figure 3.31).

    In the centre of one face a design is painted in rough red lines. There is a large central cross with small crescent finials at the end of each arm and a fairly large and a smaller bear paw motif at top left.

    Quality – Excellent.

    Condition – Good. Some slight evidence remains of the holes made by pins used to fasten the mat around the shaman user.

8. **Technical Description:**

    Warp:

    Material: Unspun reed. Occasionally, at irregular intervals the lengths are renewed by laying another length of reed in beside the first one.

    Count: 5-6 per cm.

    Selvages: At either side of the mat a pair of warps, similar to the wefts, forms a simple selvage.

    Order: Perfectly plain.

    Weft:

    Material: Indian hemp Z2S with a strong twist in the plying.

    Count: 2 per 2cm, spaced Tabby A, 7mm, Tabby B, 13mm, and repeat.

    Order: 2 wefts of identical colour and material are used alternately.

Construction:

Field: Plain warp-faced tabby; the combination of the heavy very closely set warp, which compresses and expands easily under pressure, with the lighter wefts, which are widely spaced in pairs creates a strong repeating weft-wise textural banding (Figure 3.31).

Starting Edge: A weft yarn double the width of the mat provides the first two passages of the weft. This starting yarn is folded double at one side and the two ends are tied off in a knot at the other side. The reed warps, which are double the length of the mat, have been folded at the top to make two warp ends, which are held in order by the weaving in of the two starting wefts (Figure 3.32).

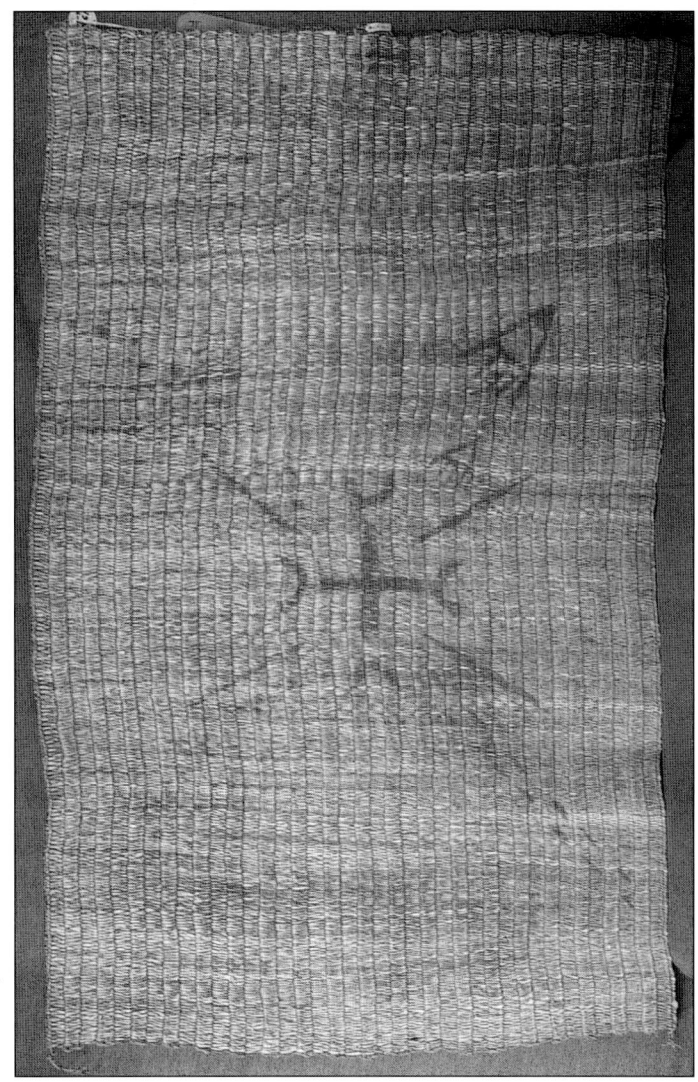

3.53 Shaman's cape with painted design. Canadian Museum of Civilization II-C-321.

Side Edges: A pair of warps similar to the wefts is woven in simple tabby down either side of the mat. Around them the wefts turn in pairs, always maintaining their order as Tabby A and Tabby B as they move down the side of the mat to the next passage of wefts (Figure 3.35).

Finishing Edge: the warp ends are woven in by the last two shots of tabby weft and are held firmly in place by weaving every second warp end back up through these last two shots of weft before cutting it off. The alternate warps are cut off just below the passage of the last weft (Figure 3.40).

9. **Decorative Techniques:** Painted designs applied to one face of the mat with heavy and rather rough bright red lines.

10. **Comments:** For shamanic use.

11. **Comparative Material:** Both material and technique are the same as with other mats collected by Teit (II-C-285, 299, 322, 323, 324) but the painted decoration makes this one unique.

Conclusion

This essay is the first detailed analysis of Nlaka'pamux rush, reed and silver-willow bark mats. It offers new information on the choices and variety of weaving techniques used by mat makers at the start of the twentieth century. In our selected sample uniformity is noted in the use of warp-faced tabby on reed and rush mats and the use of twined weave on composite fibre warps. The greatest variations in mat techniques were found in the finishing edges. This suggests that different weavers made the mats in the Canadian Museum of Civilization collection. Further analysis of mats in other collections may lead to the identity of individual weavers. The American Museum of Natural History collection may be particularly useful because of the names associated with specific mats.

Dorothy Burnham's observant eye has created a clearer understanding of the range and types of Nlaka'pamux mats in the Canadian Museum of Civilization collection. Scholars can now compare and contrast mats in other museum collections based on the following categories:

Reed Warps
a) warp faced tabby with textural banding in the weft
b) twined weave with undulating lines
c) tabby with rows of twined weave at start and finish

Composite Warps
a) twined weave with surface design created by pattern warps
b) twined weave, plain

Her analysis of design, colour arrangements, and weaving techniques has also provided a better understanding of the decoration of rush, reed and silver-willow bark mats. These detailed studies have made available to scholars, weavers and members of the Aboriginal community the unique character of traditional Nlaka'pamux woven mats.

Endnotes

1. Personal communication September 1999.
2. This plant, *Elaeagnus commutata* or Silverberry (Turner 1998:169) is commonly called silver-willow in the Nlaka'pamux community. The term silver-willow will be used in this paper.
3. The Canadian Museum of Civilization also has a number of Nlaka'pamux cedar bark mats, capes and skirts. This paper however, focuses only on the rush, reed and willow bark weavings.
4. The exhibit titled *Earthline and Morning Star* was part of a larger exhibition titled, *Threads of the Land: Clothing Traditions from Three Indigenous Cultures*.
5. See Tepper 1994.
6. Teit's collector's notes for artifact CMC II-C-347.
7. The participants included Louis Dick, coordinator, Maggie Shuter, Mary Ann John, Ethel Isaac, and Sarah McLeod.
8. Holmes 1896:18.
9. The earliest archaeological evidence of twined technology in this area is a pair of sandals (carbon dated to 9300 [250±] BCE) discovered in the Fishbone Cave of Nevada, Fraser 1989:5.
10. See for example Fowler 1990.
11. See for example Howay 1918, Willoughby 1910, Hawkins 1978.
12. See for example Wright 1991, Schlick 1994, Harless 1998.
13. See for example Haeberlin 1928, Emmons 1993, Laforet 1984, 1990, Bernick 1998.
14. See for example Burnham nd, Samuels 1982, 1987, Wells 1969, Gustafson 1980, Sparrow 1998.
15. See Turner 1998, Turner et al 1990, Gunther 1988, Steedman 1929.
16. See Tepper 1987.
17. See Laforet nd.
18. For a review of Teit's life, collecting history and contributions to Anthropology and to the welfare of the Native people see Tepper this volume, also Wickwire 1979, 1993, 1998, Campbell 1994, Fenn 1997.
19. Items of woven clothing in CMC collection include capes, skirts, caps, leggings, and slippers.
20. For a discussion on the anonymity of informants and crafts people see Tepper this volume, Jacknis 1992, Wickwire 1993.

21. Teit 1900:190.
22. Artifact documentation, American Museum of Natural History.
23. Antko died in 1899, but Teit may have retained examples of her handwork. Futher research may help identify these weavers.
24. This mat was collected by C.F. Newcombe between 1895 and 1901.
25. See Teit 1900 and artifact documentation American Museum of Natural History model canoe #343-8707.
26. Turner 1998:120.
27. Peterson 1963:251.
28. Amaron 2000:74.
29. Amaron 2000:72.
30. Whiteford and Rogers 1994:59.
31. Teit 1900:188.
32. Teit 1900:188-190.
33. Teit 1900:190.
34. Teit 1900:192, Laforet and York 1981, Rice 1991.
35. Teit 1900:196.
36. Teit 1900:195.
37. Teit 1900:196.
38. For a description of the process see Sampson 1991, Turner 1998:122.
39. Bone needle - American Museum of Natural History artifact 756-9347 ab.; metal needle - American Museum of Natural History artifact 723-9191.
40. Teit 1900:199.
41. Teit 1900:196.
42. See for example Peterson 1963.
43. These two diagrams have previously been published, Tepper 1994.
44. Materials used for shamanic head coverings appear to have been everyday objects adapted for ceremonial purposes. Mandy Brown, a Nlaka'pamux elder, recalled when she was a child seeing a shamanic performance in which the healer wore a hemp sugar sack to cover his face and head. Personal communication, 1994.
45. Teit 1900: plates XIX, XX.
46. Teit 1930.
47. Teit 1900:360.
48. American Museum of Natural History artifact documentation record.
49. Canadian Museum of Civilization artifact documentation record.

Glossary

The following definitions are taken from Burnham 1980 or prepared by Dorothy Burnham.

S-twist: When the twist of a thread around its axis follows the direction of the central bar of the letter, S, the thread is said to be S-twist, S-spun, or S-ply.

Tabby: Basic binding system or weave. Usually one weft thread passing over and under the warp threads. Also called plain weave.

Twining: Weft twining - Simple form of weaving performed manually... Two, or more, weft threads are twined around each other in an "S" or "Z" direction, as they enclose each warp end, or group of warp ends, in turn.

Warp: The longitudinal threads of a textile; those that are arranged on the loom

Warp faced tabby: A tabby weave in which the weft threads are hidden by the closely spaced warp threads. The side of a textile on which the warp predominates.

Weave: System of interlacing the threads of warp and weft, according to defined rules in order to produce all or part of a textile.

Weft: The transverse threads of a textile.

Z-twist: When the twist of a thread around its axis follows the direction of the central bar of the letter, the thread is said to be Z-twisted, Z-spun or Z-ply.

Z2S: Notation indicating that a thread is composed of two strands each spun with a Z-twist have been plied together with an S twist.

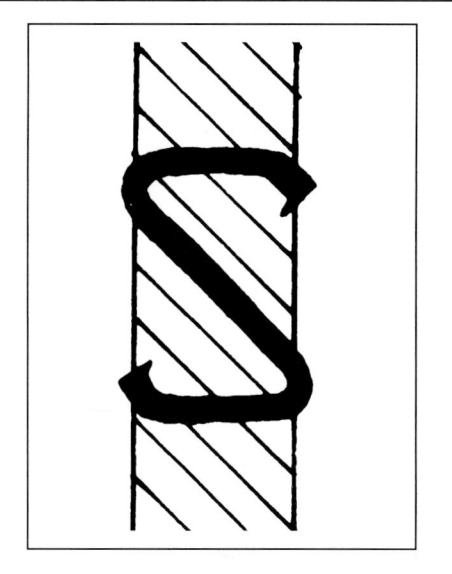

The Observant Eye: Analyzing Nlaka'pamux Woven Mats

3.54 S-Twist spin. Burnham 1980:136.

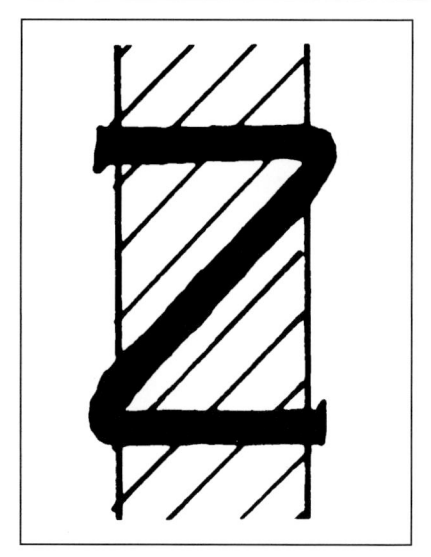

3.55 Z-Twist spin. Burnham 1980:192.

3.56 Tabby weave. Burnham 1980:139.

Works Cited

Amaron, Beryl
    2000 More than Useable Tools: Towards an Appreciation of Nle'kemx Fibre Technology as a Significant Expression of Culture. Masters Thesis University of Northern British Columbia.

Bernick, Kathryn
    1998 *Basketry and Cordage from Hesquiat Harbour British Columbia*. Victoria: Royal British Columbia Museum.

Burnham, Dorothy,
    1980 *Warp and Weft: A Textile Terminology*. Toronto: Royal Ontario Museum.

Burnham, Harold B.
    nd   *The Salish Weaving Complex and Other Papers*. Unpublished papers.

Campbell, Peter
    1994 'Not as a White Man, Not as a Sojourner': James A. Teit and the Fight for Native Rights in British Columbia, 1884-1922. *left history* 2(2): 37-57.

Emmmonds, George T.
    1993 *The Basketry of the Tlingit and The Chilkat Blanket*. Sitka: Sheldon Jackson Museum.

Fenn, Catherine J.
    1997 Life History of a Collection: The Tahltan Materials Collected by James A. Teit. *Museum Anthropology* 20(3): 72-91.

Fowler, Catherine S.
    1990 *Tule Technology: Northern Paiute Uses of Marsh Resources in Western Nevada*. Smithsonian Folklife Studies, no. 6. Washington: Smithsonian Institution Press.

Fraser, David W.
    1989 *A Guide to Weft Twining and Related Stuctures with Interacting Wefts*. Philadelphia: University of Pennsylvania Press.

Gunther, Erna
    1988 Ethnobotany of Western Washington: The Knowledge and Use of Indigenous Plants by Native Americans. Seattle: University of Washington Press.

Gustafson, Paula
    1980 *Salish Weaving*. Vancouver: Douglas and McIntyre.

Hawkins, Elizabeth
    1978 *Indian Weaving, Knitting, Basketry of the Northwest*. Saanichton BC. Handcock House.

Haeberlin, Herman, J.A. Teit and H.A. Roberts
    1928 Coiled Basketry in British Columbia and Surrounding Region. *Annual Report of the Bureau of American Ethnology for 1919-1924*, 41: 119-484, Washington: Government Printing Office.

Harless, Susan E. ed.
    1998 *Native Arts of the Columbia Plateau: The Doris Swayze Bounds Collection*. The High Desert Museum. Seattle: University of Washington Press.

Holmes, William Henry
    1896 Prehistoric Textile Art of Eastern United States. *Annual Report of the Bureau of Ethnology 1891-1892*. 13: 3-46, Washington: Government Printing Office.

Howay, F.W.
    1918 The Dog's Hair Blankets of the Coast Salish. *The Washington Historical Quarterly* vol. IX (2): 83-92.

Jacknis, Ira
    1992 'The Artist Himself': The Salish Basketry Monograph and the Beginnings of a Boasian Paradigm. In *The Early Years of Native American Art History*, ed. Janet Catherine Berlo, 134-161. Seattle: University of Washington Press.

Laforet, Andrea
    nd. *Song Notes: James A Teit Wax Cylinder Recordings*. Canadian Museum of Civilization Unpublished manuscript.
    1984 Tsimshian Basketry. In *The Tsimshian: Images of the Past, Views for the Present*, ed. M. Seguin, 215-280. Vancouver: UBC Press.
    1990 Regional and Personal Style in Northwest Coast Basketry. In *The Art of Native American Basketry: A Living Legacy*, ed. F.W. Porter, 281-198. Contributions to the Study of Anthropology, no. 5. New York: Greenwood Press.

Laforet, Andrea and Annie York
    1981 Notes on the Thompson Winter Dwelling. In *The World is as Sharp as a Knife: an Anthology in Honour of Wilson Duff*, ed., Don Abbott, 115-122. Victoria: British Columbia Provincial Museum.

Orchard, William C.
    1926 *A Rare Salish Blanket*. Leaflets of the Museum of the American Indian, Heye Foundation, New York, no.5.

Peterson, Karen Daniels
    1963 Chippewa Mat-Weaving Techniques. *Anthropological Papers Smithsonian Institution, Bureau of American Ethnology* Bulletin, 186, nos. 63-67. Washington: U.S. Government Printing Office.

Rice, Harvey S.
    1991 Native American Dwellings of the Southern Plateau. In *Spokane and the Inland Empire: An Interior Pacific Northwest Anthology*, ed. David H. Stratton, 83-107. Pullman Washington: Washington State University Press.

Rogers, Nora
    1983,
        Some Rush Mats with Warp Movements as Patterning. In *Celebration of the Curious Mind*, eds. Nora Rogers and Martha Stanley, 9-20. Leveland Colorado.

Sparrow, Debra
    1998 A Journey. In *Material Matters,* eds. Ingrid Bachmann and Ruth Scheuing, 149-156. Toronto: YYZBooks.

Sampson, Amelia Sohappy
    1991 Tule Mat-Making: A Yakima Tradition. In *A Time of Gathering: Native Heritage in Washington State*, ed. Robin K. Wright, Thomas Burke Memorial Washington State Museum Monograph 7, 186-188. Seattle: Burke Museum.

Samuels, Cheryl
    1982 *The Chilkat Dancing Blanket*. Norman: University of Oklahoma Press.
    1987 *The Raven's Tail*. Vancouver: University of British Columbia Press.

Schlick, Mary D.
    1994 *Columbia River Basketry: Gift of the Ancestors, Gift of the Earth*. Seattle: University of Washington Press.

Steedman, E.V.
    1929 The Ethnobotany of the Thompson Indians of British Columbia. *Bureau of American Ethnology 45th Annual Report, 1927-28*. Washington: Smithsonian Institution.

Tepper, Leslie
    1987 *The Interior Salish Tribes of British Columbia: A Photographic Catalogue*. Mercury Series 111, Ottawa: Canadian Museum of Civilization, National Museums of Canada.
    1994 *Earth Line and Morning Star: Nlaka'pamux Clothing Traditions*. Hull: Canadian Museum of Civilization.

Teit, James A.
    1900 The Thompson Indians. *American Museum of Natural History, Memoir 2(4): Publications of the Jesup North Pacific Expedition*. 1(4):163-390.
    1930 Tatooing and Face and Body Painting of the Thompson Indians, British Columbia. In *Forty-fifth Annual Report of the Bureau of American Ethnology for 1927-1928*, ed. Franz Boas, 397-439. Washington: U.S. Government Printing Office.

Turner, Nancy J.
    1998 *Plant Technology of First Peoples in British Columbia*. Royal British Columbia Museum Handbook, Vancouver: University of British Columbia Press.

Turner, Nancy J., Laurence C. Thompson, M.Terry Thompson, Annie Z. York
    1990 *Thompson Ethnobotany: Knowledge and Usage of Plants by the Thompson Indians of British Columbia*. Memoir no. 3, Victoria: Royal British Columbia Museum.

Wells, Oliver N.
    1969 *Salish Weaving: Primitive and Modern*. Sardis, BC: Oliver Wells.

Whiteford, Andrew Hunter, and Nora Rogers
    1994 Woven Mats of the Western Great Lakes. *American Indian Art Magazine* 19(4):58-65.

Wickwire, Wendy
    1979 'Jimmy Teit' Anthropologist of the People. *Nicola Valley Historical Quarterly* 2(2): 4. Merritt, British Columbia.
    1993 Women in Ethnography: the Research of James A. Teit. *Ethnohistory* 40(4): 539-562.
    1998 'We Shall Drink from the Stream and So Shall You': James A. Teit and Native Resistance in British Columbia, 1908-22. *The Canadian Historical Review* 79(2): 199-236.

Willoughby, Charles C.,
    1910 A New Type of Ceremonial Blanket from the Northwest Coast. *American Anthropologist* ns January-March 12(1): 1-10.

Wright, Robin K. ed.
    1991 *A Time of Gathering: Native Heritage in Washington State*. Thomas Burke Memorial Washington State Museum Monograph 7. Seattle: Burke Museum.

Acknowledgements

During the last ten years, many people have contributed their support, time and creativity to my study of Nlaka'pamux material culture. I would like to thank Chief Robert Pasco, Chief George Saddleman, Chief David Walkem, Chief Bryron Spinks, Chief Nathan Spinks, and Chief Gordon Antoine who supported the research programs. I am grateful to Debbie Abbott, Harold Aljam and the other members of the Nlaka'pamux Nation Tribal office and the Nicola Valley Tribal Association office for their assistance.

I would particularly like to thank Mandy Jimmie, Mandy Brown, Pearl Hewitt, Jean York, and Mabel Joe. They have generously shared their knowledge of Nlaka'pamux history and material culture. Sigurd Teit, Curator at the Merritt Museum, is a valued colleague and friend. The late Theresa Albert, tanner, bead worker and seamstress, is remembered for her important contributions to the research and revitalization of Nlaka'pamux knowledge.

I would also like to thank Albert Heyman, Dorothy Burnham, Judy Thompson, Judy Hall, and Elliot Tepper for reading these papers and making valuable editorial comments and suggestions.

Section 4
Eastern Woodlands Studies

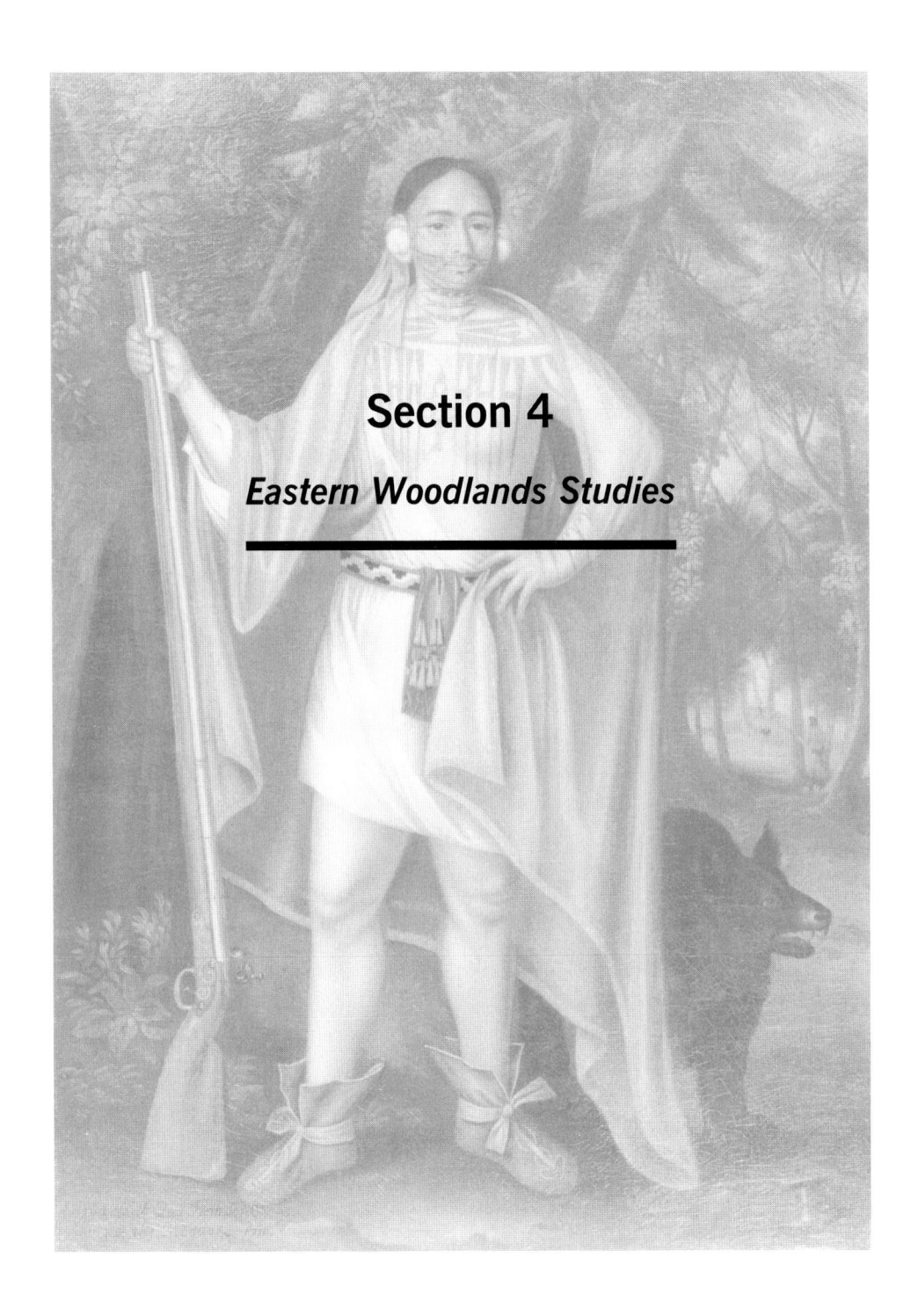

Sa Ga Yeath Pieth Tow by John Verelst, 1710.
Courtesy National Archives of Canada, Ottawa C-92419.

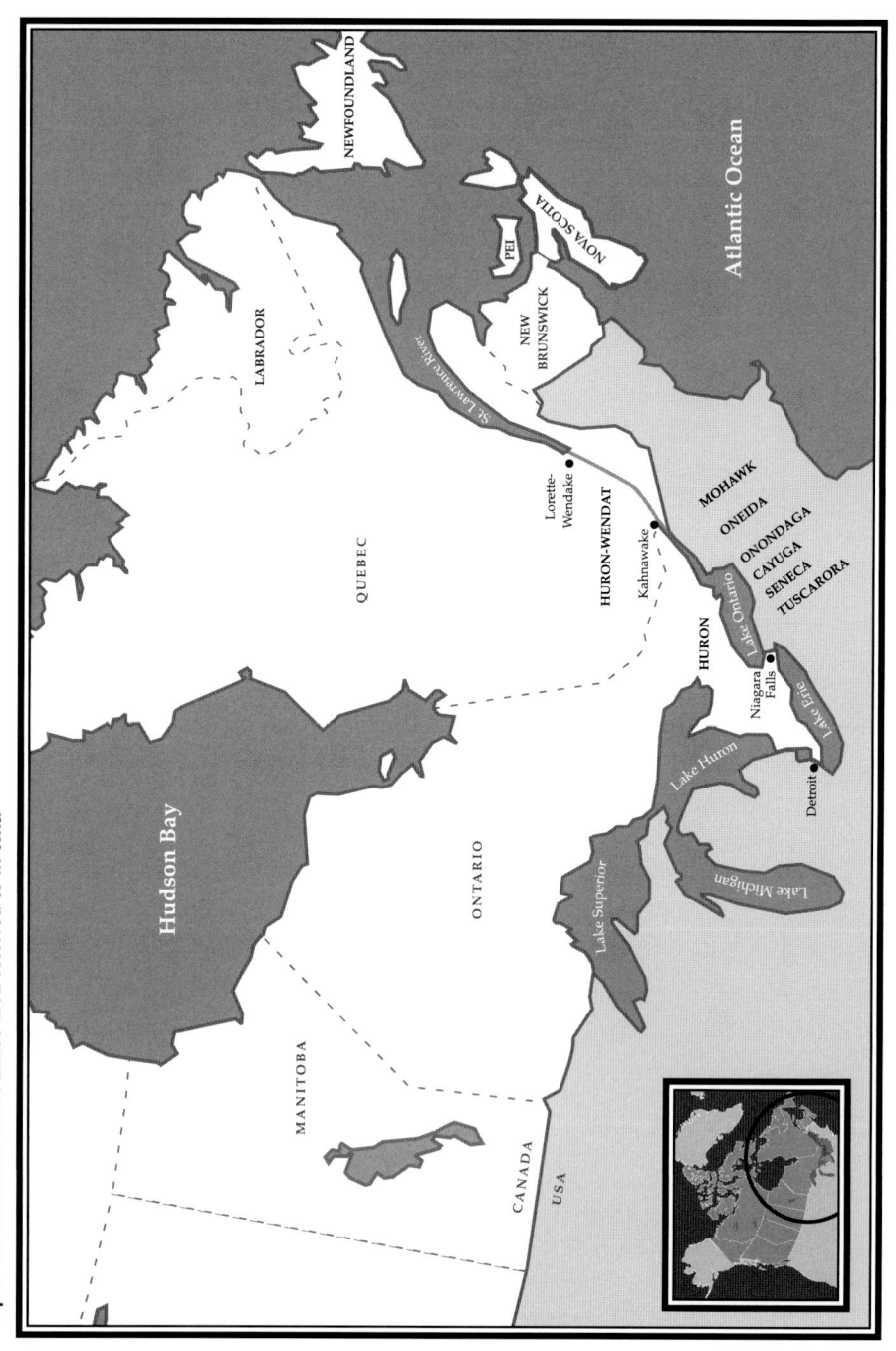

Map of St. Lawrence-Great Lakes area referred to in text.

"To Make Them Beautiful": Porcupine Quill Decorated Moccasins From the St. Lawrence-Great Lakes

Judy Hall

In all these objects, everything was done to make them beautiful.

Dorothy K. Burnham[1]

Introduction

The Canadian Museum of Civilization's ethnographic collection from northeastern North America includes over 80 skin artifacts decorated with porcupine quills. In 1997, Dorothy Burnham and I began a research project involving these objects. We systematically studied a wide range of material which included pouches, pipe stems, headdresses, and knife sheaths. It was the beautifully decorated moccasins, however, that consistently drew our attention. We examined each pair of moccasins, noting the pattern and methods of applying the porcupine quills. We kept finding different and subtle ways of using the quills. From this analysis, Dorothy produced the drawings of decorative techniques.

This paper presents some preliminary results of our research into the approaches taken to moccasin decoration in the St. Lawrence-Great Lakes region of northeastern North America (see Map). Information on moccasins decorated with porcupine quills is drawn from several sources: historical accounts and journals of European explorers who travelled to the St. Lawrence-Great Lakes area as early as the sixteenth century, paintings by European artists, analysis of moccasins preserved in museum and private collections mainly in North America and Europe, and interviews with contemporary quillworkers. Historical accounts from the sixteenth to eighteenth centuries provide descriptions of the materials and decoration of moccasins. Examples in museum collections give tangible form to these general references. During the late eighteenth and early nineteenth centuries, moccasins were extensively ornamented with porcupine quills applied in intricate techniques that testify to the complexity of this decorative art. However, by the mid-nineteenth century, most women were no longer decorating moccasins, or, for that matter, other objects, with porcupine quills. This decline can be attributed, in part, to the increased popularity of imported materials as decoration and to consumer demand. Today, nearly 150 years later, a few artists are once again using porcupine quills to decorate skin garments, including moccasins.

The purposes of this paper are three-fold. The first is to describe the techniques identified to date on two styles of quillworked moccasins from the late eighteenth and early nineteenth centuries and to compare approaches to decoration. The second is to place quillwork on moccasins into a broader historical framework by discussing early examples of this decorative art from northeastern North America and the factors that contributed to its subsequent decline. Ultimately, however, the research and technical analysis presented here could contribute to the revitalization of the use of porcupine quills on moccasins by present and future generations of artists.

The paper is divided into four sections. The first, "Worthy of Admiration", brings together historical accounts and artifactual evidence to illustrate that porcupine quill decoration on moccasins is a long-established and highly developed artistic tradition. The second section, "Very Neatly Interwoven", compares quillwork techniques on two moccasin types from the late eighteenth and early nineteenth centuries. "Moosehair, Beads, Nuns and Consumers" discusses some of the factors contributing to the decline of this decorative art by the mid-nineteenth century. The final section, "Carrying on the Tradition", looks to the future and the revival of porcupine quill decoration on skin garments by contemporary artists.

"Worthy of Admiration": Early Moccasins from Northeastern North America

Very little is known about the style and decoration of moccasins before the late eighteenth century. General information on moccasins from the St. Lawrence-Great Lakes region of northeastern North America, however, can be gleaned from written descriptions in the journals of European missionaries, travellers and explorers from the sixteenth to eighteenth centuries. The few extant examples of early moccasins in museum collections provide another source of information.

The written narratives reveal that moccasins of this period were fashioned from a variety of animal skins and were richly adorned with vibrant colours.

One of the earliest references to decorated footwear from this area comes from the journal of André Thevet, the Royal Cosmographer of France, who was near Quebec and the St. Lawrence River in 1555 to 1556. Thevet noted that:

> *Canadian women wear …shoes … made of [tanned leather] and fancy work …These [women] do not go bare-legged but have shoes made of tanned and well-worked leather, enriched with divers colors which they make from herbs and fruits.*[2]

Samuel de Champlain, who stayed with the Huron[3] in the early seventeenth century, also remarked on the variety of skins "of deer, bear and beaver" used to make moccasins.[4]

Porcupine quills used as clothing decoration are referred to in the journal of Father Gabriel Sagard-Theodat, a Recollect of St. Francis, who travelled among the Huron in 1624. The women, he wrote,

> *make a kind of leather game-bag or tobacco-pouch, which they work in a manner worthy of admiration with porcupine quills, coloured red, black, white, and blue, and these colours they make so bright that ours do not seem to come near them in that respect.*[5]

The Huron also decorated other clothing items, including moccasins, with porcupine quills: "Some of them [Huron women] have also belts and other finery made of porcupine quills dyed crimson red and very neatly interwoven."[6]

Moccasin construction and porcupine quill decoration were also noted by Father Joseph François Lafitau, who lived with the Iroquois (Mohawk) at Sault St. Louis (Kahnawake) from 1712 to 1717:

> *The leggings have no feet and are tucked into moccasins of a single skin with no heel and no strong leather sole. It is puckered over the toes of the foot, where it is sewn with cords of gut to a little leather tongue. Then it is taken up with ties of the same skin, passed through holes cut at regular intervals and tied above the heel after being crossed on the instep of the foot…Different sorts of threads are interwoven very neatly with moose, buffalo and porcupine skins [quills] dyed in different colours.*[7]

Early examples of decorated footwear from northeastern North America are today preserved in European museums. Since the first European explorers, missionaries and adventurers had travelled to North America in the sixteenth century, they had collected objects to take back to Europe as gifts or as personal mementos. Some of these objects were incorporated into Royal collections, such as the Royal Cabinet of Carlos III in Madrid, Spain and the King's Collection in Paris, France which contained material "deposited by the official voyagers who brought the objects to their Sovereign as proof of their

"To Make Them Beautiful": Porcupine Quill Decorated Moccasins

contact"[8] with indigenous people in the New World. Moccasins are particularly well represented in these early collections, most likely due to their availability, portability and their functional and aesthetic appeal. As with many objects in museum collections, reliable documentation as to their origin has been lost over time. Some evidence does suggest, however, that the moccasins discussed below originated in the St. Lawrence-Great Lakes region of northeastern North America.

Several pairs of moccasins decorated with porcupine quills at the Musée de l'Homme in Paris may be the earliest examples from northeastern North America preserved in museum collections. One pair from this collection is illustrated in Figure 4.1. These moccasins possibly were collected by Jacques Cartier in the Upper St. Lawrence region between 1534 and 1542.[9] Even if the sixteenth century date cannot be confirmed, subsequent collection history documents that they were part of the Collection of the King and the Museum of Antiquities in 1794. Each moccasin is made from deerskin, dyed black, in one-piece construction with a vertical heel seam and a centre front seam that continues under the toe. The heel seam, upright ankle lapels, and centre front seam are decorated with natural white and dyed red and black porcupine quills applied in line, whipped running stitch (Figure 4.2) and folded, zig-zag, single quill (Figure 4.3) techniques on sinew thread. The geometric design of repeated triangles on the ankle lapels is achieved by alternating the colour of the quills. The five-lobed motifs on each side are applied in line technique (Figure 4.2). The upper edge of the ankle lapels is worked in identical quill colours in single quill edging (Figure 4.4).[10]

4.1 Moccasins. Northeastern North America. The soles have been damaged. Length: 20.5 cm (8"). Courtesy Musée de l'Homme, Paris 78.32.265.

Fascinating Challenges

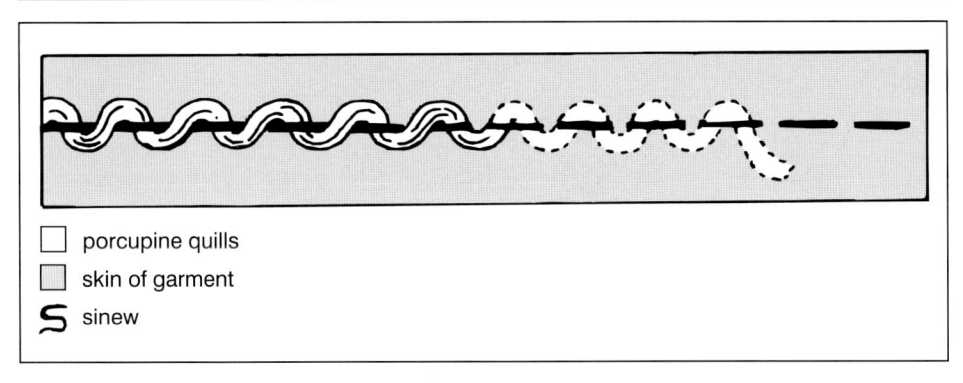

4.2 Line, whipped running stitch technique. In this technique, the porcupine quill passes over and under a line of sinew running stitches. (DB)

Two pairs of moccasins in the Museo de América in Madrid have similar characteristics of cut and decoration.[11] They may have been acquired for the Royal Cabinet of Carlos III assembled before 1762[12] and probably originated in northeastern North America "within the region of French colonial influence."[13] One pair, illustrated in Figure 4.5, was originally made from a single piece of tanned smoked skin with a vertical heel seam, centre front seam and downturned ankle lapels. The skin is gathered over the toes. The centre front and heel seams are overlaid with natural white and dyed red and yellow porcupine quills applied in line, whipped running stitch (Figure 4.2) and folded, zig-zag, single quill (Figure 4.3) techniques. Fragments of quills are all that remain of the edging on the ankle lapels, which "consists of a quill-wrapped leather thong attached to the edge by yarn stitches."[14]

By the beginning of the eighteenth century and probably earlier, some women were decorating moccasins with imported materials in addition to porcupine quills. The new materials included glass beads, metal cones, fabric and silk ribbon brought to North America from Europe. In the eighteenth century, European travellers commented on the use of porcupine quills and imported materials as moccasin decoration, and remarked on the high value placed on the new materials by the makers. For example, Isaac Weld, an Irishman travelling in the eastern United States and Canada between 1795 and 1797, observed that moccasins

> *are tastefully ornamented with porcupine quills and beads; the flap [ankle lapel] is edged with tin or copper tags filled with scarlet hair, if the moccasin be intended for a man, with ribbands [ribbons] if for a woman. An ornamented moccasin of this sort is only worn in dress, as the ornaments are expensive and the leather soon wears out; one of plain leather answers for ordinary use.*[15]

A pair of moccasins in the British Museum in London illustrates this decorative style (Figure 4.6). The moccasins are similar to those worn by

"To Make Them Beautiful": Porcupine Quill Decorated Moccasins

Sa Ga Yeath Qua Pieth Tow, an Iroquois (Mohawk) Chief, in a portrait by John Verelst painted in 1710 (Figure 4.7). Each moccasin is made from tanned skin in one-piece construction[16] with vertical heel seam and upright ankle lapels. A variation in the cut of the moccasins from those illustrated in Figures 4.1 and 4.5 can be seen in the curved seam at the toe. Red, yellow and white porcupine quills are applied to the centre front seam, the seam across the toe and the ankle lapels in line, whipped running stitch (Figure 4.2) and folded, zig-zag, single quill (Figure 4.3) techniques. The upper edge of the ankle lapels is bound with alternating colour blocks of orange and white quills in single quill edging (Figure 4.4). Predominantly white and blue glass beads, and also a few green and yellow beads, outline the centre front, toe and heel seams. Tassels of red dyed animal hair are inserted into imported metal cones to form a spaced fringe around the ankle. Natural white porcupine quills are wrapped around the skin thongs that attach the fringes to the ankle

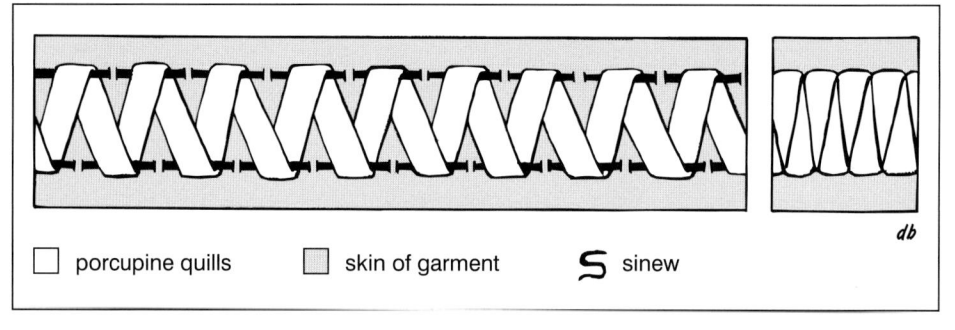

4.3 Folded, zig-zag, single quill technique. In zig-zag quillwork, the porcupine quill is held by two rows of stitches in a sequence of over, under, over, and under which produces the characteristic zig-zag effect. (DB) A running stitch secures the porcupine quills in this and subsequent drawings; a backstitch was also used.

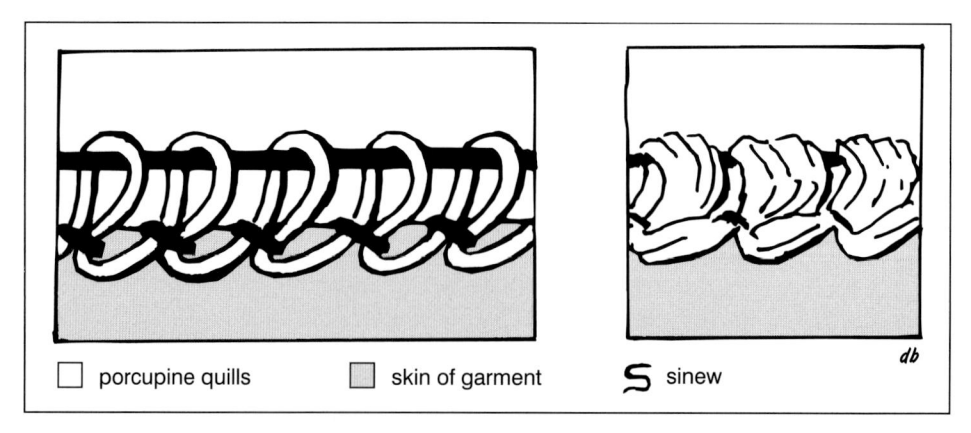

4.4 Edging technique, single quill. A porcupine quill is passed through a slanting sinew stitch taken on the edge of the skin. It then is looped over a sinew cord and back through the same edge stitch before moving to the next slanting stitch and repeating the movement. There are several variations of this technique. The diagram on the right gives the appearance of this version. (DB)

Fascinating Challenges

4.5 Moccasins. Northeastern North America, 18th century. No collection documentation prior to 1865, however, may be from the collection of Pedro Franco Davila before 1762 for the Royal Cabinet of Carlos III. The ankle lapels are photographed upright. Length: 24.5 cm (9 ½").
Courtesy Museo de América, Madrid 13953-1,2.

4.6 Moccasins. Northeastern North America, probably early 18th century. Acquired from the Yorkshire Philosophical Society Museum, York, England. Length: 22.0 cm (8 ¾").
Courtesy The British Museum, London 1921.10-14.84.

"To Make Them Beautiful": Porcupine Quill Decorated Moccasins

lapels (Figure 4.8). An account from the late eighteenth century refers to the aesthetic appeal of these metal cone fringes on Iroquois moccasins: "The quarters are ornamented about the ankle with small pieces of brass or tin, fastened with leather strings, which make an odd jingling, when they walk or dance."[17]

As we have seen from these examples from possibly the sixteenth to eighteenth centuries, moccasins from northeastern North America were made from one piece of skin cut with a vertical heel seam and a centre front seam. A variation in the pattern produced a curved toe seam as illustrated in Figure 4.6. The moccasins were decorated with porcupine quills in natural white and dyed

4.7 Sa Ga Yeath Qua Pieth Tow (Sagayenkwaraton), an Iroquois (Mohawk) Chief, by John Verelst, 1710. Oil on canvas. Courtesy National Archives of Canada, Ottawa C-92419.

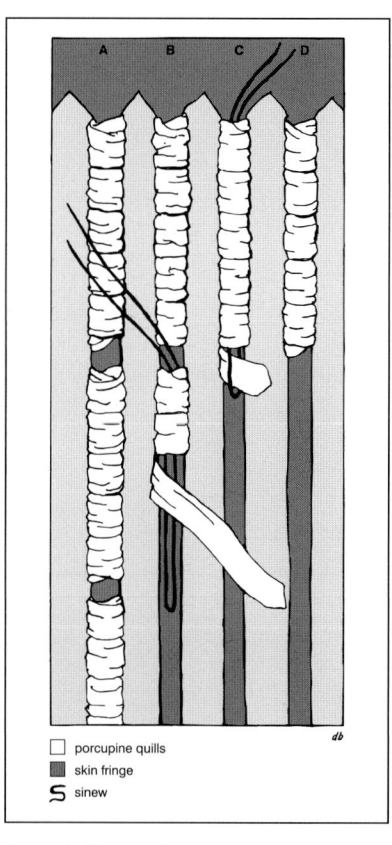

4.8 Quill wrapping. The same technique used to wrap fringes with porcupine quills also wrapped the skin thongs on the metal cones.
A. Finished strand
B. Finished section and incomplete wrapping showing insertion of sinew loop
C. Quill end enclosed in sinew loop
D. Finished section with quill end drawn up and sinew removed (DB)

red, yellow, orange and black, applied using a limited number of line, folded and edging techniques. Imported materials, such as glass beads and metal cones, were often added as secondary decorative elements. These moccasins may represent early decorative styles of the magnificently ornamented moccasins of the late eighteenth and early nineteenth centuries as discussed in the following section.

"Very Neatly Interwoven": Techniques of Porcupine Quill Decoration on Moccasins in the late Eighteenth and early Nineteenth Centuries

Moccasins collected in the St. Lawrence-Great Lakes region in the late eighteenth and early nineteenth centuries were elaborately ornamented with porcupine quills applied in intricate and complex techniques that reflected the maker's extensive technical skill and creative artistry. Moccasins, decorated in styles attributed to the Iroquois (particularly the Seneca) and Huron-Wendat[18], are well represented in museum collections, providing a body of examples for the comparison of approaches to decoration. Although the cut of the moccasins was similar, the porcupine quills were applied in different techniques and combinations of techniques to produce variations in design. Moccasins in the collection of the Canadian Museum of Civilization will serve as examples of these two decorative styles.

Figure 4.9 illustrates a pair of moccasins in a style attributed to the Iroquois (Seneca) in the early nineteenth century. Each moccasin is made from tanned smoked skin in one-piece construction with down-turned ankle lapels. The moccasins are sewn with a vertical heel seam that is gathered just above the sole, and a centre front seam using sinew thread. The skin is gathered around the toe. Porcupine quills in red, blue, yellow and white are applied directly to the skin along the centre seam in a single lane of folded, zig-zag, single quill (Figure 4.3) flanked by concentric rows of line, overcast core, decorative (Figure 4.10) technique. The same quillwork techniques are applied directly to the ankle lapels in a bilaterally symmetrical design that is identical on each side. The ankle lapels are also bound with silk ribbon[19] and edged with a single row of white glass beads illustrating the use of imported materials. Many of the motifs on the moccasins reflect Iroquois cosmology and spirituality. For example, the double-curve may represent branches of the Great Tree of Peace,[20] a symbol of strength, unity and diplomacy among the Iroquois.

The following additional line and folded techniques have been identified to date on this style of decorated moccasin: line, whipped running stitch (Figure 4.2); folded, straight, two-quills, alternating and interlaced[21] (Figure 4.11); folded, straight, six-quills, interlaced (Figure 4.12); folded, zig-zag, two-quills,

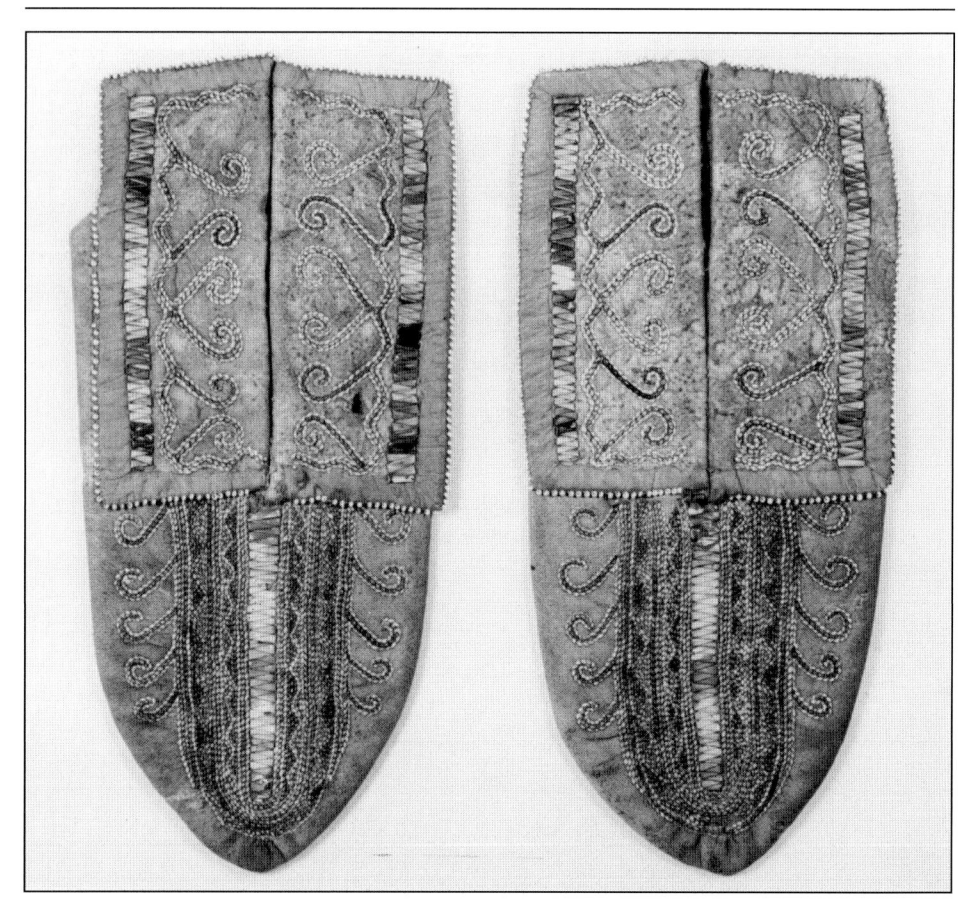

"To Make Them Beautiful": Porcupine Quill Decorated Moccasins

4.9 Moccasins, decorative style attributed to the Iroquois (Seneca), early 19th century. Collected by Arthur Speyer. Originally acquired near Buffalo, New York in 1836.
Length: 25.0 cm (9 ¾"); Width: 12.0 cm (4 ¾").
Canadian Museum of Civilization III-I-1309 a,b.

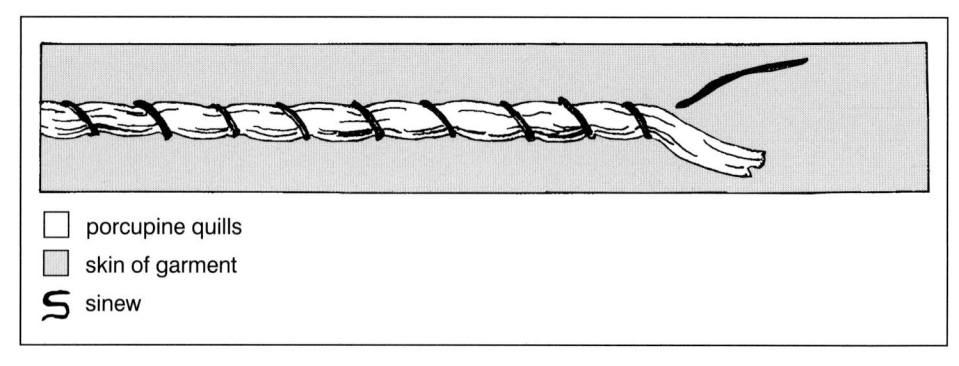

- ☐ porcupine quills
- ☐ skin of garment
- S sinew

4.10 Line, overcast core, decorative technique. In this technique, the porcupine quill is laid on the skin and oversewn with sinew stitches. (DB)

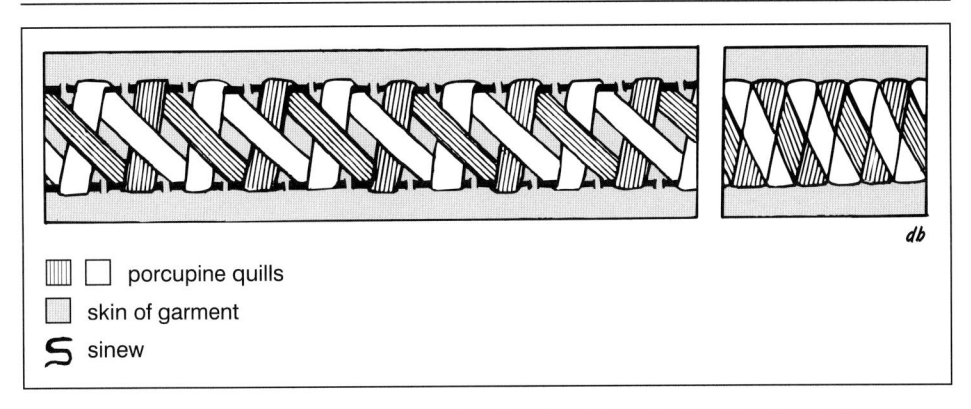

4.11 Folded, straight, two-quills, alternating and interlaced technique. In straight quillwork, the porcupine quills are held by two rows of stitches in a sequence of under, over, over, under. This technique uses two quills of contrasting colour, working first with one and then with the other in the same sequence of movement: under, over, over, under. Where the two quills pass each other, between the rows of stitches, one quill is carried over the other before being held down by the sewing. (DB)

alternating[22] (Figure 4.13); folded, zig-zag, two-quills, alternating and interlaced[23] (Figure 4.14); folded, zig-zag, three-quills, interlaced[24] (Figure 4.15); and folded, zig-zag, four-quills, interlaced (Figure 4.16). Variations in the colour and number of quills and the method of folding the quills produced the intricate patterns seen on this type of moccasin.

In contrast, a different decorative effect is achieved on the pair of moccasins illustrated in Figure 4.17, attributed to the Huron-Wendat at the end of the eighteenth century or early nineteenth century. These moccasins are similar to those worn by Nicholas Vincent Isawanhoni, a Huron Chief from Lorette near Quebec, in a lithograph dated 1825 (Figure 4.18). Like the moccasins in Figure 4.9 already described, each of these moccasins is made from a single piece of tanned smoked skin with down-turned ankle lapels, vertical heel seam and centre front seam (Figure 4.19). The skin is gathered around the toe and sides of the foot. It is in the decoration, however, that differences between these two styles of moccasins can be recognized. The centre front seam and ankle lapels of the moccasins in Figure 4.17, for example, are overlaid with porcupine quills woven on bast fibre on a bow loom (Figure 4.20). On the centre front, the woven strip tapers towards the toe, a narrowing achieved by decreasing the rows of quills from nine to three lanes. Each side of the ankle lapels is worked in geometric designs: four diamonds on one lapel, representing four nations of the Huron Confederacy[25], and three triangles on the opposite in white, red, and black quills on a blue background. The diamond motif is repeated along the centre front seam. In addition, the moccasins are decorated with porcupine quills in three folded techniques: zig-zag, single quill (Figure 4.3), zig-zag, two-quills, alternating[26] (Figure 4.13),

"To Make Them Beautiful": Porcupine Quill Decorated Moccasins

4.12 Folded, straight, six-quills, interlaced technique. Moccasin (detail) along centre seam on main foot. Courtesy Indianermuseum der Stadt Zurich, Zurich Nr 5.

■ ☐ porcupine quills
☐ skin of garment
S sinew

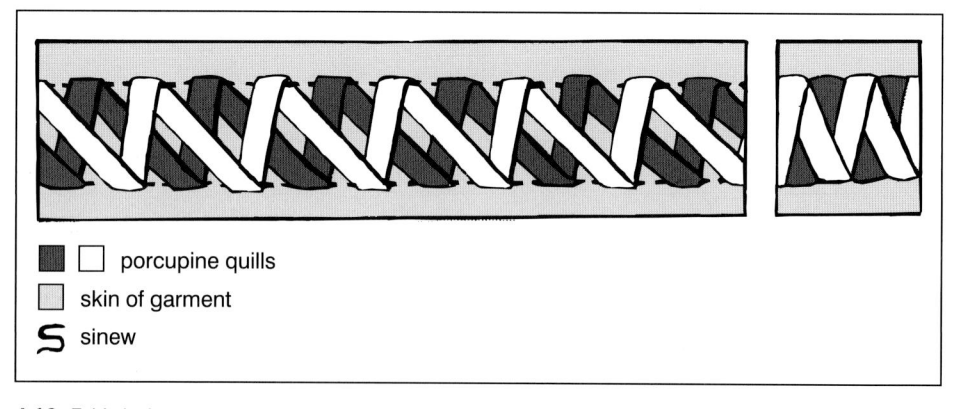

4.13 Folded, zig-zag, two-quills, alternating technique. In this version, two porcupine quills of contrasting colour are used alternately, each being held down by every second stitch. The resulting effect is of a line of zig-zags of one colour against a background of the other colour. (DB)

■ □ porcupine quills
skin of garment
∫ sinew

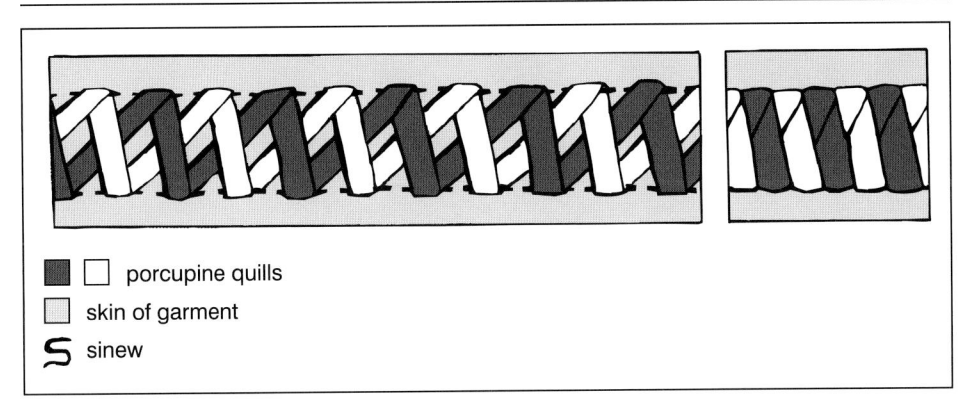

4.14 Folded, zig-zag, two-quills, alternating and interlaced technique. Two porcupine quills of contrasting colour held by alternate stitches, as described in Figure 4.13, are interlaced in a regular sequence resulting in a pattern of interlacing V-shapes.(DB)

4.15 Folded, zig-zag, three-quills, interlaced technique. Moccasin (detail) three central rows. Outer rows are in folded, straight, two-quills, alternating and interlaced (Figure 4.11). Courtesy University of Pennsylvania Museum, Philadelphia. NA 4945.

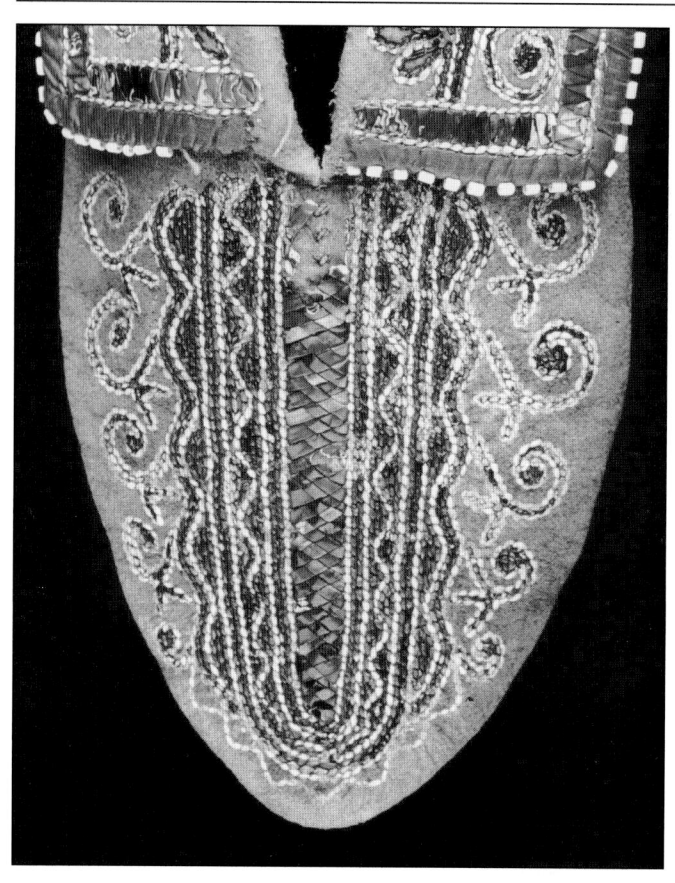

4.16 Folded, zig-zag, four-quills, interlaced technique. Moccasin (detail) along centre seam on main foot. Courtesy Peabody & Essex Museum, Salem E26,326.

and zig-zag, two-quills, alternating and interlaced (Figure 4.14). The latter two techniques are combined in the same row to produce subtle variations in design and colour. The very ingenious way of joining the loom weaving and the line of folded, zig-zag, single quill is illustrated in Figure 4.21. In this way, the folded quillwork anchors the bow loom weaving to the skin and also serves as a decorative edge. Two additional techniques have been identified on this style of decorated moccasin: line, whipped running stitch[27] (Figure 4.2) and folded, zig-zag, two-quills, double layer[28] (Figure 4.22).

In summary, differing approaches to moccasin decoration have been revealed by detailed analysis of quillwork techniques on a large number of moccasins of the styles illustrated in Figures 4.9 and 4.17. As the moccasins in Figure 4.9 illustrate, Iroquois (Seneca) women applied porcupine quills in combinations of line and folded techniques. It was in the latter techniques that they excelled: up to six quills were interwoven to produce intricate combinations of design and colour. Huron-Wendat women, on the other hand, used a limited number of folded techniques involving only one or two quills. They were, however, masters in the art of bow-loom weaving, a decorative art tradition also found

4.17 Moccasins, decorative style attributed to the Huron-Wendat, late 18th century. Collected by Arthur Speyer, formerly in the collection of Sir John Caldwell who was an Officer in the 8th Regiment of Foot during the American Revolution. Caldwell was stationed at Niagara and Detroit. Length: 25.5 cm (10"); Width: 12.0 cm (4 ¾"). Canadian Museum of Civilization III-H-432 a,b.

further west in the Great Lakes area and among Athabaskan groups (see Thompson, this volume).

Differences between these two decorative styles can also be seen in the designs on the moccasins. Porcupine quills applied in wavy and straight lines, circles, double-curves, stylized floral motifs and curvilinear designs were worked directly on the skin of Iroquois (Seneca) style moccasins in bilaterally symmetrical compositions in identical colour combinations.[29] On most Huron-Wendat style moccasins, woven quillwork bands in different geometric patterns in the same quill colours overlaid the ankle lapels[30] as illustrated in Figure 4.17. Less frequently, the panels were woven with identical geometric designs in the same colour combination,[31] or in identical designs with the same colours in different combinations.[32]

"To Make Them Beautiful": Porcupine Quill Decorated Moccasins

4.18 Nicholas Vincent Isawanhoni, a Huron chief, La Jeune Lorette near Quebec, 1825. After Edward Chatfield. Hand-coloured lithograph. Courtesy National Archives of Canada, Ottawa C38948.

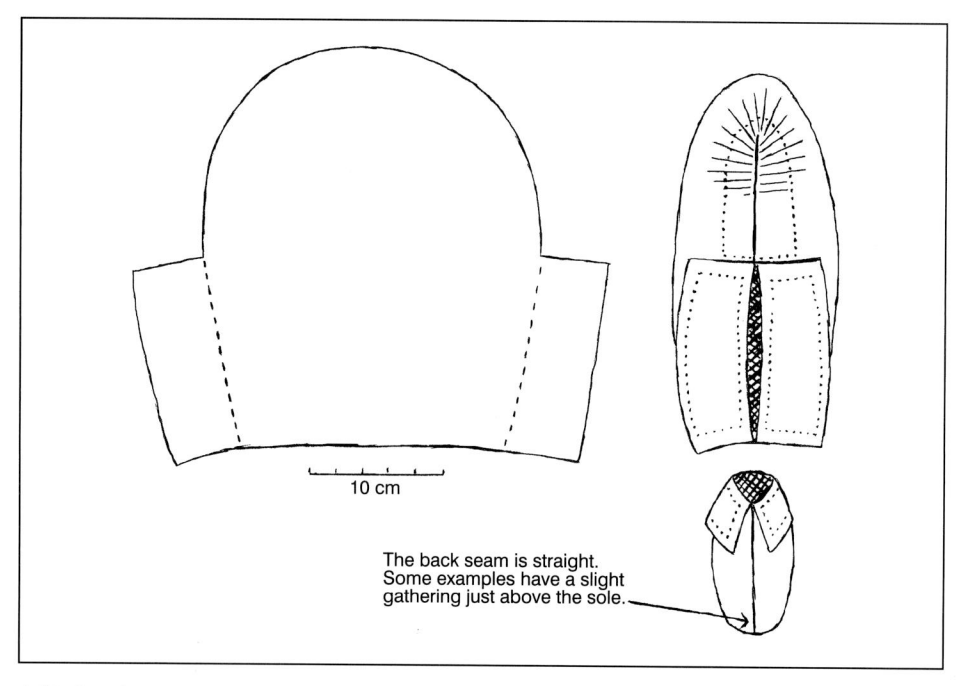

The back seam is straight. Some examples have a slight gathering just above the sole.

4.19 Cut of moccasins illustrated in Figure 4.17. Canadian Museum of Civilization 111-H-432 a,b.

4.20 Loom-woven technique. In an actual band, only the porcupine quills show. Every second warp thread is held firmly on a bow; the intervening warps are supplied by porcupine quills inserted by the weaver. As the short length of a porcupine quill runs out, or if another colour is desired, the end of the porcupine quill is pushed down to the back and a new quill worked in. (DB)

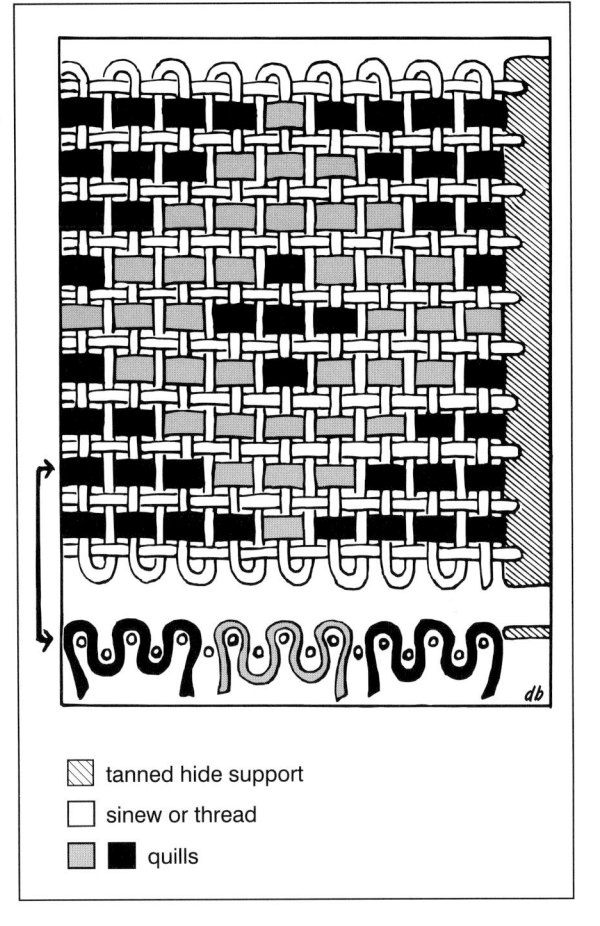

⬚ tanned hide support
☐ sinew or thread
▨ ■ quills

Moosehair, Beads, Nuns and Consumers: the Decline of Porcupine Quill Decorated Moccasins

By the mid-nineteenth century and possibly earlier, the use of porcupine quills for moccasin decoration had declined in the St. Lawrence – Great Lakes region. The introduction of imported materials, promotion of local decorative resources, and production for the European and American tourist market all contributed to the decline of this decorative art. Changes in moccasin decoration among the Huron-Wendat and Iroquois will serve as examples.

Dyed moosehair, applied in geometric designs to clothing and other objects, was a long-established artistic tradition among the Huron-Wendat.[33] Influenced by the Ursulines and other nuns in Québec, Huron-Wendat women used dyed moosehair in stylized and naturalistic floral motifs to decorate commodities destined for sale to European and American army personnel and travellers in Québec or at Niagara Falls and other tourist destinations.[34] By the late eighteenth century, moosehair, dyed vibrant colours, was applied to moccasins and other garments in highly conventionalized patterns of dense floral

"To Make Them Beautiful": Porcupine Quill Decorated Moccasins

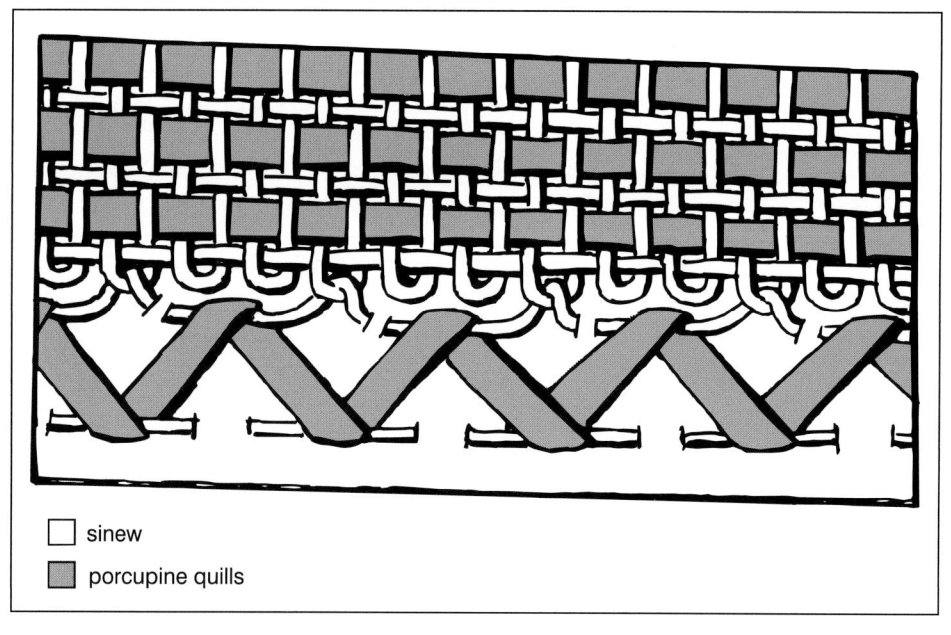

4.21 Join between weaving. In all versions of folded quillwork, the porcupine quills are secured by passing them backwards and forwards through two parallel rows of stitches. In this case, however, the line of folded quillwork is used to attach the strip of bow loom weaving to the skin. As usual, one row of quills is folded around sinew stitches in the skin; the other row is carried through the weft edge loops of the weaving. If this is done on both sides, the weaving is held firmly in place. The folded quillwork, therefore, performs a useful as well as an ornamental function. (DB)

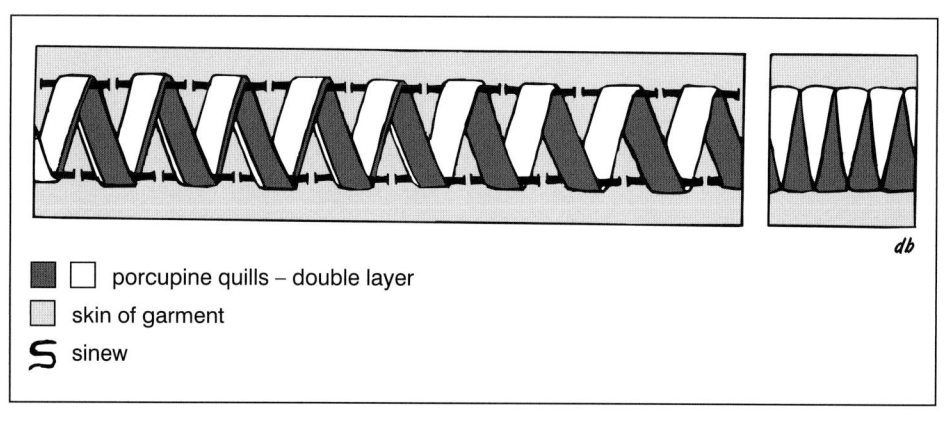

4.22 Folded, zig-zag, two-quills, double layer technique. By using a double layer of porcupine quills of contrasting colour, the zig-zag effect is strongly enhanced with first one colour showing and then the other. (DB)

— 254 —

designs, scrolls, and curves.[35] As the moccasins in Figure 4.23 illustrate, porcupine quills and moosehair were often combined as decoration. On this example, collected in 1832, porcupine quills in folded, zig-zag, single quill (Figure 4.3) technique form the bands around the ankle lapels and the toe; moosehair produces the stylized floral and dot-and-circle motifs on the upper foot and outlines the designs on the ankle lapels.[36] The moccasins in Figure 4.23 also show how Huron-Wendat women altered the cut of the moccasins to accommodate European taste. As Ruth Phillips has observed: "The deep cuff flaps, practical for travel and bad weather, have been replaced by a flat ankle panel embroidered in imitation of the vanished cuff."[37] Some moccasins combined both flat panels and down-turned ankle lapels.[38] Specialized foot-wear in the form of European lady's boots[39] and evening shoes[40] decorated with moosehair or a combination of porcupine quills and moosehair were also made during the mid- to late nineteenth century.

By the mid-nineteenth century, moccasin production for a souvenir market had become a major industry. During a visit to Lorette-Wendake in 1854 to 1855, Johann Kohl, a German traveller, remarked on the large number of objects that were being sent to Niagara Falls for sale. Kohl met a Chief in the village who

> *seemed indeed to carry on quite a wholesale trade .., for he had great tuns and chests full of mocassins (sic) embroidered with flowers ..., all made by the women of the village, and which are, I believe, destined to be sent to Montreal, and thence probably to Niagara and New York.[41]*

By 1898, making moccasins had become the second most important economic activity in the community after skin tanning. In that year, for example, 140,000 pairs were shipped to dealers in Canada and the United States.[42] These moccasins were decorated with simple designs in moosehair.[43] Mass production was to have an effect on moccasin decoration as extensive work in porcupine quills was time-consuming and, therefore, not viable economically.

Among the Iroquois, imported materials and consumer demand also contributed to the decline of porcupine quills as moccasin decoration. Glass beads and fabric became increasingly popular for ornamenting moccasins and other garments. For example, by the early nineteenth century, some moccasins of the style illustrated in Figure 4.9 were decorated with porcupine quills on the upper foot, but the ankle lapels were overlaid with silk ribbon or wool stroud adorned with bead embroidery.[44] The addition of European square-toed leather soles to some porcupine quill decorated moccasins represents a modification of this traditional Aboriginal style for European consumption.[45] By the 1850s, Iroquoian women were making moccasins with fabric (generally velvet) ankle lapels and vamps richly adorned with multi-coloured floral beadwork, meant for their personal use and for sale to tourists and travellers at Niagara Falls and other tourist areas.[46]

4.23 Moccasins. Huron-Wendat type, early 19th century. Collected by Count Albert-Alexandre von Pourtalès probably at Niagara Falls in 1832. Length: 28.0 cm (11")
Courtesy Berne Historical Museum, Berne, Switzerland Po 74.403.18 a,b.

"Carrying on the Tradition"[47]: Contemporary Porcupine Quill Decorated Moccasins

The styles of porcupine quill decorated moccasins illustrated in this paper have not been made for over 150 years. During the twentieth century, only a few artists continued to decorate skin moccasins with porcupine quills.[48] Some Iroquois and Huron-Wendat today, however, are reviving the art of porcupine quill decoration on moccasins and other garments. For example, in 1987 Richard Froman (Wa-La-Has-Keh), a Mohawk living in New Jersey, made the pair of tanned moose-skin moccasins illustrated in Figure 4.24. He worked yellow and red dyed quills on waxed dental floss in folded, zig-zag, single quill (Figure 4.3) technique on separate pieces of skin. These were then

4.24 Moccasins made by Richard Froman (Wa-La-Has-Keh), Mohawk, 1987. Received Honourable Mention in the Quillwork Category in the competition "The Decorated Moccasin" organized by The Bata Shoe Museum in Toronto in 1986 to 1987 in cooperation with the Native Arts Foundation. Length: 27.5 cm (10 ¾"). Courtesy The Bata Shoe Museum, Toronto P87.0152 a,b.

sewn over the centre front seam and to each ankle lapel. Glass beads, fringes of dyed animal hair inserted into metal cones and silver brooches were added as decorative features.

Several Huron-Wendat artists in the community of Wendake, Québec, also make moccasins, as well as other skin garments, which are decorated with porcupine quills. One of these artists, Diane Savard "Kawina", became interested in porcupine quillwork through her paternal grandmother and other elders. She has been making garments decorated with porcupine quills for about 30 years and is proud to carry on this part of her heritage.

> *I started working with porcupine quills in the 1970s when there were a number of powwows where people wore traditional clothing decorated with moosehair and porcupine quills. I learned quillwork from elders in the community like Marianna Picard.*[49]

Savard decorates skin moccasins around the gathered vamp and ankle lapels using unflattened porcupine quills dyed red, yellow, green, brown and black with bark, roots, and flowers. Following the evolution of moccasin production in her community, Diane Savard designs moccasins for herself and her family and for tourists in Canada, the United States and Europe. In addition to moccasins, she makes dresses, headbands, necklaces, belts and hats decorated with porcupine quills and beads. She derives inspiration for her work from her imagination, but also from historic photographs and illustrations of objects in museum collections. The analysis of quillwork techniques on moccasins and the detailed drawings and descriptions by Dorothy Burnham presented in this paper will provide another source of information on which contemporary artists like Diane Savard can draw.

Moccasins decorated with porcupine quills were a long-established artistic tradition in the St. Lawrence-Great Lakes area until the mid-nineteenth century. The detailed study of these objects in museum collections, in association with historic paintings, oral histories and community traditions, could play a part in the revival of this vibrant art by contemporary quillwork artists who are seeking to re-create this magnificent aspect of their cultural heritage.

Acknowledgements

The research presented in this paper could not have been possible without the many colleagues in museums in North America and England who provided access to the collections. I would like to thank Dr. Christian Feest who verified the quillwork techniques on the moccasins at the Musée de l'Homme, Paris and the Museo de América, Madrid illustrated in this paper. Dr. Ruth B. Phillip's work on the Northern Woodlands section of the exhibition The Spirit Sings: Artistic Traditions of Canada's First Peoples provided some examples of porcupine quill decorated moccasins in European museums. Her research on Northern Woodlands art has been a valuable resource. François Vincent of the Conseil de la Nation Huronne-Wendat in Wendake, Québec provided advice and interviewed the artists. Finally, I would like to thank Jonathan King, Judy Thompson, Dorothy Burnham and Peter Hall for critically reading the paper and providing many useful comments.

Endnotes

1. Personal communication, 1999
2. Thevet 1986:13,45
3. Notes on nomenclature. Huron, Huron-Wendat and Iroquois are used in this paper due to their familiarity to the general reader. Members of the Iroquois community often refer to themselves as Haudenosaunee; Mohawk as Kanien'kehaka; Cayuga as Gwe-u'-gweh-o-no'; Onondaga as O-nun'-dä-ga-o-no'; Seneca as Nun-da'-wä-o-no'; Oneida as O-na'-yote-kä-o-no'; Tuscarora as Dus-ga'-o-weh-o-no'. Variations also occur in the spelling of these names.
4. Champlain 1929:1,132
5. Sagard-Theodat 1939:102
6. ibid.:144
7. Lafitau 1977:2, 29, 97
8. Fardoulis-Vitart 1979:1
9. ibid.:54; Feest in Garrido 1992:21. Other early moccasins from northeastern North America at the Musée de l'Homme include 78.32.138, 78.32.143, 78.32.137,

78.52.149 from the Collection of the Kings; also 78.32.129 probably brought to France around 1721; 34.33.15; 34.33.17; 34.33.18.

10. Identification of the quillwork techniques on these moccasins and on the pair in the Museo de América in Madrid is from photographs; verified by Dr. Christian Feest, personal communication, April 2000.

11. Also, a pair of moccasins decorated with porcupine quills in the Museo Cospiano e dell'Istituto delle Scienze, Bologna, Italy may date as early as 1677. Laurencich-Minelli and Filipetti 1983:213,222-3, Plate 2a.

12. Collected by Pedro Franco Davila; Garrido 1992:21

13. Feest in Garrido 1992:29

14. Feest, personal communication, April 2000

15. Weld 1800: 454-455, 473

16. for pattern drawing see Sager 1995:41

17. Loskiel 1794:50

18. Reliable information on the origin of these two decorative styles of moccasins was either not recorded by the collectors or has been lost over time in museum records. Moccasins worn by Huron-Wendat in the early 19th century, however, can be seen in paintings by Edward Hatfield (see Figure 4.18). Iroquois (Seneca) moccasins decorated with porcupine quills, comparable to those discussed in this paper (Figure 4.9), are illustrated in Morgan 1850: Plate 1; 1852: Plate 11.

19. probably originally red but faded to beige and pink

20. Phillips 1998:241

21. Canadian Museum of Civilization III-I-1331; National Museum of the American Indian, Washington 23/8598, 01/1141; University of Pennsylvania Museum, Philadelphia NA 4945; Musée d'Ethnographie, Neuchâtel, Switzerland 1Va200; Museum für Völkerkunde, Frankfurt am Main NS30019; Museum für Völkerkunde, Berlin 1V B 117; Bata Shoe Museum, Toronto P81.316, P82.199; Peabody Museum Harvard, Cambridge 41-72-10-24400; private collection in Ewing 1982:258

22. Canadian Museum of Civilization III-I-1385; National Museum of the American Indian, Washington 01/1141; private collection in Ewing 1982:257

23. American Museum of Natural History, New York 50.2/2474; Detroit Institute of Arts, Detroit 1988.32; Bata Shoe Museum, Toronto P82.189; National Museum of the American Indian, Washington 01/1141; private collection in Ewing 1982:257

24. private collection in Ewing 1982:258

25. Personal communication Michel Groslouis, Huron-Wendat Cultural Association, Wendake, Québec December, 1998

26. Canadian Museum of Civilization III-H-462; National Museum of the American Indian, Washington 24/2012; The British Museum, London 1972 Am 13.13

27. The British Museum, London 1972 Am 13.13; National Museum of the American Indian, Washington 19/6342; Museum für Völkerkunde, Berlin 1V B 216

28. Canadian Museum of Civilization III-H-462; McCord Museum, Montreal ME940.1.1.1-2; National Museum of the American Indian, Washington 24/2012, 19/6341, 17/6317; The British Museum, London 1972 Am 13.13

29. an exception is at the University of Pennsylvania Museum, Philadelphia NA 4945

30. Peabody Museum Harvard, Cambridge 49325 (circa 1812); The British Museum, London 1972 Am 13.13; Berne Historical Museum, Berne, Switzerland Can 6A (1803-1826 in Thompson 1977:125); Museum für Völkerkunde, Berlin 1V B 216; National Museum of the American Indian, Washington 17/6317

31. National Museum of the American Indian, Washington 19/6342

32. Canadian Museum of Civilization, Hull III-H-462; National Museum of the American Indian, Washington 19/6341 (circa 1790); Völkerkunde-Abteilung, Hannover 755/56; Denver Art Museum, Denver 1966.389 (1813-1816 in Conn 1979:61); McCord Museum, Montreal ME940.1.1.1-2; The Horniman Museum and Library, London SE23 3PQ (courtesy Dorothy Burnham).

33. Turner 1955; Speck 1911:2

34. Phillips 1998: Chapter 4

35. Turner 1955:50

36. Thompson 1977:142

37. Phillips 1990:30; Phillips 1998:252. Berne Historical Museum, Berne, Switzerland Can 12 (in Thompson 1977:127-128); Canadian Museum of Civilization III-H -427

38. Museum für Völkerkunde, Vienna 11977 a,b

39. Royal Albert Memorial Museum and Art Gallery, Exeter, England E740 in Phillips 1998:253, Figure 6.60. The circle is worked in porcupine quills in folded, zig-zag, single quill technique (Figure 4.3).

40. Victoria and Albert Museum, London T10+a-1929 in Phillips 1998:253, Figure 6.59.

41. Kohl 1861,1:180

42. Gérin 1901:553

43. Speck 1911

44. American Museum of Natural History, New York 50.2/2474; National Museum of the American Indian, Washington 13/5376; Detroit Institute of Arts, Detroit 1988.32; Bata Shoe Museum, Toronto P82.189; Peabody & Essex Museum, Salem E21451; private collection in Ewing 1982:259; Morgan 1850: Plate 1.

45. Bata Shoe Museum, Toronto P81.316, P80.1672

46. Morgan 1850, 1852. Iroquois beadwork is the subject of the travelling exhibition "Across Borders: Beadwork in Iroquois Life" that opened at the McCord Museum, Montreal in June 1999. For beadwork as tourist commodities see Phillips 1998 and Gordon 1984.

47. Diane Savard interviewed by the Conseil de la Nation Huronne-Wendat, Wendake, Québec, March 2000

48. For example, Marianna Picard, Wendake, Québec; also moccasins in the National Museum of the American Indian, Washington 6/322 documented as Iroquois (Seneca), Cattaraugus Reservation, New York, 1940s; American Museum of Natural History, New York 50/8131 documented as Iroquois (Seneca), New York, early twentieth century.

49. Interviewed by the Conseil de la Nation Huronne-Wendat, Wendake, Québec, March 2000.

Works Cited

Champlain, Samuel de
>1929 *The Works of Samuel de Champlain*. Ed. H.P. Biggar. Vol. 3, Pt.1, [1615]. Toronto: The Champlain Society.

Conn, Richard
>1979 *Native American Art in the Denver Art Museum*. Seattle: University of Washington Press.

Ewing, Douglas C.
>1982 *Pleasing the Spirits: A Catalogue of a Collection of American Indian Art*. New York: Ghylen Press.

Fardoulis-Vitart, Anne
>1979 The King's Collection and the Ancient Collections of Curiosities in the Collections of the Musée de l'Homme. Ph.D. diss., Paris.

Garrido, Araceli Sanchez
>1992 Plains Indian Collections of the Museo de América. *European Review of Native American Studies* 6:2: 21-29.

Gérin, Léon
>1901 The Hurons of Lorette, *Report on the Ethnological Survey of Canada*. British Association for the Advancement of Science, Appendix 111. London.

Gordon, Beverly
>1984 The Niagara Falls Whimsey: The Object as a Symbol or Cultural Interface. Ph.D. diss., University of Wisconsin, Madison.

Kohl, Johann Georg
>1861 *Travels in Canada, and through the States of New York and Pennsylvania*. Trans. Mrs. Percy Sinnett. 2 vols. London: George Manwaring.

Lafitau, Joseph François
>1977 *Customs of the American Indians Compared with the Customs of Primitive Tribes*. Ed. and trans. William N. Fenton and Elizabeth L. Moore. 49 (2). Toronto: The Champlain Society.

Laurencich-Minelli, Laura, and Alessandra Filipetti
>1983 Per le collezioni americaniste del Museo Cospiano e dell'Istituto delle Scienze. Alcuni ogetti ritrovati a Bologna. In *Archivio per l'Anthopologia e la Etnologia*. Firenze.Vol. CX111: 207-225.

Loskiel, George Henry
>1794 *History of the Mission of the United Brethren Among the Indians in North America*. Pt. l. London: Brethren's Society for the Furtherance of the Gospel.

Morgan, Lewis Henry
>1850 Report to the Regents of the University, Upon the Articles Furnished to the Indian Collection. *New York State Cabinet of Antiquities Annual Report* 3: 65-97. Albany.
>
>1852 Report on the Fabrics, Inventions, Implements and Utensils of the Iroquois. *New York State Cabinet of Antiquities Annual Report* 5: 69-117. Albany.

Orchard, William C.
- 1971 *The Technique of Porcupine-Quill Decoration Among the North American Indians*. 2d ed. New York: Museum of the American Indian, Heye Foundation.

Phillips, Ruth Bliss
- 1987 Archives. Northern Woodlands section of *The Spirit Sings: Artistic Traditions of Canada's First Peoples*. Canadian Museum of Civilization Archives.
- 1990 Moccasins Into Slippers: Woodlands Indian Hats, Bags, and Shoes in Tradition and Transformation. *Northeast Indian Quarterly* Winter: 26-36.
- 1998 *Trading Identities: The Souvenir in Native North American Art from the Northeast, 1700-1900*. Seattle: University of Washington Press.

Sagard-Theodat, Father Gabriel
- 1939 *The Long Journey to the Country of the Hurons*. Ed. George M. Wrong and trans. H.H. Langton. Vol. XXV. Toronto: The Champlain Society.

Sager, David
- 1995 The Possible Origins of the Blackfeet Crooked Nose Moccasin Design. *American Indian Art Magazine* 20 (4): 36-43.

Speck, Frank G.
- 1911 Huron Moose Hair Embroidery. *American Anthropologist*, new ser. 13(1):1-14.

Thevet, André
- 1986 *André Thevet's North America: A Sixteenth-Century View*. Ed. and trans. Roger Schlesinger and Arthur P. Stabler. Kingston and Montreal: McGill-Queen's University Press.

Thompson, Judy
- 1977 *The North American Collection. A Catalogue*. Berne: Berne Historical Museum.

Turner, Geoffrey
- 1955 *Hair Embroidery in Siberia and North America*. Pitt-Rivers Museum, University of Oxford Occasional Papers on Technology 7. Oxford: B.H. Blackwell, Ltd.

Weld, Issac, Jr.
- 1800 *Travels through the States of North America, and the Provinces of Upper and Lower Canada, during the Years 1795, 1796, and 1797*. London: John Stockdale.

Epilogue

Although the authors of this volume have had the "lion's share" of Dorothy's time and talents during the past decade, many other staff of the Canadian Museum of Civilization know her, have worked with her, and admire her greatly. The final section of this book is an opportunity for them to express their appreciation.

Christina Bates, Ontario Historian

Dorothy Burnham's curiosity, attention to detail, generosity and abiding interest in the human spirit is, of course, not confined to her work in ethnology. I had the pleasure of consulting with Dorothy on an aspect of a history exhibition *Hold Onto Your Hats!* One theme of the exhibit was rites of passage, and Dorothy approached me about the bridal tiara and orange blossom wreath that was worn by her mother to her wedding in 1908, and later, by Dorothy herself, in 1944. These were on exhibit at the Canadian Museum of Civilization during 1995-6.

Understanding the importance of artifact context and documentation, Dorothy provided me with all the details of the weddings, a family tree, and a lovely photograph of her parents' wedding, which she kindly allowed me to copy. Always interested and helpful with other people's research, Dorothy also lent me photographs of her young mother and siblings over several years, which have been invaluable to me in my research on children's clothing.

In her life and work, Dorothy Burnham always manages to combine expert professionalism with personal warmth. I have been lucky to have benefited from both these attributes.

Fascinating Challenges

Photograph by Paula Mitas Zoubek, 1997.

Kelly Cameron, Collections Manager

I became very used to seeing Dorothy bent closely over layout tables at Asticou and here at the Hull site, carefully examining a wide variety of First Nations clothing. She always had a moment to look up from her work and happily tell you what she is concentrating on. I have learned about fabrication techniques, both from short conversations with Dorothy, and by looking at her amazing drawings. She is always delightful to speak with, and I can only hope to have the energy and vitality she exudes all the time.

Genevieve Eustache, Head, Archives and Documentation

I first met Dorothy Burnham in 1993, when she offered to donate a large number of her drawings of Native clothing to the Archives of the Canadian Museum of Civilization. At first, I was intimidated by the "personage", but as I got to know her, I was amazed by her warm and open attitude. Every week, we would meet in her apartment and go through a very systematic process of inventorying the drawings. Then we would have tea, often in the living room where we would listen to the children playing in a schoolyard close by. Dorothy was interested in everything that was going on in the town, and she confessed to me that she was going to miss the children's brouhaha when she moved out to the countryside. Once, when I mentioned the noise the kids were making, she said, "You know, I will miss them. Their noise is life."

Julie Hughes, Textiles Conservator

On the occasion of the 10th Anniversary of the Costume Society of Ontario - Eastern Branch, Dorothy Burnham, a pioneer in Canadian textile history and recipient of the Order of Canada, kindly offered her original drawings from *Cut My Cote* for use in a special scarf designed by Canadian textile artist Paula Mitas Zoubek, and produced by the C.S.O.-Eastern Branch. *Cut My Cote* was published by the Royal Ontario Museum in 1973. Still in print, this groundbreaking work continues to offer scholars and artists inspiration today.

To honour this extraordinary woman, and to celebrate the production of the scarf, the C.S.O.-Eastern Branch hosted a formal reception for Mrs. Burnham on Sunday, June 15, 1997, in Ottawa. Overwhelming love and admiration were expressed during this event by the many friends from across Canada and abroad who were able to attend.

The funds generated from the sale of the scarves continue to provide the Eastern Branch with resources to offer improved programming events. We wear our scarves with great pride.

Stephen Inglis, Director General, Research and Collections

Dorothy Burnham's long-standing and generous contributions to the Canadian Museum of Civilization programs are well known to those working in research and with collections. I hope this volume will widen that appreciation.

The range of Dorothy's expertise and its relevance to the Museum's collections is truly remarkable. I first encountered her work while studying the collections of folk art, and benefited from her research on the history of Canadian textiles to better appreciate the vestiges and continuities of some techniques in current production. Dorothy's work also informed the description of parts of the collections of fine craft.

It has been a pleasure to watch the ways in which Dorothy has continued her research and collaborative work on the history and ethnology collections. Her ethnographic and technical background and long career of museological experience have been a quiet but extremely significant part of our strength.

Stella Labonté, Volunteer Services

It is impossible in a few lines to do justice to the contribution that Dorothy Burnham has made to the Canadian Museum of Civilization as a volunteer. It all started soon after the new museum building opened in 1989. Her life had been dedicated to textiles and she chose the Canadian Museum of Civilization to benefit from her expertise. Her long service and wholehearted dedication as a volunteer almost went unnoticed because she never kept track of her hours. I recorded 4,141 hours and I'm certain this total does not reflect all the time she devoted to work for the Museum.

I have nothing but admiration and respect for this great lady whose life and career are an inspiration to us all. Despite her dazzling spiral of accomplishment, she managed to stay "human" and make friends with "ordinary" people by making them feel special. Only one word can be said and it is a very sincere THANK YOU. I wish you well, Dorothy.

Paul Lauzon, Conservator

For a period of several months, twice a week Dorothy Burnham used a desk in the Conservation Laboratory to study and draw different ethnographic artifacts. Every time she found something interesting in the fabrication of the particular artifact she was studying she would point it out to one of us. Inevitably, all the conservators would gather around, and she would give us an impromptu lecture on that particular object. Her enthusiasm was contagious, and we would always look forward to her next visit.

John Moses, Native History Researcher

I first had the pleasure of getting to know Dorothy during the course of my work as an assistant conservator in the Museum's artifacts lab. This was during the conservation work for the *Threads of the Land* exhibit. Dorothy would be down in the lab frequently, consulting with curators and conservation staff on different aspects of the clothing selected for the show. Although she was involved in undertaking detailed examinations of these various items and producing equally detailed line drawings of each piece, she always had a kind word and an enthusiastic greeting for everyone in attendance. She always took the time to explain to the more junior of us exactly what she was doing, sharing so generously of her own knowledge and experience. As my work at the Museum has continued as a researcher in the Ethnology division, I've continued to benefit from the wealth of information that Dorothy has generated during her career. Her published work remains an invaluable reference and research tool, and will stand as her legacy to researchers, curators and conservators at this Museum and others for years to come. Her generosity of knowledge and spirit has been a gift and inspiration to all those who have had the pleasure of working alongside her.

Nia:wen, Dorothy

List of Contributors

Dorothy Burnham is a former Curator of Costumes and Textiles at the Royal Ontario Museum, Toronto. She has received national and international acclaim as a museum worker, museum exhibition organizer, author and expert on textiles, particularly those of Canadian origin.

Judy Hall is Curator of Eastern Woodlands Ethnology at the Canadian Museum of Civilization. She is also responsible for the ethnographic collection from the Arctic.

Pearl Hewitt is a Cook's Ferry Band Councillor and works for the Band looking after the needs of the community. As a Band Councillor she is working to enforce Aboriginal rights and ensure that Aboriginal lands are protected for future generations. She continues to weave silver-willow bark capes for special commissions.

Ingrid Kritsch has worked across the Canadian North since 1977 as an archaeologist, ethnographer and historian and is currently the Research Director of the Gwich'in Social and Cultural Institute.

Leslie Tepper is Curator of Pacific Coast Ethnology at the Canadian Museum of Civilization. She was formerly Curator of Plateau Ethnology.

Judy Thompson is Curator of Western Subarctic Ethnology at the Canadian Museum of Civilization.

Karen Wright-Fraser is a young Gwich'in fashion designer and seamstress. She runs an Aboriginal arts and crafts business called "Whispering Willows" which keeps her very busy, along with being a full-time mother and wife. Karen makes white hide dresses, shirts, vests and jackets for weddings and graduations. She has been overwhelmed with orders, since traditional dress has made a strong comeback in the western Arctic during the past decade.

CONTENTS

Introduction 7

German Cycles in Reichswehr and Wehrmacht 12

Hand and Foot Heating of the Heavy Cycle 24

The Coat for Cycle Drivers and Passengers 36

Requisitioned Cycles 89

Captured Cycles 142

Cycles of the Allied Forces 149

The Kettenkrad 175

Model Motorcycles 179

Afterword 200

Introduction

In the autumn of 1993, my book "Motorcycles of the Wehrmacht" appeared. Until then, I had determined that the motorcyclists had been treated only superficially in the compilation of military history between 1935 and 1945. And yet they were the ones who were often drafted into military service along with their motorcycles and then sent "into the field" with those street machines. Surely this was done with the mistaken notion that it would all be over in a matter of weeks. Measured by the first lightning victories against western and eastern neighbor countries, this assumption was quite justified. The fact that the war would eventually last nearly six years, and that German soldiers would see action from Norway to Africa and from the Atlantic to the Volga could not be foreseen, even by the experts. And in all these theaters of war, many motorcyclists had to do their duty, most of the time on street machines that were not suitable for off-road action.

With this viewpoint in mind, the thought was awakened in me of portraying the action of these very motorcyclists—whether messengers or rifle-

Reichswehr members with their BMW R 62, as seen in 1928. The R 62, the first BMW machine with a 750 cc engine, was introduced to the Reichswehr in that same year. Note the original factory paint.

"The greater the power, the more important its control." For this reason, sporting competition was of great importance to motorcyclists, including those with heavy sidecar rigs. Here the BMW R 12 sidecar units make final preparations for a race. The cycles still have wide fenders and aluminum footboards.

men — in a special book, showing them for once as they fulfilled their duties on their "iron horses" in war- and prewar times.

My request for appropriate action photographs was echoed by many Wehrmacht veterans and their heirs. A multitude of personal photos were sent to me. While one man's memories of his machine were still fresh and lively, another might express doubt as to whether his motorcycle was a DKW 350 or 350.1. Or was it a K 800 or K 800/W by Zündapp? In my euphoria over the multitudes of motorcycle pictures sent to me, showing the greatest variety of machines, I often had doubts as to the correct identification of the cycle types. A certain blurriness in some of the submitted photo material also contributed to this. For the most part, they were photos that were "shot" by a comrade's hand, not pictures taken by a professional photographer; then too, they had come through the strictest censorship before they had been cleared for publication. Sometimes the fact that a cycle was thoroughly covered with dirt added to the problem. But the idea for such a book generally inspired positive feelings. Many a man will remember his military service when he looks at the circa 200 action photos. But there are also many interested people of the postwar generation who have been impressed by the great variety of motorcycles used by the German troops. In addition, many action pictures, which make obvious the simply unimaginable situations faced by the motorcyclists and their cycles on the Russian or North African fronts, will astonish the beholder.

All of this has contributed to the fact that, once again, a great number of personal action photos of military motorcyclists have been made available to me. These include photos of cycles in action that are not included in the first book. Although some of the contributors supplied detailed information about the technical data of his motorcycle, this volume is not to be a reference work to quench the motorcycle fan's thirst for technical information. With the great numbers of different cycles that were used by the Wehrmacht between 1934 and 1945, the detailed listing of all technical data of all onetime Wehrmacht machines would burst the confines of this book. Sufficient books on the subject, which contain data on practically all the types of motorcycles built in the factories and used in the Wehrmacht until 1945, are available on the market. For that reason, the photo captions in this volume will give only the major details of the illustrated cycles. The pictures shown in this book are intended rather to give an impression of the motorcyclist's action in everyday military service. It will document how and where the troops actually used their cycles, which either came off the assembly line as Wehrmacht machines or were requisitioned from private owners. The spectrum thus extends from the peacetime training of the motorcyclists at barracks or training camps in Germany, through the sportlike maneuvers such as the Harz winter trips, Teutoburger Wald trips, etc., to the grim wartime action on all fronts in Europe and North Africa.

A BMW R 62 of the Reichswehr in winter service. On good roads this machine attained a top speed of 115 kph.

Motorcyclists in the last war! In Russia, driver and machine froze in the biting cold or sank into bottomless mud in the wet season. In North Africa, the fuel "boiled" in the tanks of the cycles, while the drivers on their low solo or sidecar cycles had to swallow the clouds of desert sand constantly thrown up by the heavier vehicles ahead of them. That all these hardships "welded" the small numbers of motorcyclists and their passengers together into a loyal comradeship is proved by many action photos. After all, the motorcyclists were popular "meeting points" for their own comrades within their units when they wanted to find out what was new. They were the ones who had reports to bring, columns to lead into specific areas of action, officers to transport or missions to carry out as scouting troops. There were many opportunities to exchange news. And again and again, there are photos of individual motorcycle messengers who sat proudly on their machines for their comrades to photograph.

Civilian drivers were also invited to participate in off-road sporting events along with military motorcyclists. The competition was close, for civilian and military drivers often drove the same kinds of cycles. Here is a Horex S 5 with Stoye sidecar.

While the first volume contains exclusively photographs of German and captured cycles, the material to follow will also illustrate the action of motorcycles by nations that were then Germany's enemies. Thus the emphasis will be on the American, British, Belgian, French and Dutch military cycles.

The previous volume provided detailed information on the training of the motorcycle drivers in the Wehrmacht and within the framework of pre-military training in the motor-sport schools of the NSKK, as well as the variety of motorcycle types utilized between 1935 and 1945. There was also much information on the painting of the heavy Wehrmacht machinery and the conditions for obtaining the motor vehicle service medal. This information will thus not be repeated here. On the other hand, there will be more information on the so-called "cycle coat", since this piece of clothing was originally made only for motorcyclists. In addition, there will be more information on motorcycle heating, which was introduced for heavy Wehrmacht cycles in the middle of World War II, and which was unknown to many interested parties of the postwar generation.

At the beginning of the thirties, off-road motorcycle sports created a new type, the "steel-nerved" modern motor sportsman, able to handle a variety of demands, who became the model for the cyclists in the Reichswehr and Wehrmacht. Here is a picture from the "German Wehrmacht" series published in 1935.

German Cycles in the Reichswehr and Wehrmacht

An attempt to arrive at a definite number of the types of motorcycles used by the Reichswehr and Wehrmacht here would be a dangerously big job. The variety of types obtained by the Reichswehr and Wehrmacht in the usual way — leaving out requisitioned and captured cycles — was simply too great to allow an absolutely complete coverage in a book of this size. Along with the well-known manufacturers such as BMW, NSU, Victoria, DKW, Zündapp, Triumph, Ardie and Puch, there were a number of other, lesser-known brands that were given state contracts. It must not be forgotten that the motorcycle business was more or less stagnant until the thirties. In the year 1924 alone, there were more than 500 motorcycle manufacturers in Germany, and they all wanted to make a good profit. Only as of 1933 did the German industry gain a series of advantages, such as driver's-license freedom for the 200 cc class, no taxes on any motorcycles, import limitations and export support measures.

A not inconsiderable upswing was undoubtedly also experienced by the German motorcycle industry because of the increased introduction of motorcycles into the Reichswehr and later Wehrmacht. Just the establishment of the motorcycle rifle troops as of 1935, and their use of sidecar machines, also furthered their use by the private sector. There were actually no special army machines that were used only by the troops.

For example, the Zündapp works introduced their K 400, K 500 and K 800 civilian models at the Berlin Auto Salon at the beginning of the thirties. BMW was able to create a technical sensation with the 750 cc R 12. This machine was the first series-production cycle to feature a telescopic front fork with hydraulic shock absorbers. From then on, orders in the millions flooded the German motorcycle factories. From good sporting machines there suddenly sprang, "overnight", "Wehrmacht motorcycles." An immense expansion took place particularly in the realm of sidecars. In particular, the K 500 W, K 800 W and, a few years later, the KS 600 W were introduced into the Reichswehr and Wehrmacht in great numbers as solo and sidecar cycles. At the same time, a lucrative business developed in the German sidecar market in both the civilian and mili-

The "spanking clean" BMW R 35 as it was introduced into the Wehrmacht in 1935. This medium Wehrmacht cycle with its telescopic fork without shock absorbers replaced the BMW R 4 solo cycle used until then.

tary sectors. Countless entrepreneurs used their striking sidecar designs to attract business from the great motorcycle manufacturers. In pure war production, especially for the two heavy sidecar machines, the BMW R 75 and the Zündapp KS 750, which produced their own sidecars, the uniform sidecars made by Stoye, Royal and Steib were also used.

As already noted, a final list of all Reichswehr and Wehrmacht motorcycles is not possible. Yet it can be mentioned that DKW and NSU, with their NZ or OSL models, were widely used as Wehrmacht equipment. Ardie delivered several thousand of its 125 model to the Wehrmacht between 1939 and 1943. Triumph and Victoria were also granted Wehrmacht contracts. This variety of makes will be documented by the following action pictures.

Members of the "LAH" in a parade in December 1934. The BMW R 11 cycles are equipped with uniform sidecars. The crews still wear their black uniforms and Model 16 steel helmets from World War I.

The BMW R 11 cycle with flatbed sidecar carrying a light grenade launcher during off-road training in 1935. The crews here are still wearing Model 16 steel helmets of World War I vintage—and with maneuver bands.

"Hard is the path to mastery!" In the Reichswehr era, particularly talented motorcyclists were already displaying their acrobatic arts on their cycles. At left is a BMW R 57, above a Zündapp K 500.

Victoria KR 6 "Bergmeister" drilling under difficult conditions. The KR 6 was used by the Reichswehr as of 1933, almost always as a sidecar machine. These sidecars were built by the Kali firm of Oberursel.

The robust BMW R 4 of 1932 in Reichswehr service, here with "Chief" H. Reiter in 1935. The pressed-steel frame and curved handlebars are easy to see.

A photo from the series "Das Neue Reich", showing the awarding of letters of recommendation to the participants after a mission in the East. At right is a Victoria KR 35 of 1929; the other cycles are both KR 20 machines of 1930.

The caption on this picture from the series "Die Deutsche Wehrmacht" says: "Our motorcyclists are practicing repairs and fixing flat tires. The expertise they gain is also shown happily at sporting events."

Not only driving skill was stressed among the cycle units, but so was orientation by using maps. A vitally important skill for motorcyclists, as they often had to rely on their own resources during the war.

Identified by their white armbands, participants in the "Sauderland orientation drive" of the mid-1930s in a BMW R 12 motorcycle-sidecar combination.

Between 1929 and 1934 the Reichswehr put a large number of BMW R 11 motorcycles into service. The machine proved especially suitable for use with a sidecar on account of its sturdy box-section frame.

The Zündapp K 500 W machine, which was introduced into the Wehrmacht in 1937. The sidecar, made by the Royal firm in 1937, was also sold to civilians as the Type S 2 sidecar, and was still equipped with a door.

In many further training trips, driving ability and orientation in unfamiliar terrain were enhanced in drills. Here a motorcycle team on a BMW R 12 of the Luftwaffe is seen during a brief orientation drill.

Under the shelter of these trees, the motorcycle messengers of an unidentified unit have set up their bivouac during the advance into Latvia.

The Wehrmacht version of the NSU 601 OSL, made in 1939. The fishtail on the end of the exhaust pipe, which made more room for the saddlebags, can be seen clearly. The enlarged fuel filler for canister filling can also be seen. The Wehrmacht machine was also fitted with a motor shield plate below on the frame.

Meeting at a checkpoint after brief orientation, the motorcycle messengers on their BMW cycles are about to continue their training trip in 1941. Notice the drivers' helmets too: while two of the silky-matte Model 35 helmets bear the black-red-white emblem on the right and the Army adler on the left, the third driver wears a matte helmet without emblems.

Then as now, the military off-road machines attract young people's attention while the motorcycle messengers take a short break in an isolated village (in the Harz Mountains, 1941) during their off-road training. In the background is a BMW R 12.

Correct reading of maps was one of the criteria that a good motorcyclist had to fulfill. Constant practice in unfamiliar terrain sharpened his sense of orientation. At left is a BMW R 12 solo, which was used by the Wehrmacht as of 1935; at right is a BMW R 35. Note the telescopic fork with its rubber sleeves.

Motorcyclists lead the troops into a new position. A quick look at the map and the position change is carried out. Mistaken orientation could have catastrophic effects for the troops who followed. At left is an old BMW R 4 built in 1932.

Hand and Foot Heating on the Heavy Cycle

The Wehrmacht leadership at that time had surely taken the horrors of the Russian winter of 1941-42 into consideration and ordered the installation of hand and foot heaters on the heavy BMW R 12 and R 75 Wehrmacht motorcycles. The motorcycle drivers and their passengers on the unprotected cycles were at the mercy of "Jack Frost", with his coldness that reached -50 degrees Celsius and icy east wind. With the installation of hand and foot heaters, the physical damage to hands and feet that had occurred more and more frequently up to then. Technical problems surely must have been the reason why this additional equipment could not be installed on the other light motorcycles.

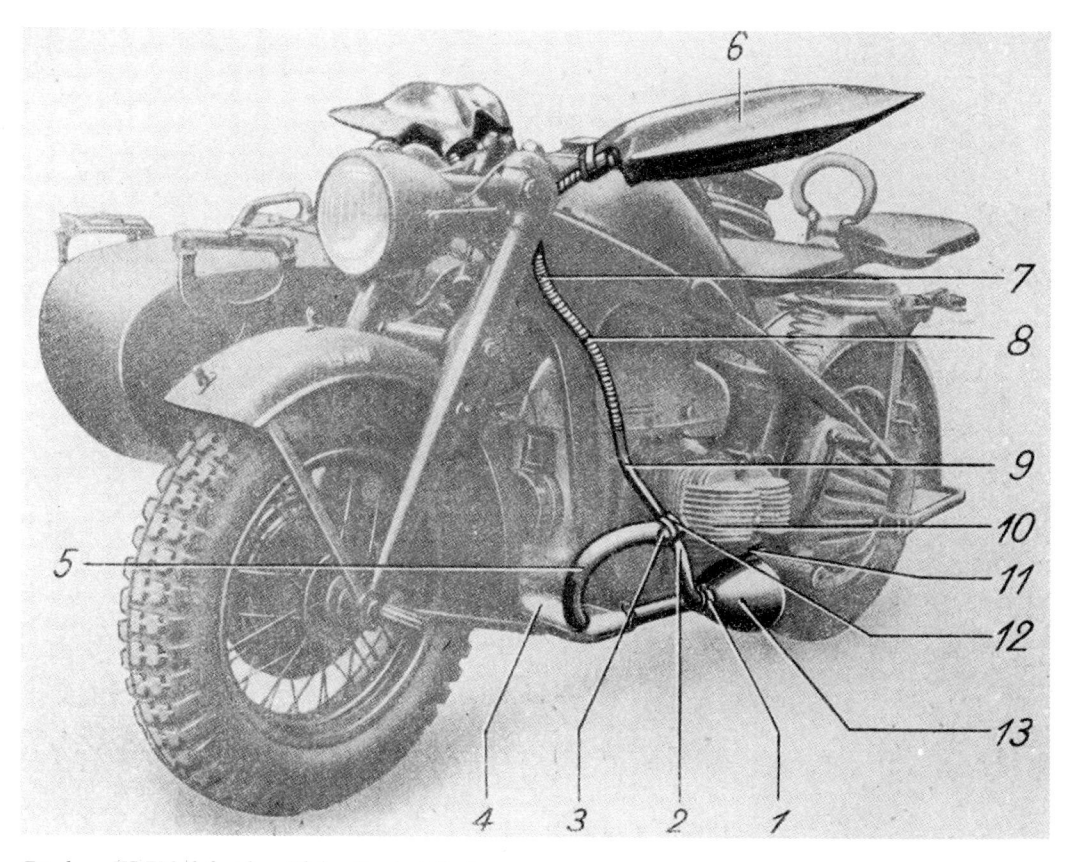

Zündapp KS 750, left side, with heating installed.
1. *Clamp*
2. *Pipe joint*
3. *Head bolt*
4. *Exhaust manifold*
5. *Exhaust pipe joint*
6. *Hand protector*
7. *Metal heat duct*
8. *Bofa clamp*
9. *Heat takeoff duct*
10. *Cylinder block*
11. *Holder*
12. *Heat takeoff flange*
13. *Foot warmer*

The installation of hand and foot heaters was not done at the factory, but had to be carried out at military workshops according to Service Instruction 632/6 of 8/12/1942. For this installation, kits were available, containing only the required parts for the particular type of motorcycle. According to the details in the instruction book, spare parts could also be ordered from the manufacturer. The motorcycle heaters were made by the Triumph works in Nürnberg.

The Hand and Foot Heating System

To heat the motorcycle, some of the exhaust gases from the engine were ducted off for heating. For this purpose, the engine's exhaust system was tapped several times right after the engine cylinder, and the hot gases were ducted to the individual heaters through pipes or metal tubing. The heaters were right next to the feet, on the handlebar grips, and in the bottom of the sidecar.

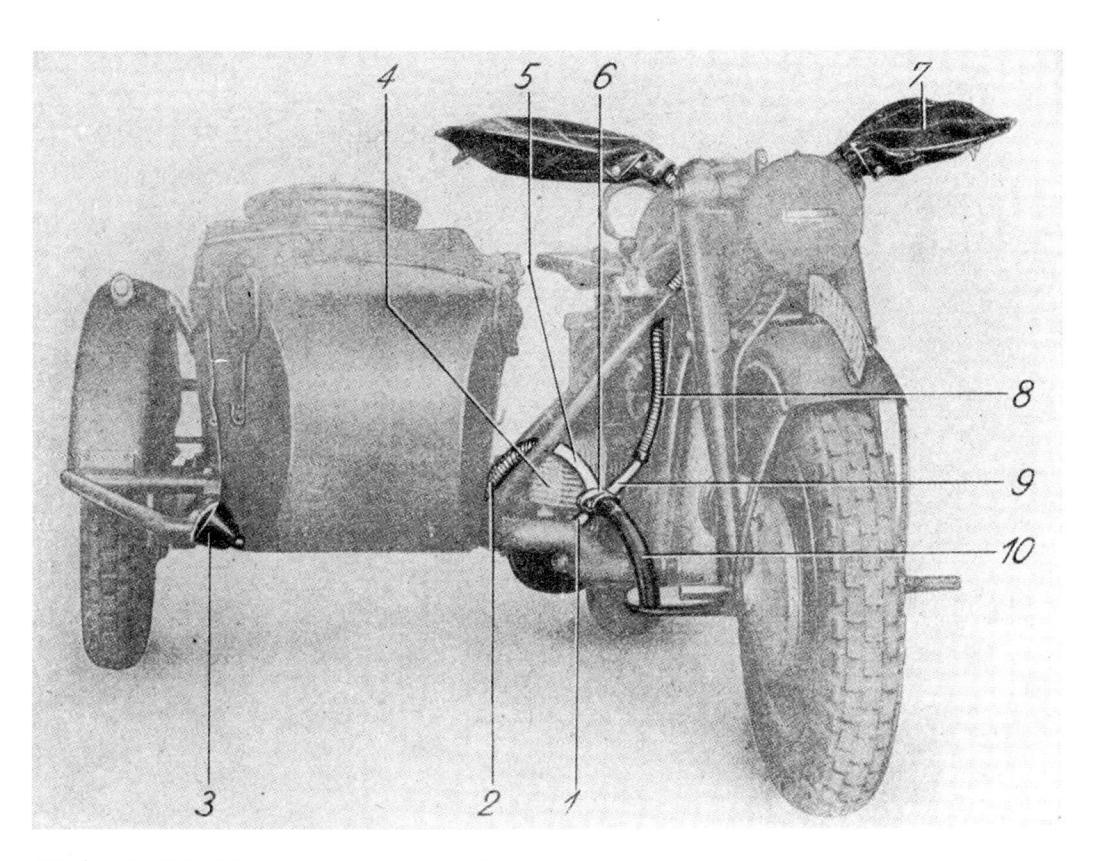

Zündapp KS 750, right side, with heating installed.
1. Heat takeoff duct
2. Metal heat duct
3. Sound damper
4. Cylinder block
5. Heat takeoff duct
6. Heat takeoff flange
7. Hand protector
8. Metal heat duct
9. Heat takeoff duct
10. Exhaust pipe joint

The Hand Heater

From two intake pipes, the hot gases were ducted to the right and left hand warmers. There the hot gases, depending on the position of the butterfly valve in the duct of the hand warmer, flowed more or less intensively out of the exit slits of the hand warmer into the area of the leather hand protector. Regulation of hand heating was done by turning the regulator lever located under the steering grip.

The Foot Heater

The hot gases intended for the foot heater were ducted directly to the foot warmers through the tube narrowers leading down to the right and left. Through a system of sheet-metal baffles, the hot gases, depending on the position of the butterfly-valve control, flowed more or less strongly out of the funnel-shaped housing directly onto the feet.

The foot heater was regulated by turning the butterfly-valve control on either foot warmer.

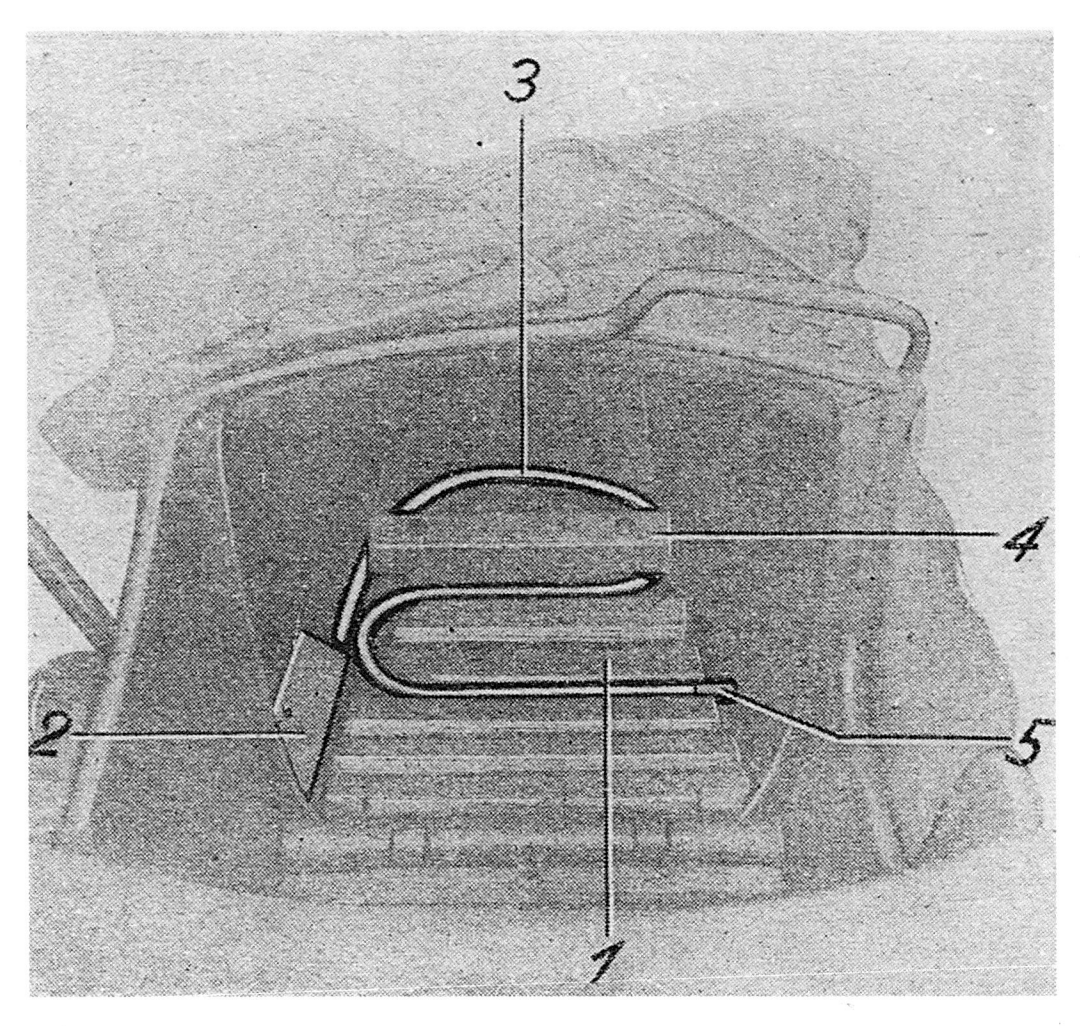

Sidecar with heating duct installed.
1. *Wooden frame*
2. *Heating shield*
3. *Heating duct "snake"*
4. *Footrest*
5. *Sound damper*

The Sidecar Heater

The hot gases were ducted through a metal tube from the third heater pipe on the right side of the cycle to the heating coil of the sidecar. At the end of the heating coil, which curved through the members of the wooden frame, the muffler with its built-in butterfly valve control determined how much heat passed through. According to the setting of the butterfly valve control, more or less heat was radiated from the heating coil to the interior of the sidecar.

Closing Notes

Before starting the motor, one had to close the butterfly valves for heating on the handholds, in order to prevent the escape and ignition of unburned gases in the hand protector. Otherwise: "stabbing flames!"

If parts (foot warmers or mufflers) were lost, the open heating had to be shut off until the parts were replaced, so that the still-burning gases would not escape and cause any damage or smell.

Members of a paratroop unit in their "bone bags" on a Zündapp KS 750 cycle. Note the camouflage cover on the headlight as well as the hand and foot heaters. Ahead of the driver's left foot, the funnel-shaped foot warmer can be seen clearly. The metal heat duct for the hand heater is also easy to see.

Before the motorcycle messengers' quarters in encircled Demjansk is a BMW R 12 in winter camouflage. This cycle also had hand and foot heating, as can be seen by the left and right heaters on the handlebars.

The VB and battery troop of a heavy launcher battery taking part in a paratroop drill outside Blankenburg in the Harz on December 6, 1943. The Zündapp KS 750 sidecar cycle is towing two light trailers, loaded with 13 men and two weapon and equipment containers. Note also the hand and foot heating. The two hand protectors and the foot heater are easy to spot.

Man and machine are marked by tough action in trackless terrain. The driver, in his long cycle coat, is taking a break with his Zündapp KS 750. Note the tube connecting the hand and foot heaters to conduct hot air to the handles and the foot heaters.

The motorcycle crew, in their long cycle coats, has stepped aside to let their DKW NZ 350 be seen clearly in their photograph.

Motorcycle messenger Obgr. H. Günther with his winter-camouflaged BMW cycle in encircled Demjansk. Despite the presence of hand protectors, this driver's motorcycle has no hand or foot warmers.

A scout troop marches out. The multi-talented motorcycle messengers were also called upon for services of this kind.

The scout troop takes a break. With carbines at the ready, the men get a brief rest.

The BMW R 35 is easily recognized. The successor model, the R 4, had a great BMW innovation: a telescopic fork. More than 15,000 of this model were built between 1937 and 1940, with the greater part of them going to the Wehrmacht.

Here is another motorcycle crew in their typical cycle coats. Note than the Zündapp K 600 sidecar cycle is equipped with normal road tires.

Motorcyclists of the "Grossdeutschland" Panzergrenadier Division (white steel helmet on the sidecar) ride through a destroyed French city in the summer of 1940. In the foreground is a BMW R 12 sidecar cycle, behind it a BMW R 35.

This picture speaks for itself! This heavy BMW, seen in a Russian winter, has a box mounted on its sidecar and a snow chain on the sidecar wheel, plus a temporary coat of chalk camouflage. The exhausted crew utilizes a brief stop to get a little rest.

This motorcycle messenger rides an NSU 501 OSL built in 1936. This is the Wehrmacht version with carrying cases and a covered headlight.

This is obviously a parade lineup with BMW R 12 cycles, taken in prewar days, since the headlights are not covered. In addition, all the cycles—with the exception of the one at the left—are still equipped with wide front fenders.

"This way!" the motorcycle messenger's arm movement appears to be saying. His BMW R 12 cycle is obviously equipped with a flat front fender.

A motorcycle rifle platoon with its BMW R 12 cycles has turned out for field maneuvers.

The Protective Coat for Motorcycle Drivers and Passengers (Kradmantel)

One of the most eye-catching pieces of clothing used by German soldiers between 1933 and 1945 was undoubtedly the protective coat for motorcycle drivers and passengers, the so-called Kradmantel).

This sought-after piece of clothing, which at first was introduced into the Reichswehr exclusively for motorcycle drivers and passengers, issued only to those specific people, and allowed to be worn only while in service using a motorcycle, enjoyed the greatest popularity among junior and senior officers in all branches of the service over the course of the years.

With the introduction of greater numbers of motorcycles into the German Army, the question was also explored of how the motorcyclists could be better protected against the roughness of the weather. No other vehicle drivers were exposed to weather conditions so vulnerably as the motorcycle drivers and their passengers on the solo and sidecar machines. In particular, the motorcycle messengers, who were constantly on duty, were mercilessly exposed to wind and weather, ice and snow. Here the rubberized, watertight cycle coat afforded a certain protection from the weather for the motorcyclist. As with all pieces of clothing and equipment, the cycle coat also underwent numerous changes in terms of color, shape and basic material during the prewar and war years.

In the General Army Communique No. 85 of 1934, the introduction of the cycle coat as a piece of clothing for specified personnel was made known officially, after wearing tests of special clothing and equipment for motor vehicle personnel had been concluded. The upper collar was

This crew is awaiting the start of the Teuteburg Cross-Country Orienteering of 1936. The wide aluminum stripes can be seen clearly on the driver's upper arms. Thus this is a group of non-commissioned officers.

made of ordinary cloth of field gray. The wearing of insignia of rank on the cycle coat was not foreseen at that time. To differentiate the levels of rank, varying aluminum braid, two centimeters wide, was worn on the upper arm of the coat experimentally, with two braids for commissioned and one for non-commissioned officers. This identifying mark, though, was not a success, so that as of 1937 this braid was replaced by removable shoulder straps and pieces. Enlisted men wore no insignia of rank, but sometimes wore shoulder pieces.

As of 1935 too, the material and color of the upper collar were changed several times. At first the upper collar was made of field-gray cloth. As of mid-1935 (HM 1935, No. 288), it was then made of field-gray insignia cloth. By the end of the same year, dark bluish-green insignia cloth was already being used, and in mid-1940 this was replaced by fatigue-shirt cloth. While the lower collar was originally made of field-gray cloth, a rubberized material was used from 1936 to the war's end.

To achieve the intended protection from the weather, the coat reached to slightly beyond mid-thigh. The two front parts and the one-piece back were sewn together with vulcanized thread. The two front parts overlapped each other greatly, and ran diagonally from the beltline up to the opposite shoulder. The high-set collar could be closed with a rubberized cord.

The back piece consisted of an open lower section with a vulcanized central panel. Under it was a material that would let air in, so that air circulation between the body and the outside air was assured.

The broad central fold of the back was slit from the bottom to the beltline. The lower corners of the coat could be wrapped around the legs and buttoned in place to serve as trouser legs. On the other hand, it was also possible to button the four edges of the coat up, using patented coat buttons. This way the motorcyclist had, on the one hand, more freedom of movement for his legs, while on the other hand, the corners of the coat could not get caught in the front-wheel spokes. On each side there was one deep inside pocket.

The different collar colors can be seen clearly here. While the coat collar at left is covered with dark blue-green emblem cloth, the other two coats have collars of field-gray cloth.

With the official introduction of the cycle coat, the following accessory equipment and clothing was also made available for drivers and passengers:
—1 pair of safety goggles,
—1 knitted woolen "pullover jacket",
—1 pair of "overleggings",
—1 pair of "overgloves."

The cost of the listed accessory equipment and clothing, including that of the cycle coat, was estimated in HM 1934, No. 85, as approximately 70 Reichsmarks per person.

This motorcyclist, with his Zündapp K 800 W cycle, has buttoned the lower tails of his coat around his legs like trousers. The 8 cm long strap with which the left front part is bound is also easy to see.

This motorcycle messenger of the staff of Panzerjäger Unit 87 of the 25th Division wears a long cycle coat, the large inside pocket of which can be seen clearly. His BMW R 4 cycle makes a "shining" impression, though it dates from 1932. The picture was taken in Norway in the summer of 1943.

The motorcycle messenger, with the tails of his typical cycle coat "wrapped around his legs like trousers", stands before his veteran BMW R 4 military cycle. The rear container and the engine shield mounted on the lower frame are easy to see here.

These BMW R 75 cycles are being serviced away from the front. These machines are still equipped with large front fenders and handles. Note also the bracket on the sidecar to hold a second storage case.

This BMW R 75 from a later production run, painted a dark yellow, already has the later front fender of the narrow type. The tropical filter can be seen above the tank. The right saddlebag bracket has already fallen victim to rough wartime conditions.

A boat sunk in the Meuse-Schelde Canal serves the crew of this BMW R 12 cycle as a makeshift bridge. The large fender with which the BMW R 12 went into service in 1935, but which filled up very quickly with mud and was thus replaced by a thinner type later, is easily seen.

A motorcycle unit with their BMW R 12 sidecar machines. These cycles with the wide front fenders and footboards instead of footrests were part of the first Wehrmacht delivery in 1935.

The number 44 in the background documents the last winter of the war: 1944. In front of it is a motorcyclist on his Zündapp cycle, presumably a KS 600 W.

Obviously, this is a peacetime training trip of a motorcycle rifle company from an SS armored reconnaissance unit. The lack of headlight covers and the shining cleanliness of the Zündapp KS 750 cycles indicate this.

The fate of a BMW R 75 sidecar cycle. Note the filter unit on the fuel tank. The vehicle has obviously been burned out.

"Comrades meet" around this BMW R 75. Note the lack of a headlight cover and the knobby tires. Obviously, this photo brings back memories.

Two cycles that were very seldom seen: at left, a DKW NZ 500 with sidecar, at right a Puch 200.

The sidecar cycles were often loaded far beyond their usual limits, as is true of this Zündapp KS 750. But one could ask practically anything of these strong and stable sidecar cycles. Note the added spare fuel canister.

44

This rough and ready motorcycle messenger on his Zündapp K 500 takes a bit of refreshment from his field flask. Note the tactical symbol of a cavalry regiment on the cycle's frame.

These motorcyclists take a short break in the Polish campaign, while dead horses lie beside the road, covered with branches.

This press photo surely helped to recruit volunteers as motorcycle messengers. It shows the driver on his Zündapp K 500 W, which was already delivered to the Wehrmacht as special equipment in prewar days.

Equipped with his carbine and gas mask, this motorcycle messenger poses for a photo on his DKW NZ 250. The cycle still has a front license plate, which was eliminated in 1943.

A brief pause in a backland area. This small group has gathered around the Zündapp KS 750 cycle for a memorable photo. Note the missing front fender.

Members of the 6th Panzer Division crossing the Dina River near Ostrov. The picture shows, among others, a BMW R 12 solo machine, with a BMW R 12 sidecar unit beside it.

With all their strength, the crew pushes their heavily loaded BMW R 12 sidecar cycle up a slope. The cycle still has the wide front fender. Note also the soldiers who could only camouflage themselves for winter with a white steel helmet.

The driver and passenger of a BMW R 12 cycle observe the damage to a light armored scout car in France in 1942.

A motorcycle messenger's group makes its last preparations for a scouting mission in the Storaya-Russe region of Russia.

To deliver important messages, the motorcycle messenger with his nimble machine is now, as then, a vital link in the military chain of command. This messenger rides an NSU 251 OS Wehrmacht cycle, officially called the D 605/7, with an engine shield on the lower frame.

Members of an unidentified unit and their cycles are being transported by rail. In the foreground is a BMW R 12, in back an Ardie, which was used by the Wehrmacht in the first months of World War II as the VF 125.

Finally bread has arrived . . . and the crew of this BMW R 12 are happy to receive their vital rations.

Two motorcycle messengers on DKW NZ 350 cycles, here in the version that was introduced into the Wehrmacht in great numbers as couriers' cycles. Note the knobby tire on the front wheel of the right cycle, as well as the messengers' good supplies of ammunition.

Checking the sidecar attachment of a BMW R 12. In the background is the tactical symbol of the motorcycle riflemen, the stylized wheel and motorcycle handlebars.

Motorcycle messenger H. Günther driving his BMW R 12 sidecar cycle in icy Russland in the winter of 1942-43.

Motorcycle messenger W. Peyn of the Infantry Regiment Staff of an infantry division, on his light Triumph 250/1 cycle at Schlüsselberg. The 250 cc cycle, modified for the Wehrmacht, was produced as of 1940, but was not off-road capable and required too much servicing for rough wartime use.

A press photo on a postcard, meant to demonstrate that the BMW R 75 cycle could handle rough conditions.

The BMW R 75 cycle with a tire chain on the sidecar wheel in the Russian winter. This wheel had its own drive.

Motorcycle messengers servicing their machines at Insterburg, East Prussia, for the last time, a few days before the advance into the Baltic region.

Two days before the beginning of the Russian campaign, these motorcyclists are preparing for action in the vicinity of Meissnerrode, East Prussia.

Members of an NSKK (National Socialist Motorized Corps) on a training mission in Hamburg. The leading cycle is the light 125 cc "Phänomen", Type Ahoi. This small cycle was made exclusively for the messenger, emergency and rescue services in cities.

Several other cycle types of the same NSKK unit; from left to right, DKW RT 100, Phänomen Ahoi 125, DKW RT 100, DKW KS 200. The others are presumably DKW RT 100.

This too could happen to a good motorcyclist in Russia. In trackless terrain it was not always easy to keep hold of a heavy machine, this one presumably a BMW R 71.

In the lee of a cemetery wall, the motorcycle messenger group has settled down for rest. Note the variety of cycle types.

Although the motorcyclist is in the foreground of this picture, many details of his heavy Zündapp KS 750 cycle can still be seen, particularly the three leather saddlebags.

Motorcyclists had to suffer particularly from rough weather, and often enough they had to literally push their machine, this one a BMW R 12, out of the mud with their own muscle power.

Motorcyclists of the II. Unit, Artillery Regiment "LAH" with their various sidecar cycles at the Baumholder training camp in 1940.

This picture surely would not have been released by the strict censors of military officialdom. The picture shows a Triumph BD 250 W, 12,000 of which were delivered to the Wehrmacht, this one loaded with all the motorcycle messenger's equipment.

Sidecar cycles were also used to transport equipment. This BMW R 75 cycle is seen in the encircled Demjansk area in the spring thaw.

A Zündapp K 800 W, equipped with an MG 34, and its crew in their long cycle coats. Note also the smooth tread of the cycle's front wheel.

The portrayal of military motorcycles should basically extend only to the year 1945. Nevertheless, the author would like to show the readers these pictures of Wehrmacht cycles that have been restored by an enthusiast since 1945.

The restored Zündapp KS 750 solo cycle is painted dark green. The leather coveralls of the driver are made up of American components.

A restored Triumph 500 built in 1933, a one-cylinder machine with fresh oil lubrication and "Tiger" fork.

On a Zündapp K 500, this motorcycle messenger traverses a corduroy road in the swampy area around Gorki-Meletcha. Such "road conditions" place high demands on man and motorcycle.

An artillery observation post is being set up in an open field. The motorcycle messengers on their BMW R 35 cycles are ready to carry orders. Note the saddlebag on the front wheel of the cycle at right.

Engineers have built a makeshift bridge over the Meuse to carry, among others, these motorcycle troops across the river.

A close-up view of a Zündapp KS 750 after crossing a swampy area.

A lineup of competition cycles on the occasion of a cross-country reliability trial. Such off-road sporting events served to train the drivers and make them more familiar with their cycles. Most of the cycles here are BMW R 12 types with wide front fenders.

This motorcycle messenger was obviously surprised by the photographer while repairing his DKW SB 500.

The calm before the storm! During rail transport, this motorcyclist had stretched out for a sunbath beside his Zündapp KS 750. The seat cushion from the sidecar serves as his pillow.

This BMW R 75 cycle serves as a towing tractor for a 7 cm field gun and "team transport wagon."

The Zündapp Works did not advertise their cycles only in the civilian sector. From 1938 to 1941, more than 18,000 of these KS 600 W machines alone, combined with a sidecar built by Zündapp itself, were delivered to the Wehrmacht.

Only very rarely was the heavy Zündapp KS 750 used as a solo cycle, as here. The sidecar was probably removed because of technical problems.

This BMW R 75 cycle with high-mounted air filter was photographed in Russia in 1942. The photo contradicts the general impression that the R 75 with the high filter was used only in the African theater of war.

A rather unclear photo, but the Zündapp K 500 W is easy to recognize. The K 500 W saw service as both a solo and sidecar cycle. This example has an unusually good tire profile.

Members of a repair unit with a Zündapp KS 750 cycle in Volkov, Russia in 1942. Note the knobby tires, very different from those of the earlier K 800 or K 600 types.

A pause during a training trip. Note the BMW R 75 cycles as this unit's uniform equipment.

Members of the 24th Panzer Division advancing in Russia in 1942. The picture shows BMW R 75 cycles, among others.

Off the beaten track, the heavy sidecar cycles often got stuck in deceptive mud puddles, as happened to the staff of a rifle brigade with their BMW R 75 cycle.

With his carbine in his hand, this cycle rifleman watches over his Zündapp K 800 W with opposed four-cylinder engine. Since the machine did not have a driveshaft to the sidecar, it was unsuitable for service in trackless terrain.

The heavy Zündapp K 800 W sidecar cycle was already in service with the troops in 1934. The 22 HP, four-cylinder engine was in use until the war's end.

In uncensored photos taken by participants in the war, the sharpness of the picture often leaves something to be desired, as here, where a Zündapp KS 750 tows a single-axle uniform trailer.

On this BMW R 75, the curved cover over the fuel tank, made to hold the high-mounted air filter, is easy to see. The lid holds, among other things, a replacement felt filter element.

A member of Panzer Regiment 25 in the winter of 1939-40, on a BMW R 35 medium cycle. The R 35 produced 14 HP and was used by the Wehrmacht between 1937 and 1940. The military version was painted field gray, instead of the usual black finish with white stripes, plus saddlebags and a headlight cover.

The messenger unit of I.R. 220 at rest in the village of Petershof in 1942. In the middle is a requisitioned Zündapp K 500, at far left a DKW NZ 350, at far right a captured French Terrot 500.

Motorcycle messengers of the division staff of the 30th I.D. after a brief "cigarette break" beside a Russian cottage, along with their BMW R 35.

The heavy Zündapp K 800 W cycle with typical leather saddlebags was almost always used with a sidecar. But the tires were too narrow to handle, for example, the mud in Flanders.

A motorcycle messenger of the II. Unit, "LAH" Artillery Regiment, on a Zündapp KS 600 W. The 600, which reached the troops in 1937, was also not an ideal Wehrmacht cycle. It differed from the civilian version only in its gray paint job, headlight cover and saddlebags.

The heavy BMW R 75 near an Autobahn rest stop outside Nürnberg. The R 75 was used only for military purposes, though BMW advertised this machine in a "civilian" brochure and proudly pointed out the sidecar drive.

Motorcycle messengers and their comrades meet by a supply truck. This Zündapp sidecar cycle belongs to the Guderian Panzer Group, hence the "G" on the sidecar.

The motorcycle messenger is always a "lone warrior." Control of his machine, a good sense of orientation and the ability to read military maps quickly and accurately make a good motorcycle messenger, like this one on a DKW NZ 350.

"Our Wehrmacht—The Messenger" is the title of this postcard picture from the Third Reich, showing a motorcycle messenger on a DKW NZ 350.

The Zündapp K 500 W painted tan, as large pieces of equipment, including motor vehicles, were as of 1943.

This too is part of wartime life! The crew of this BMW R 12 get more than just quarters from the villagers.

This motorcycle messenger in riding breeches, probably a member of a horsedrawn unit, with his captured Gnome et Rhone cycle in a souvenir photo.

The messenger on his BMW R 12 delivers a message. The passenger, with a stick grenade in his boot, has already dismounted.

In the dusty background we faintly see a horsedrawn unit. In front is a BMW R 12 with its crew. The cycle has a wide front fender and a second headlight on the sidecar.

Picture #137 from the album "The German Wehrmacht", with the caption: Motorcyclists go over a barrier. The motorcyclist has to go everywhere, on or off the road. Thus he must learn to get his heavy machine over all kinds of obstacles.

The uniform cycles of a Luftwaffe unit are Zündapp K 600 W machines.

A press photo with the caption: "Motorcycle riflemen are always at the enemy's heels." At left is a BMW R 12 with an added bracket to hold personal equipment on the sidecar, at right probably a DKW NZ 350.

A field parade of an unidentified unit in 1935. The tactical symbol on the cycle in the middle and its equipment suggest that this is a motorcycle rifle unit, established as of 1935 and almost always equipped with BMW R 11 and R 12 cycles.

Deceptively idyllic! A BMW R 4 and its crew's tent are, after all, military equipment.

The outward appearance of the two heavy Wehrmacht cycles made by Zündapp. Above is a KS 750, below a K 800 W. Note the different types of tires.

The leading motorcycle messengers show the following troops the way to march.

An unidentified unit makes its last preparations for the attack on Russia in June 1941. At right is a BMW R 12, at left an armored radio car.

A close-up photo of a NMW R 12. The right cylinder, the swinging saddle for the passenger, a part of the right footboard and the right coil spring of the driver's saddle can be seen.

To this day, motorcycle messengers provide important service for every troop leader. This messenger is seen riding a DKW NZ 350 over fifty years ago.

Requisitioned Motorcycles

Even today, there is probably no soldier who is usable in as many ways as the motorcyclist on his fast and mobile machine, even though at that time units and groups, established during the war, were equipped with a variety of solo and sidecar cycles of the most varied manufacture and design, some of which were called into war service from the civilian sector and often came to a bad end in the most literal sense of the word if a small special part for a specific cycle could not be delivered quickly. In this case, the motorcyclist generally made progress if he knew his machine inside and out and could use a few primitive means of making his cycle run again.

Within the framework of universal military service, as well as later in the war, all privately owned motorcycles were confiscated and turned over to the Wehrmacht for war service, in addition to the Wehrmacht cycles themselves. Knowledgeable personnel from the motorcycle industry were called in as "evaluators" for procedures in which they had the task of estimating the value of confiscated motorcycles in Reichsmarks, so that the owners could be reimbursed. As a rule, these motorcycles were then resprayed in Wehrmacht color, while the civilian license number was often

Off to war with whitewall tires! Two highly polished sidecar cycles were called into Wehrmacht service. At left, probably a Standart with a sporting sidecar built by Steib of Nürnberg, at right a Triumph 350 and Steib No. 36 sport sidecar with star decor.

retained. In certain places, the additional marking "WH" was added, since the army had the greatest need for motorcycles. Time and again, action photos show that sometimes repainting was dispensed with and the machines were sent to the front in their "civilian clothing."

Luftwaffe men on a BMW R 12 cycle. The aerodynamic sidecar was made by Royal. BMW worked closely with this sidecar maker. The weather protection was not part of the Wehrmacht equipment of the R 12, so this is obviously a requisitioned cycle.

A military policeman on his requisitioned Triumph 500 Tourensport. By its license plate (IX...), the machine was registered in the province of Westphalia. The added WH shows that it was requisitioned by the Army. It can also be seen that the Wehrmacht paint is already flaking off the engine.

A last look is given to these requisitioned motorcycles of various types before they are turned over to the troops. In the foreground is an NSU 351 OSL.

91

A short rest during a training trip on shining clean cycles. In front is a Zündapp KS 600 with a heavy Stoye sidecar. Zündapp preferred Stoye sidecars for their K 500 and KS 600 cycles. In back is a K 500 solo.

This requisitioned 750 cc BMW R 11 sidecar cycle with civilian license plate from the city of Münster (IIA...) has already been fitted with a passenger seat and saddlebags for military service.

Motorcyclists in Russia with problems. Often enough, the German soldiers and their vehicles encountered terrain conditions such as are shown here, with a despairing soldier with a BMW R 35 and the crew of a BMW R 12 stuck in the mud. Note the spare fuel canister on the sidecar. The R 35 is a requisitioned machine with IA license plate, from the Berlin area.

Only with the help of comrades was it possible for this motorcyclist to get his BMW R 12 up a steep slope after crossing a river in the encircled Demjansk area. The requisitioned cycle still has aluminum footboards and protectors.

The 125 cc Ardie of this jolly driver is a requisitioned machine. Along with the civilian license plate (IM... for the province of Saxony), the letters WH have been added on the front fender. The exhaust system mounted on the back of the cylinder was typical of this make of motorcycle.

This Zündapp cycle, which cannot be identified precisely, was surely used as a fast means of carrying messages from the field command post in the background.

These motorcycle messengers eat their rations from the saddles of their NSU 351 OSL. They belong to a division command post set up between the villages of Opatcha and Norvoskett.

RUNDSCHREIBEN
der Kundendienst-Abteilung Wagen - Räder, München

Gruppe Fahrgestell	No. 4
München, am 19.6.43 KMT 516/Lf	
Für BMW Vertreter des Inlandes	151

Schweres Kraftrad 750 ccm mit Seitenwagen (angetrieben)
BMW Baumuster 750/275 (R 75)

Gummimanschette zur Gabelabdichtung

Zur Erzielung eines besseren Staubschutzes haben wir eine Abdichtung der Vorderradgabel durch Gummimanschetten eingeführt, die in der Serienfabrikation ab Fahrgestell-Nr. 762 259 eingesetzt hat. Diese Gummimanschetten sollen nach Möglichkeit bei allen bisher an die Wehrmacht gelieferten Krafträdern des Baumusters 750/275 (R 75) nachträglich eingebaut werden. Diesbezüglicher Antrag an das OKH ist gestellt.

Zum nachträglichen Einbau werden benötigt:

2 Dichtungen vollst.	275 1 82 014 00	je 1.40 RM	2.80 RM	
2 Einspannstücke oben	275 1 82 069 o	je 2.45 "	4.90 "	
4 Sechsk.Muttern dazu	Kr 751 M 6	je -.05 "	-.20 "	
4 Federringe	A 6,4 DIN 127	je -.01 "	-.04 "	
4 Schellen vollst.	275 1 82 026 o	je -.40 "	1.60 "	
Muttern und Schrauben)				
BM 4x20 DIN 86 M4 DIN 934)	je Schelle 1 Stück			
2 Gummimanschetten	275 1 62 021 o	je 2.70 "	5.40 "	
2 Überwurfmuttern	275 1 62 235 2	je 2.05 "	4.10 "	

Gesamtbetrag 19.04 RM

Diese Teile können über den zuständigen Heimat-Kraftfahr-Park bei den BAYERISCHEN MOTOREN WERKEN A.G., Zweigniederlassung Eisenach, Ersatzteil-Abteilung P 250, Eisenach, Rennbahn 1, bezogen werden.
Bei den Maschinen, Motor-Nr.753 808 mit Motor-Nr.757 250 kommt die in der Gabelverschlußschraube eingebaute Entlüftung in Fortfall.
Für diese Maschinen sind zusätzlich

2 Gabelverschlußschrauben 275 1 62 030 o   je 1.55 RM   3.10 RM

zu bestellen.

Bei Lieferung der Teile zum nachträglichen Anbau wird eine Einbauanleitung mitgeliefert. Der Umbau lässt sich sehr leicht durchführen.

Sturz der Maschine

Im Rundschreiben Nr. 1 Gruppe Fahrgestell v.1.5.42 ist auf Seite 7 unter der Skizze übersehen worden, daß auch das Maß für das Baumuster 750/275 (R 75) anzuführen ist. Dieses Maß haben wir unseren Herren Vertreter bereits mit dem Rundschreiben Nr. 108 vom 6.2.42 und auf Seite 6 des Rundschreibens Nr.1 Gruppe Fahrgestell, bekanntgegeben. Wir bitten, auf Seite 7 des genannten Rundschreibens unter der Skizze hinter dem Maß 6-12 mm zu ergänzen: "R. 75 : 2 - 3 mm".

BAYERISCHE MOTOREN WERKE
Aktiengesellschaft

Nachdruck auch auszugsweise verboten!

The introduction of rubber sleeves on the front fork of the BMW R 75 heavy motorcycle is often mentioned with various dates in the literature. Here is a copy of a letter from the BMW AG on June 19, 1943, according to which this modification to the fork has been introduced into series production with chassis number 762259. It is also interesting that this letter was sent to BMW agents.

A restored BMW R 75 with rubber bellows, from the German Museum in Munich.

This 1/9 scale model also shows the rubber bellows clearly.

The front wheel of this DKW NZ 250 shows its excellently profiled off-road tire. Its shield and headlight, though, have fallen victim to wartime action. The two-tone paint on the fuel tank shows that it is a requisitioned machine.

Repairing an NSU 251 OSL in the field. This is obviously a requisitioned machine. The saddlebags and the fishtail end of the exhaust pipe are missing, as is the passenger seat.

Often the requisitioned motorcycles were sent into service in their civilian paint, as has been done with this sidecar cycle.

Badly damaged Wehrmacht cycles, obviously gathered as sources of spare parts, are loaded onto a railroad car.

Food bringers of the Guderian ("G") Panzer Group, The driver at right, on a BMW R 61, has a thermos container on his back. Behind is a BMW R 12 cycle. Its wide front fender is easy to see here.

Motorcycle messengers with Zündapp K 500 W solo cycles in occupied France, 1940. Note in particular the middle cycle with its extensive load of personal baggage.

A corporal with his rifleman's braid and heavy BMW R 12 Wehrmacht cycle at his parental home in the Breslau area.

The motor pool of a unit has its picture taken. At right are two Zündapp KS 600 W cycles.

To get help for their wounded comrade quickly, the medics made use of the motorcycles' maneuverability, as with this BMW R 12 in a Polish city.

Eating their rations at the officials' sidecar of a BMW R 12 during training in 1935.

This motorcycle messenger on his Puch S 4 is leaving a French fort in which the German Wehrmacht has taken up quarters in 1940.

These motorcyclists and their machines attract the attention of passersby. At left is a Zündapp KS 600 W, at right the special Wehrmacht version of the Derby as a light two-cycle DBK 200 ggf. 250 W cycle.

Members of a mountain division have taken quarters in this hotel. The picture shows a requisitioned NSU 501/601 T.

The unit has moved into an abandoned barnyard. The crew of the Zündapp K 500 W cycle maintains contact with the battalion.

The Zündapp K 500 W, recognizable by its long shift lever, was used as both a solo and sidecar cycle.

An interesting picture, showing exclusively "purebred" Wehrmacht vehicles, with no requisitioned ones. Among others, Zündapp sidecar units and K 800 W solos and BMW R 4 cycles can be seen here.

An antitank unit advances. The solid ground only hints at what it will be like in trackless terrain. In the foreground is a BMW R 12 sidecar cycle.

This motorcycle messenger had his picture taken with his BMW R 12 as a memento of his visit to Belgium in the war year of 1940. Note the wide front fender.

A communications center was established in this building on the Russian border. At right is a BMW with a machine gun. The motorcycle messengers await further orders.

The repair troop fixes a damaged BMW R 12 cycle. Note the camouflaged workshop truck.

Bicycles and motorcycles for the troops are loaded onto a train for transport. The picture shows a BMW R 5.

The unit moves out of the sheltering lowlands to change position. In the foreground are two BMW R 12 sidecar cycles.

Santa Claus is coming! Members of a Luftwaffe unit, far from home, have used their BMW R 12 to transport Christmas trees. Note also the gas mask used to cover the headlight.

When camouflage paint and chalk were in short supply, only the steel helmets were painted white in snowy country. Here is a Zündapp cycle in the Russian winter of 1942.

This motorcycle messenger group is taking a rest in southern France. The picture shows Puch cycles, which were built between 1938 and 1940.

This picture shows a Zündapp KS 600 W sidecar cycle. The special Type 39 sidecar was developed by Zündapp in collaboration with the Stoye firm of Leipzig.

Two motorcycle messengers with their DKW SB 500 of 1936. The SB models, with their three-speed motors, were replaced by the NZ series at the end of 1937. The two drivers, wearing cycle coats with dark blue collars, stand before their quarters in 1941.

The armored scout car has made a stop for technical reasons in the shelter of the woods. The motorcycle messenger, on what appears to be a DKW KM 200, maintains contact with the head of the platoon.

"Prepare to march" says this postcard picture, showing DKW 350 of 1934 with armature steering.

In the shelter of a wall that has taken some direct hits, the motorcyclists take a rest with their BMW R 75 cycles.

Such acrobatics during technical service were surely the exception. Yet the sergeant is obviously in command of his Victoria KR 6 Bergmeister with its sidecar.

This motorcycle crosses the Alsatian border into France. The rear part of the folding shield panel has obviously been lost already.

The products of the Austrian manufacturer, Puch, were also used in the German Wehrmacht, like this 250 cc S 204 made from 1929 to 1933.

Advancing into Poland in 1939. Engineers have built a pontoon bridge across a river, and the motorcyclist on his Zündapp KS 600 W leads the following troops across it.

Poland, 1939: a Zündapp KS 600 W follows the command car.

A requisitioned NSU 501/601 T with a sidecar on the left. For civilian use, Zündapp preferred the advantages of having the sidecar on the left side.

Requisitioned vehicles that were used in the French campaign, including a Horex.

A press photo meant to show the interest of the Hitler Youth in this DKW RT 3 PS. This light 98 cc motorcycle was also used by the Wehrmacht, but exclusively in Germany for courier service and training purposes.

A sidecar cycle of unknown make in Wehrmacht service in Holland, 1940. In any case, it is a requisitioned cycle, if not a captured one.

This BMW R 11 of 1932 is fitted with a streamlined Stoye sidecar, though BMW preferred sidecars built by Royal.

Flanked by makeshift antitank barricades on the French-Belgian border, this motorcycle messenger passes by on his requisitioned NSU 601 OSL.

The 350 cc Victoria KR 35 WH "Pionier" medium motorcycle was regarded as the best solo cycle in the Wehrmacht. This is a requisitioned cycle from the Hesse region (VH...).

A standard 500 Kurier made by the Swabian firm of W. Gutbrod. The Kurier was built between 1935 and 1939 had a 494 cc motor producing 16 HP. This is obviously a requisitioned machine, as it is not known that Gutbrod received Wehrmacht contracts.

A requisitioned BMW R 61 that went into military service with its owner in 1939. The license plate indicates an Austrian home town. Here in the field, the cycle formed a centerpiece for this photo of its driver and his comrades

The motorcyclist makes his own repairs to his BMW R 4. This is also a requisitioned machine; the license plate (IH...) indicates registration in Pomerania. The motorcyclists often knew their machines very thoroughly, particularly when they took their own cycle with them into military service.

A proud motorcycle messenger on his DKW NZ 250. This is obviously a requisitioned machine, since—unlike the Wehrmacht version—it lacks saddlebag brackets, a passenger seat, and the shield in front of the generator cover.

Two motorcycle messengers who were drafted into the army along with their private cycles. At left an NSU 501 OSL. As can be seen from the emblem on the left side of the tank, this is a machine made by the NSU-D-Rad United Vehicle Works AG of Neckarsulm. At right a DKW SB 500.

On the advance in Latvia. The exhausted motorcycle messengers are taking a break in the shade of a barn. The picture shows a requisitioned BMW 600 Sport with civilian license IA... for the district of Berlin.

Two requisitioned DKW NZ 250 cycles. The light trim stripes on the tanks are easy to see, and the headlights are not covered. In the background is a Phänomen Granit 30.

This requisitioned Zündapp DB 200 still bears the civilian license IE... for the province of Brandenburg. The Wehrmacht gray DB 200 W special version was very popular as a lightweight messenger's cycle on account of its reliability.

Many requisitioned cycles that had looked classy in civilian life on paved roads had big problems in pathless terrain, as does this DKW SB 350.

The last preparations are made on this requisitioned Victoria KR 35 B from the Berlin district, to prepare it for wartime service. Obviously, message pouches had to be attached to the cycle. In the background is a BMW R 4.

Three happy young non-commissioned officers with their requisitioned NSU 501/601 T sidecar cycle from the Berlin district (IA...) The headlight has been given a makeshift covering.

Motorcyclists and passengers with their requisitioned cycles, from left to right, probably a BMW R 4 and a Hercules 200.

This is what happened to a motorcyclist when he, on his unprotected machine, had to catch up with columns of vehicles wreathed in clouds of dust to deliver messages or handle traffic safety. The cycle is a requisitioned NSU 501/601 T from the Leipzig district.

This proud non-commissioned officer rides a requisitioned BMW R 11. The Wehrmacht version was used by the Reichswehr until 1934. Note the horn attached to the left side, not included on the Wehrmacht version.

These civilian motorcycles from various manufacturers are being considered for requisitioning. The picture was taken in Döberitz near Berlin.

This BMW R 16 cycle with Stoye sidecar, once glistening in gloss paint, came from the province of Hessen-Nassau (IT...) and was requisitioned for military use.

This motorcycle with IIZ civilian registration was requisitioned in the district of Swabia. It is obviously a Triumph S 350 of the 1936-37 series.

The rear license plates on these requisitioned cycles were repainted with WH (Wehrmacht-Heer) lettering.

This civilian motorcycle, of undetermined make, obviously was also requisitioned for military service.

In the Russian theater of war, this member of a Pak unit is seen with his requisitioned NSU 351/501 OSL.

In front of a field hospital in a French town, we see a requisitioned Triumph STM 500 cycle with Sport Sidecar No. 25, which sold for 195 Reichsmark.

A DKW SB 500, built in 1936 for the civilian market, seen in Wehrmacht service.

This luxurious sidecar cycle, made by the Austrian firm of Felber, was also requisitioned for Wehrmacht use.

Next to an abandoned armored scout car is a requisitioned NSU 351/501 OS from the Berlin district (IA...).

A captured French captain from Cherbourg is taken away in a Triumph S 500 cycle with Steib sidecar.

A civilian Zündapp KK 200, which was also requisitioned for use in the Wehrmacht.

These gleaming cycles, obviously just requisitioned for training, surely got a coat of dark gray Wehrmacht paint later. From left to right, an NSU/D-Rad 351 OSL, DKW SB 350 early version, and DKW SB 350. In the background is a DKW SB 500 with Steib No. 36 Sport Sidecar, made of shining sheet aluminum, painted with a star and selling for 220 Reichsmark. Note also the Wehrmacht identification on the headlights.

For a Medical Corps drill in 1939, these vehicles were requisitioned and turned out for inspection at Cochem on the Mosel. From left to right, a BMW R 61 with Royal sidecar, a BMW R 11 with unidentified sidecar, and probably a DKW SB 500.

A requisitioned DKW SB 500 from the Berlin district (IA...) in use as a messenger's cycle for a heavy artillery unit.

In their sidecar brochure for 1935, the NSU-D-Rad United Vehicle Works AG of Neckarsulm advertised this NSU luxury sport sidecar, suitable for the 501 OSL shown here, for 295 Reichsmark. This machine was requisitioned for military use and lettered WH on the front fender. Behind it is probably a Standard 500 with civilian sidecar.

Here is a "parade" of requisitioned cycles, at left an NSU 351/501 OSL, then a DKW 500 SB with Steib sidecar and a DKW SB 350.

This training troop with its requisitioned motorcycles has stopped on a country road in northern Baden. In the foreground are civilian motorcycles of various types. Note the sidecar with the particularly big star in the background.

"With thoughts of home"—thus could this photo of two motorcycle messengers and their machines be inscribed. The cycles are obviously requisitioned DKW SB 500 types.

The despairing expression on this motorcyclist's face makes a strong impression as he pushes his BMW R 61 through a swampy region. The R 61 was not a true Wehrmacht machine and thus fully unsuitable for off-road conditions.

A requisitioned cycle of unknown make, with a dynamo to operate its compressed-air horn. The compressor is attached to the front wheel by means of a [Bowdenzug].

In the mid-thirties there was much competition among the motorcycle manufacturers. As of 1934, Zündapp put its heavy K 800 model on the market, to be used almost always as a sidecar machine, as in this photo. Many of these machines must have been requisitioned by the Wehrmacht and repainted in field gray when World War II began.

Captured Motorcycles

For the actual Wehrmacht cycles and the requisitioned types taken from the civilian realm, the problem of supplying spare parts could usually be solved—even though with considerable difficulty. As long as the German factories had not been fully destroyed by enemy bomb attacks, supplies were forthcoming, though usually behind schedule. In addition, the German motorcyclists and repair-shop personnel in the army units and groups were familiar with the types of motorcycles from their own country.

The situation was different for captured cycles. Here the German drivers often suffered from insufficient knowledge of how to maintain these cycles properly. Since there was also the problem of finding spare parts, captured machines had no great "chance of survival." One exceptional case was that of cycles whose places of manufacture were in areas occupied by the Germans, or those for which plentiful spare-part supplies could be captured. In particular, during the western campaign, numerous motorcycles fell into the hands of the German Wehrmacht. These included several French brands that were taken over by the Wehrmacht and used for their own purposes. Among these cycles there were, in particular, those made by Terrot, Rene Gillet, and Gnome et Rhone. The last brand included the most frequently used captured French machines in the Wehrmacht. For the utilization of this product, a German service manual was prepared, so that the German drivers and mechanics could become more familiar with their maintenance. This was Service Manual (D) 605/29 of 4/28/1944, "Heavy [p. 143] Motorcycle 800 cc with Sidecar (driven by) Gnome Rhone (f) Type AX 2, Equipment Description and Servicing Manual.

In addition to technical data on the cycle, it included a thorough description of the machine, service instructions for starting the motor as well as braking, maintenance tips and repair instructions, amplified by numerous illustrations.

Another motorcycle that was used by the German Wehrmacht but cannot be classified as a captured cycle in the literal sense, and for which a

The barber has arrived! At right is a captured French Gnome et Rhone cycle.

German service manual was prepared, was the Italian Gilera. With the same contents, this manual was listed as D 618/39, Motorcycle 500 cc, Gilera (i), Type 500 LE Militaire, of 11/10/1944.

No less familiar to the German Wehrmacht were the Belgian FN (Fabrique National), Sarolea and Gillet 750 cycles. German service manuals for these cycles were, to be sure, not available. Now were there German-language service and repair manuals for the various British brands that were captured at Dunkirk.

With the use of captured motorcycles in the German Army, the problem of finding usable vehicles was surely complicated rather than lessened.

Driver Hanns Kletzer and passenger Uffz. Kilian of the 14th Panzerjäger Company, 185th Infantry Regiment, on a captured French Terrot 350, built at Vichy in 1941. They wear the typical protective motorcycle coat.

Members of the 14th Company, I.R. 220, on the advance in Lithuania. In the foreground is a captured French Gnome et Rhone of 1941, with sidecar. The army version of the Gnome et Rhone had an 804 cc side-valve opposed engine with a separate drive for the sidecar wheel. German servicing instructions, introduced especially for this make, was meant to make handling these cycles easier for German drivers.

Such perfect winter camouflage for army vehicles can be found very seldom in action photos. In this case, the cycles cannot even be identified. They were presumably captured.

These cycles were brought to a repair shop to be repaired. In the middle is a French Terrot 500 OHW.

This motorcycle messenger of the 14th Company, I.R. 220, was photographed on his captured British Norton 16H cycle in an East Prussian town.

Members of the 58th I.D. at rest in a Russian town. Among their vehicles was this captured Belgian FN 1000. The renowned Belgian Fabrique National works built this cycle for the Belgian Army in 1938.

A captured cycle "on the other side." This member of the Northamptonshire Regiment enjoys the ruggedness of his captured German Zündapp KS 750.

The American Indian Chief military cycle in the hands of German soldiers. This was probably a machine captured from the British, since Britain ordered large numbers of these Indian motorcycles in 1941.

This captured cycle, probably a Belgian FN M 86, surely has been in German service only a short time, since the original troop markings are still to be seen on it.

Motorcycles of the Allied Forces

Among the other nations taking part in World War II that used numerous solo and sidecar motorcycles between 1939 and 1945, we can list, among others, Belgium, Holland, France, Italy, Britain and the USA. The designs and uses of these cycles were just as various as those within the German Wehrmacht. As examples, we can mention the heavy American Harley-Davidson solo and sidecar cycles on the one hand, and on the other, the little 98 cc Welbike machines used by the British airborne troops. In between there were numerous medium and heavy motorcycles of various designs. To the extent that action photos of these cycles could be obtained, they are published here. The fact is that the Allied forces also simply "militarized" many civilian motorcycles and put them to use in the war.

A French René-Gillet two-cylinder sidecar machine with a French crew. Many of these cycles were captured, repainted and given new tactical symbols by the Germans, and then used very intensively by the Wehrmacht. This is obviously a civilian machine, as the paint on the tank shows.

These are not captured German machines in the Netherlands Army. These BMW cycles were obviously introduced into the Army regularly. At left is a BMW R 61. This model came out in 1938, and most of them were delivered to the German Wehrmacht. At right is a BMW R 12 sidecar cycle. Both machines had extra components (lights, horn) added to them.

Members of the 41st Netherlands Infantry Division on German BMW R 61 cycles, produced in Germany for export.

"The Flying Flea", as this 125 cc Royal Enfield light motorcycle used by the British airborne troops was called, was either dropped by parachute inside a pipe frame or brought to the scene in Horsta freight gliders.

The French Terrot 750 sidecar cycle was made between 1933 and 1937. Note the makeshift headlight shield and the knee protection.

The one-cylinder British BSA M 20, with its 500 cc and 13 HP, was among the medium cycles used by the British Army. Note the homemade front fender.

A damaged Belgian Gillet 750 sidecar cycle after a German air raid in 1940. The Gillet was the most often-used cycle in the Belgian Army.

A motorcyclist fixes a flat tire on a Norton 16H cycle.

The motorcyclist has to enlist the help of a Dutch boy in wooden shoes with his British Ariel W/NG cycle. Despite good ground clearance, the cycle was not made to handle these ground conditions.

The British Big Four sidecar cycle, made by Norton. This machine was usually used for reconnaissance purposes. The sidecar drive could be turned on or off by hand.

British soldiers on a Norton Big Four are greeted warmly in liberated Holland.

The German BMW R 12 was godfather to the American Harley-Davidson. About a thousand cycles of this type were made for testing in the U.S. Army.

Motorcyclists in the Netherlands try out American Harley-Davidson motorcycles made in 1940.

The light-loaded British Norton 16H in Africa. This originally civilian type of cycle received only a few minor modifications to be ready for military service.

A British motorcycle messenger on a Norton 16H is trying to cross a shallow brook without getting his feet wet.

The American Indian Chief with sidecar. These cycles, made in Springfield, Massachusetts, were ordered by the British in 1941.

A radio troop of Polish army men on an American Indian Chief with sidecar.

The British BSA 1000 cc saw service with the motorized Netherlands hussars. The so-called "Colonial version", an export model with a foot clutch, good ground clearance and sidecar at the right, was built until the end of 1939. The last machines were turned over to the Netherlands military forces.

A British Matchless G3, which unlike the G3L was equipped with a parallelogram fork. has lost its headlight in the war. The driver wears a typical British motorcycle messenger's helmet.

This British soldier takes a nap on his Matchless G3L. The G3L was essentially identical to the G3, but had a lighter engine and frame. The machine was fast enough to be utilized to keep order during marches. Note the rear brackets to hold saddlebags.

Technical service for the BSA M20 cycles of a British unit. Over 12,500 M20 motorcycles were delivered to the British armed forces.

A British BSA M20 in the North African theater of war. The otherwise stable front fender, as well as the headlight lens with its cover, have already fallen victim to the war. On the other hand, the spoked front wheel with its Universal tire profile, is easy to see.

The Belgian FNSM sidecar cycle with an unusual body. Note also the makeshift hitch for the two-wheel trailer.

Members of the Belgian Army on maneuvers in the country with the FN 1000 SM sidecar cycle. This machine, equipped with a 1000 cm opposed two-cylinder four-stroke motor, was built from 1939 to 1940. The FN was one of the first motorcycles with shaft drive. Note the profile of the front tire.

Along with the two prewar models at left, we see a British Matchless G3L made in 1942. The long telescopic fork and the rear stand are easy to see.

British Matchless G3L cycles in liberated Eindhoven, Holland, in 1944.

At left is a Big Four with a machine gun, at right a Norton 16H.

This Big Four was equipped with a machine gun on a swiveling mount. Note also the rough tire profile.

Another variation of the Norton Big Four, this one equipped with a grenade launcher; the sidecar body has been removed and the launcher barrel's two-legged mount attached to the frame, along with two ammunition boxes.

The simple but rugged sidecar of the Big Four. Note the easy access to the passenger seat.

One of the most curious motorcycles that saw service in World War II was the British Welbike. This folding "motorcycle" was used by airborne troops.

The Welbike with its handlebars folded down. The frame consisted of four tubes running in pairs above and below the motor and uniting at the steering column and rear axle. The wheels, tank, seat, handlebars and motor were attached to the frame.

A air bases the Welbike was used gladly by ground personnel to cover long stretches of ground in comfort. It was ideal for such purposes too.

Barbed-wire fences formed no obstacle for the Welbike. One simply lifted it over.

The Welbike was folded up and put into a container for parachuting. The cylindrical container had a diameter of 38 cm and was dropped, bike and all, on a parachute.

The American airborne troops used the Cushman motor scooter. After the jump, the paratrooper could get on it and get to a predetermined meeting point quickly.

After the drop, the Welbike was lifted out of the container . . .

. . . and was ready for action in moments.

Here the difference in size between the British airborne soldier and the little Welbike is easy to see.

A restored Royal Enfield, 126 ccm displacement, seen in postwar days. This small motorcycle, already shown elsewhere as "the Flying flea" used by the British airborne troops, is not equipped with the cylindrical muffler usually mounted ahead of the crankcase.

The Cushman had a one-cylinder four-stroke industrial motor of 244 cc displacement. The machine was crude and simple but made the paratroops very mobile when they landed.

The unsprung front fork and fat 6.00 x 6 size front tire of the Cushman, which was a practical means of transportation that allowed a quick assembly of the airborne troops when they landed.

A Maid of All Work—
The NSU HK 101 Treaded Cycle

Probably the most striking "motorcycle" that saw service during World War II was the HK 101 treaded cycle made by NSU. The inspiration for its development and the financial support for it came from the Army Weapons Office. The development itself was taken over by the NSU Werken AG in Neckarsulm. Although this is not a motorcycle in the strict sense, it is usually mentioned along with the usual motorcycles nevertheless. Because of its uniqueness, it thus deserves to be considered in this volume.

The treaded cycle was a product of the tractor program of the army leadership at that time. The production figures also confirm this statement. For the year of 1940, only 140 examples were built.

"A maid of all work", thus was the treaded cycle described in a press release by the NSU Werken AG in 1941. In fact, the manifold uses of the treaded cycle led to its being produced until 1948 for use in German forestry and agriculture.

During the war, the treaded cycle was regarded as the only truly off-road-capable light messenger, courier and scouting vehicle. This is presumably why the vehicle was counted among the motorcycles. In all, some 8500 of them were put into service by the war's end. Experts estimate that there are still about a hundred of these vehicles from wartime and postwar production still in existence, some of them used in vineyards, others preserved and protected by fans as the apple of their eyes.

The NSY treaded cycle in action. In the wet season of the Russian winter, ground conditions like these were typical.

Treaded cycles of the paratroop artillery forces in action in North Africa.

The treaded cycle served as a towing tractor for the light guns of the paratroop artillery in Normandy in 1942.

Here the treaded cycle sees service as a communications vehicle in Tunisia, North Africa.

After the war, the treaded cycle found many uses in agriculture and forestry.

Model Motorcycles

In portraying military action vehicles from the days of war and service, one often uses factory-new vehicles as a basis. This may occur because no action pictures are available, or to show the interested reader certain details on the portrayed object, which because of its war service would only be seen partly because of camouflage or other factors.

In this volume of pictures, some of the most important motorcycles, which saw action either on the German or the Allied side, shall be shown as exact-scale miniatures. These are plastic models in various scales, which were made out of available kits. Thus this chapter of the book at hand will not only contribute to the completion of the action pictures, but also serve the model builder as a valuable aid in the building and detailing of his own models.

For some time now, some of the most interesting motorcycles have been on the market as 1/9 scale kits. For the fan of these historical makes, there are thus not only kits of German motorcycles available. On the Allied side, the American Harley-Davidson WLA 45 and the British Triumph 3HW have been reproduced in scale models. On the German side, it was naturally the heavy Zündapp KS 750 and BMW R 75 sidecar types. When one considers that these kits have been sold worldwide, it is not surprising why the model industry has chosen these legendary German cycles. They were part of the concept of the German motorcycle messenger and rifle troop in all theaters of the war.

Nor is it surprising that these two types of cycles have also appeared on the model market in solo form. As solo cycles, though, these models actually look as if they are missing something, since the connection for the driveshaft of the sidecar is present on the right side of the rear axle, but the sidecar itself is missing. Nevertheless, these two solo cycles, because of their excellent details, are also very interesting to behold.

A very interesting model — which can compete very well with the original in terms of precision of detail — in the HK 101 tread cycle by NSU, likewise in 1/9 scale. Since it is so often ranked among the actual motorcycles by many readers, it shall be added to the military motorcycle models here.

The portrayal of these motorcycles in military versions would be incomplete if we did not show the interested reader the model of the BMW R 75 with sidecar in its postwar civilian form. The model, finished in gloss black paint, with many stripes of trim and chromed parts, scarcely lets one imagine that the original once appeared in field-gray paint at the gates of Moscow.

Motorcycle with Footboard—
the Harley-Davidson WLA 45

With 739 cc displacement and a top speed of 23 HP at 120 kph, the American WLA 45 was more or less comparable with the Zündapp KS 750 and BMW R 75 Wehrmacht cycles. Purely externally, this type of cycle differed from all other models in that it did not have footrests, but rather true footboards on both sides of the engine block or gearbox. This feature has been retained for all heavy Harley-Davidson machines to the present time.

Since this model also consists of a number of individual parts, its assembly requires much patience and care. Particularly in the area of the engine block and gearbox, and the footboards with the shift lever, one can only assemble it one step at a time. The gluing together of different types of material—particularly the rubber and plastic parts—causes no difficulties as long as one uses a one-component adhesive. For example, the typical rubber dirt catchers of the Harley can be attached to the appropriate plastic parts in a matter of seconds.

The models shown here were made in various colors and finished with matte green paint, generally the customary color of the Harley-Davidson, and in a light tan color for use in desert regions.

The American Harley-Davidson WLA 45 in 1/9 scale, painted tan, with a pair of captured boots on the passenger seat.

The same model, painted matte gray. The so-called "cowboy saddle" is clear to see. The engine block and gearbox are a treasure chest for a detail fanatic.

The two-section tank of the WLA 45. The tachometer is mounted atop the tank. Note also the two filler caps and the screw closing of the oil dipstick.

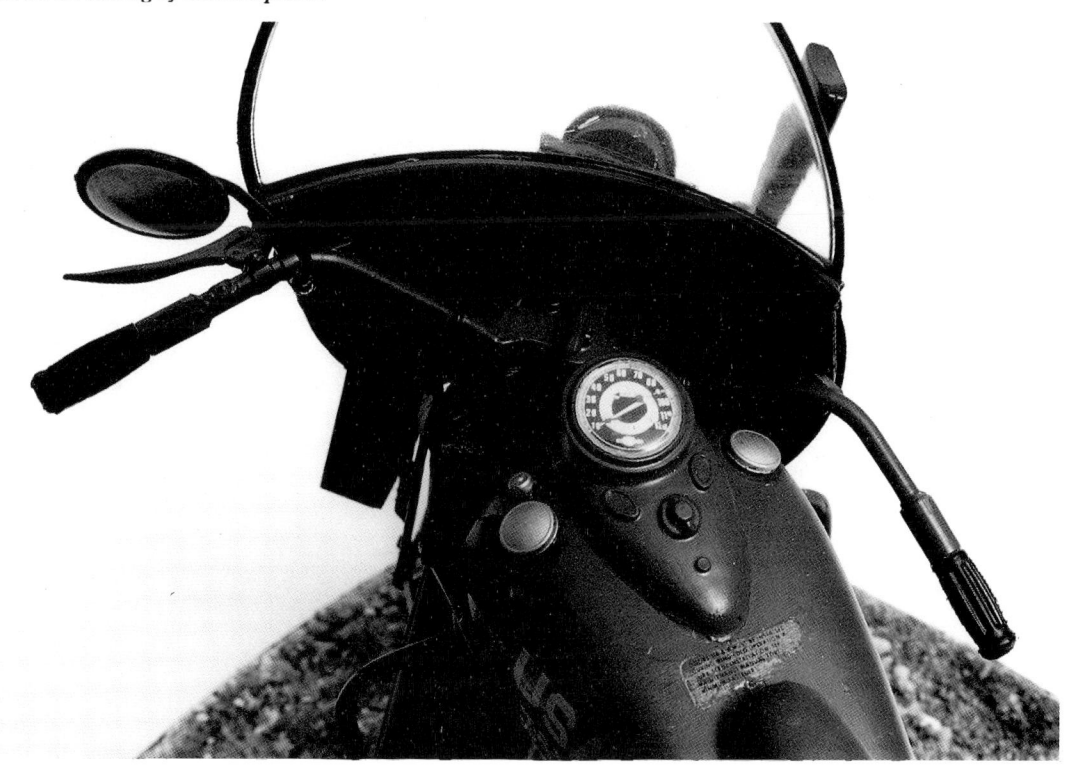

Tropical Triumph—
the single-cylinder British Triumph 3HW

The original version was built especially for war service by the Triumph firm. A similar version was already on the market for civilian use before World War II. Since this comparatively "light-footed" motorcycle nevertheless met the most stringent requirements, the Triumph 3HW was used by the Royal Army in all theaters of war—particularly in the Southeast Asian area.

Of the 1/9 scale models depicted here, the Triumph 3HW is surely the model that presents the lowest degree of difficulty in terms of assembly. The pieces fit together well and the detailed instructions also contribute to the ease. Only in the realm of the sprung trapeze fork does one need some dexterity, so that the entire mechanism can be operated after the assembly of the model.

The motorcycle was painted tan for tropical service. Behind the back seat, a rolled-up tent canvas and a small shovel were attached. The typical British motorcyclist's helmet and a machine pistol complete the model.

The original of the 3HW was used mainly by the British Navy. The model features a spring-mounted parallelogram fork and one-cylinder block motor.

A good chance to compare the model with actual action photos is provided by these pictures of the model of the British Triumph 3HW. Above is the tan military model; below the restored machine in civilian paint.

The fine details of the Triumph 3HW model, with the battery box, air pump and saddle with its coil springs.

It takes considerable dexterity to assemble the parts of the spring-mounted trapeze fork.

Renaissance on Three Wheels—
The BMW R 75 Model with Sidecar, Civilian Version

In the mid-fifties, motorcycles with sidecars were a common part of the everyday street scene. They were even called "the little man's car." In the first years after the war, they were often products of necessity and served their drivers splendidly as means of transportation. Among the heavier types was, in particular, the BMW R 75 type. At numerous motorcycle meets today, these machines still attract great admiration. When parking by means of the reverse gear is demonstrated, these machines and their drivers have the full attention of the public.

This renaissance also began early in the field of model building, and the civilian version of the BMW R 75 with sidecar has long been on the market. All the features that identified the military model as a rifle unit's vehicle have been removed, so that this kit is not at all to be regarded as a copy of the military kit. Even the plastic material has been colored black, and the completed model is meant to be painted in gloss black.

The BMW R 75 of the "economic miracle" era in 1/9 scale. Gloss black paint and many stripes of trim typify this postwar model, which includes all the attributes of a military model.

From this perspective, the original's good ground clearance is visible on the model too.

The dark green BMW R 75 sidecar cycle in the fiery paint job of a motorcycle fan.

Asymmetrical Two-Track Vehicles—
The BMW R 75 and Zündapp KS 750 Sidecar Models in Military Form

Although sidecar motorcycles, as asymmetrical two-track vehicles, constitute a technical curiosity and are also not easy to drive, they were still very popular among young and old alike in the time of the Economic Miracle. Was this popularity attributable to the experience of the motorcycle riflemen in World War II?

Next to the Zündapp KS 750 with sidecar, the BMW R 75 was probably the best-known of the off-road motorcycle units used in World War II. These two special machines reached the troops in the middle of the war.

Here too, the modelmaking industry has placed two very excellent 1/9 scale kits on the market. Both of them are characterized by a wealth of individual parts. The connections for the driveshaft and the shift lever for road and off-road gears in particular have been worked out very impressively. The machine-gun mount with the MG 34 can be mounted optionally on either model.

The BMW model can also be made in tropical form—with its air filter mounted higher up—, while the Zündapp model is equipped with cycle heating. Both models fascinate through their precision of detail. It can also be noted that the BMW model is equipped with rubber folded bellows on the front-wheel fork.

The Zündapp KS 750 sidecar cycle with dark gray paint, with a calendar picture making it look real.

The machine-gun mount holds the MG 34 on the sidecar of the Zündapp KS 750 cycle.

There was much storage space inside the heavy sidecar. As seen in many original photo the sidecar was often loaded to its very limits. The heating coils of the cycle heater can be seen here.

This model of the heavy BMW R 75 cycle has been made excellently by its manufacturer. The model features rough-profile tires. The model above is the tropical version, the one below is painted dark gray.

The rubber bellows and the flat front fender—the so-called thin wing—can be seen clearly here.

The rough tire profile is strikingly realistic.

Lone Warrior—
Zündapp KS 750/1 solo, military version

Those who admire heavy solo machines regard the Zündapp KS 750/1 solo as a desirable creation. In fact, the original machine was very seldom seen in the theaters of war in this version, because the sidecar had to be removed on account of technical problems. Nevertheless, the kit of this classic motorcycle is very popular among model builders. The precision of detail and fitting of the individual parts of this model are outstanding.

And then come the many extras! Beginning with a folding spade above the canteen flask and cooking utensils, on to the woolen blanket—everything is there that a motorcycle messenger would need as a "lone warrior." The author has added a few more utensils to this kit and has to say, "This model is alive!"

As is true of the other 1/9 scale models, the Zündapp KS 750/1 solo has numerous moving parts. In particular, the sprung handlebars and the rear seat, made with a return spring, deserve mention. Both units call for particular care during assembly in order to make sure that the parts function properly.

The Zündapp KS 750/1 solo in model form. Among the real cycles shown in this book, the solo cycle could be found only once.

The connection for the sidecar drive can also be seen clearly in the 1/9 scale model.

The model can optionally be equipped with several pieces of equipment, such as tent canvas, folding chair and light Panzerfaust.

The Soldier's Dream—
the BMW R 75 solo

The makers of model motorcycles have filled the kit of the BMW R 75 solo with a blend of fantasy and reality. This solo cycle is without a doubt a true scale model of the original. But it never left the assembly lines of BMW in this stage of completion, as the need for cycles at the front had to be met. A BMW R 75 solo never saw action as an official Wehrmacht cycle. Even so, this model will make the heart of any "oldtimer freak" beat faster.

Here too, the optional installation of the tropic air filter is possible. The front-wheel fork is designed as a so-called telescopic fork and—unlike the sidecar cycle—does not include a folded rubber bellows. On the other hand, this model includes two knee-protector panels, such as can be seen very often in pictures of the sidecar cycle. And the wide front fender—which marked the first generation of this cycle—is particularly noticeable on this model. Nor was equipment stinted on. Whether in tan or dark gray Wehrmacht paint, this model truly enriches a collection of military motorcycles.

Another special version portrays the BMW R 75 as a solo cycle. This is the tropical version with the high-mounted air filter. Without a sidecar, one has a good view of the shift lever.

Further identifying marks of the BMW R 75 sidecar cycle are the wide front fender and the absence of rubber bellows.

The BMW R 75 solo looks at home in front of a calendar picture.

And still smaller—
The BMW and Zündapp solo and sidecar cycles and the NSU treaded cycle in 1/35 scale

In a somewhat smaller version than that of the models shown up till now, the Tamiya firm, for example, offers the German BMW R 75 and Zündapp KS 750 Wehrmacht cycles in both solo and sidecar form, as well as the NSU treaded cycle. Along with the pieces of equipment for the cycles, these kits also offer appropriate figures of drivers, passengers and infantrymen. Even though the precision of detail cannot compare with the models shown already, what with the smaller scale, these are still impressive miniature versions of these onetime Wehrmacht cycles.

The BMW R 75 with sidecar, including four 1/35 scale soldiers, made by Tamiya.

These two solo cycles, BMW R 75 and Zündapp KS 750, are available in 1/35 scale model kits.

NSU treaded cycle models in varying scales.

A Maid of all work—
the NSU treaded cycle

A plentitude of functioning individual parts on this 1/9 scale model affords insight into the structural technology of treaded vehicles at that time. Beginning with the movably mounted road and drive wheels, to the handlebars and the steerable front wheel, a wealth of finely detailed work awaits the model builder before this model is finished.

The 1/9 scale NSU treaded cycle with camouflage paint.

The disc front wheel with the handlebars surely helped to take this vehicle out of the towing program for motorcycles.

Under the motor hood is the 1.6-liter Opel motor.

Afterword

The volume at hand includes no final list of all the motorcycles that saw service in the time period in question—neither on the German nor the Allied side. It is rather the purpose of this documentation to introduce to the historically interested reader the variety of different cycle types that the military forces used and took into battle in those days.

Beyond that, the published photographic material is meant to provide an impression of the daily activities of the motorcycle rider in peacetime and in the military service of these "motorized hussars" in all theaters of war. Stress is therefore given not to the censored photos of the press photographer, but to the snapshots "shot" with the private cameras of the individual soldiers—with all their failings in terms of subjects and sharpness. Thus in many cases the cycle in question is not shown totally, or parts essential to its identification are obscured by people or other vehicles. It is understandable that in these memorable photos, the person stands in the foreground. Then too, the "steel horse" is sometimes totally covered with dirt, so that it is not always possible—particularly in the case of the many requisitioned cycles—to identify the exact type of machine. But this does not decrease the value of the documentation. Rather it is these factors that reveal authentically the action of the motorcyclists on their cycles, which often enough were totally unfit for off-road action.

This book is dedicated to all the motorcyclists of those times, no matter which side they were on.

Critical notes on this book are welcomed by the author. Perhaps photographic material from the readers will make possible the publication of another documentation of this interesting subject.

Horst Hinrichsen

A look into the driver's compartment of the treaded cycle. It looks more like that of a larger vehicle than of a motorcycle.

The NSU treaded cycle with uniform trailer and three soldiers is on the market in 1/35 scale.